POLITICS AND THE ENDS OF IDENTITY

Politics and the Ends of Identity

Edited by
KATHRYN DEAN

Aldershot · Brookfield USA · Singapore · Sydney

Published by
Ashgate Publishing Ltd
Gower House
Croft Road
Aldershot
Hants GU11 3HR
England

Ashgate Publishing Company
Old Post Road
Brookfield
Vermont 05036
USA

British Library Cataloguing in Publication Data

Politics and the ends of identity. - (Avebury series in
        philosophy)
        1. Identity 2. Identity - Political aspects
        I. Dean, Kathryn
        126

Library of Congress Catalog Card Number: 97-73873

ISBN 1 85972 372 1

Printed in Great Britain by The Ipswich Book Company, Suffolk.

Contents

List of contributors

Luis Castro Leiva is Director of the History of Ideas Unit at the Instituto Internacional de Estudios Avanzados (IIDEA) at Caracas. He teaches philosophy at Universidad Simon Bolivar and political theory at the Universidad Central de Venezuela.

Kathryn Dean teaches in the Department of Political Studies, School of Oriental and African Studies, University of London. Her research interests include ideology, collective action and communications theory.

Paul Hirst is Professor of Social Theory at Birkbeck College, University of London. He is a member of the *Political Quarterly* editorial board, the *Renewal* advisory board and the Charter 88 Executive. His books include *Associative Democracy* (1994).

Ronald Inden is Professor of South Asian History and South Asian Languages and Civilizations, Associate Member, Anthropology, University of Chicago, and Professorial Research Associate, School of Oriental and African Studies, Centre of South Asian Studies, University of London. His work focusses on the history and metaphysics of representational practices in relation to India in the medieval and modern world.

Sudipta Kaviraj teaches in the Department of Political Studies, School of Oriental and Africa Studies, University of London. He has previously taught at the Jawaharlal Nehru University, Delhi. His main fields of interest are political theory and Indian politics.

Robert Meister teaches political theory and legal studies at the University of California at Santa Cruz, where he is also affiliated with the graduate programme in the History of Consciousness. Among his recent publications are *Political Identity:*

Thinking Through Marx (1990), 'Sojourners and Survivors: Two Logics of Constitutional Protection' and 'The Logic and Legacy of *Dred Scott'*. He is presently working on two books whose provisional titles are *Nations in Recovery: Living in the Aftermath of Evil and Love* and *Justice: Legitimations of Moral Inequality in Western Thought.*

Noël O'Sullivan is Professor of Political Philosophy at the University of Hull. His books include *Fascism* (1983), *The Problem of Political Obligation* (1986), and *The Philosophy of Santayana* (1992). He is presently writing a book on European political thought since 1945.

Tim Stringer lectures on East Asian government in the Politics Department at the University of Buckingham. He is researching theories of democracy and mass politics in Japan and China.

Charles Tripp is Senior Lecturer in Politics with reference to the Near and Middle East at the School of Oriental and African Studies, University of London. He is presently working on a study of Islamic responses to capitalism.

Zafer F. Yörük is a PhD student in the Department of Government, University of Essex. His research interests include ideology and discourse analysis. He is the author of a number of articles on Turkish identity, the Kurdish question, nationalism and post-analytical philosophy and is a regular contributor to an English language newspaper in Turkey.

Acknowledgements

This volume began as a seminar series and conference organised by the Department of Political Studies, School of Oriental and African Studies, University of London during 1993-94. My thanks are due to all who contributed to our meetings, as well as to the contributors to the present volume. I wish also to thank the British Academy and the School of Oriental and African Studies, whose financial contributions made the project possible. Others who deserve grateful mention here include Sudipta Kaviraj, who suggested the topic, and Noël O'Sullivan and Tom Young, who offered valuable advice and support at key moments in the editorial process. Finally, I must thank Joyce Hutchinson for her unfailingly cheerful technical support.

1 Introduction: politics and the ends of identity

Kathryn Dean

The term 'identity politics' which has been in use since the early 1980s implies that, before that time, politics had been in some sense free of identity. This surely cannot have been the case. '[R]ecognition', says Calhoun, 'is at the heart of the matter' of identity.[1] It is through recognition that individuals acquire a sense of self, of place, of capacities, characteristics, entitlements and/or obligations. In this sense, identity has been indissociable from the business of politics, much of which is about the formation and dissolution of such identities. Identity, whether conceptualized as 'given' (natural) or 'constructed' (social), is that which endows groups and individuals with a place, a function, a purpose and, in the modern world, as Kaviraj argues below (chapter 2), with the capacity for action.

If it is the case that identity is indissociable from modern politics, we need to ask about the significance of the proliferation of identity politics in recent years. As Gorz suggests, the widespread use of the concept and preoccupation with identity questions suggest, not that identity is a novel phenomenon, but rather that identity can no longer be taken for granted.[2] Recognition of the requisite kind is not forthcoming. That is to say, the social conditions for the maintenance, within the individual, of a distinct and stable sense of self are not in place. It will be of interest, then, to establish what these conditions might be. This will be one of the tasks of this introduction whose overall purpose is to fill in the background necessary to place the individual papers which make up this collection. In the process of doing this, basic questions about the meaning of identity and the conditions needed for its formation and maintenance will be posed and a method for addressing these questions will be suggested. The answers to these questions will show that identity is always a social and collective matter, a claim that will be further supported by an examination of the link between identity and collective action in different contexts. Of particular interest here will be collective action oriented to the 'nationalization' of cultures threatened by enforced meetings with western colonialism, since several of the papers in this collection are concerned with the identity effects of such meetings. Finally, the emergence of a new kind of identity politics as well as of what appears to herald a political project oriented to the end of identity, namely, the politics of difference, will be examined and assessed.

1

As a preliminary, the concept of identity will be explored through a brief examination of the work of Erik Erikson whose name is closely associated with identity questions. As Inden points out (chapter 3), the concept of identity was first used and developed by Erikson in the immediate post-1945 period. Inden has strong reservations about Erikson's work, indeed he urges us to reject the very notion of identity which that work privileges. The reasons for this will need to be explored later. Some of Erikson's ideas, though, remain useful in terms of helping to clarify the issues at stake in identity politics and of aiding systematic thought about this confused and confusing topic. For reasons which Inden looks at, Erikson is concerned with the development of a strong sense of identity in individuals in industrialized countries, this sense being described as follows:

> [a] sense of identity means a sense of being at one with oneself as one grows and develops; and it means, at the same time, a sense of affinity with a community's sense of being at one with its future as well as its history – or mythology.[3]

While Erikson is preoccupied with the formation of individual identities, he stresses the necessarily social relational character of these identities. Individuals only feel at home in the world if they develop a strong sense of personal, individual identity which resonates with and finds its validity in an accompanying collective identity. Individual identities can only be formed within stable group identities:

> The term identity expresses ... a mutual relation in that it connotes both a persistent sameness within oneself (selfsameness) and a persistent sharing of some kind of essential character with others.[4]

Human beings have a need to be recognized, to be responded to, given function and status, and these needs require the existence of a fairly stable group with the will and resources to transmit its specific way of organizing experience to each new generation. Indeed, the establishment of an '"average expectable" continuity in child rearing and education' is 'a matter of human survival', Erikson claims. Young people need a stable environment which allows them to develop in a culturally and psychologically consistent way which will fit them for an adult status ensuring a sense of competence and usefulness and of recognition by other members of the group.[5] However, identity is not gained once and for all time. Identity formation is a never-ending process or 'evolving configuration' which requires a balance between continuity and discontinuity such as to enable the individual to absorb new developments and to meet new demands without suffering from 'identity diffusion'. By the latter term Erikson means 'a split of self-images, a loss of centrality, a sense of dispersion and confusion, and a fear of dissolution'.[6]

The conditions of possibility for the formation of new identities are described by Erikson under three headings as follows:

2

One is *factuality,* that is, a universe of facts, data, and techniques that can be verified with the observational methods and the work techniques of the time. Then, there is an inspiringly new way of experiencing history as unifying all facts, numbers and techniques into a *sense of reality* that has visionary qualities and yet energizes the participants in most concrete tasks. And, finally, there must be a new *actuality*, a new way of relating to each other, of activiating and invigorating each other in the service of common goals.[7]

In the absence of any of these, no 'true identity' can be formed. I take it that *factuality* coincides with the empirically verifiable dimensions of identity formation i.e. the natural and social environment within which individuals are situated and the ways in which a group is organized to meet its subsistence needs. *Sense of reality* coincides with the *worldview* or *imaginary*, the culturally specific set of values and categories which serves to constitute, interpret and evaluate the world. *Actuality* coincides with the *institutions* which produce the social relationships through which this worldview is lived.[8]

Having drawn out of Erikson's work the basic elements needed to discuss questions about identity formation and dissolution, I want to explore further the social requirements for the formation of stable identities. The vehicle for this exploration will be Jurgen Habermas' work *The Structural Transformation of the Public Sphere*.[9] Although it is ostensibly concerned with the category of the bourgeois public sphere, this work is paradigmatic for any attempt to discuss the formation of stable identities under modern conditions, both collective and individual, whether such identities be seen as desirable or not. This is because it brings to our attention the significance (for identity formation) of the historically and culturally novel conditions associated with the emergence of the structural differentiation which is one of the constitutive characteristics of the modern world. While the differentiation of spheres tends to be taken for granted in discussions about identity, it is crucial to highlight its importance in producing both the liberal individual and the bourgeois class. The notion of liberal individualism is constitutive of the institutions which have produced and been produced by western modernity and which have, to a greater or lesser extent, been exported to or imposed on nonwestern populations. Habermas' work allows us to think further about the relationship between the modern western form of differentiation and the emergence of what have been, until the 1980s, the taken-for-granted identities of politics in liberal democracies, namely, those of the bourgeois subject and of class. It makes clear the specific social and cultural conditions required for the formation of such identities. If questions about identity are discussed in relation to the degree of modern differentiation experienced by a particular population, understanding of the different forms that identity and modernization have taken where differentiation has scarcely begun may be facilitated.

I

Modernity, identity and the bourgeois public sphere

Modernity as the differentiation of spheres

Modern societies are societies in which human activities are fragmented through the division of labour and the differentiation of spheres. What the latter refers to is the 'splitting' and parcelling out between different spheres – the economic, the political, the familial and the cultural – of a totality of social action. This splitting demands or allows different values, orientations and behaviours in the different spheres. Activity in the economic and political spheres is (or should be) rational, 'functional' and impersonal, oriented to strangers for specific and limited purposes; activity in the intimate sphere of the family is (or should be) loving, loyal and affectionate; activity in the cultural sphere is expressive and aesthetic.[10] The differentiation of spheres and the accompanying distribution of dispositions – rationality, affect, expressivity – are associated with the belief that the modern world institutes a purely functional form of the social, a form whose institutions are guided wholly by a specific kind of rationality preoccupied with efficient and effective action upon 'things'. The claim that the spheres of economic and political activity should be rational and functional is related to the claim that the modern world has liberated (or offers the possibility of liberating) pure humanity from the shackles of custom, tradition, superstition; that it has liberated (or offers the possibility of liberating) pure functionality from cultural constraints. Liberated, culture-free rationality will be the basis of a liberated, self-activating subject and liberated functionality will be the basis of mastery of the natural world. However, the very notion of a pure 'functionality' is in itself a cultural notion, as Castoriadis, for example, points out. What is presented as rational-objective-universal, as based wholly on nature and reason is, in fact, a cultural-symbolic set of institutions.[11] The full significance of this becomes clear only when the attempt is made to impose apparently culture-free institutions on other cultures. This will be considered further below.

Capitalism and the state are 'first order institutions' (Castoriadis' description) of the modern world which are avowedly characterized by pure functionality. They are also the institutions which oversee a complex, never to be precisely delineated, multi-faceted nexus of processes whereby different aspects of human activity became detached and institutionalized in separate spheres over a period of about two hundred years in western Europe.[12] The impersonal economic and political spheres result from the disembedding of individuals from premodern corporate relationships found in the extended family, guilds, clans or tribes, and reincorporated into the state.[13] It is on the basis of this 'fateful differentiation of cultural components' that capitalism can represent itself as transparently rational, productive, objective and universal, or as Sahlins puts it: '[e]verything in capitalism conspires to conceal the symbolic ordering of the system'.[14] It is on this basis that spheres of activity can be assessed

4

in terms of 'utility' and pronounced to be rational or irrational. It is on this basis that activities considered to be outside the sphere of pure rationality and utility can be considered to be somehow optional, or surplus to strict social requirements; a matter for private, individual choice apparently without social implications or consequences. Habermas' work will be discussed here as an account of the 'identity effects' which accompanied this differentiation. While his primary task is the exploration of the category of the bourgeois public sphere, that exploration leads him to analyze the requirements for the production of both a self-conscious bourgeois class and the individual bourgeois subject. Therefore, the same method and materials can be used to analyse both the public sphere and the constitution of individual and collective identities. It should be noted here that the complexity of these objects 'precludes exclusive reliance on the specialized methods of a single discipline', as Habermas says of the category of the public sphere.[15] Both require a multi-disciplinary approach which is at once sociological and historical.

Politics and identity: the bourgeois public sphere

Briefly, Habermas traces the emergence of a bourgeois public sphere during the second half of the eighteenth century in England, France and Germany. This bourgeois public sphere was a 'forum in which the private people, come together to form a public, readied themselves to compel public authority to legitimate itself before public opinion'.[16] Here debate took place over the rules governing 'relations in the basically privatized but publicly relevant sphere of commodity exchange and social labour'.[17] The bourgeois public sphere, which was constituted by the 'private' sphere mediated between society (as an aggregation of private individuals) and the newly depersonalized state i.e. the state which had attained 'relative autonomy' from the person of the monarch.[18] These private people had developed specific identities through a nexus of institutions, intimate (familial), private (economic and cultural) and public (the state). The intimate sphere consisted in the property-owning, non-producing bourgeois patriarchal family. Individual productive property which was at the free disposal of the family head underpinned the family's autonomy and the father's authority. An increasingly rich cultural sphere composed of printed material of various kinds as well as theatres, museums and concert halls was essential for the formation of the specific identity of the liberal, introspective and autonomous individual or subject.[19] The emerging constitutional state was to be the guarantor of property and other liberal rights and of the impersonal functioning of the free market. In short, the different spheres were mutually constitutive although apparently governed by different values and logics. Some elaboration of this is in order.

In his account of the public sphere Habermas presupposes the Freudian model of the patriarchal bourgeois family. This family instituted 'permanent intimacy' as against older forms of communality found in the extended and directly productive family. It served as the essential socializing agent whereby, in spite of the illusions of freedom, 'strict conformity with societally necessary requirements was brought about'.[20] This was a conformity based on self-mastery rather than habituation. Self-mastery required that the individual must not merely do the right thing, but do it for the right reasons. This is the Freudian Oedipal model which stresses the role of the stern patriarchal father in the production of the individual (male) capacities just mentioned. Habermas is here drawing on the model as developed by the earlier Frankfurt School; the model socialized and historicized, in other words.[21]

The parents/child relationship was part of a wider set of institutions all of which served to inform and reinforce the particular kind of individuation which seems to have flourished in certain strata of the new bourgeoisie for about a hundred years from the mid-eighteenth century. The privatization of the family was expressed and advanced in architectural changes whereby lofty raftered halls were replaced by separate rooms having distinctive functions. The house became a home for each individual rather than for the family as a whole. It was a place where privacy could be enjoyed.

In this respect literature, which could be read in privacy within the redesigned family home was of particular importance in constituting the introspective, self-disciplined individual. Reading here was active and educational, oriented to self-improvement through the critical absorption of philosophy and literature, of moral weeklies and critical journals. It was, in addition to the cultural products of concert-halls, theatres and museums, the vehicle whereby bourgeois individuals developed a subjectivity marked by interiority, or psychic inwardness and self-consciousness.[22] This was an inwardness, though, which was not solely concerned with self-cultivation; it was an inwardness which was to be constitutive of a new politically significant phenomenon called public opinion, public opinion here being the outcome of the public use of individual reason. The products of the new dedicated cultural sphere made an important contribution to the constitution of a new kind of individual equipped with a strong sense of self *and* a strong social sense.[23] This social orientation found its first expression in literary salons which therefore functioned as a kind of training ground for more explicitly political discussions in the more masculine environment of coffee houses.[24] The coffee houses were the congenial public spaces within which culturally and socially nourished individuals interacted with one another so as to produce an informed and self-confident collective public opinion.

The capacity to produce such 'inner-directed' individuals was linked to the economic functions of the patriarchal family as property-owner, or, as Habermas puts it: 'The economic demands placed upon the patriarchal conjugal family from without corresponded to the institutional strength to shape a domain devoted to the development of the inner life.'[25] Autonomy was maintained through the ownership and control of productive property as the heads of bourgeois families had a crucial social role to play where production was being transferred from the family to a dedicated 'economic' sphere. The inner sense of certainty formed in the familial and

6

cultural spheres was internally, necessarily related to the outer sense of certainty derived from ownership and control of means of production.

Clearly the subject under discussion is a class-specific product, i.e. the bourgeois subject. Capitalist industrialization, by its very nature, required that property ownership – the necessary basis of individual self-cultivation – be limited to a minority of the population. The remainder would have neither the property nor the leisure to embark on the kind of education and to develop the necessary cultural experiences that self-cultivation required. For the majority, individual conformity to the new disciplinary requirements of emerging industrial production was induced in a variety of ways ranging from early paternalistic arrangements whereby social relations were based on the principle of kinship to later, more large-scale and impersonal institutions which sought to fabricate disciplined, docile individuals through surveillance, or the 'gaze'. Here, discipline would have been imprinted through drilling; mastery would have been imposed and would require no sense of an individual 'interior' or 'consciousness' of which the disciplined activity would be the direct expression. Whereas the bourgeois individual would have been the Kantian autonomous individual, the new working-class individual would have been the docile and therefore heteronomous individual, and necessarily so.[26]

Nevertheless, as Habermas points out, the bourgeois public sphere achieved its fullest expression when operating on the fictitious equation of the bourgeois privatized property owner and humanity as such. In fact, private and public spheres were marked by ambiguity, in the sense that the bourgeois was a privatized individual who was both:

> owner of goods and persons and one human being among others, i.e., *bourgeois* and *homme*. This ambivalence of the private sphere was also a feature of the public sphere, depending on whether privatized individuals in their capacity as human beings communicated through critical debate in the world of letters, about experiences of their subjectivity or whether private people in their capacity as owners of commodities communicated through rational-critical debate in the political realm, concerning the regulation of their private sphere.[27]

This constitutive ambiguity or contradiction held the likelihood of degeneration into a politics of 'interest'. It was this split between *bourgeois* and *homme* that was to be the focus of the young Marx's critiques, as will be seen later.[28]

The fictitious equation of bourgeois and humanity was underpinned by a universalist liberal discourse. The self-interpretation of the bourgeois experience was that it was the experience of a rational, universal (therefore culture-free) humanity and following logically from this interpretation the bourgeois public sphere was theoretically open to all.[29] However, the translation of theoretical into empirical openness would have required a social base consisting in a community of petty commodity producers, as Habermas himself points out. Only in such a community would the other institutional precondition – a social realm in which ownership of the means of production was 'relatively widely and evenly distributed' – pertain. Only in such a community would a general interest in the protection of property truly express the general interest.[30]

In this case, the constitution of a collective political identity enabling a newly-emerging bourgeoisie to assert itself against monarchy and aristocracy required a combination of 'private' and 'public' institutions having mutually reinforcing effects. That is to say, the different spheres within which the bourgeois individual acted, the intimate or familial, the economic, the cultural, the public, would all reinforce and sustain the individual characteristics of rationality, self-discipline and public-spiritedness while at the same time allowing for the expression of non-rational or affective orientations in the intimate sphere, of expressive, aesthetic and social orientations in the cultural sphere which in turned merged into the congenial public sphere where sociality joined 'interest' in the discussion of matters of shared concern such as the regulation of the emerging market system. Not only would the political identity of the (male) bourgeois allow of effective political action but it would fulfil the human requirement for recognition and for a sense of place and human relationship.

Habermas' work enables us to think about the emergence of a new worldview with the material, theoretical and social resources required to sustain durable collective and individual identities of the kind specified by Erikson. From Erikson's point of view, such individuals would have had a strong sense of self; a sense of inner and outer security derived on the one hand from a long, continuous process of education of a particular kind and, on the other hand and relatedly, from the recognition of individuality given willingly by one's peers. Such recognition would be related to participation in public discussion ensuing in the formation of a public opinion of sufficient significance to act as a constraint on the activities of monarchical power; this constraint being exercised in support of the general interest in respect for private property and for the other civil rights acclaimed by an emerging bourgeoisie.

The work shows both the historical and cultural specificity of a 'human nature' claimed by liberals to be universal, natural, or given. It shows, in effect, that the bourgeois subject is constituted by a range of private and public, economic, familial and cultural institutions.[31] Here we have the beginning of essentialism as domination, of the claim that one culturally specific form of human being represents humanity as such. This is a theme which has come to the fore so powerfully both in social theory and in identity politics in recent years; a theme to which I shall return below.

Habermas offers an account of the public sphere which reveals the constitution of individual and collective identities oriented to individual and collective forms of action which are congruent with one another, or which moved in the same direction, as it were. What should be clear from the foregoing is that insofar as the public

8

sphere functioned as Habermas claims, it was because specific kinds of individuals had been constituted by a multiplicity of congruent institutions so as to render them suited to participation in this public sphere. Individual identities were congruent with the kind of public or political identity required for the specific kind of participation expected. The bourgeoisie was numerically small enough to allow of efficient and effective coordination through a combination of print communication (including the speedily growing number of books, magazines and periodicals) and the face-to-face contact which took place in coffee-houses, salons and clubs of various kinds. Nevertheless, the kind of functional, mutually constitutive relationship between different spheres needed to maintain this form of the social would have demanded, in addition to enabling structural conditions, an unprecedented combination of political judgement and skill and of the freedom to exercise such judgement and skill in the appropriate manner.[32]

As further differentiation followed with the development of industry, and as mass politics came to replace the elite politics in operation during the period with which Habermas is concerned, the problems of functionality and coordination would become acute. While Kaviraj (chapter 2) does not frame his questions about identity, modernity and collective action primarily in terms of functionality and coordination, his paper does enable us to think about these problems more systematically. What he is interested in is the way in which collective identities change as the modern emphasis on the plasticity of the world gives rise to attempts to transform it. These attempts require the transformation of premodern group identities from identities of 'being' into identities of 'doing'. The production of an agentive 'we' requires the fusion of imagination, knowledge and power. Kaviraj's suggestion is that we can begin to understand how the 'we' is constituted if we manage to unite the insights of Anderson and Foucault. This interesting theoretical fusion will help us to understand, not only the successes but the failures of such political projects. It will enable us to deal with questions on which Habermas is silent, namely the national imaginary and discipline.[33] Given these additions, we may begin to understand two things: how the successful inculcation of a sense of identity (in the Eriksonian meaning of the term) helps to create and maintain coherence out of radically fragmented liberal capitalist forms of the social and how, in consequence, projects requiring collective action may be successful.

II

Identity and collective action: the bureaucratic model

Collective action and the nation-state

Differentiation fragments the totality of social activity needed to satisfy the needs of a given population in such a way as to require sustained coordinating activity to ensure the congruence and functionality of the fragments. It also fragments the social bond. Although the 'free market' is considered by some to be the wholly satisfactory means of ensuring coordination in such societies,[34] much, or even most of the responsibility for this has fallen to the state. Where the state has succeeded in constituting its population as a nation, this task of coordination has been rendered less difficult.

The nation-state is perhaps the most powerful model of collective action available to us. It is the institutional complex which reunites the fragments resulting from modern differentiation by ensuring the coordination of different and necessary elements, and by reuniting the emotional and the rational in a form which is supportive rather than subversive of state projects. The ideal marriage of nation and state is a rare event which brings together the apparently contradictory orientations of the emotional and the rational, those orientations which the commonsense of modern intellectuals wishes to see kept apart. In a sense, what is in question is the re-institution of kinship at the level of the state. Kinship is used here to refer to social relations which cannot be characterized purely as 'affective', 'interested' or 'rational'. That is to say, affect, self-interest and rationality are fused rather than differentiated in social relations governed by kinship. Such relations are to be contrasted with instrumentally rational relations which are held to pertain between modern individuals in the economic and political spheres.[35] Where kinship is allied to an efficient state bureaucracy the result is a powerful collective identity, an identity, that is, with both the emotional strength and cognitive and organizational scope to carry out the most demanding collective tasks.[36] The reinstitution of the kinship principle at the level of the state is the institution of a new 'we' having capacities which would have been beyond the scope of premodern groups. In short, the most durable kind of collective action in the modern world will be the result of the combination of solidaristic social relations organized on the kinship principle and a powerful and efficient bureaucratic apparatus. Where the personal or kinship element is present in the shape of the nation, individuals will have a strong sense of national identity and will therefore support collective actions of a bureaucratic kind. However, there are different kinds of collective action ranging from the purely bureaucratic and impersonal to the purely solidaristic, spontaneous and personal.[37] In some cases of bureaucratic action, popular support may amount to little more than passive acquiescence in state activities. Of interest in this respect is the brief post-1945 period in western Europe when the nation-state in alliance with a revitalized capitalism oversaw a period of remarkable stability and prosperity. During the early years of this period, state projects were accepted by individuals as in some significant sense theirs also. Let us see how this came about.

Inden argues, on the basis of a discussion of the work of Erikson (chapter 3) that the emergence of the concept of identity during the early post-war period was related to the need to subordinate individuals to the purposes of western states. He uses the concept of transcendence to explore the relationship between individual and society as posited during this period. Identity was intended to do the work of stitching together the supposedly irrational individual and the supposedly rational state. At this time, he says, the populations in question accepted the invitation to imagine themselves as members of a nation to which they owed their supreme loyalty. Thus were emotions 'mobilized' (Inden's word) in support of the nation-state. Here I want to emphasize the relative congruence attained by the different spheres of activity during this period. A combination of nationalist rhetoric (nourished by the recent experience of fighting against a terrifyingly destructive enemy), Keynesianism and disciplinary practice underpinned by a consensus established by EuroAmerican elites and expressed in the Bretton Woods agreement led to a quarter century of stability during which activities in the different spheres were coordinated both inter- and intra-nationally. For a short time, during the quarter-century following 1945, welfare state capitalism in the countries of the west managed to institute a form of the social which appeared to offer the kind of secure basis for collective and individual identities prescribed by Erikson.[38]

The welfare state instituted respect for workers in that it represented a partial decommodification of labour, that strange entity which, while embodied in human beings, is seen by capitalism to be a 'factor of production' and therefore, along with other factors of production, subject to the requirements of the market. A new kind of recognition of the working class as organized labour was instituted. In effect, the most dehumanizing aspects of industrial capitalism were marginalized as the welfare state and official concern with full employment catered to many of the material and psychological needs of the labour force. While work may have been for the most part unsatisfying, continuous employment in reasonably well-paid jobs with safeguards against the fears of sickness, unemployment and old age did offer some sense of security, competence and usefulness and, in addition, offered the means of selfexpression and/or development in the familial and cultural spheres. As the state became the welfare state, some substance was given to the idea of the state as nation-state, the state as community. As social rights were added to civil and political rights, membership of the nation-state became more substantial and loyalty to the nation state (expressed most importantly perhaps during this period in the readiness to pay taxes) could be demanded in good faith.

Keynesianism, then, was not just a set of economic prescriptions for reinstating capital accumulation and economic growth but a metanarrative which linked the fates of different classes and strata within the nation-state, which recognized the humanity, usefulness and needs of the hitherto marginalized. Membership of class and nation-state was reconcilable and could form the basis for stable individual identities. Capitalism was saved from itself in the sense that the most brutal and divisive effects of the 'free market' were eliminated or minimized by means of political, bureaucratic action. The working class was successfully coopted through a combination of the concessions described above and the spread of a relatively new kind of enjoyment, namely the consumption of commodities. In a very real sense, decommodification in some areas, as manifested most impressively in public health services, was made possible through more intensive commodification in others.[39]

Since the 1970s the vulnerability of the model of collective action which in part produced this state of affairs, (of one, that is, in which the bureaucratic element is preponderant) has become increasingly clear. The bureaucratic model of collective action is characterized by impersonal means of organization and coordination. It is action carried out by elites as experts on behalf of or upon the population at large or targeted strata of the population. What it requires from a collectivity is compliance rather than active involvement. In fact, such action can be carried on without any conscious engagement of the population involved. It is therefore a world away from the kind of action discussed above in relation to the constitution of the bourgeois subject. The bourgeois subject is active and self-disciplined, with strong *inward* and *outward* orientations. These two orientations are mutually constitutive since a strong sense of self endows the individual with the sense of competence needed to act in public and acting in public brings rewards which are not reducible to the satisfaction of 'interests'. The result is a sense of unity or continuity between the individual and the social rather than the kind of radical disjunction which is found where individuation takes the form of 'possessive' or utilitarian individualism.[40]

If we follow the logic of Habermas' argument about the structural transformation of the public sphere, we will see that the institutions which emerged out of the postwar settlement constitute quite a different kind of individual – one who is more passive and 'privatized' – than the bourgeois subject. In fact, Habermas, following the analysis of various members of the Frankfurt School, dated the decline of the bourgeois subject to the transition from liberal to organized capitalism, a transition which transformed the family head from independent property owner to functionary in a system over which he had no control.[41] In addition, the cultural sphere was transformed through a new kind of commodification which altered the content of cultural products so that these were no longer of the kind needed – educational, critical, challenging – to constitute the introspective, critical subject. Now cultural products were designed to amuse, to entertain, to pacify, rather than to stimulate and educate. They debilitated or rendered empty and vacant the individuals who consumed them. In short, they served to intensify a political passivity which bureaucratic collective action was tending to produce in any case, so that in this respect, political-administrative and cultural institutions were moving in the same direction.[42] However, this political passivity can be accompanied by (or transformed into) resistance to paying through taxation for any public services from which the individual cannot expect to receive direct benefit and to any collective projects which may require individual self-sacrifice of any kind. In effect, the strong sense of a 'we' which in the beginning supported the kinds of redistribution required by the welfare state begins to dissolve. As the brief era of postwar prosperity and stability comes to an end, the fragility of bureaucratic action unsupported by either the active commitment or mere compliance of the relevant populations becomes clear. Before going on to discuss this, I want to move the focus from the 'centre' to the 'periphery' by which I mean, in this case, those colonial countries whose populations were mobilizing for independence just at the time when the 'centre' was enjoying a period of unprecedented stability.[43] This change of focus should enable us to understand further the relationship between identity and action in the modern world.

III

Identity and collective action: the solidaristic model

The view from the periphery

So far, the emphasis has been on politics and identity within modernity's home. Having begun with a discussion of what was to become the normative model of individual and collective identity in the modern west, I have looked at the way in which developments within the west have served to undermine the necessary bases for producing the bourgeois subject and later the emergence of movements offering fundamental challenges to this model will be explored. However, we are very much concerned in this volume with the view from outside the west. Several of the papers in this collection discuss these questions from the points of view of meetings, more or less enforced, between the west and the nonwest. Yörük (chapter 4) offers us, in his analysis of the formation of the modern Turkish republic, an example of the most enthusiastic and vigorous espousal of western ideas of civilization and development. Guided by the theoretical framework of Laclau and Mouffe, he traces the emergence of an identity crisis during the late Ottoman period which opened the way for the Kemalist nationalist project. This project required the repression (through 'discursive externalization' rather than either physical expulsion or death) of Muslim and Kurdish identities. In short, the construction of the new Turkish nation demanded the cultural homogenization of the population in question.

Zörük discusses the 'Kemalist grand-narrative' as borne by the 'Turkish historical thesis' which attempted to establish civilizational credentials through the repression of the 'Oriental dimensions of Turkishness' and of 'alien-Islamic accretions'. Here imagining the nation required the identification of a 'constitutive (and inferior) outside' whereby the superior and desirable identity could be constructed. However, this cultural homogenization required, not only the production of new meanings, symbols and rituals, but accompanying and supportive economic and social changes, as Zörük makes clear in his discussion of Kemal's 'populist' politics. With these points in mind, let us consider in a very general sense, the relationship between identity and modernization in the colonial and postcolonial or peripheral states.

Colonialism represented the most dramatic and embodied challenge to the cultures (and therefore identities) of nonwestern peoples. In certain cases, the assertion or reassertion of independence from the west has required the mobilization of whole populations under the banner of nationalism. To what extent had the nationalisms of the independence movements constituted a solidaristic collective actor – a collective actor, that is, combining emotional, cognitive and organizational strengths – prepared to participate in the task (at once more prosaic and more heroic) of making these countries modern in some real sense? What part did questions about identity play in the success or failure of such mobilizations? A few words about culture will be in order as we move to considering this question further.

Culture and identity

It has been seen in the discussion of Habermas' work on the bourgeois public sphere that the cultural sphere played a key part in the constitution of the bourgeois subject. As we know, culture has also assumed an unmistakable importance in contemporary discussions about identity and difference, so it will be useful, before proceeding further, to take a closer look at the range of references of this capacious term.

Culture is used in two broad senses in the social science literature: first, to indicate the total, distinctive way of life of a given population – culture as a particular way of relating to nature and other humans or culture as all 'learned' behaviour; second, to refer to a specialized or single aspect of human life, namely the meaningful or the symbolic and, relatedly, to the body of meanings and symbols produced in the dedicated cultural sphere, or culture as expression.[44] The broad conception is considered to be of little use in the social sciences for two reasons: one, it is so all-encompassing as to lack any analytical purchase on the empirical world; two, the distinctive and insulated, isolated or autonomous cultures which it presupposes are not to be found in the contemporary world. While these criticisms are well made, there are also problems relating to the use of the narrow conception. For one thing, it tends to efface the fact that all human activity is meaningful, thereby facilitating the naturalization of culturally-specific western conceptions of activity described as 'economic'. Further, by equating meaning with specialized production in the cultural sphere, it is in danger of divorcing meaning from materiality and of forgetting the necessary connectedness of the different spheres of activity. This can result in a culturalism every bit as misleading and reductive as its 'other', namely economism.

It is necessary to retain the two conceptions of culture if we are to understand some of the connundra of identity politics in the contemporary world and, particularly, if we are to understand the view from the periphery, rather than from the centre. The differentiation of spheres and the narrow conception of culture has encouraged the perception that parts of a particular culture (as total way of life) considered useful or desirable may be abstracted and adopted by different cultures

14

without assimilating those parts considered less useful or desirable or even downright undesirable. The possibility of picking and mixing had been discussed from the second half of the nineteenth century onwards by Chinese, Japanese, south Asian and African intellectuals who attempted to extract sometimes the 'universal', sometimes the 'technological' from the unwanted culture of the west so as to retain cultural integrity while at the same time gaining the power to repel or eject the west. Clearly the presence or absence of colonialism makes a significant difference in relation to the freedom to choose cultural items in this way. However, beyond this question of choice regarding details, there is the fact that the kind of action required to protect a nonwestern culture necessitates the adoption of some fundamental western values and practices, among these the adoption of a numerical or quantitative conception of individuals, groups and their relationships, as Kaviraj makes clear (chapter two). Whether this aspect of modernity can be adopted without shredding these reactive cultures is a question which can be explored in the first instance by considering the the case of Japan.

Culture and the nation-state

As is well known, Japan was the first nonwestern culture to make the transition to modernity without, apparently, losing its unique identity. Japan became modern without becoming western, perhaps.[45] Or, as some would see it, Japan's transformation was incomplete.[46] Stringer (in chapter 5 below) discusses this 'incompleteness' and considers its effects in relation to the determination of the post-1945 United States forces of occupation to remedy it. He also explores attempts of various postwar Japanese intellectuals to explain it. Notable here is the work of Maruyama, who looked for a dissolution of Japan's 'family state' and for an accompanying depersonalization of politics. Clearly, although the advanced division of labour required for industrial production had been attained in Japan, it had not been accompanied by the process of differentiation discussed above. That is to say, the distribution of activities between the different spheres – i.e. the political, the economic, the cultural, the familial – had not been accompanied by the fragmentation of human orientations – i.e. rationality, expressivity, affect – as expected by the western model. Because this fragmentation had not taken place, institutions which were nominally of a western kind would be governed by kinship (in the sense defined earlier) rather than by (instrumental) rationality. There is a suggestion in Stringer's paper, too, though, that it was precisely the personal (or kinship) character of Japanese politics that may help to explain its late nineteenth century success. It is this suggestion that I want to follow up to suggest why Japan did manage to industrialize and put in place apparently modern political and economic institutions while somehow maintaining its coherence or identity during its first stage of modernization following the Meiji Restoration of 1868. This will help us to understand the problems facing other nonwestern countries attempting to effect the 'great transformation' during the mid-twentieth century.[47]

The first obvious point is that Japan was a culturally homogeneous society so the cultural work of imagining the nation was not so strenuous as it had to be elsewhere (for example in the Turkish case discussed by Yoruk in chapter 4). The claim to nationhood (as expressed most vividly through the symbolism and rhetoric of the Emperor system) made sense in terms of the felt experience of individuals in Japan. Put another way, the kinship model of social relations which is implied in the claim to nationhood[48] could be imposed without doing too much violence to pre-existing social relations and group structures at the popular level. At the same time, disciplinary (bureaucratic) resources were already extensive and were rapidly adapted to the needs of modernization by an unusually dedicated, cohesive and intelligent elite.[49] In Kaviraj's terms (chapter 2), imagination and discipline were combined and oriented to the same ends.

The Japanese case represents a dramatic episode of identity politics in the sense that Japanese elites mobilized the population to undertake and successfully complete the modernizing task so as to preserve the unique Japanese identity against western encroachments. Kinship was put to work in support of bureaucratic action, although, as Stringer argues, the price of politicizing kinship in this way was to become extremely high in due course. Here a national identity was successfully constituted out of suitable raw materials so as to preserve a culture (as a total way of life) which is somehow seen to have survived the transformations required by modernization and all its works.

This collective political identity required both internal and external recognition: within the state, intra- and inter-group mutual acceptance of common membership of the state which would thereby become a *nation*-state; without the state, acceptance that political elites had the support of populations which could be persuasively characterized as constituting a *nation*.[50] In relation to these related requirements, the advantages enjoyed by Japan were little replicated elsewhere. If we turn to the post-colonial states, neither cultural homogeneity nor an adequate supply of administrative resources was likely to be available. Furthermore, the colonial state had had effects which exacerbated the difficulties associated with these disadvantages. Let us explore these points in a little more detail.

In these states, the kind of cultural homogeneity which had aided Japanese elites in their tasks was singularly lacking.[51] State boundaries had been drawn with a view to colonial administrative effectiveness and did not take account of the distribution of cultures in relation to such boundaries. Not surprisingly, the administrative and cultural boundaries did not match. This might not have mattered had premodern corporate or kinship cultures been significantly weakened under colonialism, thereby producing the disembedded individual with nowhere to go except the state *and* had the new state had the resources, including most significantly, the bureaucratic capacity, to offer the kinds of protection against hardship which welfare states are expected to deliver.[52] In relation to the first of these, colonialism had in

16

many ways served to enhance, rather than undermine kinship. One of the ways in which this happened was through the policy of 'indirect rule', that is, the exercise of political power through the medium of indigenous authorities. This resulted in a kind of bastardized system of traditionalist rule which became the partial basis for 'tribal' politics. More strongly, it is arguable that the concept of tribe and the idea that each person belongs to only one tribe was a colonial import. Tribal categories were, if not actually invented, then hardened, simplified, bureaucratized through the work of missionaries, anthropologists and colonial officials so that identities were transformed in the manner discussed by Kaviraj (chapter 2) in relation to India. In Africa, for example, what colonialism did in its quest for manageability, predictability and 'countability' was to constitute groups as having mutually exclusive memberships bearing certain characteristics and of individuals as permanent members of particular tribes. This was done by means of the use of tribal names on forms, the formation of tribal councils by colonial officials, and by enthusiastic accounts of 'their' tribes by anthropologists and missionaries. Colonial conceptions were made real because they became the practical basis for administrative boundaries and were reproduced in relationships between colonial officials and local populations.[53] In short, far from depleting them, the colonial state replenished the sources which nourished the kinship model of social relations, so that, (and this allows me to deal speedily with the second point) such resources as were available to the state were used, not to put in place the institutional nexus needed to build up and provide universal welfare for the population overall, but to build up specific kin groups, or 'tribes' and to buy off opposition.

This readiness to view the state as a source of largesse rather than as an object of obligation, was in itself the product of colonialism. The state itself was a colonial product and necessarily associated with the colonizer. It was therefore seen either as an evil to be avoided or as a dispenser of resources in the form of, for example, comparatively lucrative positions in the civil service. Furthermore, elites engaged in anti-colonial struggles gained much of their support through promises that independence would procure through the state a way of life modelled on that of the colonizers. In fact, the combination of a history of reluctant contact with the colonial state, on the one hand, and a politics of mobilization grounded in promises of future largesse to be derived from the independent state, on the other, led to a situation which indicated a bleak future for innovating political elites in these countries.

To summarize, colonialism had not initiated a process of 'disembedding' individuals from their corporate groups. Neither had the differentiation of spheres advanced in any real sense. Hence the splitting or separation of human orientations i.e. of the affective from the rational and their distribution among different spheres had not taken place, a separation which is at the basis of modern institutions, including those of liberal democracy. Nevertheless, in postcolonial states the community was mostly imagined as a collectivity of enfranchised individuals.

However, elite imagination was not (and could not be) instituted beyond the formalism of constitution-writing.[54] The pre-existing culture was inhospitable to attempts to reconstruct the population as an aggregate of individuals. Social relations continued to be governed by kinship, but this was kinship that functioned at a subnational level in the interests of subnational groups.[55] The state did not 'capture' kinship as had the Japanese state, but neither was kinship at the subnational level privatized as in the western European manner. Worse, because the state was associated with the colonial power, it became the object of predation rather than of moral attachment (which remained tied to 'kin' or 'tribe') and the resources available to the state became the basis of revitalizing kinship groups.[56] The modern was assimilated to the premodern, as it were.[57] The subnational kin group continued to be the source of both emotional and material satisfactions for individuals in many postcolonial countries.

To express the situation in terms of Erikson's criteria for the formation of new identities, there was a radical disjunction between *factuality, sense of reality* and *actuality*. The *sense of reality* (worldview or imaginary) of liberal democratic capitalism (or of socialism) advanced by indigenous elites (unlike that advanced in Japan by the Meiji elites) received no support from (in fact was actively subverted by) *factuality* and *actuality*. In this case, identity could not do the work of harnessing popular energies to the task of creating a modern society; the state did not become a nation-state.

Having discussed one version of identity politics in relation to the post-colonial periphery, I shall now return to the centre to consider the revolt against technocracy and the disintegration of the Keynesian postwar settlement which together initiated a new kind of identity politics.

IV

Towards identity politics

Identity politics is a term used to distinguish a form of political action concerned with 'symbolic' (cultural) rather than 'distributional' (economic) injustice. Used in this sense, it is held to be distinctive from class politics, or the politics of interest. Whether the symbolic and the distributional can be kept separate in this way is an interesting question which is discussed by Meister (chapter 8) in terms of the relationship between exploitation and domination.[58] Certainly many of those who see themselves as engaged in identity politics have taken as their point of departure a rejection of the preoccupation with matters material or economic. In this section, I shall be discussing two strands of identity politics: first, a politics based on the rejection of the identities formed by liberal democratic capitalism; second, a politics arising from the alleged 'crisis of recognition' produced by the effects of global changes over the past twenty years. It is not always easy to keep these two strands separate, nevertheless the following discussion will attempt to do so.

Modernity and the 'violence of abstraction' [59]

Habermas discusses the bourgeois public sphere largely from its 'good side' i.e. as a convivial, educative, enabling sphere in which the narrowness of the private gives way to the outward expansive orientation required for the discussion of public interests. Others, most notably Marx in 'On the Jewish Question', focus on the 'bad side' of the early bourgeois world and its politics.[60] Marx sees bourgeois politics in terms of alienation, a much abused and capacious concept which in Marx's work is used to refer to the loss of control *and* of a sense of human connectedness or sociality which the differentiation of spheres and capitalist industrial production bring in their train.[61]

Marx had claimed that the capitalist mode of production could offer no basis for satisfying human relationship and recognition. Rejecting Hegel's claim that such recognition would be available through the state, he argued that what is recognized there is 'political man [who] is only abstract, artificial man, man as an *allegorical, moral* person'. What goes unrecognized is 'man in his sensuous, individual, and *immediate* existence'.[62] For the young Marx, the split between 'man' and 'citizen' is a fatal and destructive one which offers the individual the freedom of 'a monad isolated and withdrawn into himself' and reduces the political community to the status of a means of preserving the rights to property and self-preservation.[63] The early account of alienation in the political sphere was replaced in the later works by an emphasis on the effects of alienation and instrumental rationality[64] in the economic sphere. The result of the capitalist subsumption of all to the requirements of profit-making is the 'emptying out of the human content' as the individual is sacrificed to a world which is entirely external to her and which uses her as a means to increasing surplus value. From this point of view the 'childish world of antiquity appears ... as loftier' because 'it does not sacrifice the human individual to an entirely external world'. It provides 'satisfaction from a limited standpoint; while the modern gives no satisfaction'.[65]

Marx's early critique of the bourgeois capitalist world prefigures many of those developed during the 1960s when the humanist version of Marxism became quite powerful for a time.[66] The intellectual and political radicalism of that period had many sources, including the civil rights and the anti-Vietnam war movements. What I want to focus on here is the critique of a modern universalism which during the 1950s had become institutionalized as the large-scale, anonymous, standardized organizations of mass-producing or 'organized' capitalism. The identities of liberal democratic capitalism, those of class, of worker, of consumer, of voter, were seen, (by a vocal minority of the young 'post-materialist' generation) not as liberatory or satisfying, but as efficient forms of constraint, even of domination, which leave the individual feeling increasingly isolated, lonely and overwhelmed. 'Technocracy's children' were in revolt against a world ruled by techne, against a 'totally administered world'.[67] The spread of impersonal bureaucratic relations came to be perceived as oppressive even where these were intended to increase general wellbeing. What came to be emphasized was, not the security and comfort of an unprecedently prosperous way of life, but rather its standardizing, ordering, disciplining and depersonalizing effects. During this period, the new cultural politics of the young constituted, in effect, a demand for the removal of bureaucratic obstacles to the expression and enjoyment of an authentic sense of self. This was a kind of new romanticism concerned to revitalize the romantic rather than bourgeois subject. It expressed a concern with 'postmaterialist' issues and was thus seen as antithetical to the routinized politics of 'interest' i.e. a politics concerned only with questions of economic distribution.[68] This new preoccupation with self-realization, with the 'postmaterial' and 'cultural' became the basis of a new kind of identity politics as disappointment with the outcome of the 'events' of the late 1960s was translated into disillusionment with the 'Marxism of the parties' (Wallerstein's phrase[69]) which was now seen to be implicated in the universalism, economism and rationalism of the liberal capitalist version of modernity.[70] It is here we can mark the beginning of what was to become identity politics.

Identity politics and the revolt against abstraction

The revolt against abstraction is a revolt against the violence of conceptualizing persons in terms divorced from their concrete, felt, embodied experience of the world. More strongly, abstraction and universalism are seen as forms of mystification whereby one form of human being is privileged above all others. It is useful to begin thinking about this in relation to the dichotomous form of thought which is now widely seen to be specific to western cultures and to be expressed in binary systems of classification which lie at the base of an allegedly universal, essential conception of human nature. This system of classification is derived from the rules of formal logic relating to principles of identity and noncontradiction. The principle of identity states that if something is A, then it is A and only A. The principle of noncontradiction states that nothing can be both A and not-A. Related to these is the principle of the excluded middle which states that everything must be either A or not-A. These principles are seen to be the basis for constituting a politics of identity in which A stands for the white, male bourgeois in relation to whom all other forms of identity are assessed. From this point of view, the worldview of liberal capitalism is a worldview organized according to dichotomies which sort people, whether individuals, groups or whole populations, into superior/inferior. Here the public/private dichotomy is equated with the universal/particular dichotomy and both are seen as foundational for others such as masculine/feminine and rational/irrational. In effect, recognition can be of a positive or negative kind. Negative recognition

20

results in exclusion from the public sphere of matters which are seen to be of purely private concern and therefore of no political concern or interest. It may also, and more strongly, lead to exclusion from participation in decision-making about matters of shared, public interest. At the same time, negative recognition, or the presence of an entity which is different and inferior, is constitutive of the positive. Here there is an emphasis – absent from Erikson's account of identity formation – on the constitutive relationship of identity and difference, with the western binary classification system inevitably translating difference into inferiority.[71]

Those who feel themselves to be relegated to the second term of the binary have a choice of strategies available to combat such injustice. First they can set out to demonstrate that they possess the attributes necessary for promotion to the first term, or, that their true identities are being concealed by means of a socializing process designed to allocate them to inferior positions. Put another way, they can claim that their natural human attribute of rationality is being denied expression, or that they are being denied some fundamental human rights. This is the strategy adopted by intra-state groups such as liberal feminists as well as by certain anti-colonial nationalist movements. As discussed earlier, Yörük (chapter 4) gives an account of one version of this strategy i.e. the Kemalist early twentieth century modernization programme whose goal was the constitution of the Turkish nation-state.

The second strategy available to the marginalized is to embrace and valorize the stigmatized identity, proclaiming it superior to the supposedly universal and rational identity to which it is opposed. This is the strategy adopted by radical feminists as well as by some groups using ethnicity or the nation as markers of distinctiveness. To a certain extent, the Islamic intellectual discussed by Tripp (chapter 6) is engaging in this kind of strategy. Tripp is concerned with the attempts of one Islamic intellectual to preserve an Islamic identity (or culture in the broad sense) in the face of western intrusions of a capitalist kind; to protect a total way of life expressive of a distinct spirit and set of values. In attempting to think his way through this problem, the intellectual is almost imperceptibly drawn onto the ground of western culture by incorporating into his thought notions of the 'economic' which emanate from an alien culture and which may be antithetical to the preservation of a unique Islamic culture. This is the conundrum faced by all groups who adopt this strategy.

Third, the marginalized can reject the existing classificatory system, together with the very attempt to attribute fixed positions or identities to individuals and groups within it. This is the strategy which is referred to as the 'politics of difference', which is discussed by O'Sullivan (chapter 9) below and about which I shall have more to say following further discussion of identity politics.

Identity politics and the rage against reason

What came to be described as a 'rage against reason' was in the first instance a rage against the alleged misuse of reason through its equation with a socio-historically, culturally specific conception of reason, namely instrumental rationality.[72] Members of the Frankfurt School had built on the work of Marx and Weber to reveal the limited character of such rationality.[73] This task was now taken up and given a new twist by radical feminists on behalf of women in general and by nonwestern (as well as some western) intellectuals on behalf of the nonwest.[74] These focused on the gender and cultural-historical specificity of the allegedly universalist identities described earlier (and the forms of knowledge which both supported and were supported by them). They charged that universalist claims serve to cloak a reality which is white, male and western; a reality which expresses and valorizes some human characteristics while suppressing and devaluing others. Radical feminists were particularly critical of the public/private split which was rejected as the institutional expression of this bogus universalism and which served as the means of effacing the constitutive role of 'private' activity in relation to the 'public'.[75] The Islamic intellectual discussed by Tripp considers the socially destructive implications and consequences of the individual/society split and engages in the attempt to construct a politics of identity which acclaims a distinct, homogeneous, essential Islamic identity over against a threatening western 'Other' (chapter 6).

Those espousing identity politics in this sense demanded, not the inclusion of groups in question into a fundamentally unaltered form of the social but, rather, the transformation or avoidance of a harsh, impersonal and individualistic politics held to be gender and/or culturally specific in favour of a community-based politics.[76] An important move towards this end was the constitution of a new morality, a new epistemology and a new psychology, as the partial basis for the reconstitution and valorization of an identity which embraces those human orientations and faculties which have been 'privatized' and therefore demoted by liberalism (as well as by an economistic Marxism). For many radical feminists, an important element of that valorization is to 'promote' reproduction – i.e. pregnancy, birth, maternity – from the merely biological or natural to the socio-historical or cultural.[77]

Radical feminism constitutes an attempt to create a new culture which is as revolutionary (in its implications at least) as the earlier bourgeois transformation.[78] This new culture strikes at the foundation of welfare state capitalist forms of the social by questioning the gendered division of labour particularly as it is expressed in the nuclear family.[79] In striking at the nuclear family, it is endangering the production of the individual, whether this individual be seen as the bourgeois subject described by Habermas in the work discussed above, or as the docile individual required by a mass producing capitalism and described by, for example, Foucault and Althusser.[80] The thrust of much of radical feminist writing on this topic is towards a new kind of communitarian individualism. It remains unclear, though, how, in the absence of new institutions supportive of new kinds of family structure, such an individual can be brought into being.[81] While neoliberal capitalism is certainly open to the demands of liberal feminists, its institutions are antithetical to the constitution of communitarian individuals.

In relation to this point, Castro Leiva's discussion of the enforced meeting between Latin American republicanism and neoliberalism (chapter 7) makes clear the contradiction between the communitarian individualism espoused by the former and the utilitarian individualism produced by the latter. The republican communitarian individual is a unique individual possessing 'singularity of character' which is the product of a self-conscious process of self-disciplined self-cultivation whereby the agent becomes the object of aesthetic moral appraisal. The conformist individual required by contemporary neoliberalism as it manifests itself in Latin America embodies a contractual conception of selfhood which is conceived of as a bundle of quantifiable and measurable desires or as a purchaser of utilitarian identification. Whether or not these two kinds of individualism can coexist is the question which Castro Leiva addresses. In relation to this question of individualism, radical Islam attempts to avoid what it sees as the worst excesses of western possessive individualism by, for example, creating economic institutions based on Islamic rather than western capitalist values. As mentioned earlier, though, this is also a politics which incorporates an ambiguity or even contradiction relating to the relationship between sameness (in this case Islam) and difference (the west).[82]   Tripp's essay (chapter 6) on the attempt to develop an Islamic economics traces the way in which the foreign discourse infiltrates and subverts sophisticated attempts to evade it, since the very acceptance of a separate sphere of economics is the acceptance of a fundamental western cultural 'item'.

Having considered identity politics as a response to the 'violence of abstraction', let us now move on to consider another interpretation of the origin of identity politics, namely, that it is the outcome, not of a principled rejection of an arid universalism and essentialism, but rather, of 'a crisis of recognition'.

Identity politics and the crisis of recognition

The 'crisis of recognition' thesis has been put forward most persuasively by Axel Honneth.[83]   The thesis sees identity politics as the outcome of a combination of economic and cultural changes which many have described under the rubric of globalization, a process which, it is claimed, is transforming the world into one place.[84] This, apparently, is the new reality with which we must all come to terms; a new reality marked by the reappearance of unmistakable extremes of wealth and poverty, as well as new forms of insecurity and the intensification of change in the industrialized world. Change encompasses new forms of economic organization cutting across the boundaries of national economies; a new international division of labour connected to the wide-spread speedy industrialization of parts of Asia; associated with the last, a transfer of industries from Europe and North America to these newly-industrializing areas with accompanying occupational changes. The transformation of western societies from industrial societies to 'knowledge' societies diminishes the power of the organized working class and leads to claims about the demise of class politics at a time when the triumph of one stratum of the bourgeoisie appears undeniable.[85]

The new technologies, referred to above, accompany (indeed make possible) changes in the global division of labour. These technologies allow of more flexible working arrangements and social relationships. Self-employment, part-time work, short-term contracts, begin to take the place of life-time employment, of predictable and graduated career structures. There is a new temporariness in the structures of both public and private value systems which means that both public and private relationships are marked by transitoriness. Short-termism and adaptability, pluralism, fragmentation and change are upheld as new values.

For employed as well as the growing pool of the long-term unemployed, these changing conditions are likely to be experienced as insecurity, the loss of a strong sense of place in the world and of the capacity for political action. All boundaries are experienced as porous, all allegiances as temporary, all contracts as short-term. The criteria pinpointed by Erikson as essential for 'true identity' become difficult, if not impossible, to fulfil as the postwar settlement guaranteeing recognition for organized labour begins to unravel. As unemployment increases, the role of work in ensuring a sense of usefulness and competence and recognition by other members of one's group is undermined; state-provision of universal welfare benefits is undermined as higher levels of unemployment, together with the growth of aging populations and the intensifying of feelings of insecurity on the part of the middle class create a widening gap between resources needed and willingness and ability of the taxable to be taxed.[86] The Keynesian settlement is replaced by a neoliberalism which stresses self-interest, self-reliance, flexibility, the free market and entrepreneurship. This neoliberalism is quite different from the earlier liberalism whose institutions (described in the first section of this introduction) produced (and were reproduced by) the bourgeois subject.

The preoccupation with flexibility derives from the conviction that a capitalism, freed from earlier forms of political regulation and armed with the technological means of moving resources around the globe apparently at will, requires populations to be permanently mobilized to respond to its demands. As Inden remarks (chapter 3) these developments are endowed by commentators such as Reich with the power and intransigence of a force of nature and so it becomes imperative for collective action to be mobilized to produce the kinds of persons (highly skilled in the new technologies, highly mobile and flexible and therefore radically disembedded) required to attract capital. At the same time it is clear that a sizable minority of persons in the 'post-industrial' countries will remain surplus to capitalism's requirements.[87] It is in such a world that culture in the narrow sense, (in the sense, that is, of a body of 'meanings', representations, etc., produced by specialists in a dedicated sphere) becomes an important (for some apparently the only) source of identity. This is a culture which is increasingly disembodied in the sense that it is separated from the social practices of which it was originally both shaper and product (e.g. various

24

forms of sport which are now 'consumed' as images in the isolation of one's home rather than being engaged in directly or watched along with others at the place of play). Honneth is exercised by what he sees as the intensification of that process of commodification which Habermas noted in relation to the early twentieth century period. Such a process – one which results in the *'fictionalization of reality'*[88] – leaves individuals as passive consumers of images rather than active participants in a living popular culture, or in Appadurai's more striking phrase, fantasy becomes 'a social practice' in the sense that 'ordinary lives today are increasingly powered not by the givenness of things but by the possibilities that the media (either directly or indirectly) suggest are available.'[89] Honneth, who takes the view that culture is 'both the bearer and the ideology of capitalist growth processes' will see no contrast here between fantasy and the given, since fantasy now becomes the capitalist product par excellence. From this point of view the electronic media and the fantasies which they disseminate are, along with the speeded-up consumerism characteristic of the contemporary world, manifestations of systemic imperatives and therefore an intrinsic part of the 'givenness of things'.[90] Here the preoccupation with fantasies is a manifestation of a 'crisis of recognition' as fantasies take the place of earlier identities grounded in a sense of place and of function derived from location within the family and the occupational structure. The cultural sphere replaces the famial and economic spheres as shaper of identities and as the output of the 'culture industry' increases through the remarkable proliferation of technologies described above, the turnover in 'identities' also increases. Thus we move towards a politics of difference which seems to herald the 'end of identities'.

However, Meister (chapter 8) offers quite a different account of the source and appeal of an identity politics nourished by consumerism and productive of the 'post-bourgeois' subject. Meister's concern is that a socialism preoccupied with questions of exploitation and distribution is failing to notice that the debate has effectively moved on in that a concern with domination rather than exploitation is what characterizes the contemporary world. Identity politics derives from this concern and this concern may be met by a capitalism which has moved on from utilitarian justifications for its existence. It is from this point of view that he contends that sometime during the 1980s, capitalism ceased to be defensive about its propensity to produce more desires than it could satisfy. Meister makes his case through a reworking of the Freudian concept of ambivalence (in relation to gain and loss) by way of the Nietzschean concept of the will to power (whereby self-assertion and self-sacrifice are inextricably linked). He claims that acquiring new desires, even where these are incapable of satisfaction, may be experienced as in itself a good, or, put another way, desires can be 'beyond satisfaction'. The twist is that these desires are related to the will to power. This needs to be understood by an 'interest' politics focussed exclusively on questions of gain and the politics of distribution. What also needs to be understood is the way in which capitalism caters to such desires. By this account, the apparent worldwide triumph of consumerist capitalism is related to the desire for personal sovereignty rather than for gain (as socialists have assumed) and this in turn should be understood as the struggle for cultural dominance. Identity politics and what Meister refers to as 'the consumer revolution that is creating one world' are intimately related as domination becomes a more urgent cause for concern than exploitation. What is required, claims Meister, is an analysis and politics which shows the relationship between exploitation and domination rather than privileging one at the expense of the other. Let us now turn to the politics of difference in which questions about exploitation have become muted, or have been eliminated altogether.

V

Identity and the politics of difference

The politics of difference and the end of identity

Groups who wish to bring new claims into the political arena now have the choice of doing so, not under the banner of 'identity' but of 'difference'. What is meant, though, by the politics of difference? This is by no means a transparent category. What was described as identity politics in section four can equally be described as a politics of difference in the sense that it rejects the homogenizing thrust of western universalism and proclaims either a competing, equally essential identity or an ineradicable and wholly desirable cultural plurality. However, I am here reserving the term 'politics of difference' for the apparently more radical rejection of the western model which, as mentioned above, seems to herald the end of identity itself. While the politics of difference shares with identity politics the rejection of the universalist, essentialist claims of the west, it also rejects the strategy of identity politics as discussed in the previous section.

The politics of difference rejects the second strategy on the grounds that it merely replaces one essentialism by another. For example, difference feminists criticize radical feminists on these grounds and charge that the latter are in danger of dominating, rather than liberating women. Their strategy will have the effect, even if this is not the intention, of sacrificing women's diversity on the altar of the alleged identity of universal woman, in the way that liberalism and Marxism sacrifice human diversity on the altars of the (male, white) subject and of class respectively. Postcolonial theory makes similar arguments in relation to questions about ethnicity.[91] From this point of view, the problem is the very preoccupation with identity, which, by its very nature, excludes the possibility of emancipation. What emancipation requires is not the constitution of a strong sense of collective identity, but, on the contrary, the positive recognition of difference which in turn requires the abandonment of all talk of identity and of the danger of essentialism which such talk

26

appears to secrete. Here the fear is expressed that the fundamentalism of liberal capitalist modernity will be replaced by other fundamentalisms no less antithetical to human freedom.

So, difference politics goes beyond identity politics when it makes the further claim that identity *tout court* is both impossible and undesirable. The pluralization of identities required by identity politics is insufficient to guard against the perils of domination and essentialism. In fact, the concept of identity and the attempt to establish stable, durable identities with which the concept is associated, are seen to be ineradicably related to the illegitimate project of mobilizing popular energies in support of elite projects of various kinds. For this reason, Inden (chapter 3) advocates the jettisoning of the concept from the social science lexicon and its replacement by concepts such as participation and agency which do not have the effect of engulfing individuals in the projects of others. However, in abandoning identity and essentialism he does not move directly to a constructivist position, which tends to efface the givenness and durability of cultures. Indeed, he points to evidence of the resilience of Indian culture in the face of a new flourishing consumerism. In this case, there appears to be a resistance to sliding from identity to difference.

At its most extreme, difference politics finds theoretical support in the postmodernist claim about the decentring of the subject.[92] Here the subject is seen, not as the model for autonomous human being in the world but, rather, as the most notable evidence of modernity's (i.e. the west's) quest for domination. By this account, modernity is nothing but the darkness of this quest; it has no bright side. Talk of emancipation is merely a gloss on what is in fact a project to remake the world so as to control it. The end of modernity, then, is at once the end of the western project to rationalize, disenchant, standardize and dominate the world and the beginning of the possibility of the untrammeled enjoyment and tolerance of difference. This, very briefly, is the kernel of poststructural and postmodern positions insofar as these translate into the politics of difference.[93]

The adoption of the prefix 'post' is an expression of the refusal or inability to refer to anything 'real', or enduring in the world. It is an expression of what Baudrillard describes as the 'death of referential reason'.[94] It is the characterization of the entity in question in terms of what it is not rather than what it is. This characterization is associated with the freedom and flight from fixed identities into a playful world of polysemy, of a 'surplus of meaning' or discourses which serve as a rich resource for the postmodern individual.[95] To attempt to confine the individual within any one of the many identities available to her in the contemporary world is to attempt to dominate that individual. The end of identity does not presage the end of human health and happiness. On the contrary, human happiness lies in the freedom to choose and discard identities. There is no trace of the fear, which we find expressed in Erikson's work – as discussed by Inden (chapter 3) – that the lack of a stable sense of identity may leave individuals open to extremist political interpellations. Here we are far from Erikson's project and claim that human health and happiness require stable identities. What takes its place is the idea of experimental self-creation and re-creation through the experience of diverse forms of life. Here, in place of the newly-marginalized turning to fantasy in the absence of more concrete markers of identity such as family and work, we have the celebratory and principled advocacy of a 'permanent revolution' in identities which means in effect, the end of identity. The resulting 'lightness of being' is to be celebrated because it will remove the possibility of the kind of sustained collective action which produced the myriad forms of domination with which western imperialism and colonialism are associated. For critical theorists such as Honneth, it is to be deplored because it leaves the individuals thus constituted culturally, socially and politically impoverished and therefore open to the many subtle forms of manipulation produced by contemporary capitalism. Moreover, Honneth sees the preoccupation with culture which characterizes the theory and practice of the politics of difference as a manifestation of the 'loss of the social', his claim being that the term difference refers to the conviction that 'the biographical peculiarities of every individual subject, its specific manner of self-creation, can better unfold the fewer the normatively encompassing bonds and contexts it is involved in.'[96] Before concluding I want to consider the implications of this 'loss of the social' in relation to collective action.

Identity, difference and action

It was stated earlier that politics and identity are mutually constitutive in that the recognition of an entity – individual or group – as having certain functions, purposes, rights and/or obligations is a prerequisite for participation in politics. For this reason, the demand for such recognition, together with the exercise of demonstrating one's worthiness to be recognized, have been, and continue to be, the stuff of politics. Whether or not we continue to use the concept of identity to refer to whatever it is that claims and gains this recognition is an open question. As has been seen, some argue that there are good reasons (related to the way in which identity has been used to manipulate and even dominate individuals) for abandoning the concept. However, the phenomenon to which the concept refers, i.e. a sense of self – both collective and individual – seems to be a prerequisite for effective political action.[97] If this is accepted, then it becomes difficult to imagine how a politics of difference might be pursued in the world. This is the problem which O'Sullivan (chapter 9) explores. He looks for, but does not find, a politics of difference which is simultaneously coherent and fundamentally different from that which difference politics wishes to eliminate i.e. rights-based liberal democracy. Neither Derrida nor Levinas, neither Rorty nor Connolly, can produce such an entity. O'Sullivan's account of Anne Phillips' attempt to create a politics of 'presence' which avoids the intellectualism and abstraction of conventional liberal politics is of particular interest, since what it shows is the apparently unavoidable consequence of avoiding 'essentialism'.[98] This consequence is a return to liberal democratic, therefore individualistic, rights-based politics. If no assumptions can be made about what constitutes the salient identity of individuals, then access to the public realm must be open to all individuals as individuals. Given this state of affairs, it is no surprise that O'Sullivan finds Chantal Mouffe's account of difference politics returning, as he says, 'full circle' to the 'classical theory of civil association' which accommodates diversity in a 'non-purposive framework of formal rules'.[99]

Here difference politics is a politics in the service of individuals who are free to pursue their individually-chosen, private purposes. The difference between the individuals posited by difference politics and utilitarian, possessive individuals is, apparently, that the former are motivated by 'identity' and the latter are motivated by 'interest'. However, if we recall the centrality of the identity-constituting properties of the cultural sphere in the contemporary period, we may be forced to conclude that nothing much separates these individuals since they are both gaining their ends through the consumption of commodified entities. They are both attaining their ends directly through capitalism which is by these means replenished and revitalized. However, this is not the end of the matter. While the utilitarian individual was also the docile, disciplined individual and therefore available (in however minimal a sense) for social purposes and susceptible to the appeals of nationhood, the contemporary individual (at least in the AngloAmerican world) is, as Honneth has noted, resistant to the demands of the social, at least insofar as these demands emanate from the state.[100]

We are apparently a world away from those collective transformative projects, discussed by Kaviraj (chapter 2) which required for their completion a sense of collective identity and the readiness of individual members of the group to be 'enumerated' (and therefore in some sense stripped of their individuality) and placed in a hierarchy of positions as dictated by the project in question. Here the end of identity is the mobilization of popular energies and collective resources in pursuit of ends which may or may not be to the direct benefit of those involved. Difference politics appears to rule out such projects by associating them necessarily with a modernity which is inherently dominating. As has been seen, there is a resistance on the part of contemporary individuals (in the west, at least) to being absorbed into projects not of their own making. Identity can no longer be a means to the ends of others. It is an end in itself.

If modernity sets up a pressure towards agentive collective agencies and therefore collective identities oriented to doing, as Kaviraj claims, are we now experiencing a transition from these to new kinds of identities of being? Or, put another way, are we witnessing the replacement of instrumental or economic motivations for political action (in which identity functioned as a means) by cultural motivations whose goal is the creation and preservation of particular group and/or individual selves (in which identity is an end in itself)? While the logic of difference politics appears to rule out any sustained group membership (which will have the tendency to congeal into relationships of domination), identity politics of an 'essentialist' kind is flourishing in many parts of the world, as we know. Yörük's account of the dissolution of Kemalism (chapter 3) reveals the unstable coexistence of 'flag politics', neoliberal consumerism (which could become the basis of difference politics) Kurdish nationalism and Islamism in contemporary Turkey.

On the other hand, those who hold to the innateness of 'interest' motivations will find a reminder, in Hirst's paper (chapter 10), of the historical and cultural specificity and novelty of such motivations. Hirst reminds us of the continuing relevance of Carl Schmitt's friend-enemy relations and of the variability or 'open-ended' character of issues and motivations that define the political. In this case, he returns to seventeenth century western Europe and the origins of the nation-state in the religious wars of that period. At this time, religious motivations and conflicts formed much of the content of politics. At the same time, the Peace of Westphalia marked the beginning of the privatization of religion through its 'nationalization' (in the sense that state and religion would ideally become coterminous, as it were). This nationalization and subsequent privatization of religion, which was as necessary to state-building as the internal pacification of territories, according to Hirst, could only come about through international means. It thereafter became the partial basis of a cultural distinctiveness and homogeneity which would lend credence to future nationalist claims.

However, as has been made abundantly clear in recent years, religion will not remain privatized. In any case, the distinctiveness of motivations and of activities posited and to some extent constituted through the modern differentiation of spheres can lead us astray in our attempts to understand the well-springs of political action. While the privileging of interest motivations is misleading, there is no avoiding interest politics in a completely monetized, commodified society, even though difference politics appears unaware of this. The politicization of culture by the politics of identity and difference is accompanied by the economization of culture by the politics of interest but neither culturalism nor economism will enable us to comprehend these processes satisfactorily.

Conclusion

It has been argued here that the preoccupation with identity can only be understood in relation to the differentiation of spheres which is the defining characteristic of the modern world. Beginning with a consideration of the early bourgeois public sphere, the way in which a sense of identity, both collective and individual, served both to create a capacity to act collectively and to give individuals a sense of self, of place, of function and of relationship was explored. What was found was that, for a short period at least, a new sense of identity appeared to serve individual and collective ends. It could only do so, however, through the coordination of processes and practices in the different (emergent) spheres i.e. the economic, political, cultural and familial. Since such coordination requires good fortune, political skills of an exceptional kind and a receptive environment it is to be found only rarely in the modern world. Therefore, a sense of identity is difficult, if not impossible, to maintain under modern fragmented conditions, although for a quarter century following the end of World War Two, this difficult feat was apparently accomplished in the west. During this period identity served the function of harnessing the energies of individuals to collective, state-driven purposes, in part because the attainment of those purposes was compatible with (indeed was implicated in) the welfare of the individuals in question. In the contemporary world, capitalism as described by Marx in *The Communist Manifesto* becomes once more a reality, as solidity melts and permanence gives way to temporariness. This is what accounts for the intense preoccupation with identity in recent years, when globalizing processes have endangered or removed the bases for identity constructed in the west after the Second World War.

As we have seen, there is a separate but related question arising from the allegedly deviant and inherently unsatisfactory character of social relations instituted by capitalism; social relations marked by instrumental rationality and all that this term implies. From this point of view, the stability of the post-1945 quarter century could not have continued indefinitely, even in the absence of the various shocks which ended the economic growth upon which it depended. During the 1970s, critiques of capitalism shaded into critiques of modernity as disillusionment with economistic Marxism set in. Radical politics now moved from the economic to the cultural sphere, in both centre and periphery. During the 1980s, as neoliberalism revitalized a free-market capitalism which began to lay a heavy economizing hand on all within its grasp, class politics, or the politics of interest, fell silent (or was reduced to the occasional whimper) and ceded to the politics of identity and difference.

In relation to the periphery, we have noted attempts both to follow the western path to modernity and to preserve intact the nonwestern cultures which modernity seems bound to assimilate. Regarding the first, what have been noted are the peculiar difficulties (relating in part to the strengthening of kinship relations effected by colonialism itself) faced by postcolonial countries attempting to undergo a speeded-up, intensified process of modernization, which is to say, differentiation of spheres of activity, disembedding of individuals from kinship groups and depersonalization of social relations held to be economic and political, all of these in turn oriented to the increase in economic growth. Here, identity served the purpose, not of constituting the nation-state needed to achieve collective goals, but rather of enhancing conflict between kinship groups struggling over the spoils of state. Regarding the second, it has been seen that attempts to preserve nonwestern cultures in the face of modernity have been marked by contradictions in the sense that the very attempt to do so involved engagement with the west on western terms. Defence against modernity required the incorporation of elements of modernity itself.

Finally, the possible homogenizing effects of globalization have been referred to above. However, given the continuing heterogeneity of cultures, of histories and of contemporary experiences found in the world today, the claim that globalization is constituting the world as one place is not convincing. Certainly, the picture offered in *The Communist Manifesto* of a capitalism recreating the world in its own image seems more relevant now than it did in the mid-nineteenth century. The economic reforms in China and the collapse of the Soviet Union have extended the reach of capitalism quite significantly and the advent of new technology has given it the means of integrating and coordinating processes and practices in different parts of the world to quite a remarkable degree. Furthermore, the diffusion of electronic media of communication have given us the means of imagining the world as one place in the sense used by Anderson in relation to the nation.[101] So we appear to have both the disciplinary and imaginary means of constituting a collective identity with global reference. However, if we accept that identity is constituted by difference, this claim will be unpersuasive. In any case, before concluding that the world is indeed becoming one place through globalizing movements of persons, culture and other commodities, and, perhaps more significantly, through the introduction of capitalist industrial social relations in new areas, we need to bear in mind two fundamental factors which are likely to prevent the production of social and cultural homogeneity in the short or even medium term. The first of these is that as new countries industrialize, old countries deindustrialize or 'dedevelop'. The result is a kind of unevenness within the centre which up to now has been found only in the periphery. This is one source of heterogeneity. The other is the differing capacities and propensities of nonwestern cultures to resist complete absorption by the west. It is only if we allocate a determining role to what really is experienced globally, i.e. the consumption of both images (through the electronic media) and of commodities in general, that we can make claims about a homogenizing globalizing process. As should be clear by now, such culturalism is as misleading about the world as is the economism which is its complement. As the papers in this volume make clear, the 'end of history' in this sense is not in sight.

Notes

1   Calhoun (1994), p. 20.
2   Gorz (1994), p. 24.
3   Erikson (1974), pp. 27-8.
4   Erikson (1959), p. 102.
5   Ibid., p. 151.
6   Ibid., fn.7 pp. 122-3.
7   Erikson (1974), p. 33.
8   It should be noted, though, that these are analytical rather than empirical

distinctions. The institutions (actuality) would 'fabricate' individuals on the basis of both the empirical (factuality) and symbolic (sense of reality) resources available. For the account of institutions used here, see Castoriadis (1987).

9   Habermas (1989).

10   Giddens (1990) offers an account of some of the effects of 'disembedding'.

11   See Castoriadis (1987) for an excellent, historically informed philosophicalaccount of these developments.

12   See Appleby (1978) for an account of the seventeenth century origins of the discursive construction of the 'economic'. Tribe (1981) takes up the story as it unfolds in the eighteenth century.

13   For more on this, see Kalberg (1993).

14   Sahlins (1976), p. 220. See also Gudeman (1986).

15   Habermas (1989), p. xvii.

16   Ibid., pp. 25-6.

17   Ibid., p. 27.

18   A key development here was the point at which the state apparatus began to assume an independence from the monarch, in other words, the point at which power was transferred from a person to an impersonal apparatus. As the state apparatus began to assume an independence from the personal sphere of the monarch, the courtly society began to drift towards the town where it came to have an influence on the emerging new bourgeoisie. What might be described as the organic intellectuals of the bourgeoisie, Habermas' 'bourgeois avant-garde of the educated middle class' acquired the art of critical rational public debate through its contact with the courtly world. It was when the court lost its central position in the public sphere that 'reason' could 'shed its dependence on the authority of the aristocratic noble hosts' and 'acquire that autonomy that turns conversation into criticism and *bons mots* into arguments' (Habermas 1989, p. 31).

19   By subject here I mean the introspective, self-activating, self-disciplined individual. See Cascardi (1992) and Touraine (1995). Both of these authors focus on the 'contradictions internal to the culture of modernity' (Cascardi 1992, p. 3), contradictions relating to the relationship between subjectivity and rationalization. Touraine sees 'modernity' as a state of civil war between the principles of subjectivity and of rationalization. By subjectivity, Touraine means *'an individual's will to act and to be recognized as an actor'* (Touraine 1995, p. 207 - italics in original). How to resist a reductive conception of modernity (one which equates it with rationalization) and ensure the triumph of subjectivity is the problem Touraine sets out to resolve.

20   Habermas (1989), p. 47. Nevertheless, it should be noted that Habermas, a few lines earlier, had referred to this development as 'psychological

33

emancipation', ibid., p. 46.
21   See Adorno & Horkheimer (1979); Horkheimer (1972).
22   Whyte (1960) gives a useful account of the emergence of self-consciousness in the modern world.
23   This is the individual that Durkheim was later to refer to as the Kantian individual, in contrast to the self-interested, calculating utilitarian individual. See Durkheim (1973).
24   Habermas has been criticized by feminists for making too little of the exclusion of women from the bourgeois public sphere. See, for example, Ryan (1992).
25   Habermas (1989), p. 157.
26   For a brief discussion of the variety of disciplinary procedures used during the nineteenth century, see Perrot (1979). See also Foucault (1979), Pollard (1963) and Thompson (1967, 1978b). According to Thompson (1978b) paternalistic relations were predominant in England until the 1840s. In France, on the other hand, according to Pollard, paternalistic relations survived to a significant extent until the end of the century. The work of Elias (1994) remains an indispensable guide to the long-term emergence of 'discipline'.
27   Habermas (1989), pp. 55-6.
28   Marx (1994).
29   However, for Habermas (here echoing a claim made in *The German Ideology*) this self-interpretation converged with the 'objective function' of the bourgeoisie in the sense that the emancipation of the emerging 'civil society' from absolutist rule was in the general interest.
30   Habermas (1989) p. 86
31   The extent to which a new radical bourgeoisie was in existence during this period is a matter of some controversy. For works which confirm (in broad terms) Habermas' account, see Kramnick (1990) and Eley (1992). According to Eley: 'The value of Habermas' perspective has been fundamentally borne out by recent social history in a variety of fields' (p.294). The researches of Perkin (1985) offer a different view, namely that the English bourgeoisie was reluctantly radicalized by means of the Corn Laws in 1815.
32   Elias (1994) is an important resource of insight on these questions.
33   Mass integration and mass discipline would not have become an urgent concern in the late eighteenth century and Habermas' historically specific account of the bourgeois public sphere does not require a consideration of these questions.
34   Hayek (1986) provides one of the most powerful statements of the effectiveness, efficiency and even moral desirability of the market. Parsons (1977) offers the most systematic attempt to deal theoretically with the

problem of integration in the modern world. See also Luhmann (1982); Alexander and Colomy (1990). Althusser (1990) offers a Marxist account of differentiation and the problems of integration.

35   Hirschman (1977) offers an excellent account (from a history of ideas perspective) of how and why the latter became normative in the west.

36   For more on this see Calhoun (1982, 1991).

37   Tarrow (1994) offers a useful account of these matters.

38   See Lash & Urry (1987); Marglin and Schor (1990); Piore & Sabel (1984).

39   Offe (1984) discusses the role of the state in 'rolling back' commodification during the postwar period.

40   See Carrithers et. al. (1985) for more on different conceptions of the individual. The term 'possessive individualism', is Macpherson's (1964).

41   Held (1980) gives a useful introduction to the work of the Frankfurt School.

42   Habermas (1989).

43   These terms are unsatisfactory in many respects but appear less misleading than the vocabulary of 'thirdworldism' so, following their introduction here, they will be used without quotation marks. What is becoming clear now is the comparative fluidity of 'centres' and 'peripheries' as the industrial developments in east and south east Asia open up the possibility of the emergence of a new centre to replace that of EuroAmerica.

44   For a useful and succinct overview of the conceptual debates, see the papers in Haferkamp (1989). See also Bauman (1973); Featherstone (1989); Inglehart (1990); Wallerstein (1991).

45   Arnason (1995),

46   Parsons (1951).

47   Polanyi's famous phrase (1957).

48   I am aware that this conception of the nation is partial in the sense that a civic model of nationalism exists which privileges a universalist, citizenship based model. See Hall (1993) for a succinct discussion of different models of nationalism and the nation. See also Chatterjee (1986) who discusses these questions specifically from the point of view of the nonwest.

49   This transition may not have been quite as speedy as would appear by glancing at the date of the Meiji Restoration – 1868. At this point, Japan had many of the characteristics deemed of crucial importance in the modernizing process, including high levels of literacy and an efficient bureaucracy which included effective local government. For more on this see Steenstrup (1976).

50   It should be noted here that, in the Japanese case, favourable bureaucratic and cultural 'raw materials' were not sufficient in themselves to constitute the new nation state. The Meiji 'reforms' met popular and elite resistance and required both negotiation and coercion for their successful implementation.

See Ikegami (1996). Tilly (1990) has interesting things to say about the importance of bargaining in the constitution of durable nation (or national) states.

51   In relation to Africa, John Dunn comments: 'The plethora of languages and the multiplicity of pre-colonial and colonial units of social and political membership has rendered effective localist representation an aggressive solvent of the somewhat gimcrack national unity of African states' (Dunn 1990, p. 153).

52   Ayoade (1988) argues that retreat into subsistence agriculture remained a possibility for Africans as late as the 1980s. That this option was even considered says much about the lack of 'infrastructural' power in African states. For more on infrastructural power, see Mann (1984).

53   Ranger (1983, 1993) discusses the 'invention' of ethnicity in colonial Africa. Ekeh (1990) proposes a new normative critical language as a means to combat the continuing problem of tribalism in post-colonial Africa.

54   In this, as in many other respects, the example of the French Revolution is salient. Here a whole raft of legislation was designed to 'disembed' the individual from local and familial networks so as to free him (her?) for untrammeled membership of the nation-state. At the same time, policies designed to create absolutely separate private and public spheres were introduced. These included the rationalization of the judiciary and the taxation system and the elimination of the role of private enterprise in public finance. For more on these matters, see Bosher (1970); Forrest (1991). Bosher describes the resulting transformation as 'the invention of an administrative weapon for social and political domination [which] ... was capable of mobilizing the financial resources of the nation to a degree Louis XIV could hardly have imagined' (Bosher 1970, p. 313). Price (1975) offers a persuasive account of the cultural obstacles to the pursuit of such rigorous differentiation in one post-colonial African country.

55   See Ranger (1983, 1993).

56   For an interesting general discussion of this problem see Ekeh (1975). Ekeh argues that there are two 'publics' in African countries – the 'primordial' and the 'civic'. The primordial public 'is moral and *operates on the same moral imperatives as the private realm*' of '*primordial groupings, sentiments, and activities*' with which it is 'closely identified'. The civic public is 'historically associated with the colonial administration' and '*is amoral and lacks the generalized moral imperatives operative in the private realm and in the primordial public*' (Ekeh 1975, p. 92, italics in original).

57   It should be noted here that 'kin' and 'tribe' are both used to designate, not necessarily a 'blood' relationship, but a specific kind of of social relationship diametrically opposed to the impersonal legal rational model. For an account of the continuing vitality of African kin groups in this

sense, see Meillassoux (1980). Lonsdale (1981) offers an excellent account of the 'unevenness' that resulted from the African encounter with the west.

58   We may wonder about the utility of this distinction in relation to the politics of independence movements in colonial states where symbolic and distributional questions were and are intimately connected. Fraser (1995) questions its use also in relation to class politics. She suggests that the history of class movements reveals a more complex history than this dichotomy suggests. As she says: 'Those movements have elaborated class not only as a structural category of political economy but also as a cultural-valuational category of identity .. Thus, most varieties of socialism have asserted the dignity of labour and the worth of working people, mingling demands for redistribution with demands for recognition' (Fraser 1995, p. 75).

59   Marx's work is an early critique of this peculiarly modern kind of violence. The expression 'violence of abstraction' is borrowed from Sayer (1987).

60   See Marx (1994).

61   See Marx (1977).

62   See Marx (1994) p. 49

63   Ibid., p. 47. Clearly, what Marx sees is not the Kantian or bourgeois subject but the utilitarian or possessive individual.

64   While this term is not used by Marx he does discuss the phenomenon to which the term refers.

65   Marx (1973) p. 488.

66   Anderson (1979).

67   Gorz (1989); Keane (1984); Marcuse (1986). The phrase 'technocracy's children' is Roszak's (1970).

68   Inglehart (1977); Roszak (1970).

69   Wallerstein (1991).

70   Baudrillard (1975) discusses this connection. For an account of the political sociological effects of disenchantment with Marxism, see Boggs (1988). See also Gitlin (1994).

71   See Laclau (1990) pp. 32-3.

72   See Bernstein (1986).

73   Held (1980).

74   Said (1978) is a key text here. See also Said (1985); Turner (1994).

75   For a useful discussion of the precarious and questionable nature of a range of distinctions or classifications related to the differentiation of spheres, see Fraser (1989).

76   Radical feminists criticized existing liberal capitalist forms of the social as organized on masculine principles of, at best, cold, impersonal notions of justice, and, at worst, domination, discipline and control. See Gilligan (1982) for an account of the 'justice' perspective allegedly developed by

boys and the 'care' perspective allegedly developed by girls. The former is associated with impartiality and universalizable (abstract) principles arrived at on the basis of the capacity for disinterested reflection; the latter is associated with partiality, situated, concrete concerns, with intimacy and personal feeling.

77 See Gallop (1989) for more on this. In fact, Gallop, influenced by Keller (1985), questions the utility of the absolute split between biology and history. Pateman (1988), argues for a 'sexually differentiated' view of citizenship which rejects the antithesis of reproduction and citizenship by asserting the political importance of motherhood.

78 However, it is a less ambitious and comprehensive project than was that of the bourgeoisie which embraced economic as well as political, cultural and social changes. In fact, as has been argued above, the bourgeoisie *created* these distinctions, although this expression of the matter is too clear-cut and voluntaristic. It would be more correct to say that these differentiations were overdetermined by intentional action (including theory-formation and direct practical action) and by congruent wide-scale and long-term changes which had not been directly willed by anybody.

79 The feminization of the labour force in liberal capitalist countries is also having this effect, of course.

80 Althusser (1984); Foucault (1979). See also Sampson (1989).

81 Benjamin (1990) offers a feminist psychoanalytic account of the family and subjectivity.

82 Chatterjee (1986) discusses this question, as does Geertz (1963).

83 Honneth (1995a, 1995b).

84 The proliferation of literature on globalization now matches that on culture. See, for example, Cox (1992); Hirst & Thompson (1996); King (1991); Miyoshi (1993); Panitch (1995); Piven (1995);

85 Gorz (1989, 1990).

86 Reich (1991); Head (1996). See also Kennedy (1993).

87 Wilson (1996).

88 Honneth (1995a) p. 223 (italics in original).

89 Appadurai (1991) pp. 198, 200. This is one of several claims about the social significance of fantasy in the contemporary world. See also Baudrillard (1994); Fuss (1989) ch. 6; Honneth (1995a), ch. 13.

90 Baudrillard (1993) offers the most provocative account of the contemporary world in terms of the 'end of production'. See also Kellner (1992).

91 Turner (1994).

92 This blanket use of the term postmodernism is highly criticized in certain quarters. See the papers in Butler & Scott (1992). However, in this case it is justifiable since all 'post' forms of thought are agreed on this one matter i.e. the decentring of the subject.

93   It should be noted here that a less dramatic position than that described here – one which does not move from the deconstruction to the elimination of the subject – can be found in the 'difference' literature. See the papers in Butler & Scott (1992).

94   Baudrillard (1993).

95   Laclau & Mouffe (1985) offer a sophisticated version of this approach, one, though, which, unlike other versions (e.g. Butler 1990) does not deny the necessary link between indentity and action.

96   Honneth (1995a), p. 226.

97   Laclau and Mouffe (1985) discuss this question.

98   This term is in quotation marks because its meaning is far from clear. It can refer to the claim that one culturally and/or class specific form of the human being is in fact the real, essential and therefore normative form of human being. It can also refer to the related but separable claim that human beings have essences which are biological and which therefore determine or condition their identities. While the latter claim has been the basis for the former in the case of the bourgeois subject (as well as for the 'negative' or exclusionary recognition discussed above) it is possible to hold a weak version of this claim without going on to make universalist claims for one culture at the expense of all others. In fact, the fear that the second entails the first has led to the espousal of extreme positions claiming a complete disjunction of the biological and the socio-cultural, positions which find their theoretical support in deconstruction, poststructuralism and Lacanian psychoanalysis. Once the cultural sphere itself is conceived as being radically unstable, and as in a state of continuous flux, we have arrived at the theory of difference which underpins difference politics. For more on essentialism, see Brennan (1989); Calhoun (1994); Fuss (1989); Laclau & Mouffe (1985). Fuss attempts to break down the dichotomy between essentialism and constructivism which, like all dichotomies, conceals more than it reveals.

99   The difference is that the range of issues to be addressed by these means includes some unimagined by the founding fathers of this theory e.g. gender, sex, race, environment. Given this difference, it might be wondered whether the form of the public sphere can contain such contents.

100 Where collective action remains vibrant in the west it tends to avoid conventional political institutions in favour of concrete, local engagement with immediate and visible problems. Examples include actions against road building programmes and actions organized to reclaim unused land (The Land is Ours). However, it is too early to assess the significance of such actions. What seems clear from the considered reflections of social movement theorists such as Melucci is that, since the 1980s, collective actions have tended to be carried out by networks of multiple memberships

with constantly changing means of identification. The organizational form of these small groups is a goal in itself; it is an expression of rejection of the instrumental rationality of dominant institutions; it expresses 'being' rather than 'doing'. Furthermore, this 'being' is a being marked by short-term, reversible commitments, multiple and challengeable leadership and ad hoc, temporary organizational structures. Hence the use of the term 'nomad' by Melucci. These groups arc highly resistant to any attempts to 'solidify' or institutionalize a way of life or set of social relationships. Their members must be left free to remake or refashion themselves at will. See Melucci (1989).

101   Anderson (1991).

References

Adorno, T. & Horkheimer, M. (1979), *Dialectic of Enlightenment*, Cumming, J. (trans.), Verso: London.

Alexander, J.C. & Colomy, P. (eds.) (1990), *Differentiation Theory and Social, Change*, Columbia University Press: New York.

Althusser, L. (1984), 'Ideology and the Ideological State Apparatuses: Notes towards an Investigation', in *Essays on Ideology*, Brewster, B. (trans.), Verso: London.

____ (1990), 'Contradiction and Overdetermination', in *For Marx*, Brewster, B. (trans.), Verso: London.

Anderson, B. (1991), *Imagined Communities*, Revised edn., Verso: London.

Anderson, P. (1979), *Considerations on Western Marxism*, Verso: London

Appadurai, A. (1991), 'Global Ethnoscapes: Notes and Queries for a Transnational Anthropology', in Fox, R.G. (ed.), *Recapturing Anthropology: Working in the Present*, School of American Research Press: Santa Fe, N. Mexico.

Appleby, J. (1978), *Economic Thought and Ideology in Seventeenth-Century England*, Princeton University Press: Princeton, NJ.

Arnason, J.P. (1995), 'Modernity, Postmodernity and the Japanese Experience', in Arnason, J.P. & Sugimoto, Y. (eds.), *Japanese Encounters with Postmodernity*. Kegan Paul International: London.

Axford, B. (1995), *The Global System: Economics, Politics and Culture*, Polity Press: Cambridge.

Ayoade, J.A.A. (1988), 'States without Citizens: An Emerging African Phenomenon', in Rothchild, D. & Chazan, N. (eds.), *The Precarious Balance: State and Society in Africa*, Westview Press: London.

Baudrillard, J. (1975), *The Mirror of Production*, Poster, M. (trans.), Telos Press: St. Louis.

____ (1993), *For a Critique of the Political Economy of the Sign,* Grant, I.H. (trans.), Sage Publications: London.

____ (1994) *Simulacram and Simulation*, Glaser, S.F. (trans.), The University of Michigan Press: Ann Arbor.

Bauman, Z. (1973), *Culture as Praxis*, Routledge & Kegan Paul: London.

Benjamin, J. (1990), *The Bonds of Love*, Virago: London.

Bernstein, R. (1986), 'The Rage Against Reason', *Philosophy and Literature*, 10, pp. 186-210.

Boggs, C. (1986), *Social Movements and Political Power: Emerging Forms of Radicalism in the West*, Temple University Press: Philadelphia.

Bosher, J.F. (1970), *French Finances 1770 - 1795: From Business to Bureaucracy*, Cambridge University Press: Cambridge.

Brennan, T. (ed.) (1989), *Between Feminism and Psychoanalysis*, Routledge: London.

Butler, J. (1990), *Gender Trouble: Feminism and the Subversion of Identity*, Routledge: London.

Butler, J. & Scott, J.W. (eds.) (1992), *Feminists Theorize the Political*, Routledge: London.

Calhoun, C. (1982), *The Question of Class Struggle: Social Foundations of Popular Radicalism during the Industrial Revolution*, Blackwell: Oxford.

____ (1991), 'Indirect Relationships and Imagined Communities: Large-Scale Social Integration and the Transformation of Everyday Life', in Bourdieu, P. & Coleman, J.S. (eds.), *Social Theory for a Changing Society*, Westview Press: Boulder, CO.

____ (ed.) (1992), *Habermas and the Public Sphere*, The MIT Press: London.

____ (ed.) (1994), *Social Theory and the Politics of Identity*, Blackwell: Oxford.

Carrithers, M., Collins, S. & Lukes, S. (eds.)(1985), *The Category of the Person: Anthropology, Philosophy, History*, Cambridge University Press: Cambridge.

Cascardi, A.J. (1992), *The Subject of Modernity*, Cambridge University Press: Cambridge.

Castoriadis, C. (1987), *The Imaginary Institution of Society*, Blamey, K. (trans.), Polity Press: Cambridge.

Chatterjee, P. (1986), *Nationalist Thought and the Colonial World: A Derivative Discourse?*, Zed Books: London.

Cox, R.W. (1987), *Production, Power and World Order*, Columbia University Press: New York.

____ (1992), 'Global Perestroika', *Socialist Register*, Miliband, R. & Panitch, L. (eds.), The Merlin Press: London, pp. 26-43.

Dunn, J. (1990), 'The Politics of Representation and Good Government in Post-colonial Africa', in *Interpreting Political Responsibility: Essays 1981-1989*, Princeton University Press: Princeton, N.J.

Durkheim, E. (1973), 'Individualism and the Intellectuals' in Bellah, R.M. (ed.), Traugott, M. (trans.), *On Morality and Society: Selected Writings*, Chicago University Press: Chicago.

Ekeh, P. (1975), 'Colonialism and the Two Publics in Africa: A Theoretical Statement', *Comparative Studies in Society and History*, 17:1, pp. 91-112.

____ (1990), 'Social Anthropology and Tribalism in Africa', *Comparative Study of Society and History*, Vol. 32, No. 4, Oct., pp. 660-700.

Eley, G. (1992) 'Nations, Publics, and Political Cultures: Placing Habermas in the Nineteenth Century' in Calhoun.

Elias, N. (1994), *The Civilizing Process: Vol.1. The History of Manners, Vol.2. State Formation and Civilization*, Jephcott, E. (trans.), Blackwell: Oxford.

Erikson, E.H. (1959), *Identity and the Life Cycle*, International Universities Press, Inc: New York.

____ (1974), *Dimensions of a New Identity*, W.W. Norton & Co. Inc.: New York.

Featherstone, M. (1989), 'Towards a Sociology of Postmodern Culture', in Haferkamp.

Forrest, A. & Jones, P. (eds.) (1991), *Reshaping France: Town, Country and Region during the French Revolution*, Manchester University Press: Manchester.

Foucault, M. (1979), *Discipline and Punish: The Birth of the Prison*, Sheridan, A. (trans.), Penguin Books: Harmondsworth.

Fraser, N. (1989), 'What's Critical about Critical Theory? The Case of Habermas and Gender', in *Unruly Practices: Power, Discourse and Gender in Contemporary Social Theory*, Polity Press: Cambridge.

____ (1995), 'From Redistribution to Recognition? Dilemmas of Justice in a "Post-Socialist" Age', *New Left Review*, No. 212, July/Aug., pp. 68-93.

Friedman, J. (1992), 'Narcissism, Roots and Postmodernity: The Constitution of Selfhood in the Global Crisis', in Lash & Friedman.

Fuss, D. (1989), *Essentially Speaking: Feminism, Nature and Difference*, Routledge: London.

Gallop, J. (1989), 'Moving Backwards or Forwards', in Brennan.

Geertz, C. (1963), 'The Integrative Revolution: Primordial Sentiments and Civil Politics in the New States' in Geertz, C. (ed.), *Old Societies and New States*, Free Press: New York.

Giddens, A. (1990), *The Consequences of Modernity*, Polity Press: Cambridge.

Gilligan, C. (1982), *In A Different Voice: Psychological Theory and Womens' Development*, Harvard University Press: Cambridge, Mass.

Gitlin, T. (1994), 'From Universality to Difference: Notes on the Fragmentation of the Idea of the Left', in Calhoun.

Gorz, A. (1989), *Critique of Economic Reason*, Hendyside, G. & Turner, C. (trans.), Verso: London.

____ (1994), *Capitalism, Socialism, Ecology*, Turner, C. (trans.), Verso: London.

Gudeman, S. (1986), *Economics as Culture; Models and Metaphors of Livelihood*, Routledge & Kegan Paul: London.

Habermas, J. (1989), *The Structural Transformation of the Public Sphere*, Burger, T. & Lawrence, F. (trans.), The MIT Press: Cambridge, Mass.

Haferkamp, H. (ed.) (1989), *Social Structure and Culture*, Walter de Gruyter: New York.

Hall, J.A. (1993), 'Nationalisms: Classified and Explained', *Daedalus, Reconstructing Nations and States*, Special Issue, Summer, pp. 1-27.

Hayek, F.A. (1986), *The Road to Serfdom*, Routledge & Kegan Paul: London.

Head, S. (1996), 'The New, Ruthless Economy', *New York Review of Books*, Vol. XLIII, No. 4, 29 February.

Held, D. (1980), *Introduction to Critical Theory: Horkheimer to Habermas*, University of California Press: Berkeley.

Hirschman, A. (1977), *The Passions and the Interest: Political Arguments for Capitalism before its Triumph*, Princeton University Press: Princeton, N.J.

Hirst, P. & Thompson, G. (1996), *Globalisation in Question – the International Economy and the Possibilities of Governance*, Polity Press: Cambridge.

Honneth, A. (1995a), *The Fragmented World of the Social: Essays in Social and Political Philosophy*, State University of New York Press: New York.

____ (1995b), *The Struggle for Recognition: the Moral Grammar of Social Conflicts*, Anderson, H.J. (trans.), Polity Press: Cambridge.

Horkheimer, M. (1949), 'Authoritarianism and the Family Today', in Anshen, R.N. (ed.), *The Family: Its Function and Destiny*, Harper: New York.

____ (1972), 'Authority and the Family', in *Critical Theory: Selected Essays*, Herder & Herder: New York.

____ (1974), *The Eclipse of Reason*, Seabury: New York.

Ikegami, E. (1996), 'Citizenship and National Identity in Early Meiji Japan, 1868-1889: A Comparative Assessment', in Tilly, C. (ed.), *Citizenship, Identity and Social History, International Review of Social History*, Supplement 3, Press Syndicate of University of Cambridge: Cambridge, pp. 185-221.

Inglehart, R. (1977), *The Silent Revolution*, Princeton University Press: Princeton, NJ.

____ (1990) *Culture Shift in Advanced Industrial Society*, Princeton University Press: Princeton, NJ.

Jameson, F. (1991), 'The Cultural Logic of Late Capitalism', in *Postmodernism or, the Cultural Logic of Late Capitalism*, Verso: London.

Kalberg, S. (1993), 'Cultural Foundations of Modern Citizenship', in Turner, B.S. (ed.), *Citizenship and Social Theory*, Sage Publications: London.

Keane, J. (1984), *Public Life and Late Capitalism: Towards a Socialist Theory of Democracy*, Cambridge University Press: Cambridge.

Keller, E.F. (1985), *Reflections on Gender and Science*, Yale University Press: London.

Kellner, D. (1992), 'Popular Culture and the Construction of Postmodern Identities', in Lash & Friedman.

Kennedy, P. (1993), *Preparing for the 21st Century*, Harper Collins: London.

King, A.D. (ed.) (1991), *Culture, Globalization and the World-System*, Macmillan: London.

Kramnick, I. (1990), *Republicanism and Bourgeois Radicalism: Political Ideology in Late Eighteenth-Century England and America*, Cornell University Press: London.

Kumar, K. (1988), *The Rise of Modern Society: Aspects of the Social and Political Development of the West*, Basil Blackwell: Oxford.

Laclau, E. (1990), *New Reflections on the Revolution of Our Time*, Verso: London.

Laclau, E. & Mouffe, C. (1985), *Hegemony and Socialist Strategy*, Verso: London.

Lash, S. & Friedman, J. (eds.)(1992), *Modernity and Identity*, Blackwell: Oxford.

Lash, S. & Urry, J. (1987), *The End of Organized Capitalism*, Polity Press: Cambridge.

Lonsdale, J. (1981), 'States and Social Processes in Africa: A Historiographical Survey', *African Studies Review*, Vol. XXIV, Nos. 2/3, June/Sept., pp. 139-225.

Luhmann, N. (1982), *The Differentiation of Society*, Holmes, S. & Larmore, C. (trans.), Columbia University Press: New York.

Macpherson, C. B. (1964), *The Political Theory of Possessive Individualism: Hobbes to Locke*, Oxford University Press, Oxford.

Mann, M. (1984), 'The Autonomous Power of the State: its Origins, Mechanisms and Results', *Archives Europeennes de Sociologie*, 25, pp. 185-213.

Marcuse, H. (1986), *One Dimensional Man: Studies in the Ideology of Advanced Industrial Society*, Routledge & Kegan Paul: London.

Marglin, S.A & Schor, J.B. (eds.) (1990), *The Golden Age of Capitalism: Reinterpreting the Post-War Experience*, Clarendon Press: Oxford.

Marx, K. (1973), *Grundrisse: Foundations of the Critique of Political Economy*, Nicolaus, M. (trans.) Penguin Books: Harmondsworth.

____ (1977) *Economic and Political Manuscripts of 1844*, 5th edn. Lawrence & Wishart: London.

____ (1994), *Early Political Writings*, O'Malley, J. (ed. & trans.), Cambridge University Press: Cambridge.

Meillassoux, C. (1980), 'From Reproduction to Production: A Marxist Approach to Economic Anthropology', in Wolpe, H. (ed.), *The Articulation of Modes of Production: Essays from Economy and Society*, Routledge & Kegan Paul: London.

Melucci, A. (1989), *Nomads of the Present: Social Movements and Individual Needs in Contemporary Society,* Keane, J. & Mier, P. (eds.), Temple University Press: Philadelphia.

Merchant, C. (1980), *The Death of Nature: Women, Ecology and the Scientific Revolution*, Wildwood House: London.

Miyoshi, M. (1993), 'A Borderless World? From Colonialism to Transnationalism and the Decline of the Nation-State', *Critical Inquiry*, 19, Summer, pp. 726-51.

Offe, C. (1984), *Contradictions of the Welfare State*, Hutchinson: London.

Panitch, L. (1995), 'Globalisation and the State', *Socialist Register*, Panitch, L. (ed.), The Merlin Press: London, pp. 60-93.

Parsons, T. (1951), *The Social System*, The Free Press: New York.

⎯⎯ (1977), *The Evolution of Societies*, Prentice Hall: Englewood Cliffs.

Pateman, C. (1988), *The Sexual Contract*, Stanford University Press: Stanford.

Perkin, H. (1985), *Origins of Modern English Society*, Ark Paperbacks: London.

Perrot, M. (1979), 'The Three Ages of Industrial Discipline', in Merriman, J.M. (ed.) *Consciousness and Class Experience in Nineteenth Century Europe*, Holmes & Meier: New York.

Piore, M.J. & Sabel, C.F. (1984), *The Second Industrial Divide: Possibilities for Prosperity*, Basic Books: New York.

Piven, F.F. (1995), 'Globalizing Capitalism and the Rise of Identity Politics', *Socialist Register*, Panitch, L. (ed.), The Merlin Press: London, pp. 102-16.

Polanyi, K. (1957), *The Great Transformation*, Beacon Press: Boston.

Pollard, S. (1963), 'Factory Discipline in the Industrial Revolution', *Economic History Review*, Vol. 16, No. 2. Dec. pp. 254-71.

Price, R.M. (1975), *Society and Bureaucracy in Contemporary Ghana*, University of California Press: London.

Ranger, T.O. (1983), 'The Invention of Tradition in Colonial Africa' in Hobsbawm, E. & Ranger. T.O. (eds.), *The Invention of Tradition*, Cambridge University Press: Cambridge.

⎯⎯ (1993), 'The Invention of Tradition Revisited: The Case of Colonial Africa' in Ranger, T.O. & Vaughan, O. (eds.), *Legitimacy and the State in Twentieth Century Africa*, Macmillan: London.

Reich, R.B. (1991), *The Work of Nations: Preparing Ourselves for 21st-Century Capitalism*, Simon & Schuster: New York.

Roszak, T. (1970), *The Making of a Counter Culture: Reflections on the Technocratic Society and its Youthful Opposition*, Faber & Faber: London.

Ryan, M.P. (1992), 'Gender and Public Access: Women's Politics in Nineteenth-Century America', in Calhoun.

Sahlins, M. (1976), *Culture and Practical Reason*, The University of Chicago Press: Chicago.

Said, E.W. (1978), *Orientalism*, Routledge & Kegan Paul: London

⎯⎯ (1985), 'Orientalism Reconsidered', *Race & Class*, 27, 2, pp. 1-15.

Sampson, E.E. (1989), 'The Deconstruction of the Self', in Shotter, J. & Gergen, K.J. (eds.), *Texts of Identity*, Sage Publications: London.

Sayer, D. (1987), *The Violence of Abstraction: The Analytic Foundations of Historical Materialism*, Basil Blackwell: Oxford.

Steenstrup, C. (1976), 'Did Political Rationalism Develop along Parallel Lines in Premodern Japan and in the Premodern West? Prolegomena to a Comparative Study', *Journal of Intercultural Studies*, No. 3.

Tarrow, S. (1994), *Power in Movement: Social Movements, Collective Action and Politics*, Cambridge University Press: Cambridge.

Taylor, C. (1992) 'The Politics of Recognition', in *Multiculturalism and 'The Politics of Recognition'*, with commentary by Gutmann, A. (ed.) et. al., Princeton University Press: Princeton, NJ.

Thompson, E.P. (1967), 'Time, Work-discipline and Industrial Capitalism', *Past and Present,* 38, Dec. pp. 56-97.

____ (1978a), 'The Poverty of Theory or An Orrery of Errors', in *The Poverty of Theory and Other Essays*, Merlin: London.

____ (1978b) 'Eighteenth-century English Society: Class Struggle without Class?', *Social History,* 3, 2, May, pp. 133-65.

Tilly, C. (1990), *Coercion, Capital, and European States: AD 990 - 1990*, Basil Blackwell: Oxford.

Touraine, A. (1995), *Critique of Modernity*, Basil Blackwell: Oxford.

Tribe, K. (1981), *Genealogies of Capitalism*, The Macmillan Press: London.

Turner, B.S. (1994), *Orientalism, Postmodernism and Globalism*, Routledge: London.

Wallerstein, I. (1991a), *Unthinking Social Science: The Limits of Nineteenth-Century Paradigms*, Polity Press: Cambridge.

____ (1991b), *Geopolitics and Geoculture: Essays on the Changing World-System*, Cambridge University Press: Cambridge.

Wilson, W.J. (1996), *When Work Disappears: The World of the New Urban Poor*, Knopf: New York.

Whyte, L.L. (1960), *The Unconscious before Freud*, Basic Books: New York.

Acknowledgements

I am grateful to Angus Stewart and Charles Tripp for comments on earlier drafts of this introduction.

2   Collective forms in modern politics

Sudipta Kaviraj

There is a feature of modern political sociology which is ubiquitous but goes relatively unmarked. This is the astonishing frequency of attribution of intentional verbs to entities which are not individuals. In any hard-headed analysis of political language these sentences would appear immediately suspect, particularly in a general atmosphere of dominant methodological individualism. Still in any standard text talking about modern societies, we read unsurprised of nations going to wars, peoples fighting for their rights, classes deciding to enter into terminal conlficts. Accordingly, we find nothing startling about statements that the British were ruling over Indians or the Algerians fighting the French for independence, or the Americans keeping the peace. This appears to be a development in modern language to describe some persistent features of the modern political world. Probably such attribution of action verbs to collective agencies would have appeared inappropriate to describe premodern political worlds. Action and agency in the ancient or medieval world appear to be quite different in the way significant actions were commonly attributed. There kings declare wars upon one another. Individual heroes fight others or hordes of others. Conspirators often kill rulers or tyrants, but that shows an acute desire on that individual's part to end tyranny, and not an action in which large collectivities are shadowily involved. The point is seen clearly in the nature of modern wars. When rulers made wars in premodern times, it is true those were prosecuted with the help of armies; but, crucially, the entire people of their kingdoms do not seem to stand behind these armies in the way they seem to do in the modern world. The whole population of a country is assumed to be abstractly involved in the acts of their governments. This is demonstrated by the negative fact that if some people have to dissociate from what their government is doing they must signal that by taking formal recourse to passive resistance or civil disobedience. The reason a Russell or a Sartre has to undertake civil disobedience is precisely because otherwise they would have been assumed to be in support of the actions of their states. There would have been a complete subsumption of their agencies within the agency of their state. In a political world arranged like this, a shot fired by a Serbian nationalist against an archduke of Austria takes on peculiarly collective meanings. All Serbs are in some sense implicated in the act; and its victims or objects are all Austrians; and that incident sets in motion a war in which, in fact, not merely all Serbs and Austrians, but indeed whole populations of most European states get inescapably entangled. Thus the contrast between modern and premodern times in terms of the relation between people and the governments they live under is quite real, because this kind of language brings into representation a crucial feature of the modern state.

Yet there could remain considerable unease at this hasty and absentminded use of language about political events. First, there is always a suspicion of an inappropriate, because overextended, attribution of these actions. Not all Serbs massacred Muslims in the recent conflict in Bosnia; neither did all British exploit the Indians, nor all Indians fight for freedom from British rule, nor are all Americans involved in keeping the peace in the world, or are painfully concerned about its fragility. Should we use these statements in the face of the utter improbability of such groups arriving at any semblance of a decision to sanction or empower or condone such acts? Secondly, there is further inappropriateness in the casual way in which the composition is put to use. We use the verbs of action in relation to these highly internally complex and divided social collectivities as if they were simple and single individuals. We tend to ascribe an action to the whole class of proletarians in nineteenth century England with the unproblematic simplicity with which it can be ascribed to a single rebellious factory worker. Despite such problems, why is this such a persistent feature of our language about the political world?

There can be two possibilities: the first is to extend to this case the argument that ordinary language about the world should always be taken with critical mistrust. It should not be assumed that users of these statements always mean what they say. If pressed with objections, that language would slowly make room for these internal complexities. Statements like those are then simply convenient shorthand expressions. These can be seen as commonsensical descriptions which serve the purpose of unrigorous communication of ordinary journalism or conversation, but which must be given up in more rigorous understanding of how actions take place. Alternatively, it can be argued, extending a suggestion from theorists who argue the primacy of practice, that ordinary language is a more accurate register of real life and contains a peculiarly sly ability to grasp reality that escapes more officious 'theoretical' languages. This manner of speaking does register something significant about the way modern political life is organized. This paper would suggest that the second line of thinking should be explored, rather than dismissed too easily. Language is usually an accurate reflection of the historical world. This is true in this case as well. This way of speaking reflects a particular way of doing things which has been extended if not perfected by modernity, and which has particularly significant implications for the understanding of modern politics.

I

It is interesting that the current philosophical literature does not show a substantial interest in the theory of *collective* action.[1] A theoretical tradition in social science which takes collective action seriously treats it primarily as a branch of decision theory.[2] It deals in detail with problems such as the composition of preferences and the fit between intended and actual outcomes, but it is less curious about the mechanisms and conventions by means of which *sociologically* preferences can be melded together, or at least a plausible pretence to that effect is created. But the processes by which collective 'intentions' are created, preparatory to political action, are clearly crucial for understanding modern politics because so much of it is done in the name of such bodies. Considerations about the nature of beliefs, desires, motives, intentions and their relation to action are quite central to the analytical philosophy of action of natural individuals. But social theory neglects these questions in respect of collective actions. Is this because it is considered inherently implausible for such groups to have beliefs, desires, purposes and intentions, or intention-like states? There can be a summarily dismissive argument that asserts that to ascribe such things to collectivities is unhelpfully imprecise, and these would be exorcized after a suitable cleaning up of ordinary political language and shown to be states of individuals who comprise these groups. But this is not entirely satisfactory. Of course there is a trite minimal sense in which this is true, that without the constituent members holding similar beliefs these cannot be beliefs held by the groups. But what about actions which can only exist as collective actions, although within them, as in the case of modern war, there still remains the ineradicable discreteness of individual acts and responsibilities? Modern war is a good example of this point. In earlier times too wars could not be fought without ordinary soldiers doing most of the actual fighting. But they were either parts of armies recruited by rulers by means of mercenary incentives, or forced to join by levies. In either case, the war they fought in had little to do with their being, in any sense, part of a decision-making process by which it could be said that each individual was fighting in 'his own war'. In modern times, in many cases, there is clearly an attempt to involve the individual actor in quite a different way, either by claiming his implied assent through invoking his nation, his religion, or through a decision-making process claimed to be a democratic process, and therefore one in which he has been, however indirectly, involved. But this applies not only to wars. A large class of modern political actions/events invites the use of this peculiar kind of language. Tribes and peoples massacre each other, terrorists from unknown lands infiltrate and bomb people against whom they can feel no conceivable individual resentment. Governments, acting for entire nations, enact treaties affecting trades which seriously redistribute real economic advantage. Since they occupy so much of our political experience, we must investigate this foggy area of how such collective 'intentions' are produced and relate to group actions.

II

Consequences of enumeration

Political sociologists who work with the problem of identity in the modern world often face a curious difficulty. When we consider the outbreak of identity politics in the modern world, it seems tempting to say that it is only moderns who have identities, while premodern peoples did not. Although this appears both counter-intuitive as well as politically incorrect[3] there may be some truth in that idea. Modern identities bear a specially intimate relation to actual, intended or potential agency, which does not seem to be true in premodern contexts. Indian examples will be used to illustrate the following argument. However, it is likely that processes of collective identity formation of a distinctively modern kind will be found elsewhere as well.

Identity and collective practices

In thinking about how Indian politics has been transformed in modern times, we come across a simple but fundamental difficulty. Whether we think of religious groups, or regional groups based on language, they seem to exist earlier, but start behaving rather oddly after the coming of the British, especially after colonial rule becomes fully entrenched in a state and capable of shaping Indian society as a whole. When British rule in India came to an end, there were two successor states instead of one and the explanation of the partition which caused this most often refers to shadowy collective intentions. The partition of India has often been causally attributed to an 'intention' of the Muslim community, and in some instances, also of the Hindus, to have a separate state of their own.[4] Certainly the separation of Pakistan from British India had something to do with what India's Muslims wanted or intended, with their 'collective intention'. But neither historians nor sociologists have tried to examine more carefully what this 'collective intention' consisted in or what were the modes by which this was produced. Explanatory ideas, in any case vague and gestural, have tended to oscillate between two equally unsatisfactory poles. Either it is claimed that Indian Muslims simply 'wanted' a separate state (the Muslim League version of this history, adopted later by Pakistani nationalism), or that it was just a plan of a small minority of privileged Muslim politicians who deceived ordinary members of their community in passing it off in their collective name. More specifically, it would suggest that large political decisions about, for example, the way in which decolonization would take place, are always effectively taken by small groups of individuals – British administrators and the political elites of the Muslim community in this case. Only these groups had the means to act effectively in altering power arrangements in Indian society. Since others, like ordinary members of the Muslim community in India, were deprived of such means, they had to acquiesce in the consequences, or adapt as best they could. The exact nature of this historic decision is explained by the inequality of political means at the disposal of different layers of the social group. Even though there is an important element of truth in this demystifying explanation, it does not account for the fact that elites on both sides did not present it as a decision they took on their own, but as one which either respected or met the 'collective intention' of the entire community. Indeed, the entire language of being the 'sole spokesman'[5] implies a deliberative process of some kind, though its exact form is difficult to outline. Since then, the whole of South Asia has experienced periodic waves of political activity in which social groups like Hindus, Muslims, Bengalis, Tamils, Indians, Pakistanis have exerted themselves to do various things to themselves and to others. And one interesting feature of this political history is the persistence with which these have been represented as acts, not of individuals, but of whole communities, by virtue of some kind of non-specifiable collective decision.[6]

The trouble is that, if we call these 'identity groups', then they have a fairly long history; but they had never acted in such troublesome ways before. The standard Indian nationalist argument maintained that this was due to the stratagems of the British who played one religious group against another and encouraged them to fight in order to perpetuate their own colonial or postcolonial control. Some forms of liberal and leftist political opinion in India would still assert that present tensions between religious communities are simply long-term consequences of colonial policy; and in a sense the British, who departed half a century ago, are still responsible for what is happening today. But this explanation seems inadequate, and it has been suggested, theoretically, that there were two levels of causality in these historical processes, and that nationalists conflated these two. Certainly, at one level of political agency, some leaders of the Muslim community worked energetically towards the achievement of a separate state for 'themselves'. They had Hindu counterparts who acted through the more ambiguous ideological structures of the Congress, thus often escaping detection. British administrators evidently sought to put these divisions to use for their own purposes. However, these political moves were themselves made possible by a fundamental alteration of the cognitive map of the social world brought in by processes of colonial administration which had wide ranging practical consequences. There was a fundamental process of *enumeration* carried out by administrative and statistical processes brought in by the modern state which irreversibly altered the cognitive orientation of ordinary people towards the social world.[7] Literate or not, people in modern societies partake of these cognitive conditions. Illiterate peasants master easily the practical political implications of majority and minority existence. What is central to the discussion is the unavailability of some crucial modes of political action to communities which were constituted in the premodern fuzzy form.[8] Without the cognitive assistance of a mapped and counted world, such groups simply could not exist beyond the scale of the accessible immediate universe - neighbourhoods, localities, areas of a relatively small compass which could be connected by everyday trade and religious practices, or affected by rumours. Thus, to take an example of linguistic communities, clearly Bengalis and Tamils had existed for a long time, since these languages had existed for centuries, but before the nineteenth century we do not find Bengalis who consider their Bengali-ness a fit subject for discussion, or indeed for politically motivated action. Similarly, before modern politics came to India there were Hindus and Muslims, but the implication, the social meaning, of being a Hindu or a Muslim was not the same. One way of dealing with this difference between pre-modern and modern politics is to try to move beyond the simple, singular term, identity, and to introduce further distictions between its various modes. The conventional nationalist argument appears to be faulty on this point. Since it uses the idea of Hindu and Muslim identities rather indiscriminately for both modern and premodern periods in history, it produces the impression that these large *abstract* identities typical of modern times also existed earlier; but somehow these groups behaved much more peaceably than they do now. If this is accepted, then we are inevitably pushed towards an explanation of the difference in social behaviour by reference to religious ideology. We are forced to distinguish, as Ashis Nandy has done, between a 'traditional' tolerant religion, and an aggressive one. But the trouble with that move is that it encourages an entirely unacceptable romanticization of traditional religious practice. An alternative route is to distinguish between the sociological form of the identities themselves. That is, to assert that in traditional India 'being a Hindu' or a Muslim makes sense, as it does in modern times; but they are not the same sense. To be a Hindu or a Muslim does not mean the same thing. But how has that changed? We can try to grasp this differnce by using a distinction between a *descriptive* and an *agentive* identity. It should have been possible for people who fell in the relevant groups in fifteenth century India to grasp the idea of their belonging to a category of people called Hindus, though that did not contribute relevantly to any recognizable social, much less *political* practice.[9] They could be said in that sense to have had an identity which would have been in principle intelligible to them,[10] an identity used for possible description, not for possible action. Identities or characterizations like female, European, red-haired, parent, etc. were all intelligible descriptions which those who fell under those categories would have accepted as reasonably accurate descriptions of themselves as a collectivity. What is crucial is that no line of potential action based on a recognizable potential *interest* would have followed from such recognition. These could be called identities of *being*. By contrast, the identity of a Communist, or a Frenchman, or an Allied soldier, or Indian freedom-fighter were identities of *doing* something. These were identities which assumed their significance, indeed, their very reason for existence, from some promise of political agency. Furthermore, those kinds of agency were in their very nature 'common' or collective. They were common, and not individual in the same sense in which two people lifting a stone,which would have been beyond the power of each singly to lift, undertake a common or collective action. Making a revolution, liberating Europe from Nazi tyranny, liberating India from British rule are all similar to this example of a common or collective action, except that these are not physical in the simple sense.

But common is not a sufficiently unambiguous term, as commonness can have various forms. It is essential to discriminate between different types of collective actions or practices.[11] To take a simple example again, worshipping can be a collective practice in many discernibly different senses. If all Hindus get up at dawn and pray in their homes, this constitutes a common action. If they all gather in the evening in a temple yard, and offer their silent individual prayers to a common deity, this is also common, but in a distinctively *different* way. If they join together in collective singing in a temple, this is a third way of doing collective worship. When devotees pull the rope of the great chariot of the Jagannath temple and make it move, this goes further in the same direction. We can see a certain *direction* of movement in these examples: there is some identifiable feature of commonness which is being intensified as we go along, people being drawn together into a 'common action' rather more tightly. It seems that modernity creates a historical climate in which acts of the latter type tend to become first more imaginable, then more feasible, and finally, more probable. In the end success in the modern political world depends heavily on the relative effectiveness of various groups in mounting such actions, so that identities of doing, or agentive identities become the mark of political modernity. This helps solve one persistent problem of South Asian history. Because we can now disentangle the two ways of 'being Muslim or Hindu or Bengali'. We do not have to deny there were Hindus in the premodern world, nor do we have to suggest that they were exceptionally peaceable compared to their more violent modern successors. Some ways of being in the social world were simply not part of their sense of what was historically or socially feasible. But why?

Imagination and quasi-intentional forms

Oddly, this brings these processes in contact with a strand of modern social theory which emphasizes the plasticity of the social universe, theories which speak of imagination, invention, *l'imaginaire*, the construction of society.[12] It is inadequate, at worst seriously misleading simply to suggest that a process of 'imagination' is at work in the formation of modern nationalism, to stress only the *invention* dimension of the identity process.[13] This does not show how that identity becomes effective as an historical force, in other words, how that imagined identity makes the transition to agency. Clearly that is a matter of some importance. If some imaginations did not translate into agency, we would not have taken them so seriously. There is another related problem. The imaginations which are most often discussed in the current political literature are normally associated with nation-states, the peculiar, wholly modern combination of as intangible a thing as imagination with the fearsomely tangible instrumentalities of the modern state.[14] In fact, that intangible imagination gets deflated and regards itself as entirely unsuccessful if it fails to translate itself into that compellingly tangible form. Clearly we are not dealing with the intangible imagination, the ability of human beings to produce ideas in themselves, but also their ability to force people to accept those ideas in a form which produces institutional forms[15] and material consequences for history. The modern state of course is a set of *disciplinary* practices, as Foucault has taught us so emphatically; and the reason why this captures such an important element of the nation-state is that it points to the means by which states put in place rehearsed, easily available, set formats of collective action. To have a theory of the modern nation-state, we must therefore find a way of combining the Anderson-style arguments[16] about imagination with the Foucault-style analysis of disciplinary power. It is not easy to bring them together; but one possible line could be through an analysis precisely of those techniques which seek to give modern political action a quasi-intentional collective form.

Subjectivity and the new ontology of the social world

Foucault's work does not place sufficient explicit emphasis on some ideas that it requires as a somewhat contradictory premise for itself. Any detailed analysis of the creation of disciplinary forms in the modern world requires as a preface a discussion of a change in the ontological conception of the social world. Modernity gradually formulated a conception of subjectivity and made it fundamental to human existence in two different but related forms. Charles Taylor has given us a magisterial survey of the production of modern subjectivity; but his narrative relates entirely to the individual.[17] Yet the rise of this new kind of subjectivity is also crucial for the ever-expanding scale of modern political action. Because there are some attributes integral to this kind of individual subjectivity which make it possible to agglomerate such individual subjects into grids and pyramids, and thus to create typically modern forms of 'collective' subjectivity. The most significant feature of this process is the manner in which the connections which hold between identity, intention and action in the case of individuals are transferred to 'collective' subjects. These groups have peculiar structures or internal arrangements because of which it becomes possible to talk of them as having identities[18], containing deliberative processes which can fashion a 'collective' intention, and then engaging in an action which can in turn be attributed to these intentions and identities.

From divine to collective intentions

The frontispiece of Hobbes's *Leviathan* offered one of the earliest and best visual representations of this historical process. In that picture, tiny individual subjects produce by their combination and *subsumption*, an 'artificial', i.e. non-natural collective subject.[19] The major attraction of this constructed (artificial) collective subject is precisely its unprecedented ability to act on a scale not available earlier. This assumption of sovereignty over the social world by a collective human subject depended however on a progressive secularization of thinking. There is a slow recession of an all-encompassing divine intention, and the resumption of the space from which it was evacuated by a human collective quasi-intention in its place. There is a revolutionary transformation in the conception of this idea of plasticity.

The transition to a modern mentality about the social world contained, along with other immense changes, this fundamental alteration of premise. Premodern religious thought usually posited the existence of a sovereign divine will for which anything could be accomplished by simply willing it. At the same time, this will was cognitively impenetrable to human beings. So although the world was infinitely malleable to the divine subject, it appeared to human beings as entirely intractable. This implicit idea of a plasticity to the divine will came to be replaced by an idea of plasticity of a very different kind. The social world, including its political arrangements, came to be seen gradually as a plastic formation, made up of relations amenable to pressures, changes, particularly to *willed* transformations.[20] Yet at the same time modern social thought slowly articulated ideas about '*structures*' – relations which individuals cannot affect, conditions which cannot be shifted and to which they therefore have to adapt.[21] Thus the relations which constituted the framework of social life also exhibited a peculiar quality of imperviousness to individual desires and initiatives. The only way in which these could be bent, altered in shape, and perhaps completely restructured was by means of coordinated *collective* efforts. Some types of theories, like Marxism, would introduce an additional – cognitive – condition into the success of such efforts. To change the world, crucially, it was essential to know its structure. But even in Marx, such historical knowledge of structures could not produce the desired change entirely unassisted; it still required directed collective action. This collective or common effort which could alter and shape these structures must have a collectively quasi-intentional character, which made the ideas and efforts of large numbers of people converge on a common goal. Much of modern politics is consequently devoted to the creation of processes which can produce such deliberative convergence of common activity, a deliberative process at the end of which all participants can accept the goal as collectively devised. The idea of the plasticity of the social world was thus intimately connected to a new kind of politics which sought to produce a particular kind of outcome from the interplay of individual subjects. In an atomistic social world each person might follow his own contingent individual goal. But both the theory and practice of modern politics quickly saw the potential of collective power implicit in this only if their propensity to get dissipated into capriciously divergent individual projects could be overcome and some devices could be found which could interlock subjectivities into collective forms. Three different types of modern political agents show this peculiar ability to give to collective actions a quasi-intentional character.[22] Institutional forms of the modern state, its internal constitutive agencies, and even some interstate bodies have institutionalized deliberative practices which can produce collective actions. Nationalism brought in an alteration in the logic of identities which fused with the intentional pretensions of the growing modern state, precisely because it seemed to provide a more secure, unquestionable cultural basis of identity from which this intentionalist project could be mounted even more plausibly. Gradually, this feature spread to all types of modern identity politics. Modern identities, i.e. the characterizations that people in the modern world characteristically accept, acknowledge, covet, foster, arrange for themselves, have this active, or agentive quality: these are not identities that are given, but taken; not descriptions that men have to inhabit helplessly, but ones they assume in order to facilitate actions and for achievement of purposes consciously undertaken. To take an Indian example, traditionally, caste descriptions were ones that people had to live inside, but these were not identities to do things with, especially to change the overall structure of social descriptions from which they derived their meaningfulness. Under an electoral parliamentary system, people are still born into castes, but these have been converted into identities for doing things collectively, precisely to challenge the irremediable division of productive responsibilities and rewards that the traditional caste system imposed on all constituent groups.

The modern state as a quasi-intentional form

Analysis of action usually moves from a person or agent to an intention which is preparatory to the act, to the action itself. It is possible to introduce refinements of this basic model. Danto's work distinguishes between a basic action, its 'accordion effects' and unintended consequences.[23] More appropriately to our case, Searle suggests a distinction between an intention *prior to* action and an intention *in* the act itself.[24] It might be difficult to bring exactly parallel refinements into a model of collective action. But one rather general point can be made. The cover picture of the *Leviathan* suggests, with wonderful appositeness, an isomorphism between the acting capacity of individuals and of the artificial individual created by their covenant. It is true that, as Hobbes suggested and classical western political theory elaborated for the next two centuries, the advantage of having a state at all was precisely the advantage of possessing an instrument which provided a stable framework of collective actions in permanent readiness. This suggests a possible connection between traditional analyses of political theory and Foucault's studies of modern power, and allows us to see the history of political theory, from this limited perspective at least, as a genealogy of modern forms of political power. At times, it appears that Foucault's studies of emerging and tightening disciplines in modern society lack any identifiable purpose. Why are people interested in such processes? The question becomes more complex and acute if we accept Foucault's rejection of the easy ascription of subjects to these processes. But it is possible to see an evident consequence of the disciplinary processes: they produce an apparatus which is in permanent readiness to act. It acts on behalf of huge numbers of people, or at least claims to; and further, it can employ the collective capacity of enormous numbers for those purposes, who are already linked together by disciplinary forms. An additional curiosity of this instrument is that it is not adapted for any particular type of action, and useless for others. As the history of the modern state shows, its instituted capacity can be put to the most bewildering range of uses. The story of the modern state as Foucault tells it is a story of constant extension, intensification and refinement of these institutionalized forms of collective action.

The early modern absolutist state first elaborated and perfected these disciplinary frameworks by means of which collective actions could be undertaken with great effect. It is not accidental therefore that the structure of individual action is mirrored in the structure of collective actions undertaken by the state. In place of the natural individual as an actor, we have the collective group, the members of a political community. Similarly, in place of the agency or action intended by the natural individual, we find the convenience of a collective agency which can make possible undertakings on a scale unprecedented in earlier times. This new state capacity is used for conquest of territories, prosecution of new types of war, pursuit of collective economic objectives of a wholly unprecedented kind. The more the modern state got involved in these new goals of action, the more it was forced to alter its internal organization and give more salience to processes which yielded quasi-intentional situations, so that larger and larger collectives of people could be said to direct their agency towards some commonly understood purpose. It became all the more necessary therefore to devise frameworks of collective quasi-intentionality. It is characteristic of modern politics that not merely states, but other political actors too follow this imperative of involving abstract[25] groups in a process by which they could be said to be deliberately involved in a particular course of action.[26] With the emergence of modern nationalism, this quasi-deliberative pretence becomes more plausible. Remarkably, the establishment of modern universal suffrage democracies accentuates this trend, allowing states to act, apparently less illegitimately, in the name of the people they govern.

But quite obviously, this process tends to produce an effect of a different kind altogether. Quite simply the larger the grids of these collective forms, the weaker is the reality of such deliberative claims. Governments can reasonably claim, as the size of modern states grows steadily larger, that it is impractical to elicit the opinion of the people incessantly. And it is particularly difficult at times of emergencies. Therefore, there must be an established pattern of representation, which periodically consults the relevant constituents but leaves states free to act in their name. This introduces a troublesome, unreliable representative element into these quasi-intentional processes. Even in the best of cases, there must be large numbers of small groups and individuals caught in the interstices of these collective structures who are unhappy about these decisions, or indifferent, but who do not have the means to register their difference. Their agency, or potential agency is thus illegitimately subsumed in the collective agency of these large political actors. Quite often this degenerates into a mere pretence. Individuals who are caught up in these actions, and come to bear a very real but curious 'responsibility', rarely have the opportunity to be heard effectively, or influence decisions. Perhaps the best illustrations of this sort of case can be found in political rioting. A Muslim who is totally opposed to the communal treatment of a Hindu can be easily killed by Hindu zealots in a communal riot in India, precisely on the alleged ground of such subsumption. Still, even the most authoritarian of modern states usually carry on some pretence of deliberative connection with the people they rule over. In the Third World, an interesting question is why regimes, which have no intention of ruling by popular consent, still hold periodic elections. At least part of the answer might be found in the impression this creates that the acts of the state are sanctioned by this vague deliberative process, and are thus acts of the people. This claims an automatic representativeness of the state for its people. It is possible to reject such claims by standard democratic arguments; but supporters of these regimes can mount counter-arguments by pointing out the imperfect character of democratic representation. Similarly, political movements which work outside the framework of the state claim to not merely represent their abstract group as a whole, but do so by virtue of some deliberative process which produces an intention of that collective. Fundamentalist groups often exploit this logic successfully since provocative terrorist acts, particularly against innocent victims, tend to force communities to act as solid blocs, and this turns the claim of a conflict between abstract and 'universal' communties into a self-fulfilling prophecy.

Quasi-intentional forms and demands for transparency

It seems that this kind of quasi-intentionality as a framework for collective actions is a feature of modern times, but it might be possible to distinguish between some historical stages in its evolution. The early versions of the modern state in the west, in the form of absolutism, proved to be more effective in surviving and succeeding in this increasingly plastically conceived world, in which there was no absolute, unchangeable template made by divine artifice, and thus everything, from territorial frontiers, to processes of economic prosperity, to forms of government, were all amenable to restructuring to one's advantage. The condition for success was an institutional structure which could direct the actions of increasingly larger numbers of people in the same direction and towards an identifiably single action. Absolutism provided the first workable framework for this sort of concerted action and a collective frame by focusing the will of the state in a single centre – of an absolute monarch assisted by a growing bureaucracy. It made this possible by the enormous concentration of resources in the hands of the modern state and the intricate techniques of social command – the early bureaucracies, new types of military commands of permanent armies. These were not merely able to create enormous scale changes in directed actions, but also devised means, both in terms of intricate organization of command structures and by raising resources through a much expanded ability to tax, of making such structures of collective action *permanent*. These structures, e.g. officials for collecting revenue, for managing the state's affairs, or armies to fight a war, were not put together in an ad hoc provisional way, when the need arose. These were made permanent structures, so that their responses were more effective and instant. And because these were permanent, these could themselves be the object of learning and engineering processes which constantly looked for ways of increasing their efficiency – the processes which Foucault has generally called disciplines. One of the consequences of the invention of these forms of collective agency and quasi-intentional processes is that the society, or groups or institutions become the objects of their own cognitive and engineering efforts.[27] This process appears to enter a new stage with the arrival of the new conception of the nation, especially through the radical republicanism of the French revolution. Republicanism displaced the earlier form of direction of collective action represented by absolute monarchy. It replaced that with a new kind of collective action. It did this by devising deliberative forms, through which the necessarily divergent wills of a large number of individuals could be melded into a more focused directedness, giving more decisiveness to actions, by creating devices of constitutional or discursive precommitments of various types. One important implication of these deliberative forms was that although people had very unequal access to them, it took away from them the claim of not being consulted. Political power, while becoming more impersonal, also found a way of implicating those who had little control over its operations. Constitutional legislative procedures created a gigantic system of exercise of preference about the goal, the nature, the inflection, the instrumentalities of intended collective acts by representation and alienation. Each individual got an opportunity to say what he wished to be done in or through that act, or in other words, contributed his individual intention towards the making of an artificial one at higher levels. By accepting rules of constitutional procedure, he precommitted himself to the acceptance of the outline and form of collective quasi-intentionality, suppressing his own peculiar, individual, private proposal about that act. At every stage of the growth of representative government, this process was carried on further forward and upward, until it was possible to produce quasi-intentional objectives for the entire French or British or Indian nation. As the idea of plasticity of social relations seeped down into lower classes, pressures built up for their inclusion into the format of these quasi-intentional deliberative processes. At the same time, with their inclusion, which of course contained its own filters and subtle dispossessions,[28] these agencies became more substantial. It became more realistic to talk about the acts of a British or an Indian nation, reflected naturally in the language of reports about this world of politics, using singular verbs for these large entities.

With clearer appreciation that progress of this technique of pyramiding of effort, intent or agency, contained internal exclusions and depletions, there arose demands to make this process transparent and recursive. First, transparency required that the process by which individual agency was subsumed under such collective quasi-intentional forms must be clear to those who participated in these processes. Secondly, since gradually the question of the relation between individual and collective identities became increasingly critical, the demand grew that such representative subsumption of individual initiative should not be either simply symbolic, like a tyrant acting in the name of his people, or permanent, i.e. after the initial surrender of the right to individual action to collective agency, people could not revise that primal act.[29] Consequently, it was argued with increasing force, that these opportunities should return periodically, so that individuals could rationally monitor the effects of their own subsumption in that collectivity, or into an individual collective action, and exercise their right to alter its constitution. Clearly, democratic regimes are the most effective in creating relatively transparent quasi-intentional forms of collective action, with the further implication that they are both most stable and most painlessly flexible. But the rather unexpected corollary of this is that the quasi-intentional attachment of citizens to the acts of their states is closer than that of people living under regimes where such processes are unconvincing, perfunctory or simply deceptive.

This has a further implication for modern politics. It is part of my argument that the logic of modernity creates pressures towards the conversion of all descriptive identities, which tended to be entirely passive, into agentive forms. It does so by revealing through its cognitive processes the plasticity of social rearrangements, the provisionality of relations of domination and subjection, and by the constant examples of effectiveness of new and innovative forms of quasi-intentional organisation in distributive struggles of power and wealth. Success of some players forces others to transactively adopt similar strategies of self-organisation. It is also by this logic that most social identities tend towards assuming state or state-related forms. In the modern world, deprivation or indignity can no longer be explained by an impenetrable divine will. People are increasingly unwilling to see these as unintended consequences of acts, or effects of structures which are under no one's effective control. Modernity constantly intensifies the myth of collective and individual agency, and such things are then plausibly attributed to large political formations. Modern politics thus gives rise to a constantly proliferating repertoire of responses to large groups, in which variations between individuals are not to be seen or treated as significant. Paradoxically, in modern times human beings have shown great ingenuity in devising more general and effective forms of collective action but this has made the political world also more volatile and violent, as the room for political action of individuals is increasingly shrunk by the movement of large collectivites like nations, states, ethnicities.

Notes

1   Searle (1993) treats collective action as 'biologically primitive'. This is an interesting revision of earlier ideas about the ontological nature of collective action. But he is also not interested in the sociological forms which give collective acts their peculiar shape, and determine their effectivity.

2   Olson's work on collective action has given rise to a large and intricate body of literature which analyses collective actions from the point of view, mainly, of decision theory. Cf. Olson (1971, 1982).

3   Because one important ingredient of that form of modern piety is to treat the dead with consideration, to act with a sense of retrospective equality. Thus, suggesting that we can do something they could not seems to be diminishing them, and thus goes against the grain of the liberal sense of intergenerational equality.

4   The infelicity of such theories have been shown by the work of several modern historians of South Asia. For Pakistan especially, see the work of Jalal (1981, 1994).

5   Jinnah's claim is used as the title of Jalal's book, Jalal (1981).

6   In the South Asian context, one can think of several examples of such collective action. India and Pakistan have gone to war on at least three occasions. Identity movements of the Sikhs and Kashmiris in India, of the Bengalis against Pakistan, of Tamils against the Sri Lankan state have all purported to express such collective 'desires' of these peoples. In actual political propaganda, desire appears to be a more apposite concept than intention.

7   For the Indian discussion, see Appadurai (1993).

8   Kaviraj (1992).

9   Interestingly, until modern times such characterizations were used by outsiders, like the great Islamic scholar Al Biruni, not internally by the Hindus as a category for self-description and characterization. It was certainly not proper to any action related to religious worship or ritual conduct.

10   It is notable how awkward this is to formulate without falling into an easy anachronism.

11   The difference between actions, structures and practices is itself quite significant. For some discussions about structures and practices, see de Certeau (1986).

12   Anderson (1991), Hobsbawm and Ranger (1983), Castoriadis (1987), parts of Giddens (1991).

13   This is particularly true of Anderson (1991) and Hobsbawm and Ranger (1983). However, as both works are products of authors working within a Marxist tradition of social theory, they do not neglect social historical

preconditions or contextual factors which facilitate the acts of collective suggestion and imagination. Still, the point is that to relate the process of imagination to contextually given preconditional factors is unsatisfactory, because the process of imagination/invention itself uses quasi-intentional meanings which have to be seen in a more complex and critical fashion.

14   It is rather odd that the literature on modern politics remains resolutely divided between a strand analysing the rise of nations and another focusing on the modern state. Except in a few cases, for instance, Mann (1986) these two lines of analyses are not brought together.

15   It would be misleading to suggest that this agency must always take an institutional form in the strict sense. Crowds can often do very well as instruments of such political action; but they do not constitute institutions.

16   Though it must be said, in fairness to Anderson (1991) that his own analysis takes account of developments in technology and social practices, (e.g., his attention to print-capitalism) and is not exclusively an analysis of ideas.

17   Taylor (1986).

18   As opposed to individuals constituting them would have identities. A group of tourists at a fairground would not constitute an identity in this modern sense, distinct from the identity of the persons who constitute the crowd.

19   Oakeshott's eloquent introduction to the *Leviathan* emphasizes this accomplishment which Hobbes called a 'civic' association, Oakeshott (1975).

20   Contractualist theory in general exhibits this kind of excessive belief in the constructedness of the political universe, a feature it shares with much enlightenment thought.

21   This is clearly evident in Marxist thought, though some elements of Hegelian thinking would also emphasize the structural limits to subjectivity.

22   I.e. these can all be seen as producing in various ways something like a 'common intention'.

23   Danto (1968).

24   Searle (1983).

25   In the sense of a large group which could not have face to face contact.

26   By the involvement of an abstract or a universal group, I mean the involvement (allegedly) of *all* Indians, *all* Muslims, *all* Frenchmen and so on.

27   Beck and others have argued that this should be called 'reflexive' modernization and is a feature of the latest stage of modernity. But I think this kind of reflexivity does not appear suddenly in the late twentieth century. It arises slowly through the patterns of development I have traced and can be found in modern politics of the late nineteenth century onwards.

This is one of the principal marks of political modernity; though Beck seems to be right in showing that in late modernity reflexive transformations are often achieved without violent conflict. See Beck et. al. (1994).

28   E.g. the controversy about delegates or representatives.
29   Which, in most cases is nothing more than a legal fiction.

References

Anderson, B. (1991), *Imagined Communities*, Revised edn., Verso: London.

Appadurai, A. (1993), 'Number in the Colonial Imagination' in Breckenridge and Van der Veer.

Beck, U., Giddens, A., and Lash, S. (eds.) (1994), *Reflexive Modernization*, Polity Press: Cambridge.

Breckenridge, C. and van der Veer, P. (1993), *Orientalism and the Post-colonial Predicament*, University of Pennsylvania Press: Philadelphia.

Castoriadis, C. (1987), *The Imaginary Institution of Society*, Polity Press: Cambridge.

Chatterjee, P and Pandey, G. (eds.) (1992), *Subaltern Studies*, VII, Oxford University Press: Delhi.

Danto, A.C. (1968), 'Basic Actions' in White.

de Certeau, M. (1986), *The Practice of Everyday Life*, University California Press: Berkeley.

Giddens, A, (1991), *Modernity and Self-Identity*, Stanford University Press: Stanford.

Hobsbawm, E. and Ranger.T. (eds.) (1983), *The Invention of Tradition*, Cambridge University Press: Cambridge.

Jalal, A. (1981), *The Sole Spokesman*, Cambridge University Press: Cambridge.

____ (1994), *Democracy and Authoritarianism in South Asia*, Cambridge University Press: Cambridge.

Kaviraj, S. (1992), 'The Imaginary Institution of India' in Chatterjee and Pandey.

Mann, M. (1986), *Sources of Social Power*, Vol II, Cambridge University Press: Cambridge.

Oakeshott, M. (1975), *Hobbes and Civil Association*, Blackwell: Oxford.

Olson, M. (1971), *The Logic of Collective Action*, Harvard University Press: Cambridge, Mass.

____ (1982), *The Rise and Decline of Nations*, Yale University Press: New Haven.

Searle, J. (1983), *Intentionality*, Cambridge University Press: Cambridge.

____ (1993), *Construction of the Social World*, Allen Lane: London.

Taylor, C. (1986), *Sources of the Self*, Cambridge University Press: Cambridge.

White, A. R. (ed.) (1968), *The Philosophy of Action*, Oxford University Press: London.

3   Transcending identities in modern India's world

Ronald Inden

> When, as is currently the case, (national, social, occupational, ethnic or religious) identity is invoked and extolled on all fronts, this proves that it is *in doubt*, that it is no longer self-evident, that it is already lost.[1]

André Gorz would have us believe that our present-day concern with 'identity' arises precisely because the traditional or modern 'subjects' with which people have for some time wanted to 'identify' have themselves changed to such an extent that 'identifications' with them are no longer possible or are of dubious value. He does not, however, question the concept of identity itself. To be sure, the most common use of the term now, both in academic discourse and public discussion designates a public or private self's distinctiveness or individuality that is felt to be at risk. While that feeling may have intensified recently, it is the extension of the term, the promiscuity of its use, that is most novel. As we shall see, what started out at the onset of the Cold War as a concept applied primarily to the men of the ruling societies of modern nation-states has come to be used in relation to their others as well. Among these are women and people of minority groups, ethnicities, cultures, or races, subaltern classes; 'subnations' such as Cataluña and the Orangemen of Ulster, in Europe, or Bengal and Ilam, in South Asia; and 'fundamentalist' religious movements, ranging all the way from the Christian Right in the US to hard-line Zionists, Khomeiniism, and, in India, Hindutva. People speak quite freely now of gay and lesbian identity, men's and women's identity, African American or Han identity, and in South Asia of Dravidian, Sri Lankan Buddhist, Sikh, tribal or Adivasi, Dalit or Harijan identities.

Of what does this concept of identity consist? On first inspection, it seems simply to evoke the distinguishing names or labels people give to themselves and others, to individual persons and also to the larger aggregates with which people might identify. Often that is all people mean when they talk about identities. The situation is, however, more complicated, for, in most usages, more is usually implied in the use of the term than simply the notion of identity in the sense of naming.

Let me begin with the most obvious question. Why use the term identity to

64

designate the distinctiveness of selves? The answer is, I contend, because we are talking about a distinctiveness that arises from the equation or bringing together of two entities, the 'individual' and 'society' (usually the nation-state). I prefer to think of individuals and societies/people, whether acting singly or in combination, as agents, instruments, and patients, as makers of one another, but always in particular circumstances in one fashion or the other precisely because of the tendency of people to think of identities as self-contained entities, as essences standing underneath, behind, or outside of history. That is, society, in the guise of the modern, liberal nation-state, is considered the essential bearer of reason and the guarantor of human order, unity, and progress. The individual is its opposite. The essential bearer of emotion, it is the guarantor of individuality and authenticity. (When talking about totalitarian regimes, liberal scholars swap reason and emotion around. There we have the lone voice of reason standing up to the irrational military dictator or party leader.) Persons in discourses on identity, notwithstanding all the current verbiage about empowerment and agency, are actually treated as the patients and instruments not so much of the nation-state, but of their own emotional essence. Similarly, the nation-state itself is the patient and instrument of an Agent that stands outside history and uses it for its own ends.

Agents range from the relatively simple – persons and families – to the relatively complex – large polities and international organizations. Even the relatively simple person that goes by the name of the individual consists of contestable agentives – ego, super-ego and id, soul and body, selfish genes, computer-minds, charisma, and genius, to name but a few. Complex agents may be relatively dispersed, divided, or fractionated (Sikhs or, even more so, Indians, Pakistanis, Nepalis, and Bangladeshis living 'overseas' or in 'diaspora') or relatively unified (the Indian Administrative Service). I do not, thus, mean by agent here the individual or person, the entity taken as agent in much of social scientific discourse and often pitched against society or structure as the bearer of free will against determinism. In fact, the idea of complex agent, elaborated out of R. G. Collingwood, is meant precisely to overcome these dichotomies.[2] The 'minds' or more particularly the life-wishes of these agents may be relatively homotelic or heterotelic. The 'identity' which any of these agents has is, in the simplest sense of the term's use, the name and place another agent has given to it as a coagent, instrument, or patient as well as the name and place it has defined for itself. Reducing these differing actualities to the binary opposition of individual and society oversimplifies the world.

Agents overlap both in the sense that their activities continually affect one another and that agents claim to represent other agents. They also overlap in the sense that agents claim to belong to other, more complex agents or claim to be separate from them. The process that causes some sort of bringing together of individual and society on the part of new recruits is usually called identification or identity formation. It results in what I would call the *participation* of one agent in the activities of another. I see participation as a relational activity of different kinds and degrees. Servants may participate in their masters' lives without becoming their mere instruments. Conscripts participate in army life, though not on the same terms as their officers. Fans participate in the lives of film and sports stars. Finally, people may participate in the life of their polity in a variety of ways – working hard and paying taxes, voting or running for election; marching against perceived injustices, sabotaging the assembly line, campaigning for reform or even revolution; or by becoming computer literate, advocating free markets and human rights, buying an expensive house. Scholars have instead here insisted on speaking of identity as the result. Participation as I would define it allows a person to belong to one or more social aggregates and to retain his/her autonomy. The notion of identity, however, does not so readily allow for multiplicity and autonomy.

Implicit in the term identity itself is a strong tendency to reduce what I would take to be a process involving heterogeneous agents and possibilities to a struggle between the hostile poles of a binary opposition between individual and society. And this binary relation is itself almost always assumed to be tilted against the individuality of the person or aggregate to which an identity is attributed. Distinctiveness is at risk because it faces powerful opposition to its very existence (or to its full realization). Personal or ethnic or subnational identity is opposed by the requirements of the nation-state. Or, national identity is itself opposed by the globalizing forces of imperialist, colonialist, or free-market world orders. To put it another way, people assume that the larger identity with which persons are asked or required to identify may in fact efface or disfigure them in the process. Identification may result not in participation but in dissolution or absorption into the larger whole, a worry reiterated in regard not only to 'totalitarian regimes' but more generally to modern, industrial 'mass' society. The concept of identity is supposed to resolve the opposition it presumes to exist between individual and society by bringing about an equation or unity of those opposites, to prevent individuality from being subsumed in some social totality and ideally allowing it to fulfill itself. Reason will not be allowed to go too far, stifling a person's humanity. On the other hand, the emotions will not be permitted to have their way, producing mental and social disorder. What we might see as the Cold War of the mind's two superpowers could always break out. The uneasy truce declared between them could easily rupture, bringing on an identity crisis.

Transcendence in a radical form has been integral to this concept of identity, though it is discussed even less than participation. Society, it is assumed, transcends the individual: it is a totality whose powers far surpass those of the identifying individual who has to come to terms with it. More important is the assumption that identity transcends the past and the constraints of the lived human world. An individual can develop an identity only by transcending his own developmental past. He has to cease being a child and become an adult. Correlate to this is the assumption that a society (hypostatized as a person) can only grow or develop or mature if it is able to transcend its own past. The modernist ways of life that prevailed after World War II constituted the modernity of people as transcending, as potentially or actually rising above, some earlier medieval or traditional way of life. Life in a paradise that had only been attainable in medieval times after death and in a remote heaven would now be attainable in a utopia that was already here but not yet fully realized. In the traditional world, society transcended the individual. What distinguishes the modern world is that here the individual can or will transcend society. This is more or less what radical advocates of a free market promise. Left-liberal scholars such as Charles Taylor, Anthony Giddens and Craig Calhoun[3] concur when they argue that the modern, liberal state differs sharply from the medieval or traditional state in its concern with the dignity and uniqueness of each of its citizens. Problems of 'identity' and its 'recognition' for the individual are, they assert, distinctive of the modern world. The problem is that in much of the writing about identity modernity has been associated with reason and tradition, especially in the form of nationalism outside the Anglo-American world, has been associated with the emotions. So in order for the traditional person (usually meaning, again, a man of the national ruling society) to become truly modern, he had to transcend the traditional. But if he does, he will cease being a Bengali, Indian, whatever, lose his true, authentic self. Once again, I suggest, we have a cold war on our hands.

Participation in the 'past' is not the only thing that identity has to transcend. The idea that everyone should have an identity seems vaguely widespread. What views such as these have failed to recognize, however, is that an identity itself has to have an 'outside', another identity or the lack of an identity against which a particular identity was defined. Just below the surface in much discourse about identity is the assumption that some identities, whether personal or aggregate, come into existence and sustain themselves at the expense of others, by overcoming or winning out against siblings or classmates, business competitors, national enemies, or sports rivals. Closely connected of course is the idea that some people not only do not themselves have a stable identity and suffer an identity crisis but the idea that they cannot have an identity at all. At best they may have an associated or partial identity. Those who could have an identity during the Cold War were the men of national ruling societies, the 'subject' whose death has been so often proclaimed.

I wish here to look to look at this concept of identity as a specific, historically situated concept that scholars have used to theorize the relationship of people to their larger communities, especially the nation, since World War II. It is, I submit, the concept itself that is now at risk because of the radical rearticulations of class, nation, and person that have been taking place since around 1975 and especially since the end of the Cold War. Many younger people who see themselves as members or potential members of a rising techno-entrepreneurial elite actually find a notion of identity built around the oppositions of the Cold War confining and undesirable. Recent efforts to rethink identity as multiple, split, or hybrid, as constructed rather than essential are, I will argue, to be seen more as symptoms of these changes than as a successful relaunch of the concept itself. It would be better, I argue, to shift the discussion over the problems of participation and transcendence that simple and complex agents have in a world no longer ordered by binary oppositions. The problems of identity in India have, I argue, to be seen within this global historical setting. Many Indians belonging to the expanding, increasingly entrepreneurial and consumerist middle class see themselves, I conclude, as participating in this cosmopolitan, transnational class. They do not, however, appear to be participating in this class as most social scientists would anticipate.

Throughout I will focus on the issues of participation in and transcendence of national, international, and 'transnational' ruling societies making differing claims about how the world is and should be ordered. I am especially interested in modernist politics claims to free the world from the everyday life of the medieval or traditional, to turn the day-to-day life of the modern world into a moral or material utopia that transcends the past. Many thinkers in 'medieval' or 'traditional' India saw the person or self both as relatively heterotelic, as pursuing different goals in different situations, and as relatively homotelic, as articulating those different goals into some sort of unity. Absolutely homotelic selves, those capable of permanently transcending the everyday world, were the exception and were considered ontologically and logically possible only in limited circumstances and as the result of much striving. Among these were the Pāñcarātra Vaiṣṇavas, a disciplinary order ('sect') whose practices I have been reconstructing. According to the eighth-century texts of this order, which is ancestral to most Vaiṣṇavas of present-day India, *bhakti*, 'devoted participation' embraced the activities of everyday life as well as a special liturgy of image-honoring. It led to moments of relative transcendence of the everyday at special paradisiac sites during the course of the day, year, and life of a person and the polity of which he or she was a part. This was so, their texts claimed, because the practices of devoted participation that they commended allowed agents to become relatively homotelic. Something like permanent transcendence of day-to-day life was attainable only at death and consisted of a divine life-time of devotions carried out by a small number of homotelic adepts. Absolute transcendence of the everyday world, attainable by a very few, occurred only when the soul of the homotelic adept rejoined the undifferentiated divine personality of Viṣṇu himself. The contrast of this Vaiṣṇava representation of transcendent paradise with the modernist representations of a utopia is remarkable. Elaboration of this contrast, which reveals much about our modernist assumptions and presuppositions, lies outside the scope of this essay, yet it is important to refer to it here for two reasons. First, as we shall see, descendants of these medieval Vaiṣṇava paradises are also implicated in emergent Indian versions of a consumerist arcadia. Second, my understanding of the 'medieval' Vaiṣṇavas has come to constitute an 'outside' for me, from which vantage point I look critically at the idea of identity that has come to prevail in the human sciences since World War II.

Identity's genealogy

The notion of identity now prevalent has at least three intellectually distinct ancestries. One is supposedly Freudian coming through Erik Erikson (1902-94) or, quite differently, Jacques Lacan (1901-81). The other purports to be Hegelian, coming to us through Charles Taylor, among others. According to Philip Gleason's genealogy of the concept[4] the apical ancestor of discourse on identity in the social sciences was Erik Erikson.

Scholars at the end of World War II began to use a concept of identity to solve the problem of how the 'individual' came to participate in 'society' by which they mean the modern nation-state. They wanted to see the personality or psyche of a person as a unity but their problem was this: the primary identity of a person is, they thought, inherently emotional (sexual) and unconscious, grounded in the biological, in gender, family, ethnicity, and nationality. The secondary identity of a person, the one he acquires as an adult, is, they assumed, inherently rational, manifesting itself in science and in the political and economic life of modern society. There is thus an underlying and potentially irreconcilable opposition between personal or cultural identity and political and economic role, between one's private and public personae. During the course of adolescence this opposition is somehow reconciled. An identity, a unity that consists of the combination of opposites, emerges and the person establishes a stable, life-long relationship of participation in a nation.[5] In other words, a person whose mind is set on a unified life course, a mind that is what I shall call relatively 'homotelic' emerges.[6] As private persons, people would remain primarily emotional and individual while as public persons they would be primarily rational and social.

The place of the nation-state in this scheme was both crucial and problematic. Modern polities are national, given at birth, and carry with them the emotionality of their medieval and traditional pasts. Political leaders, liberal and Marxist alike, claimed during the period of the Cold War that people could transcend their medieval, traditional, underdeveloped condition only by participating in the ideas and institutions derived from the universal principle of reason. The nation, for these thinkers, was only the accidental, historical vehicle for these ideas and institutions and both bourgeois and socialist thinkers saw the nation as a temporary vehicle for universal values and practices, one that would dissolve eventually into a utopia – a single international polity or world government or a world-wide, stateless communism. Forward-thinking people considered the idea that a nation as such would come decisively to transcend other nations in its modernity as nationalist or chauvinist, as harking back to the barbarism of Nazism and Fascism against which both liberals and Marxists had fought the Second War. Nations, thus, like persons, had identities consisting of emotional and rational opposites. Until the world reached utopia, nations would continue to exist. They, too, would remain emotional and retain their individual cultures but to the extent that they truly manifested modernity, they would be rational and peaceful in their dealings with other nations.[7.]

Erikson's work was crucial in forming discourses on identity at the beginning of the Cold War period. I concentrate on his work in my brief genealogy. Erikson was concerned, as a psychoanalyst, with the problem of extending the insights of that discipline from the psychosexual period of childhood up to adolescence and adulthood (and ultimately to old age).[8.] Erikson had, if we may restate it historically, become keenly aware that the socialization of young people in a modern mass society did not end with the resolution of the Oedipus complex and the child's coming to terms with the old patriarchal family whose power the newly powerful nation-state had largely eclipsed. His notion of identity formation, especially as worked out in adolescence, when a youth had to come to terms with career and nation, as well as a mate, seemed to provide a way of talking about the individual and society – what Erikson called the psychosocial – without completely subsuming the individual in society, by which Erikson and others meant the absolutizing nation-state of the twentieth century.

Eriksonian uses of the term identity imply that its owner's life has a coherence or unity in its make-up and actions, an integrity of character. Implicit also is the notion of authenticity. One's life as seen by oneself and recognized by others is distinctly and rightly one's own. Erikson[9] states that he has used the term *ego identity*, citing an article as early as 1946, 'to denote certain comprehensive gains which the individual, at the end of adolescence, must have derived from all of his preadult experience in order to be ready for the tasks of adulthood'. According to him,

> It is this identity of something in the individual core with an essential aspect of a group's inner coherence which is under consideration here: for the young individual must learn to be most himself where he means most to others – those others, to be sure, who have come to mean most to him. The term identity expresses such a mutual relation in that it connotes both a persistent sameness within oneself (selfsameness) and a persistent sharing of some kind of essential character with others.[10]

Clearly this idea is essentialist and absolutely homotelic, but we should not rush to condemn this, for that is precisely what Erikson and others of the period wanted, a concept of participation and transcendence that could be both enduring and unifying because it was somehow grounded in the psychic nature of man.

Erikson and those who have directly or indirectly taken up his idea of identity have focussed on adolescence as the period in a person's life when identity, his relation of participation in the nation, formed. According to Erikson, the psychic attachments that a person formed were not the result of conscious, rational life and career choices. They were not, in other words, the result of an agent's unfolding cognitive capacities. No, this psychic attachment at issue is assumed to be the result of largely unconscious, emotional processes. (Which is why identity is a discursive entity in psychoanalysis rather than in cognitive psychology.)[11.] Almost inevitably identity is considered to be the result of some formative event, an 'identity crisis' during or after adolescence.[12]

Adolescence was important for identity formation because it was fraught with certain problems which Erikson labels 'identity diffusion'. The concept of identity may have focused on the emotional, but it did not leave out the rational. Far from it. Identity not only entailed the identification of a person with the nation, it also involved the combination of the emotional with the rational. Erikson held that primary schools in America began to bring the emotional individuality of the child into contact with the rationality of the public world, manifest as 'initiative and industry'.[13] So far as the Anglo-Saxon population was concerned, Erikson contended that the schools succeeded in training their children 'in a spirit of self-reliance and enterprise'. We could see this by comparing this experience with that of those who have recently become the 'subjects' of identity politics:

> Minority groups of a lesser degree of Americanization (Negroes, Indians, Mexicans, and certain European groups) often are privileged in the enjoyment of a more sensual early childhood. Their crises come when their parents and teachers, losing trust in themselves and using sudden correctives in order to approach the vague but pervasive Anglo-Saxon ideal, create violent discontinuities; or where the children themselves learn to disavow their sensual and overprotective mothers as temptations and a hindrance to the formation of a more American personality.[14]

It was in primary school, apparently, that these children went through an 'identity crisis' as they became partly encapsulated in the national way of life and began to transcend their minority ways. For the majority of children, however, adolescence was the period of trouble.

Adolescence was the point where a youth was called upon to bring his emotional identity, tempered by the rational values of school days, into relation with the rational requirements of the public world of work. Speaking of modern youths in general but of Americans in particular, Erikson states that 'In general it is primarily the inability to settle on an occupational identity which disturbs young people'.[15] What was the cause of the disturbances of which Erikson speaks? It was the irrationality long attributed to 'masses' or 'crowds', which he,[16] following Freud, saw as the sociological equivalent of the biological id:

> To keep themselves together they temporarily overidentify, to the point of apparent complete loss of identity, with the heroes of cliques and crowds. On the other hand, they become remarkably clannish, intolerant, and cruel in their exclusion of others who are 'different', in skin color or cultural background, in

tastes and gifts, and often in entirely petty aspects of dress and gesture arbitrarily selected as the signs of an in-grouper or out-grouper.[17]

According to Erikson, these signs were inherently psychological and not attributable as such to particular practices:

> It is important to understand (which does not mean condone or participate in) such intolerance as the necessary *defense against a sense of identity confusion*, which is unavoidable at a time of life when the body changes its proportions radically, when genital maturity floods body and imagination with all manner of drives, when intimacy with the other sex approaches and is, on occasions, forced on the youngster, and when life lies before one with a variety of conflicting possibilities and choices. Adolescents help one another temporarily through such discomfort by forming cliques and by stereotyping themselves, their ideals, and their enemies.[18]

These psychological problems of the group and of the adolescent group in particular were worrying to Erikson and others in 1950 because the reason-based institutions of modernity were spreading and national(ist) leaders, especially in the newly independent and developing countries could take advantage of the turbulence of adolescence:

> It is important to understand this because it makes clear the appeal which simple and cruel totalitarian doctrines have on the minds of the youth of such countries and classes as have lost or are losing their group identities (feudal, agrarian, national, and so forth) in these times of world-wide industrialization, emancipation, and wider intercommunication. The dynamic quality of the tempestuous adolescences lived through in patriarchal and agrarian countries (countries which face the most radical changes in political structure and in economy) explains the fact that their young people find convincing and satisfactory identities in the simple totalitarian doctrines of race, class, or nation.[19]

Close to the top of Erikson's mind was something very specific – the problem of participation in a *mass* society, as embodied in the *nation*.

The worry here was not so much how to launch a national mass society, but how to relaunch one. The Germans and Italians, and in quite different ways, the Soviets and the Americans, had already launched mass societies in the form of centralized nation-states. The Nazis and Fascists had shown that by displacing the family and school with youth organizations and the 'mass' media it was possible to mobilize the young people of a nation for a large-scale all-embracing national project – war.[20] The problem for Erikson and his contemporaries was not only how to avoid a repetition of that mobilization, but also how to continue to encapsulate people in the nation and mass society without sacrificing the individualism they saw as central to liberal polities, most notably that of the US.[21] We might add that the problem of how to remobilize for peace was also looking in over the shoulders of Erikson and his contemporaries.[22] The idea of identity seemed to pull the nation-state back from its worst excesses without requiring it to give up its absolute claims. It was, in other words, a marvelous instance of theoretical suturing.

At first it might seem that 'identities' in this new suturing of the individual to society were indefinitely plural, that people would have as many identities as there were and were about to be, nations; but this was only partially so. A healthy personal identity emerged in adolescence only to the extent that the nation itself with which a youth was to identify was itself the embodiment of values and institutions that Erikson and others assumed to be universal, those they thought were based on reason, those of the free market economy and representative democracy. These transcended the particularities of nations and persons grounded in the emotions. The identities of certain modern nations (the United States of America) and of certain aggregates of persons in those nations, the virtuous middle classes, and especially the men, the bearers of the 'Anglo-Saxon ideal', were, thus, he and others assumed, normative. The members of what I would call the nation-state's ruling society, these men were truly the 'subject' of History, capable of being essentially and fully human.

Implicit in Erikson's focus on the Anglo-Saxon ideal are two identities against which he saw that identity defined. One of these was the totalitarian racial identity of the Nazis. The other was the notion of the cultivated, autonomous, liberally educated burgher, against which the Nazis had themselves constructed their racial identity.[23] It was something like this notion of the cultivated gentleman that Erikson was trying to recuperate in the US through his theory of identity, not as a public identity but as a private self that would somehow soften the enterprising individualism of the Anglo-Saxon ideal.

The question is, what about the identities of those left out of the US ruling society of Anglo-Saxon, middle-class heterosexual men – women, racial and ethnic minorities, and sexual 'deviants'? They apparently acquired their identities not by identifying directly with the nation-state, but indirectly (women as wives or black men as faithful employees). Those who failed either directly or indirectly to fuse their different identities into one that embodied the identity of the American nation-state might instead develop what Erikson called 'diffused identities'.[24] Their identities were, in my term, heterotelic, but incapable of articulation as the nation required. Still worse, those who failed to identify with the ruling society of the American nation-state might develop 'negative identities'. They would fuse together 'an identity perversely based on all those identifications and roles which, at critical stages of development, had been presented to the individual as most undesirable or dangerous, and yet also as most real'.[25] Marginal to the life of the nation-state or alienated from it, they could cultivate an individuality that would remain private if not secret, an individuality unrecognized or even despised by the Anglo-Saxon nationals. Relief from their situation was 'often sought collectively in cliques and gangs of young homosexuals, addicts, and social cynics'.[26] These marginal people, along with children, were the people an Anglo-Saxon man transcended when, in adolescence, he formed his identity with the American nation-state.

There is also another assumption here, namely, that the emotional, personal and familial identity of a person could and would combine with the public identity he had to acquire during adolescence. Yet this notion of an absolutely homotelic self or identity that would emerge in adolescence seems to me highly problematic. One could more readily argue that the public identity a person acquired at adolescence was at the very least distinct from the private identity he or she had already acquired and would continue to cultivate throughout his or her life. It is possible, furthermore, to find many examples of disagreement about what should constitute peoples' private identity. Finally, what some leaders had advocated as public identity in one nation or period, others could advocate as a private identity in others and vice-versa. Indeed it is just such contestations that are important to today's multiculturalism.

To sum up, identity, as Erikson conceptualized it after World War II, emphasized the participation of an individual dominated by emotion in a modern nation-state itself normatively dominated by rationality, the result of which was the emergence of an absolutely homotelic mind and identity. Formation of this homotelic identity took place during adolescence when the educational institutions of a modern nation-state, constituted as a mass society, incorporated the younger members of its ruling society into itself. The identity that formed was healthy or positive, however, insofar as the nation, based on emotion, subordinated itself, through its state, to universal values based on reason. The nation-state which best did this, the United States, was conceived of as the most advanced bearer of civilization. It was a modern utopia, a society based on machines. Ever progressing, it transcended previous forms of human existence, those considered medieval or traditional. Yet it continually ran the risk of turning into a dystopia should it fail to balance the emotional, individual needs of its citizens against the requirements of mass society. There was also a nagging residual problem: those ineligible to become full members of a nation-state's ruling society – women, people of lower classes, and minorities – might fail to identify indirectly with the nation (through their participation in the lives of the men who constituted the ruling society) and form negative identities.

Erikson's idea of identity formation was timely for two major reasons. First, it seemed to avoid conceding too much to the principle of rationality in the modern world. For many, the successes of Communism, Fascism, and Nazism and the clamour of colonized peoples for independence demonstrated that the dark forces of unreason were much stronger than liberals of earlier generations had thought. Identity at once recognized the strength of reason and emotion and resolved the opposition between them. Erikson's notion of identity also argued for the individual's autonomy within the nation-state, acknowledging the opposition between the personal and national and again resolving it. Finally, it took heed of the opposition of particular and universal, when it came to the relationship of the individual to the nation and of the nation to universal values based on reason. From a different angle, it provided a new discourse for explaining why peoples had different cultures and histories, why they developed or failed to develop along the same lines. Racial explanations of difference which had been hegemonic among Europeans and Americans had become discredited during World War II. Psychological explanations could now do much of the work the racial ones had done before. Scholars such as David Riesman were ready to talk about identity in the modern US while others such as Daniel Lerner were ready to talk about the formation of collective identities in the volatile Middle East of Nasser.[27]

Erikson and his colleagues thus hoped that the notion of identity would lend a natural-seeming unity to the participation of the individual in the absolute nation-state as a free agent without yet requiring the liberal nation-state to give up its absoluteness, based on its embodiment of universal values. The oppositions between the emotional and rational, personal and national, and the particular and universal would, at the time of adolescence, resolve into a belonging together which, even though in need of continual monitoring and suturing, might appear seamless. My point is that identity as Erikson conceived it, is only one historic form that the participation and transcendence of people in their lives has taken. What I propose to do is to broaden this discussion by looking at persons as agents whose selves are relatively heterotelic or homotelic rather than as 'egos' or 'subjects' which have absolute essences. The goals that people have involve the participation in and transcendence of one another's lives in different ways and in different situations. I want to look at the lives and life-wishes of people as agents and see how they attempted to realize those life-wishes through different practices of participation and transcendence in relation to larger, complex agents, those referred to as communities or polities.

Transcendence: from the everyday to paradise or utopia

Transcendence is not a single condition. I use the term transcendence not to signify some underlying and central urge of Man that the human sciences can isolate and determine (as some in comparative religions, psychology, or anthropology might wish) but nominally, in order to create a discursive field of inquiry. We can speak of transcendence in a number of different but related senses. I begin with simpler notions of transcendence in the day-to-day and end with the notion of participation in a paradise or utopia, the idea of transcending everyday existence altogether.

Integral to any agent is what people refer to as the well-being, prosperity, success, good health, long life, or happiness that they enjoy at moments in their day-to-day lives. Collingwood, whose discussion relates to European and British discourses on the topic, distinguished between happiness or well-being as a relationship to oneself and to the world around one. Happiness in the first is virtue, in the second, power. Internally, the unhappy man is at the mercy of his passions; externally, of others: 'Essentially to be unhappy is to be in the power of circumstances, things other than oneself standing round oneself, constricting one's movements by their presence, forbidding one to do anything except what they permit'.[28] The most common term to denote a general, diffuse, and transitory happiness in Sanskritic and Persian-related vocabularies of modern South Asian languages with which I am familiar is *sukha* or *khuśī* the opposite term being *duḥkha*, used to denote misery, sorrow, discomfort, pain, and sadness. Older discourses use a language of lordship and mastery to discuss the conditions they denote in terms broadly similar to those Collingwood uses. The attainment of happiness within either of these general discourses requires the articulation of an agent's life activities such that an agent is able to rise above or transcend his or her situation while yet participating in the lives of others. Crucial here is the range of feelings – satisfaction, contentment, pleasure, elation, the glow of excitement or even ecstasy, for these in large part constitute an awareness of happiness.

Happiness or well-being is not, of course, only a consequence of participation and transcendence in the daily lives of persons. People do or are supposed to experience them as participants in more complex agents, families and communities or societies, those concerned with making a livelihood, those having to do with ways of life which tell people how to reach transcendence, and those having to do with the ordering of the human world so as to make a way of life practicable.

So far I have been talking about well-being as a moderate and relative condition of transcendence. Proponents of many ways of life, however, also promise their adherents a state of well-being or happiness consisting of a radical or absolute condition of transcendence, one in which a person lives in complete accord with the will of God or the dictates of Reason or some such. These transcendent states are defined in relation to the immanent conditions of life. Proponents of the ways of life known as the world religions of medieval Europe and India – Christianity, Islam, Hinduism, Buddhism – variously promised their followers transcendence. It existed, they claimed, as some sort of afterlife in a paradise that actually transcended the world, being in a distant land on earth or above it in a heaven. (Hindus and Buddhists went so far as to promise an ultimate condition that transcended even paradise.)

Advocates of 'modernist' ways of life known as world political and social movements – liberalism, socialism, ecologism, neoliberalism or secular humanism, modernism, feminism – have also offered their followers transcendence. They have promised to bring about personal and national or collective happiness not by transporting their followers to a heavenly paradise or even a distant land (though the early utopians did just that) but by transporting paradise to earth. They claim that the foundational principle of reason is no longer the inscrutable attribute of a transcendent God but the immanent property of humankind. By making it fully manifest in the here and now they will create a utopia that transcends their former condition.

Here we are dealing with more explicitly and consciously discursive forms of transcendence, yet they are not unrelated to everyday notions of transcendence. As Gramsci would have argued, well-being or happiness – transcendence – in everyday life and the reasons people do and do not gain it might seem self-evident, natural, or common-sense to the people involved, but they are almost always a broken-up, naturalized composite of these previously more elite 'isms'.[29]

It is important to attend to the language people use to characterize the acts or practice by which more radical and absolute transcendence is to be achieved. It is common to represent these practices as a form of travel, journeying or progressing, going on pilgrimage, or voyaging to the desired paradise, in the course of which one leaves behind the undesired condition of life. Notions of light and dark, of vision and blindness are also prominent in depicting the forms of consciousness involved. As one proceeds, one gets closer to light and further from the dark.

Crucial to the representation of the practices by which one proceeds from the everyday world to a heavenly paradise or earthly utopia is the focus on some act or other by which one may make a decisive break with the everyday. Here I refer to such terms as baptism, salvation, initiation, release or liberation. One term that figures prominently in modernist discourse is emancipation, as a result of which the freedom or liberty central to utopian existence comes to be experienced on a permanent basis.[30] To become modern is to be emancipated – either individually or collectively, gradually or suddenly – from the constraints, inhibitions, whims, exploitations, and oppressions of the medieval or traditional.

What counts as medieval or traditional depends, of course, on what sort of modernist one is. For liberals the medieval is the dark side of arcadia – a rural life shortened by back-breaking labour, famine, plague, and endemic war where initiative is stultified by the 'primordial' ties of kinship, clan, tribe, and village and material progress is prevented by religious superstition. For socialists the traditional or medieval is extended to encompass the dark side of modernity, a capitalist dystopia – rack-renting landlords and the satanic mills and child labour of commercial, industrial society, or, in the underdeveloped world, the overcrowded, disease-ridden favelas, chawls or bustees that surround the big cities.

Although many modernists represent the modern/utopia as a sharp break with such a medieval past, I contend that the emancipation they talk about has consisted to a large extent of a double process of the appropriation of the medieval itself. First, they have *secularized* the transcendent paradises of the medieval world. Medieval leaders had promised people a radical, absolute transcendence, but that was only to be available to a few in another time, after death, and in a remote place, heaven, and perhaps not even there. For the many, moments of ameliorated, relative transcendence were available at certain times, holidays and in certain locations, churches or temples and the sites of festivals and carnivals. Modern leaders claim that they will bring about a radical, absolute transcendence for the whole of society in the here-and-now. We will no longer have to wait for death and a journey to a transcendent realm that exists only far away in time and/or in place. Becoming modern will make the world of daily life itself into a paradise for the many. Those who live in the hell of the Third World, of course, were, for the time being, not eligible, as we shall see.

Second, modernists have *sacralized* the mundane and everyday. This they have done by transferring (often silently) various attributes of what they take to be the divine – certain knowledge based on reason, domination of the world, and control over affairs at a great distance (also known as omniscience, omnipotence, and omnipresence) – to the modern nation-state and its inhabitants.[31]

What supposedly made emancipation, the sacralization of the mundane, possible was the advent of labour-saving, fuel-powered machinery. Especially in German and American representations of civilization as utopia, the modern world was one that would be radically transformed through machines. Indeed, society itself would become a machine or machine-like in its organization. Whence the importance, from Hobbes on, of the image of the 'commonwealth' or state as a 'body politic' which is itself a perfect machine. As a result of this transformation, people would live harmoniously with each other – there would be no politics – and realize themselves through a variety of aesthetic and consumer activities. Some commentators, of course, were less optimistic about the outcome of modernization. They have represented the process as possibly or even necessarily resulting in a dystopia where machines become the masters of men, where rationality forces them into an iron cage.[32]

The language modernists have used in the past century or so strongly evokes the image of the modern nation-state as a vehicle that has progressed to a utopia that is itself ever-changing. During the Anglo-French imperial formation, the civilizing missions of the British and French empires were national practices, the desired outcome of which was to be transcendence of an unwanted or less desirable way of life, those deemed uncivilized or less civilized. The freedom crusade of Cold War America, arms races, and the space race, and economic development directed by five-year plans are all examples of diverse yet transcendental practices which various nations took up in the period after World War II. All of them of course required the mobilization of the emotions and not just the deployment of reason. Practices involving transcendence of the daily life of the 'past' that continues into the present are, however, by no means confined to such national projects (and to the extent that they are those projects have probably foundered). We can, I contend, also see this notion at work in the day-to-day lives of people in the nation, as I show below.

International welfare utopia after World War II

The idea that came to the fore in twentieth-century representations of utopia, especially after World War II, is that the whole of the nation is an emergent paradise, especially for its elite. People as citizens of the modern nation are supposed here not to strive for identification with an absolute represented as an invisible god in a place remote in time and space, identity with whom they will attain only after death. They are supposed to work toward identifying themselves with an absolute represented as the modern nation, an absolute that exists in the here and now. It exists as the body politic, the representation of the nation as the 'people' congealed into a single man who is a machine. This identity is, of course, defined against the image of the people as jarring molecules, warring individuals (and the notion of the community as a cooperating collective). The modern welfare state claimed that, with the aid of the natural and social sciences, it would bring about man's transcendence of nature. Through technology, the advent of the steamship and train and the automobile, and aeroplane, 'man' would overcome his bodily immobility. Through modern mass manufacturing and agriculture using fertilizers and pesticides man would overcome his dependence on particular environments. Through the spread of technically advanced medical care men and women would extend the quality and length of their lives. Centrally heated and electrically lit housing and the abundance of food and clothing would allow men and their families to become independent of the vagaries of the seasons.

These uses of machines are concerned mainly with freeing the body. Just as important were those that were to liberate the mind, assumed in these discourses to be inherently homotelic. Through telecommunications – the telegraph and telephone – people would overcome the limits of the human vocal chords and be able to talk to one another at great distances. By way of the mass media, the older print media of the book, magazine, and newspaper and the newer electronic media – film, radio, and television – people would, as McLuhan said, extend their senses and minds, making information and entertainment available on an unprecedented scale.[33] Thus, by scientifically deploying the machines of both body and mind, all people, homotelic by nature, would achieve paradise in the here and now.

Past attempts to translate the absolute order and ecstasy of God into the body politic of the nation did not always live up to expectations. The British and French had transcended their pasts and become empires, subjecting other, lesser peoples in order to bring about the liberty, world order and prosperity – civilization – that its leaders promised to the metropoles (a technical term translatable in Britain as London and the Home Counties). The subjected countries to which the British and French brought Christian and modern civilization are the countries leaders and scholars came to consider, after they gained independence, as 'underdeveloped'.

The 'developed' countries are those that have progressed to modernity. Most of these required 'reconstruction' after World War II. The problem with India was that, along with other so-called Third World countries, it had not yet attained the permanent and absolute transcendence of the past possessed by the 'advanced' nations. Which is to say that India was still a medieval country, a nation dominated by the traditional. India, according to the predominant colonialist image, had always been divided by race, language, caste, family, and creed. Its natural political condition, reflecting these divisions, was that of a feudal or post-tribal polity consisting of fractious principalities, divine kingships in which political rationality was distorted by religion. When the conflicting pieces were brought together into a single polity it was the result of conquest. The single polity that the presence of outsiders caused was inevitably an autocracy, an 'oriental despotism', for only a strong centre could counter the 'centrifugal forces' or 'fissiparous tendencies' threatening to explode the Indian body politic. It alone could remain neutral and maintain impartiality towards India's contentious castes and creeds. Colonialists thus provided Indian history with a series of imperial moments, flawed anticipations of the British empire destined to come. It, too, would originate in conquest but its transcendence would last because it would be based on the Law and not on arbitrary personal will, and on markets free from unnecessary government interference.[34]

Colonialists in this century had got into the habit of calling this imperial administrative state 'secular'. At the same time they had represented the society over which it presided as 'communalist', as so dominated by religion that the only or primary basis of political unity in the subcontinent could be the allegiance of people to either of the two large, inherently opposed 'communities', Hindu and Muslim.[35] British India, thus, consisted of two nations (as Pakistan's future leader, Jinnah was fond of saying), each based on a religion, ruled over by a secular state, the colonial equivalent of the modern, liberal state. Nehru and other Indian nationalists (including Gandhi), though forced to accept and recognize Pakistan did not accept the communalist view for the Republic of India and after independence proclaimed India a secular state that would tolerate all religions. Politically, then, independent India retained a state that had claimed to transcend its political past both legally and administratively. It still presided, however, over a society that was medieval, dominated by religion.

The reason for this was that the British had left India economically 'backward'. That, at least was the nationalist argument, concurred in by the new world ruling society that grew up after World War II and the shift away from the old French and British notions of empire as bringing civilization to the world. Nehru and some of the greater figures in his postcolonial government, as in-country members of this new ruling society, made it their highest priority to develop India. Hoping to provide it with the same sort of welfare state that the developed countries had built for themselves, they embarked on a quest for transcendence of the economic and social past through five-year plans, steel production, and dam building the story of which I tell elsewhere.

Scholars and commentators have represented the persons who were supposed to inhabit this international welfare utopia as 'abstract'[36] or 'possessive'.[37] It is the idea that the human being has an inner nature that remains essentially the same in all situations for all purposes. The idea of a person as a 'subject', as having some mental entity that underlies the apparently changing personality, is another way scholars have theorized the individual as inherently homotelic.[38] That inner nature or essence is, as is well known, reason, the capacity to make rational choices. Abstract individualism comes in two forms, the political, which focuses on a person's rights and interests and how to protect them, in the form of liberties, within a state that emphasizes 'separation of powers' and 'checks and balances'. The other is the economic, one that sees people as abstract, rationally calculating entrepreneurs and consumers acting in a 'free market'.[39]

Philosophers, social scientists, and political leaders have disagreed over which of these is primary. I would argue that during the Cold War period, political individualism, modified so as to be concerned with the extension of rights in the name of social justice, came to prevail. The complex of practices making up the welfare state, the form of polity that became hegemonic in the period, presupposes this position.

Abstract individualism of just this sort was what Erikson, working in tandem with political thinkers and leaders after World War II, took as constituting the best form of national identity. The emotionally based personal and familial identity of a young man would somehow come to terms with the requirements of the rationally based American modern national identity and a single coherent identity would emerge. The dystopian fear of being atomized in the 'mass' of a relentlessly rationalizing and impersonal machine society would be avoided and so too would the even worse fear, that of being caught up in the sociological irrationality of the mass in the guise of a distinctive and superior people or nation.

This seamless identity did not, however, materialize, even in the exemplary US, outside academic discourse and political rhetoric. Instead, 'private' and 'public' identities that people saw as quite distinct, often opposed, emerged. What Robert Bellah refers to as an expressive individuality emerged in the 1950s and 1960s.[40] This notion of individuality, loosely traceable to the early nineteenth-century Romantics, emphasized self-fulfillment through sexual love and other activities of self-expression ranging from the esthetic to the plainly hedonist (depending on who was doing the evaluating) – reading or even writing novels or poetry, taking drugs, doing transcendental meditation, travel, listening to the Beatles, and watching and discussing art films. For the upper reaches of the middle classes, especially those with a liberal education (where the humanities catered to these new needs), this notion of an expressive or creative individualism largely displaced that of religious individualism in its older form of denominational Protestantism.[41] Charles Taylor, calling on his own past work as a post-Hegelian, centers his argument about multiculturalism and recognition on a creative individualism, which Lukes describes under the heading of romantic self-development.[42] Taylor rightly argues that the self is not a given in nature but is something that requires making both by oneself and by others. Selves are, then, for him, very much historical entities. He fails, however, to point out that this notion of individualism, largely confined to the personal or private realm, is inconsistent with the notion of abstract individualism which has prevailed in civil society or the public realm. Taylor's argument thus misses the point, for what distinguishes multiculturalist demands from earlier similar demands is precisely their public locus. To make matters worse, Taylor gives prominence to the liberal representation of the modern state least capable of accommodating cultural differences, the one he calls 'proceduralism'. Some thought this new, more 'constructionist' notion of private self might displace the older productivist public self.[43.]

I have already mentioned some of the national projects through which the welfare states of the Cold War period tried to gain transcendence over their pasts and each other. Here let me point to some of the practices of daily life in the modern nation of this period that were productive of transcendence, whether in public or private life. Winning a court case or obtaining a high score on an examination as a student are examples that antedate this period. Others distinctive of it were working as a business executive in a high-rise office building for a major corporation, travelling by air in business or first class to do a job for a client, owning and driving a car, one's private vehicle of transcendence, and living in a suburb away from the problems of the 'inner' city. Getting high at a Saturday-night party, attending yoga class, going on holiday outside the country, and a quest to find just the right sexual partner are some of the private activities conducive to transcendence in which middle class people of the period might have engaged. Indeed the work of psychologists such as Abraham H. Maslow (d. 1970) focussed specifically on how 'self-actualizing' persons might go beyond the practical achievements of what I am calling abstract individualism and become 'creative' people who experienced 'transcendence' in their inner lives.[44] According to Maslow: 'Transcendence refers to the very highest and most inclusive or holistic levels of human consciousness, behaving and relating, as ends rather than means, to oneself, to significant others, to human beings in general, to other species, to nature, and to the cosmos'.[45]

These are just a few of the moments in American middle-class daily life of the period where people expected to exert personal and institutional superiority and to experience an emotional charge from doing so. Within independent India, the ruling society that emerged was embodied in the figure of the civil servant or political leader, journalist, or university lecturer. A socialist or Gandhian, he was a man who had transcended his caste and religious background (mostly high and Hindu) and claimed to live up to the nation's secular ideal. Representing himself as living austerely, his day-to-day way of participating in India's development was through self-sacrifice. He also enjoyed moments of transcendence (as did the lesser members of this ruling society) when he saw Nehru open a new dam or steel mill in a newsreel, participated in national elections, or read of Indian engagement in world affairs as one of the leaders of the neutral bloc.

The claim in the modernism of the Cold War period was that all the people of the nation should experience life in a utopia and should, accordingly, have feelings of transcendence. It is obvious, however, that the activities in which people engage and the feelings they experience are highly inflected by class, region, race, gender, and sexual orientation. What I would like to propose is that within the welfare state, the category of persons qualified for modernist transcendence par excellence were the civil servants (in government) and corporate managers (in business) of the nation. People of the professions – medicine, law, education, the clergy – were also qualified because they were in charge of making or transforming not only themselves as agents but of making or transforming the civil servants and managers. Cadres of international civil servants most exemplified the identity of the period and the United Nations was the foremost of international organizations, the utopian embodiment of universal values and of an abstract human identity. Working through it, these 'world citizens', equipped with homotelic minds, were supposed to cooperate with their counterparts in the nation-states to maintain world order (while the US and USSR rattled nuclear weapons at one another).

Transnational utopia

Now, the experts tell us, that epitome of modernity, the nation-state, especially in its welfare configuration, is out of date. There is no need for me to repeat what others have said about global integration or disintegration, about the quickening-pace-of-change sociology that now abounds. I do not want to frame the dislocations that have been occurring in the world in the past ten years or so as 'late' or 'high' modernity as 'advanced' or 'late' capitalism, or a 'risk' society. I find it amusing, however, that Gorz finds it necessary to change his idea of the traditional or medieval. The world once envisioned in Soviet communism or socialism as the quintessence of the modern and anticipated in the welfare state is now premodern.[46] I do, nonetheless, agree with Gorz and others, that major changes are taking place which do indeed pose challenges to the nation as the major social agent in which people participate, as the source of their primary 'identity'. The institutional practices for making children into nationals – universal education and national media foremost among them – have lost the capacity they had in the period after World War II to encapsulate their patients and provide them with identities that appear to reconcile the personal with the national. This is especially so for those outside the male children of the nation's ruling society – women, minorities, subnationals, and the economically oppressed.

The 'cultural identities' that have emerged in the past twenty years or so have focussed around precisely those definitions of self or community that the absolutist nation-state marginalized – feminist, gay and lesbian, Chicano or Latino, African and, very differently, Asian American in the US and others ranging from the Greater Serbia movement to the so-called Muslim fundamentalists elsewhere. Attempts to create these and other such identities are thus symptomatic of the weakening of the national identities that people saw as existing in the Cold War period. I see any number of dislocations of that identity taking place and these dislocations now make it possible for new practices of participation and transcendence to emerge. I am afraid, however, that I do not see here the rise of new postmodern identities. To a very large extent, the emergent societies that claim to speak for these larger communities can rather be seen as trying to create identities for themselves of just the sort that they had been excluded from during the Cold War period. Paul Gilroy provides one of the better discussions of this tendency.[47]

There is a problem here, though. The creation and sustenance of the identity that Erikson and others thought possible and desirable, even natural, required the existence of central national institutions, not only the state, but also others such as a national system of educational practices, including broadcasting media. Such institutions created and sustained a personal-national identity or, (more accurately, the illusion of one) in two supplementary ways. On the one hand, they encapsulated the people of the polity's ruling society, especially its youth, within them and turned them into citizens with something resembling an identity. On the other hand, they were able, more or less successfully, to subsume, marginalize, or even pathologize those seen as incapable of carrying the national identity, namely, those outside the ruling society's men. The idea that feminists, gays and lesbians, subnationalities, minority groups or ethnicities of various kinds can create and sustain unitary identities for themselves without states and their educational institutions seems highly implausible.

India is no exception. The situation there is certainly confusing. I nonetheless think it safe to say that the failure of state-directed development to produce what it had promised combined with contested demands made from precisely those largely excluded from the national ruling society, the rise of a Hinduist nationalism, and the shift toward more open markets articulate in a variety of ways with the changes signalled by talk about globalization. The consequences for identity, for the homotelic person of independent India, can be seen in many venues. Let me just look at one account from a symposium held on that topic.[48] The presentations published deal with women, tribes, Muslims, Sikhs, and the Dravidian movement in Tamil Nadu. Virtually all of them indicate that the notion of an identity of person and nation is in trouble. The article of most interest is the one that concentrates on children. Its author, Krishna Kumar points to the major difficulty faced by the Eriksonian notion of identity in its Indian rendering, the claims political leaders have made on its behalf:

The feature that stands above all others is the absoluteness of the nation. The nation to which the politician's banal words refer not only transcends all other units of collective identity and belonging; it denies to these units the moral legitimacy they would be expected to have earned following the legal legitimacy granted to them in the Constitution. The moral legitimacy of sub-national units of identity is denied by an inevitable invocation of the danger of disintegration or subversion. Appeal to the absolute ideal of the nation is made by juxtaposing all other units of identity with the risk of the nation falling apart.[49]

Two of these other identities – caste and religious – were definitely 'wrong' while regional and linguistic identities were treated more 'delicately'. They might, for example, be accorded a role in national development: 'Celebrating a major industrial establishment located in an economically poor region, a politician might well mention the contribution made by that region towards national development'.[50] Most interestingly for my purposes, Kumar turns to educational practices. The child learns to identify with family, caste, religion, village, town and region but, according to Kumar, such identities are not recognized or articulated with a national identity when the child attends school. Rather, 'The Indian school does all it can to weaken the bond children might have with their local habitat, its history, geography and culture. As an official agency, even if run privately, the school upholds the ideal of the nation as an absolute, and therefore deals only superficially, and usually disdainfully, with local matters'.[51] He goes on to argue that 'the absolute ideal of the nation which is drummed into children's ears can hardly be expected to survive the coming of adolescence'.[52] The reason for this? The adolescent, now placing his reasoning capacities in charge of his identity formation, sees through the hypocrisy that makes possible the banal representations of the Indian nation. This, he avers, leaves the adolescent in a 'residual frenzy'.[53] He or she can take up one of three broad options: migration to the West; joining a 'fanatic organisation' including, presumably the RSS, Shiv Sena or BJP, Jama'at-i-Islami, etc.; or, last, 'devoting oneself to the pursuit of money'.[54] What we can infer from this account is that the very dichotomy between particular identities and the 'universal' identity of the nation in India has, given the perceived failure of India to develop as previously envisioned, positioned Indians to see membership in some sort of new universal community as both desirable and attainable.

The main reason for this reorientation is to be found in the emergence of a new global ruling society. Robert B. Reich, President Clinton's Secretary of Labor, tells us that the US workforce is increasingly divided into what I infer are three functionally different classes. Interestingly, he says these three are no longer in a single national 'boat' but in three separate boats. 'Routine producers', the stand-bys of mass production in nationally organized industries are sinking fastest, rendered increasingly redundant by the globalization of labour and computerization. The second boat, sinking more slowly and unevenly carries 'in-person servers' who tend to the needs of the folks in the third boat, the rapidly rising luxury-liner containing the 'symbolic analysts'.[55] Also called techno-entrepreneurs, they are mostly white men, highly educated, who engage in 'problem-identifying' and 'strategic-brokering' activities. They do not sell standardized products or render personal services, they trade in 'the manipulation of symbols – data, words, oral and visual representations'.[56] Some might describe these as the elements of culture, others, as the units of information. Either way, the lives of symbolic analysts are much more focussed on telecommunications and the media than the older national citizenries they would displace. They are the rulers of what Mark Poster[57] calls a 'second age of mass media'. Comprising one-fifth of the US population, the people of this new class have incomes that 'have soared to what years before would have been unimaginable heights, even as those of other Americans have declined'.[58]

Reich represents this emergent ruling society as transcendent under the narrow rubric of 'secession'.[59] More dependent on each other and on institutions and activities going on in the 'global web' and through international networks, symbolic analysts increasingly lead lives apart from the rest of the nation. They 'can work almost anywhere there exist a telephone, fax, modem, and airport'.[60] Thus, though they tend to concentrate in certain locations – Silicon Valley, the City of London – they are not tied to any one of them; 'there are other symbolic-analytic centres to which they might relocate'.[61] The 'weights of tradition and extended family' do not 'bear heavily on their locational decisions'. Having lots of money to spend on private schools and child-care, they are 'less dependent on relatives living nearby'.[62] The sure sign of their transcendence is that they 'spend a great deal of time on the move – at meetings with clients and customers in distant cities, on temporary assignment in a factory or laboratory in another nation, at trade shows and conventions around the world'.[63]

In what looks much like the way historians have described the iniquitous organization of medieval society into estates, Reich reports that while the new ruling society has greatly reduced its dependence on the rest of the population in the nation, the dependence of that population on the symbolic analysts has increased. We thus have a world in which an estate of symbolic analysts, like the lords spiritual and temporal of Europe or the 'twice-born' of India, is serviced by an estate of supplicant serfs or Śūdras, artisans and attendants. William Gibson, guru of cyberpunk, has explicit recourse to an image of the medieval in commenting on the new arrangement:

> Tired as I am with all the hype about the Internet and the info highway, I suspect that from a future perspective it will be on a par with the invention of the city as a force in human culture. People still don't understand the Internet is transnational. Cyberspace has no borders, and that's fine with me because I had my fill of nationalism in the Vietnam war.
>
> But nation states had this honourable potential, the democratic tradition that gives people some kind of say. In the kind of global corporate feudalism that seems to be coming next, of transnational mega corporations and whole regions

of the earth run by organised crime, we may be getting something worse.

So I have a central professional duty to remain as deeply ambivalent about technology as I can, to recognise the downside. There's no knowing what any given technology will do. Look at the refrigerator: a wonderful life-enhancing product, that now looks as if it's destroying the ozone layer'.[64]

Reich, like many commentators on both right and left, writes about the rise of this new, transnational ruling society as if it were a natural event: 'The ubiquitous and irrepressible law of supply and demand no longer respects national borders. In this new world economy, symbolic analysts hold a dominant position. American symbolic analysts are especially advantaged'.[65] Commentators like Francis Fukuyama, pupil of Allan Bloom at Chicago, have gone so far as to announce under the rubric of liberal democracy that the situation which Reich describes is, in effect, the final goal toward which mankind has, with some perverse backing and filling, been striving.[66] Commentators on the left, no longer able to claim some kind of organic relationship to this new ruling society as they tenuously could to the civil servants of the welfare state and the old international order, still want to keep up the pretense of being able to call the shots. So, under the labels of postmodernism or a high modernity or a late or advanced capitalism, they, too, give the impression that what is happening is the inevitable unfolding of some world history.

Like Stuart Hall,[67] I believe that the actual configuration of social relations that Reich describes is underdetermined by the technological and organizational changes that have taken place. It is ceaseless representational activity in both a political and verbal or pictorial sense that brings about the momentary determinations. Reaganites and Thatcherites have formed the political vanguard of this rising class of techno-entrepreneurs. The centrepiece of this political movement is free-market economics which grounds itself in an economic version of abstract individualism.

Much of the New Right, it has been argued, shadows the Old Left. Here, I contend, the New Right's vision of a world that is ruled by a transnational business class which subsumes in itself the existing nation-states shadows the Old Left's hope for a world where an international proletariat would overcome national differences. The older liberals, those of the period after World War II when the US displaced the British and French empires, envisioned a world order that consisted either of an association of free nations or a federation of them ruled by a world government. Now the New Right offers us its replacement for an international order that the older Communists saw as eventually being ruled by the working class. It is the world described by Reich.

This vision departs from the idea of the world ruling society it is displacing in two major ways. First it replaces the idea of the international civil servant with the transnational techno-entrepreneur. Second, it turns a relationship of coagency that was supposed to exist between the international civil servants and the national civil servants into one of transcendence in which the international and national civil services and the agencies they administer are to be redeployed as the subordinates of the new entrepreneurial ruling class.

What is integral to both of these changes is a shift in the relation between the political and economic forms of abstract individualism. The centrist liberal modernism that prevailed from World War II until about fifteen years ago outside the former Soviet bloc allowed for *both* political and economic individualism and usually gave the edge to the political. The New Right claims, *pace* Fukuyama and the Straussites, that economic individualism should take precedence over political individualism. The latter has only a provisional or secondary existence and can be reduced to a subsidiary status or eventually even eliminated. The disintegrative effects of this new ruling society's activities on those excluded from it has, I would argue, provoked the responses that take the form of religious fundamentalism. That is, the absolutism of the economic individualism of the free marketeers is opposed by the absolutism of the religious individualism of the fundamentalists. This is especially so with respect to the global yuppies' amoral and self-centred consumption practices. Public and private identities are, in this notion of individualism, closely connected. Indeed, some personal or private practices are or may be crucial to the sense of making a public life in utopia. The satisfaction one is supposed to gain as a mall rat engaged in 'recreational shopping', for example, or the high one gets from drug-taking or participating in a rave may be enjoyed as rewards for being a senior market analyst, as a priming of oneself for the next week of work, or even as a substitute for the job one has lost. Going on expensive holidays to exotic locations reiterates one's cosmopolitan credentials. Wearing designer clothes impresses both friends and clients. Surfing the Internet and accessing the World Wide Web bring the feeling of omniscience in every aspect of life. Genetic engineering, exogenesis, cosmetic surgery, and cryogenics will soon let us overcome the vagaries of existence as transitory organisms. The cyborg, fusion of both the rational and machine component with the emotional and organic, is the apposite figure for this utopia. Within the developed countries, most notably the United States, religious fundamentalists often represent the excesses of consumerism and personal arrogance of the new class as the result of the permissiveness of an older liberalism, that is, of the expressive individualism that arose in the 1950s and displaced denominational religion, supposed to have been conceded supremacy by the modern liberal polity in the personal or private sphere under the guises of 'separation of church and state' and 'tolerance'. Within the developing countries, like India, that had followed a secular socialist path, religious nationalists aim their criticisms both at the deficient consumerism of secular socialism and at the excessive consumerism of Western and home-grown transnationals.

The identity that the symbolic analysts and their gurus, the organic intellectuals of the new rulers, Reich, Tom Peters, Alvin and Heidi Toffler, and Kenichi Ohmae, are fashioning for the new global ruling society has an essence – the economic individualism of the free market – as its core.[68] Precisely because of its global pretensions its members have great interest in manipulating national cultures and they are quite content, once these have been defanged, to strap ever-shifting 'cultural' identities, better described as styles or even fads, onto this core. Indeed, it is necessary for this global class to learn about different languages and cultures, to listen to world music and read world (magical realist) literature, use Chinese acupuncture and eat Japanese food in order to lend itself the transcendence of any one national culture that it must display in order to validate its global, cosmopolitan credentials.[69] This homo interneticus, unitary on the inside and multicultural on the outside, is the ideal that its representations in films, magazines, television, and advertising shape in our world-wish (and attendant anxieties) and it is this variety of individualism we are called upon to take up. It is, furthermore, the 'diaspora' of these techno-entrepreneurs, mostly American, that figures prominently in the imaginary of South Asians both in the subcontinent and abroad.

The main problems of identity India faces are not just whether it is to continue as an underdeveloped country or to become a developed country in a world where nation-states seem to be losing their place as the primary focuses of a unitary identity and whether, in such circumstances, India will sustain itself as a 'secular' state or become a Hindu nation with highly uncertain consequences for its many minorities – Muslims quite diverse, Dalits, Harijans, or untouchables, Adivasis or tribals, and scheduled or backward classes. The current shift of India to a free-market economic regime now means that Indians staying in India can promote themselves as symbolic analysts and join this new global class more readily than in the past for they can now do so in India itself. (The problems of participation and transcendence faced by South Asians in diaspora are, of course, different from these and quite diverse in themselves. The growing importance and visibility of a globally dispersed, yet largely American society of techno-entrepreneurs poses one set of problems for the South Asians in the United States and another for those settled in the United Kingdom.)

There is certainly plenty of talk, much of it motivated by business desires for new markets, about an increasingly prosperous middle class in India (as well as in China and the entire 'Asian Pacific'). Commentators debate over the size of this class – estimates range from 7-15 per cent of the total population – and the extent of its prosperity.[70] They do seem to agree, however, that the values of this protean class have changed. They have become more individualist and consumerist and the entrepreneur has begun to displace the civil servant as model member of the ruling society. It would, however, be premature to conclude that middle-class Indians are all becoming techno-entrepreneurs.

One place we would expect to see techno-entrepreneurs appearing, if anywhere in India, is Bangalore, its 'Silicon Valley'. My reading of a recent article on the computer industry there suggests that few if any of its computer whizzes see themselves as techno-entrepreneurs.[71] Interviews with computer experts there suggest that Indians could well find themselves tied to the largely American analysts as routine producers: 'Despite all the brave talk about lucrative, state-of-the-art client-server projects, the big software companies remain mired in coding ancient languages like Cobol for legacy systems that are three decades old. And they marginalize themselves by sending the best and brightest native sons and daughters to work for overseas software companies. Like indentured technoserfs, the workers are paid low salaries – by American standards – and bound to the bodyshoppers by contract'.[72] We are also told that there are still not many personal computers in India and few use them at home. Yet the same article does point to the possibilities for full participation in the techno-entrepreneurial class: 'Silicon Valley-style upward mobility is shocking to old-line Indian executives brought up in the tradition of nearly feudal loyalty to employers. But it is the taste of free enterprise that endows Bangalore pub life with the tang of modernity and a thrilling sense of being on the technological event horizon'.[73] Watch this space.

Overall, then, there is little reason to think that Indians or other South Asians have moved *en bloc* to participate in the transcendent utopia of a transnational class which Americans represent to the world. Indeed, there is some evidence, worth attending to, that many if not most Indians have a world-wish that is arcadian rather than utopian. That is, they envision a world in which relations of devoted participation (*bhakti*) among relatives, friends, and others deemed to belong to their society, is strengthened by the use of machinery rather than radically transformed and displaced by a cyber-society.[74] The world that the changing middle classes envision is a reworking of the 'traditional' joint family. Scrubbed free of its long-recognized problems – exploitation, gender discrimination, poverty and disease and inadequate housing – the members of this arcadia dwell, so to speak, in a permanent festival mood. This is the world of the popular Hindi film *Hum Aapke Hain Koun ...!*(1994).

Surprisingly, this is also in its main points the world which the columnist and novelist, Shobha Dé, represents in her first novel.[75] The blurb calls it 'The first truly modern novel in English by a woman ...'. The interest of this novel comes from the efforts of its heroine, Karuna, to transcend her middle-class, Nehruvian family background. Here is the account she gives of her family:

> Luxury ... was a dirty word in our house, while Education, with a capital E, of course, was one of the great gods. Like in clichéd Hindi films, the world of the rich and privileged was synonymous with the Evil Empire (oh, the hypocrisy of it all). We were trained to regard everything that wasn't 'basic' and 'essential' as frivolous and wasteful. The key word was austerity. Discipline and denial were the highest prized virtues. Children didn't drink tea, coffee or aerated waters. (Unfortunately, at our place, 'children' we remained till the day we married or left home – whichever was sooner. My aversion for milk was understandable – milk was tyranny.

My parents were not overly religious, but festivals were considered sacred. We couldn't skip any of the rituals – not even in the middle of our exams. Diwali remained the high point of our young lives.[76]

Karuna is fascinated by the media component of the techno-entrepreneurial class and the world its intellectuals imagine. The media had a strong connection with her austere middle-class family life:

Cinemas were out and so was film music. We woke up to the sounds of AIR *bhajans*. Mother was allowed to tune in to her favourite *Lok Geet* programme of songs from popular 'dramas', but that was only during the hours Father was away at work. I longed to listen to the Binaca Hit Parade broadcast by Radio Ceylon but I had to satisfy myself by hoping the neighbours would turn up their set or that Father would choose that time to go for his bath. 'Love me tender, love me sweet, never let me go', Elvis Presley would croon and I would go weak in the knees and kiss the World War II radio over the bookcase.[77]

After abortion and a divorce Karuna attempts a career in the media. She is also drawn to, then revulsed by, the private life of consumerism and parties of the Bombay rich, entrepreneurs and film-stars and their hangers-on. She finally decides that the way to suture together a life for herself is to give up the prospect of marriage (incompatible with her independence if not her 'career') and to continue staying with her parents, to whom she had returned after many years.[78] After reading in a gossip column that she was having a love affair with Girish Sridhar, a 'great art-film maker'[79] and his son, Kunal, she cries. Dé next chooses to have her heroine hear the sounds of a Ganapati procession and recall her participation in past festivals of the god:

As my weeping subsided the incessant drumming of Ganesh worshippers began to filter in. It was the tenth day of the festival, and the immersion of the elephant God had already begun. I could hear the raucous cries of *Ganapati bapa morya* and the rhythmic clanging of cymbals as the processionists made their way to the sea.

I felt like drowning myself with the deity. My mind came up with increasingly morbid images. Would I end up at the bottom of the ocean? Or continue to float, belly-up, at low tide like the plaster images of the rotund God? I stood at the window watching a small family negotiating its way through the throngs, carrying their little Ganapati carefully, a small white handkerchief on his head to protect him from the sun. A large group of rowdy mill-workers were accompanying their idol – a mammoth Ganesh straddling the globe – on its final journey with a motley brass band playing the theme from *Come September*. Right behind them was another crowd from a co-operative housing society. Their

Ganesh belonged to the 21st century. He was dressed like an astronaut. A tall cardboard rocket was fixed behind him. To go with his space-age image, these people had dispensed with the brass band. They'd hired a rock group with a Moog synthesizer. Their choice of music was also very *au courant* – George Michael and U2!

Not only is Karuna's attachment to this festival personal, it is also familial. She then recalls her Hindu moment of arcadian transcendence from the past:

The noise, the bustle, the energy eased the sorrow from my mind as I recalled the Ganesh Utsavas from the past. From the age of five till my days of trying to be a sophisticate I had participated enthusiastically in them. It was my favourite festival, even more special than Diwali. Though we didn't bring the *moorti* to our house, it didn't really matter since it came to my father's older brother's home. We were expected to be present for the *aartis*, which took place twice a day. I loved the rituals that went with the *puja*. I enjoyed watching my aunt arranging the gleaming silver and brass *thalis* alongside the altar, heaping one with flowers, one with fruit, one with *prasad*, and one with *diyas*. The smell of incense, combined with the aroma of sandalwood paste and coconut oil. Wonderful. I'd watch with fascination as the pot-bellied priest chanted the '*Sukha karata ... dukha harata ...*' and the elders joined the chorus. I'd be given tiny cymbals of my own to beat to the tempo of the prayer. It was almost hypnotic.

I felt in a trance once again as I watched the believers from my parents' home. I wanted to join them downstairs and go to the beach to perform the farewell *aarti* where dear Ganapati would be given a tearful send-off. Back to his watery home he'd go on the head of an urchin willing to wade into the sea for ten rupees and all the coconuts he could retrieve from the waves. I stood at the window for a long time, gazing at the various images of the Benign One, wondering what the hell to do with my life.[80]

It is interesting that Dé would have her heroine involve herself in the denouement of the novel with devoted participation in her family and the sacrifice of her own good, which lay in marrying Girish, the only really decent man she had had an affair with, for her family. She decides she cannot marry Girish:

Not now at any rate. Living with my parents had opened up a new dimension for me. I felt like a responsible, caring daughter for the first time in my life. They needed me. And I needed them. We had arrived at a happy situation. They didn't have a son to look after them in their old age. They had the enormous burden of an invalid daughter to cope with. Each day in their life was a major struggle to just get on with the living that remained. How could I abandon them at this point?[81]

If the novelist whose writings some see as embodying the worst of western sex and consumerism represents the modern Indian in this way, then I think we should be extremely cautious in seeing the shift to more free market practices and more extensive consumption as in themselves bringing about the breakdown of family life or the wholesale adoption of corrupt Western values.

To conclude, the presently occurring dislocations of economy, gender, and nation that go under the label of globalization, make possible the rise of new sorts of selves, associations, and polities. They do so because they undermine the forms of participation of people in nation-states that people represented as 'identities', as the transcendent realizations of a universal immanent reason fused with particular emotional nationalities and personalities. Identity may have seemed plausible in the international welfare utopia, shadowed by the polarities of the Cold War, that political leaders attempted to construct after World War II. So far, however, the only concrete alternatives to the split, but homotelic, person of the transcendent nation-state are the even more homotelic persons offered up by the new global ruling class and its country cousins, the religious fundamentalisms. The organic intellectuals of the former construe it as an omniscient, omnipotent, omnipresent network transcending national ruling societies and their identities. Spokesmen for the religious fundamentalisms fancy their ways of life as immutable and universal and also transcending any other identities. It is difficult to see how one can represent either of the homotelic minds assumed to exist here as identities. The public selves of neither the techno-entrepreneurial class nor of the religious fundamentalists are, in their view, national, they are global. Nor do they consider their public selves inherently opposed to private selves. Quite the contrary, both deny that there is any difference between public and private selves.

I think it is possible to construct lives without 'identities' – people have done so in the past and do so today – but the task of inventing persons and polities that are assumed to be heterotelic, eschew utopian transcendence, and have the capacity to displace the techno-entrepreneurial ruling society that now seems about to take hold is a daunting one. Certainly people on the left will not succeed if they ignore the political dimensions of the formation of this class by pretending that this is somehow the necessary component of a last stage of capitalism or modernity. Nor will they succeed by representing attempts to recuperate something like the failing identities of the Cold War with ethnic, subnational or sexual identities as some brave new step. These are, so far as one can tell, mostly attempts to take up the ground being vacated by the nation-state without, however, doing more than make gestures in the direction of new 'identities'. If we accept the notion of identity as a belonging together of opposites, then it is simply incoherent to talk of split, hybrid or diasporic identities, for these are nothing more than the diffused or negative identities Erikson and his colleagues saw as failed identities. Shifting from an 'essentialist' to a 'constructionist' position is not much help either, for both these positions were already implicit in the Eriksonian concept.[82] We might, however, be able to theorize more genuine alternatives if we were to look at people and their institutions as agents rather than egos or subjects and to concentrate more specifically on the participatory and transcendence aspects of the practices through which people try to make their world.

Notes

1   Gorz (1994), p. 24.
2   Inden (1990), pp. 27-9.
3   Taylor (1994); Giddens (1991); Calhoun (1994), pp. 9-36.
4   Gleason (1983).
5   Heidegger (1969) pp. 23-41 talks about identity as a belonging together of different things.
6   This term and much else that is good in this essay has been the result of discussion with and criticism from Mark Hobart.
7   Gutmann asks, 'Can citizens with diverse identities be represented as equals if public institutions do not recognize our particular identities, but only our more universally shared interests in civil and political liberties, income, health care, and education?' Here the dichotomy of the emotional/multiple and the rational/unitary is, of course, both hidden and heightened by referring to national identity as 'interests'. See Taylor (1994), pp. 3 4.
8   Erikson left Vienna for Boston in 1933. During World War II he worked for the US government on the psychology of soldiers, and wrote on Hitler and his appeal to German youth. See Coles (1970), pp. 30-2, 44, 84-99.
9   Erikson (1950), p. 101.
10   Ibid., p. 102.
11   Frosh 'Whereas psychologists prioritise intellectual over affective material to such an extent that they produce an aseptic image of a mental life without passion or content, psychoanalysts tend to downgrade cognition until ... they are in danger of being left with no detailed theory of thinking at all'. See Frosh (1989), pp. 59, 84.
12   Erikson (1969).
13   Erikson (1950), p. 96.
14   Ibid., p. 96.
15   Ibid., p. 97.
16   Erikson (1946), pp. 18-9.
17   Erikson (1950), p. 97.

18   Ibid., pp. 97-8.
19   Ibid., p. 98.
20   Elliptically referring to the Nazis and Fascists, Erikson says: 'Even though we may be forced to win wars against their leaders, we still are faced with the job of winning the peace with these grim youths by convincingly demonstrating to them (by living it) a democratic identity which can be strong and yet tolerant, judicious and still determined' (Erikson 1959, p. 98). Although family, school, and Hitler Youth, for those 15 to 18 years of age, were all supposed to have worked harmoniously together, it is clear that youth were supposed to and did shift their loyalties from home and school to Hitler Youth and Nation. Writing in 1947, Paul Oestreich concludes that 'The Hitler cult subverted the family, while it exalted the clan and presented awards to prolific mothers as if to so many armament workers' (Mosse 1966, p. 275). Excerpts from other documents on the Hitler Youth make it clear that it attracted many adolescents, next in appeal only to Hitler and his message. According to one Inge Scholl: 'But there was yet one more thing that attracted us with a mysterious force and pulled us along – namely, the compact columns of marching youths with waving flags, eyes looking straight ahead, and the beat of drums and singing. Was it not overwhelming, this fellowship? Thus it was no wonder that all of us – Hans and Sophie and the rest of us – joined the Hitler Youth' (Ibid., p. 272). Encapsulation in the Youth brought about participation in a transcendent utopia, the Third Reich, one in which the feeling of belonging to a nation (*Volk*) overrode that of merely being part of a mass: 'We believed ourselves to be members of a great, well-ordered organization which embraced and esteemed everybody from the ten-year-old boy to the adult man. We felt we were part of a process, of a movement that created a people out of a mass' (Ibid., p. 272).
21   Here one should note that Erikson takes a constructionist position: 'Democracy in a country like America poses special problems in that it insists on *self-made identities* ready to grasp many chances and ready to adjust to changing necessities of booms and busts, of peace and war, of migration and determined sedentary life. Our democracy, furthermore, must present the adolescent with ideals which can be shared by youths of many backgrounds and which emphasize autonomy in the form of independence and initiative in the form of enterprise' (Erikson, 1950, pp. 98-9).
22   Erikson continues: 'These promises, in turn, are not easy to fulfill in increasingly complex and centralized systems of economic and political organization, systems which, if geared to war, must automatically neglect the "self-made" identities of millions of individuals and put them where they are most needed. This is hard on many young Americans because their whole upbringing, and therefore the development of a healthy personality,

95

depends on a certain degree of *choice*, a certain hope for an individual *chance*, and a certain conviction in freedom of *self-determination*' (Ibid., pp. 98-9). The unconscious processes by which identity was formed made the problems of demobilization difficult and the recourse to psychoanalysis necessary. In a telling footnote, Erikson says: 'This has certain obvious implications for the "re-education" of "bad" nations. It can be predicted that no admission of having sinned and no promises to be good will make a nation "democratic" unless the new identity offered can be integrated with previous concepts of strong and weak, masculine and feminine, based on experiences in the geographical-historical matrix of the nation and in the childhood of the individual. Only a victor who demonstrates the historical inescapability of supernational aims and knows how to base them on established regional identities will make new people out of old nations' (1946, Fn. 5, p. 179).

23   Note this official pronouncement: 'The National Socialist philosophical revolution has replaced the illusory image of a cultivated personality with the reality of the true German man, whose stature is determined by blood and historical fate. It has substituted for the humanistic conception of culture, which had continued in vogue up to very recently, a system of education which developed out of the fellowship of battle' (Mosse 1966, p. 283). Some found to their disappointment that the prevalent notion of expressive individuality was not to be enhanced but effaced by participating in the Hitler Youth. One young man, Hans, '... had always believed that every boy should develop his own special talents. Thus through his imagination, his ingenuity, his unique personality, each member could have enriched the group. But in Nuremberg everything had been done according to the same mold' (Ibid., p. 273)

24   Erikson (1950), pp. 97-8; (1956), pp. 131-9.

25   Erikson (1956), p. 141.

26   Erikson (1950), p. 143; (1956), pp. 173-4.

27   Lerner (1958).

28   Collingwood (1992), p. 84.

29   Gramsci (1971), pp. 323-43.

30   Laclau has argued that classical notions of emancipation (and before it, of Christian salvation) carry with them what I would consider to be a utopia, the idea of a transparent social whole dichotomously related to a previous, oppressive totality. According to Laclau: 'Emancipation presupposes the elimination of power, the abolition of the subject/object distinction and the management – without any opaqueness or mediation – of communitarian affairs by social agents identified with the viewpoint of social totality. It is in this sense that in Marxism, for instance, communism and the withering away of the state logically entail each other' (Laclau 1992, p. 121).

31   Foucault (1977, pp. 139-40, 141, 149-50) makes the argument about the extension of disciplinary practices from the monastery to secular institutions. Voegelin (1987, pp. 107-32) makes a rather different argument. According to him, modernity involves a 're-divinization' of society as a result of the uptake, often unawares, of what he calls Gnosticism, a heretical variant of Christianity. More radical, secularist descendants deny the transcendence of God and/or Reason, claiming him or it to be fully immanent in Man. Voegelin and others, notably Karl Löwith, trace this tendency to Joachim of Fiore (1131-1202). He bequeaths to us the division of history into three overlapping periods – ancient, medieval, and modern (corresponding to the Father, Son, and Holy Spirit). Predominant Catholic Christianity confined the divine's presence on earth to the clergy. Joachim and those who can be traced to him promised a third period of history, 'new age' in which 'the church will no longer be a clerical hierarchy grown worldly but a monastic community of saints in the succession of St. Benedict, destined to cure, by an ultimate effort, a disintegrating world' (Löwith 1949, p. 146). Löwith provides a summary of Joachim (Ibid., pp. 145-59).

32   Among the many cinematic representations of dystopia are Fritz Lang's *Metropolis* (1926) and Terry Gilliam's *Brazil* (1985).

33   McLuhan (1994).

34   Inden (1990), pp. 162-88; Hutchins (1967).

35   Pandey (1990).

36   Lukes (1973), pp. 73-8.

37   Macpherson (1962).

38   Erikson used the term 'ego' rather than subject. It should not come as a surprise that scholars should have conceived of the entities that have these mental essences as 'subjects'. Implicit in the philosophical idea of a subject, of that which is 'placed under' (*subjacere*) is the idea of an ego that witnesses what goes on around it while remaining unchanged itself. Webster's represents this as the philosopher's version: 'the actual substance of anything as distinguished from its qualities and attributes; the mind, or, ego, that thinks and feels, as distinguished from everything outside the mind'. This is nothing but the older theist notion of a soul given a secular upgrade.

39   Lukes (1973), pp. 79-87, 88-93.

40   Bellah (1992), p. 162.

41   Lukes (1973), pp. 94-8.

42   Ibid., pp. 67-72.

43   Lasch writes about the failure of expressive individualism to eventuate in the social or political transformation some had hoped for in the 1960s:

'After the political turmoil of the sixties, Americans have retreated to purely personal preoccupations. Having no hope of improving their lives in any of the ways that matter, people have convinced themselves that what matters is psychic self-improvement: getting in touch with their feelings, eating health food, taking lessons in ballet or belly-dancing, immersing themselves in the wisdom of the East, jogging, learning how to "relate", overcoming the "fear of pleasure." Harmless in themselves, these pursuits, elevated to a program and wrapped in the rhetoric of authenticity and awareness, signify a retreat from politics and a repudiation of the recent past' (1979, pp. 29-30).

44   Maslow (1993), pp. 270-86.
45   Ibid., p. 269.
46   'Individual being and social being no longer coincide – and can no longer coincide – because this latter is no longer – and can no longer be – a belonging of the individual in his or her entirety to society and community – in work, lifestyle, ethics, milieu and position within the social totality – as was the case in a guild-based [medieval?] society or within the industrial working class, with its culture, solidarities, associations and counter-society [welfare or state capitalism/socialism?]. In complex modern society [=postindustrial, late modernity/ capitalism?], the differentiation of spheres of activity brings with it a differentiation of the dimensions of existence, and prevents the subject from seeking his or her unity in any of them. The multiplicity of his or her roles introduces a fissure between each of these and him – or herself' (Gorz 1994, p. 24, bracketed text mine).
47   Gilroy (1993).
48   Pattanayak (1991).
49   Kumar (1991), p. 22.
50   Ibid., p. 23.
51   Ibid., p. 23.
52   Ibid., p. 23.
53   Ibid., p. 23.
54   Ibid., p. 23.
55   Reich (1993), pp. 208-21.
56   Ibid., p. 177.
57   Poster (1995), p. 3.
58   Reich (1993), p. 224.
59   Ibid., 252-300.
60   Ibid., pp. 294-5.
61   Ibid., p. 295.
62   Ibid., p. 295.
63   Ibid., p. 295.
64   Walker (1995).

65   Reich (1993), p. 244.

66   Fukuyama (1992).

67   Hall (1988).

68   Peters (1992); Toffler (1970); Ohmae (1994).

69   Rieff (1993).

70   Kulkarni (1993); Prasannan (1995).

71   Rappaport (1996).

72   Ibid., p. 114.

73   Ibid., pp. 112, 114.

74   As Prasannan notes, the consumer habits of middle-class Indians differ from those in other 'take-off' societies, including those of the Asian Pacific tigers, those with 'Asian values'. Indians would rather buy durables than non-durables because they 'are considered life-long assets. They can be bequeathed to the son or given away as the daughter's dowry' (1995, p. 62). And, he points out, 'the durables they are still fond of are those which have no human substitute – television sets, music systems, refrigerators, motor vehicles, and so on' (Ibid., p. 64). According to Prasannan: '... for the majority of the prospering middle classes, lifestyles are not changing radically; life's comforts are. Breakfasts are still largely puris and idlis and not cornflakes; but water is from the fridge and the chutney is ground in a mixer-grinder' (Ibid., p. 63).

75   Dé (1995).

76   Ibid., p. 41.

77   Ibid., pp. 41-2.

78   Ibid., pp. 373-4.

79   Ibid., p. 337.

80   Ibid., pp. 370-1.

81   Ibid., pp. 373-4.

82   The essentialist position sees 'cultural' identity as grounded in the natural environment (an idea long discredited but now returning in new forms in ecologism), in race or genes (sociobiology), in the soul or spirit (theology, as in Christian fundamentalism), a rational human nature (cognitive psychology and free-market economics), or social position in a mode of production such as feudalism or capitalism (critical sociology, historical materialism and socialism), that is, where identity is premade by an essentialized or substantialized agent that stands outside history. The constructionist position sees identities as the result of the conscious actions of free agents. The term culture itself has become so important in discussions of identity precisely because it elides the difference between substance and action. I agree with Hall that the essentialist notion, which emphasizes being over becoming is the one that has predominated until

recently. It construes "cultural identity" as a "shared" culture, a sort of collective "one true self", hiding inside the many other, more superficial or artificially imposed "selves", which people with a shared history and ancestry hold in common' (Hall 1990, p. 223). This first or substantialist notion of identity, precisely because it is grounded in something outside the actions of transitory human agents, their institutions and practices, was not one that people made or changed. It was an absolute, something that scholars and leaders discovered and represented to those people for whom the identity at issue was relevant. Those people were, then, supposed to identify themselves with that monolithic identity. The second or constructionist notion of identity, according to Hall, 'is not something which already exists, transcending place, time, history and culture. Cultural identities come from somewhere, have histories. But like everything which is historical, they undergo constant transformation' (Ibid., p. 225). Here people acting alone, together, and against one another in a variety of ways engage in activities and practices of identification. These involve not simply an identifying with but a differing from other agents. This notion of identity is dialogical. The identity of one person or group depends on his, her, or their ongoing interactions with others. Integral here, too, is a concern for the desire for and acquisition of recognition both by those sharing in the same identity and especially from those of differing identities, those in the relation of others. The problem with the constructionist notion of identity is that it often turns out to be a mirror image of the essentialist, lapsing into voluntarism. Its proponents would have agents make themselves and one another, as it were, from scratch (*ex nihilo*). Stuart Hall (1991a, 1991b) also makes an extended argument about ethnicity and identity. On this 'debate' from the standpoint of sexual orientation, see Stein (1992).

References

Bellah, R. N. (1992), Madsen, R., Sullivan, W.M., Swidler, A., Tipton, S.M., *The Good Society*, Vintage: New York.

Calhoun, C. (1994), 'Social Theory and the Politics of Identity', in *Social Theory and the Politics of Identity*, Blackwell: Oxford.

Coles, R. H. (1970), *Erik H. Erikson: The Growth of His Work*, Little, Brown: New York.

Collingwood, R. G. (1992), *The New Leviathan: Or Man, Society, Civilization and Barbarism*, Clarendon Press: Oxford, Boucher, D. (ed.), First published 1942.

Dé, S. (1995), *Socialite Evenings*, Pocket Books/Simon & Schuster: London.

Erikson, E. H. (1946), 'Ego Development and Historical Change', in *Identity and the Life Cycle*, International Universities Press: New York.

____ (1950), 'Growth Crises of the Healthy Personality', in *Identity and the Life Cycle*.

____ (1956), 'The Problem of Ego Identity', in *Identity and the Life Cycle*.

____ (1969), *Gandhi's Truth: On the Origins of Militant Nonviolence*, W. W. Norton: New York.

Foucault, M. (1977), *Discipline and Punish*, Sheridan, A. (trans.), Pantheon: New York.

Frosh, S. (1989), *Psychoanalysis and Psychology: Minding the Gap*, Macmillan: London.

Fukuyama, F. (1992), *The End of History and the Last Man*, Free Press: New York.

Giddens, A. (1991), *Modernity and Self-Identity: Self and Society in the Late Modern Age*, Polity Press: Cambridge.

Gilroy, P. (1993), 'Nationalism, History and Ethnic Absolutism', in *Small Acts: Thoughts on the Politics of Black Cultures*, Serpent's Tail: London.

Gleason, P. (1983), 'Identifying Identity: A Semantic History', *The Journal of American History*, 69.4 (March), pp. 910-31.

Gorz, A. (1994), *Capitalism, Socialism, Ecology*, Turner, C. (trans.), Verso: London.

Gramsci, A. (1971), *Selections from the Prison Notebooks*, Hoare, Q. and Geoffrey Nowell Smith, G. (ed. and trans.), International Publishers: New York.

Hall, S. (1988), *The Hard Road to Renewal: Thatcherism and the Crisis of the Left*, Verso: London.

____ (1990), 'Cultural Identity and Diaspora', in Rutherford, J. (ed.), *Identity: Community, Culture, Difference*, Lawrence & Wishart: London.

____ (1991a) 'The Local and Global: Globalization and Ethnicity', in King.

____ (1991b), 'Old and New Identities, Old and New Ethnicities', in King.

Heidegger, M. (1969), *Identity and Difference*, Stambaugh, J. (trans. and intro.), Harper & Row: New York, First published 1957 as *Idenität und Differenz*.

Hutchins, F. (1967), *The Illusion of Permanence*, Princeton University Press: Princeton..

Inden, R. (1990), *Imagining India*, Blackwell: Oxford.

King, A.D. (ed.)(1991), *Culture, Globalization and the World System*, Macmillan: London.

Kulkarni, V. G. (1993), 'The Middle Class Bulge', *Far Eastern Economic Review* (14 Jan.), pp. 44-8.

Kumar, K. (1991), 'Ill-fitting Mask' in *Identity: A Symposium on Definitions of the Self*, Pattanayak, D.P. (ed.), *Seminar* 387 (Nov.), pp. 21-3.

Laclau, E. (1992), 'Beyond Emancipation', in *Emancipations, Modern and Postmodern*, Pieterse, J. N. (ed.), Sage: London.

_____ (1995), 'Universalism, Particularism and the Question of Identity', in *The Identity in Question*, Routledge: New York.

Lasch, C. (1979), *The Culture of Narcissism: American Life in an Age of Diminishing Expectations*, Warner Books/W. W. Norton: New York..

Lerner, D. (1958), *The Passing of Traditional Society: Modernizing the Middle East*, Free Press: Glencoe, IL.

Löwith, K. (1949), *Meaning in History*, University of Chicago Press: Chicago.

Lukes, S. (1973), *Individualism*, Blackwell: Oxford.

Macpherson, C. B. (1962), *The Political Theory of Possessive Individualism*, Oxford University Press: Oxford.

Maslow, A. H. (1993), *The Farther Reaches of Human Nature*, Penguin Arkana: New York, First published 1971.

McLuhan, M. (1994), *Understanding Media*, Routledge: London, First published 1964.

Mosse, G. L. (1966), *Nazi Culture: Intellectual, Cultural and Social Life in the Third Reich*, Grosset & Dunlap Universal Library: New York.

Ohmae, K. (1994), *The Borderless World: Power and Strategy in the Global Marketplace*, Harper Collins: London.

Pandey, G. (1990), *The Construction of Communalism in Colonial North India*, Oxford University Press: Delhi.

Pattanayak, D. P. (ed.)(1991), *Identity: A Symposium on Definitions of the Self*, *Seminar* 387 (Nov.).

Peters, T. (1992), *Liberation Management: Necessary Disorganization for the Nanosecond Nineties*, Fawcett Columbine: New York.

Poster, M. (1995), *The Second Media Age*, Polity Press: Cambridge..

Prasannan, R. (1995), 'Lifestyle: Great Indian Middle Class', *The Week* (25 June), pp. 51-2, 54-6, 60, 62-5.

Rappaport, R. (1996), 'Bangalore', *Wired* 4.2 (February), pp. 111-14, 164-70.

Reich, R. B. (1993), *The Work of Nations: Preparing Ourselves for 21st-Century Capitalism*, Simon & Schuster: London, First published 1991.

Rieff, D. (1993), 'Multiculturalism's Silent Partner', *Harper's Magazine*, (August), pp. 62-70.

Stein, E. (ed.)(1992), *Forms of Desire: Sexual Orientation and the Social Constructionist Controversy*, Routledge: New York, First published 1990.

Taylor, C. (1994), *Multiculturalism and 'The Politics of Recognition'* with commentary by Gutmann, A. (ed.), Rockefeller, S.C., Walzer, M. and Wolf, S., Princeton University Press: Princeton.

Toffler, A. (1970), *Future Shock*, Pan: London.

Voegelin, E. (1987), *The New Science of Politics: An Introduction*, University of Chicago Press: Chicago, First published 1952.

Walker, M. (1995), 'Keyboard Whiz-kid', *Guardian* (29 May).

4   Turkish identity from genesis to the day of judgement

Zafer F. Yörük

Prelude: the flag will never come down

On the evening of 14 August 1996, the world's leading TV channels broadcast shocking pictures of a Greek Cypriot youth who was shot dead by Turkish troops at a peace demonstration. Solomos Solomou was climbing up a flag pole on the Turkish side of the buffer zone which separates the two Cypruses (Turkish occupied north and the Greek Cypriot south) when he became the second victim of a four day attempt by a group of international peace activists to demonstrate against the division of Cyprus by means of forcing their way up to the north. The first victim, Anastasious Isaak, was beaten to death three days before Solomou's death, by a mob of ultra-nationalist Turks who were brought to the island to counter the peace demonstration, assisted by the Turkish police. Turkish TV channels, radios and newspapers presented the shooting as another victory against the 'enemies of Turkish flag', showing images of Solomou's last minutes – his neck and face covered with blood – whilst quoting cheerfully the Deputy Prime Minister Tansu Ciller's catchphrase: 'No one can lay a finger on the flag. Anyone who has the nerve to do that, we will break their hands!'

This was not the first time that the Turkish public has been preoccupied with the theme of the flag. In fact, the flag, and the threats against it, have been at the centre of greater hysteria in recent years. Throughout the 1990s, any occasions on which the Turkish flag and other national or religious symbols were relevant have been exploited to their very limits. National soccer matches and the street parties to say farewell to young army conscripts are two such examples. The 'nation' has come to love its flag and national anthem so much that the normal soccer league matches in recent years are opened with the national anthem and in every soccer fan's possession, there is now a Turkish flag in addition to the banner of the team that he is supporting.

In the year 1996 alone, the Cyprus shooting was the third such incident of 'flag politics'. The first serious flag affair of the year broke in February in the form of a 'put your flag up and take the opposite side's flag down' competition with Greece on the Imia (Kardak) islets of the Aegean Sea which brought the two countries to the brink of war. The crisis was resolved without a battle with US intervention, but the Turkish press did not miss this occasion as an opportunity to claim a victory.

In June 1996, another 'flag affair' shook the country: during the pro-Kurdish People's Democracy Party (HADEP) annual congress, a masked man ripped down a big Turkish flag decorating the congress hall and replaced it with a Kurdish flag. This incident did not only lead to the arrest and subsequent imprisonment of the entire HADEP leadership, but also a weird campaign was launched by the government and media asking citizens to dress their houses, shops and streets with Turkish flags, in order to demonstrate the determination of the Turkish nation to protect its flag. And the 'citizens' obeyed: the flag hanging campaign was carried out by the nation so fanatically that even a good patriot would grow sick of not being able to escape the scene of Turkish flags anywhere in the country day and night. Banners with the slogan, 'The flag will never come down, *Ezan* (call for prayers) can never be silenced, our Motherland will never be divided', decorated even the remote streets of Turkish cities, small towns and villages with hundreds of thousands of flags of different sizes. New flag shops proliferated around the country, and even the street pedlars of Istanbul, who normally sell *simit* (bread rings), or offer shoe polishing, switched quickly to selling flags.

The giant dimensions of this 'flag mobilization' and the reckless readiness of the otherwise very cautious government to risk Turkey's fragile foreign relations over the issue of the flag, indicate something beyond the familiar day-to-day manipulative tactics which any political authority would resort to in order to divert public attention away from the dislocations of social order. Turkish 'flag hysteria' needs serious consideration both as a symptomatic effect of a deeper crisis and as a metaphorical expression of the desire to resolve this crisis.

But what could be more natural than a nation becoming over-enthusiastic about its flag - the eternal dream of any good nationalist? Should this obsession with the 'national objects of desire' not be defined as an ideal situation rather than a crisis? These legitimate questions become irrelevant when we consider that the country in which this hysteria is taking place is 1990s Turkey, which has not only been facing a real threat to her territorial integrity from her Kurdish citizens, but is also governed, at present, by a political party which represents precisely what modern Turkish identity was constructed against. This is where this paper will assert its main thesis – that the abundant usage of the flag and national symbols occurs at the variant of an identity crisis in Turkey, both as its traumatic manifestation and as a proposal to overcome this crisis. Making 'flag politics' intelligible with its full meaning and implications, therefore, requires, above all, a narration of the genealogy of modern Turkish identity from its formation at the turn of the century, to its *fin-de-siecle* tendency towards disintegration.

I

Before Kemalism

For Kemalism as for any modernist discourse, the formation of the modern Turkish Republic, with its modern subjects, represents the rebirth of the Turkish nation. The discourse of this imaginary reincarnation is in fact the grounds upon which modern Turkish identity is built. The genealogy of Turkish identity in this part, however, will take a different course and will treat the formation of Turkish nation-state as the origin of the nation as a social identity – the birth of the Turkish nation – without attempting a narrative about the origins and the history of the Turks as an entity.

Social identities will be taken in this paper as components of certain discursive territory which emerge under a discursive horizon. It is on this territory, in which a common moral life, through a web of shared understandings, identities, debates and traditions, becomes possible. But this territory, or 'system', is impossible to define without a closure, which requires the definition of the 'system' with reference to its outside, that is, with reference to its difference from other systems. The act of closure thus sets the boundaries of the territory of social identities with the employment of a final discursive marker (God, the divine right of Kings, natural law, nation, etc.) which lays down the basis upon which a concept of 'us' is built, to separate an entity from its enemies, citizen from alien and member from stranger.[1]

Within a clearly defined territory, social identities have a relational character; they can be defined only in their difference from one another: I exist in my difference from you and others. The territory of social identities, however, is not merely an aggregation of different egos, but of different subject positions defined according to class, status, gender, profession, political tendencies, age, etc. Identity formation is primarily the 'identification' of individuals with certain subject positions, furnished by the system.[2]

The discursive territory of modern Turkish identity, Kemalism, which has existed under the discursive horizon of modernity, is called after the name of the founder of modern Turkey, Mustafa Kemal Ataturk. Ataturk, in turn, has been the final discursive marker which has drawn the boundaries of Turkish identity, providing the Turks with a number of subject positions with which to identify as modern subjects of republican Turkey, that is, within an overriding conception of Turkishness. The narrative of the (re)birth of the Turks as a nation corresponds to that of the emergence of Kemalist hegemony which therefore deserves detailed consideration for the purposes of this paper.

'The sick man of Europe'

The Republic of Turkey was built out of the ruins and ashes of the Ottoman Empire that collapsed with the conclusion of World War One. The agony of the Empire, however, began long before its moment of final collapse and was spread over centuries. Roughly from the late seventeenth century onwards, the medieval empire of The Ottomans had been in obvious decline *vis-a-vis* Europe, when the latter, armed with the knowledge and organization of modernity, came to challenge the Ottomans. For an Empire whose political economy was based on conquest (constant expansionism through the inclusion of non-Muslim lands under the subjection of the Sultan and Khalif), to adapt a defensive position itself meant an upturning of the whole range of conventional patterns of meanings and beliefs.

The Ottoman response to this decline came a century late in the form of a succession of modernization attempts which were initiated by reformist Sultans and statesmen throughout the nineteenth century. For the Ottomans, modernization meant, above all, the renovation and the centralization of the Empire's administration, through the replacement of the conventional institutions, primarily the military, with western-style ones. The reformist movement hoped to bring back the military and administrative strength of the Empire and to secure a place, through recognition by the west, among the emerging great Powers.

This was, however, a dangerous move for two reasons: firstly seeking a place among the western 'great powers' required a reconceptualization of the west which would disturb the Ottoman system of meanings, which was constituted in its difference from the Christian world. The west had represented, in the conventional Ottoman discourse, the precise object of the imperial conquest, that is, the lands to be conquered and people to be brought under the subjection of the Sultan and Khalif. The closure of the Ottoman social order was only possible through its definition in reference to the west as being the outside, that is, in its difference from western order. Being Ottoman meant, therefore, being outside of – and in opposition to – the Christian world as a whole; the west, in other words, was the 'constitutive outside' of the Ottoman social order.

The late Ottoman attempts to become part of the west would deprive the system of its 'constitutive outside', its essential discursive tool of closure. In sum, the reforms brought about the necessity of a redefinition of the west, and of the position of the Ottoman social order *vis-a-vis* the west, radically different from that of the conventional Ottoman discourse, a task which was not possible to achieve within the particular logic of the available system of meanings.

Secondly, and similarly, the modern discourse of the Great Powers was built on the assumption of an ontological difference of the Orient from the west, which the modern west had largely inherited from the Christian conceptualization of the world. The Orient, which conventionally meant a threat to Christianity, became, in the modern discourse, the object to 'rationalize' and to 'civilize' while maintaining its ontological status as a source of threat to 'reason' and to 'civilization'. For six centuries, the Ottoman Empire had represented the oriental challenge to the west, and its decline supplied the great powers with a golden opportunity for the elimination of any future possibility of the re-emergence of this threat while putting this chaotic entity, which was now called 'the sick man of Europe' under the domination of 'reason' and 'civilization'.

For Michel Foucault, the hegemony of medical discourse in the nineteenth century accompanied a new conception of society as a body that needed to be protected against 'social illnesses' in a quasi-medical sense. This is how, according to Foucault, the methods of asepsis-criminology, eugenics and the quarantining of the 'degenerates', were born, leading to the employment of 'remedies and therapeutic devices ... such as the segregation of the sick, the monitoring of contagions and the exclusion of delinquents'.[3] Foucault argues that this metaphorical articulation of the social body and of medicine lies at the origins of modern disciplinary practices. The term the 'sick man of Europe', therefore, implied the need both to be segregated and to be cured, that is, to be kept aside from Europe, whilst being subjected to therapy and correction from this imagined 'social body'. The overall result was that, instead of being recognized as part of the great powers, the Empire would become the field of a power struggle, the object of a politico-military game, which was then called the 'Eastern Question', between the Great Powers (Britain, Russia and France, in particular), which would gradually rip the Ottoman Empire into pieces, while postponing its inevitable death in accordance with their conjunctural interests.

Early reformism and its consequences requires for the closure of the Ottoman discursive territory a radically different definition of the 'outside' of the Ottoman social order, not only as a superior system to become a part of, but also as an enemy to be fought. However, even if a closure in terms of such a redefinition were possible, within this discursive territory where the results of the initial political and economic reforms were radically turning the conventional tables, the relational syntax of social identities would also require a redefinition.

Ottoman reformism took measures for the recentralization of the Empire, whilst concurrently attempting to institute guarantees of citizens' rights and equality and to curb the absolutism of political authority. Successive legislation was put into effect, to reorganize the conventional terms of the relationship between the Ottoman state and its non-Muslim subjects. These constitutional changes would lead the multinational Empire, which accommodated fifty different ethnicities, speaking more than ten different languages, into a process of significant transformation which would make it impossible to maintain society in the context of the traditional *millet* system.[4]

A structural adjustment of the Ottoman economy accompanied political constitutionalism in the aim of integrating the Empire into the European capitalist networks through measures for the utilization of private commercial and industrial activities. For various cultural-historical reasons, the commercial classes that emerged out of these reforms and the economic integration through foreign trade were predominantly non-Muslim, composed of Greeks, Armenians, former Europeans (Levantines) and Jews. Consequently, the effects of economic transformation were not limited to the disturbance of a traditionally static order, but led to an ironic situation in terms of political economy: whilst the Ottoman Empire was based on Islamic dominance over various religious and ethnic communities, Muslim landowners and provincial merchants were increasingly subordinated to a non-Muslim commercial bourgeoisie. The consequent resentment of the displaced craftsmen and Muslim merchants was strengthened by a disastrous famine in Anatolia in 1874 and the bankruptcy of the state treasury in 1875. In the midst of social disruption combined with an economic crisis, the ruling bureaucracy risked losing its legitimacy in the eyes of the social groups which made up the traditional order. The Ottoman social order, as a discursive territory consisting of different subject positions, was thus decisively disturbed and the Palace and bureaucracy were no longer able to legitimize their domination by depending on the conventional systems of meanings.

The inclusion of Ottoman society under the discursive horizon of modernity therefore brought about structural dislocations with the turning upside-down of conventional subject positions, and the consequent impossibility of defining the social domain as an aggregate of social identities. The discursive territory – the boundaries of which had already eroded with the changing meaning of the encounter with the west – that had provided the Ottoman subjects with a web of shared meanings and common values upon which the networks of identity/difference could operate, was decisively disarticulated: the Ottoman identity crisis had begun.

Ernesto Laclau asserts that at the variant of the dislocation of the social order, where the sense of identification with subject positions is shattered, a 'mythical space' opens up to constitute critiques of the lack of structuration of the existing order. This space is mythical in the sense that it represents what is unrepresentable with the available codes of the discursive territory, that is, the dislocations of this territory. The mythical space opens up to provide the dislocations and social demands with surfaces of inscription and through their articulation, an alternative horizon of social imaginaries is formed. In this mythical production process, which dislocations or which of the social demands are to put their stamp on the new horizon of social imaginaries is decided through a complicated process of overdetermination.[5]

At the variant of Ottoman identity crisis, a mythical space opened up with the contents of the need to redefine both the 'outside' of the Empire (in order to secure the closure of the context), and the need to redefine the relational syntax of social identities within this system. The overriding necessity that dominated this mythical space was to provide the Ottoman order with means of legitimization and maintenance, that is, repairing the damaged structure. This 'will to legitimization' would also determine the limits of the mythical space, as the reformation of the state, by effecting a transformation from above of the social system, in order for the Empire to take a more active role in the modern world.

The ultimate question of the political and ideological debate that flourished with the participation of the old and the new intelligentsia from the last quarter of the nineteenth century onwards was 'the salvation of the State'. The 'old' intelligentsia consisted of the traditional Palace bureaucracy and the *ulema* while the 'new' intelligentsia consisted predominantly of the graduates of the new imperial schools of engineering, medicine and administration, all founded around the middle of the nineteenth century in order to fill the ranks of military and civilian bureaucracy with new cadres trained on modern, western, lines. Three discourses emerged out of this debate between the traditional and modern wings of the intelligentsia, or in Gramscian terms, between the traditional intellectuals of the Ottoman order and the emerging organic intellectuals of the ruling bureaucracy.[6]

'Three modes of politics'

The first one of these three late Ottoman dreams was Ottomanism, which proposed freedom and equal rights for all Ottoman subjects, now redescribed as citizens, under a constitutional monarchy. Ottomanism was the dream of the first generation of modernist bureaucracy who, following their Jakobin coup under the leadership of Mithat Pasha, had forced Sultan Abdul Hamid II to accept the constitutional monarchy in December 1876. However, the disappointing results of integration into European modernity that produced the Ottoman identity crisis, did not allow the rule of Ottomanists to last long. The Palace bureaucracy led by Sultan were quick to regain their absolutist powers following the Russian war of 1877-8, through a counter-coup by which they dismissed the Constitution in 1878, sent the reformists into exile and executed some of the leadership including Mithat Pasha.

A new stage, the reign of Sultan Abdul Hamid II, blended with a discourse of political Islam which then attempted to restore the traditional Ottoman order under a more centralized administration. Abdul Hamid and the Palace bureaucracy redefined Ottoman society in terms of an Islamic discourse and managed to attain hegemony at the popular level by restoring the traditional balances at the expense of the non-Muslim subjects, via populist policies towards the Muslim-Turkish elements of the Empire. Abdul Hamid emphasized his title as the Khalif and spoke on behalf of the Muslim world, which, when taken along with the attempts of administrative recentralization, represented the first experience of a modern Islamic state. Islamist hegemony did not only manage to restore the conventional identities of the Ottoman order, but also provided the Muslim subjects of the Empire with a vision of Islamic unity and a clear reconceptualization of the west and the west's reformist allies in the Ottoman bureaucracy as being an external threat to the Muslim identity.

The discourse of political Islam led to the emergence of antagonisms both among the bureaucracy and intelligentsia, and between the Muslim and non-Muslim subjects of the Empire. Having fallen out of favour, the exiled reformist intelligentsia experienced a transformation by which they were reincarnated into a more radical version as the Young Turks. The growing alienation of non-Muslim ethnic groups on the other hand, was leading them to create their own social imaginaries in terms of nationalist discourses and secessionism. The Young Turk movement articulated the demands of these groups in an anti-absolutist discourse which signified a new Ottomanist vision that promised equality and federation among various ethnic and religious groups of the realm. The entire modernist Ottoman elite were won over by the ideas of the Young Turks in a short period and their struggle under the banner of Ittihad ve Terakki – the Committee of Union of Progress (CUP) that was founded as the endogenous wing of the Young Turk movement – resulted in the declaration of the second Constitution in 1908.

The Young Turk revolution carried CUP to power in 1909 with the formation of the first Parliament, which consisted of 288 deputies, with an almost ideal ethnic composition.[7] This democratic awakening was accompanied by an era of increased social and political activity: in an atmosphere of diminished censorship, political organisations and trade unions proliferated and women were allowed in schools and universities for the first time. However, after having to confront the reality of secessionism supported by European intervention, the CUP came to realize that the identities within the multinational Empire had already been decisively divided and antagonized, and any attempt at reconciliation was fore-doomed. The obstacles that they faced in the way of administrative and social reforms were increasingly interpreted by the Young Turks as extensions of the ethnic heterogenity of the Empire, or as the consequences of co-existence with Christian minorities. The Balkan War which brought the loss of the European portions of the Ottoman lands to newly independent nation-states constituted the turning point: the salvation was in constructing a political entity based on the European model of nation-state. Thus the Young Turks would relinquish the banner of 'Liberty, Equality and Fraternity' to be replaced by a one party dictatorship armed with a discourse of Turkish nationalism.[8]

Therefore, the mythical space of the late Ottoman dreams, the constitutive axis of which was the 'will to legitimization' of the Ottoman order, gave birth to a nationalist imaginary. This development of the mythical space meant that the point of reference against which the political experiences were to be measured as a success or a failure shifted from repairing the damaged structure to structural transformation. This is why in contemporary texts of Turkish history, the Young Turk experience is presented as a failure, not because with it the Empire was dragged to a catastrophic collapse, but because the Young Turks were not able to finish the job that they had begun, that is, to abolish the throne and replace it with a modern nation-state.

The Young Turks' experience was a failure by all measures: they initiated an expulsion of Armenians in Eastern Anatolia, which amounted to ethnic cleansing and genocide and reinforced xenophobia as an organic component of Turkish nationalist discourse within which such a crime had to be legitimized; they alienated Middle Eastern peoples of non-Turkish origin with nationalist discrimination which would lead the emerging Arab nationalist movements to side with the British in the world war; and they entered into the First World War on the losing (German) side. Young Turks, however, laid down at the same time all the essential elements of the future

Kemalist movement: they articulated the Muslim/non-Muslim antagonism in a quasi-anti-imperialist discourse based on a Turkish/European powers antagonism, backing their discursive move with a policy of 'national economy', that is, government promotion of industrial and commercial ventures by the emergent Muslim bourgeoisie. Young Turk nationalism, although flawed by an adventurist ideal of pan-Turkism, pronounced Anatolia as the Turks' Homeland, hence popularizing the themes of 'land' and 'nation' on the basis of Anatolian patriotism. A strong nationalist resonance was formed between these themes and the bitterness and frustration of the migrating Muslim masses from outlying Ottoman lands in the Balkans and the Caucasus to Anatolia. In other words, the alliance between the Muslim population of Anatolia and the Ottoman bureaucracy that Abdul Hamid had restored with an Islamist discourse, was renewed in nationalist terms. The ethnic cleansing of the Armenian population helped this renewal and it was, in effect, the first stage of 'Turkisization' of Anatolia.[9] Later, a 'National Struggle' against the Greek presence in the 'Motherland' Anatolia, would be carried out by this alliance under the Kemalist leadership, to finalize the project of Turkisization.

The mythical space of the late Ottoman dreams thus experienced an over-determination by the Kemalist discourse following the collapse of the Empire by the end of the First World War and the subsequent 'National Struggle', which would lead Kemalism to build the republican Turkey in its own image. The Kemalist imaginary put an end to the Ottoman identity crisis by both reorganizing the discursive territory of republican Turkey and by providing this territory with a closure through the negativization of its constitutive outside.

II

Turkish identity and its others

Orientalism and the nationalist 'will to civilization' [10]

> 'If you speak of civilization, there is just one, and that is in the west. One is either in it or out of it; there is no way in between'.
>
> Abdullah Cevdet

Partha Chatterjee suggests that the logic of Orientalism also applies to nationalist thought in the Third World. His study demonstrates that Third World nationalism is a 'derivative discourse' that acts upon the basis of the categories produced by Orientalism. Underlying this point is Chatterjee's observation:

> nationalist thought, in agreeing to become 'modern', accepts the claim to universality of this 'modern framework of knowledge'. Yet it also asserts the

autonomous identity of a national culture. It thus simultaneously rejects and accepts the dominance, both epistemic and moral, of an alien culture.[11]

The Turkist discourse of Ziya Gokalp (1876-1924) that was situated at the edge of this simultaneous rejection and acceptance constituted the theoretical framework of Young Turk nationalism and was inherited by the Kemalist discourse.

The primary question of the making of national identity in Turkey, as it was formulated by Gokalp, the most influential thinker of Turkish nationalism, was how to create a Turkish nation whose ideal was to modernize. The term *modernize* is used by Gokalp synonymously with the term *civilize*. Gokalp, an orthodox follower of Emile Durkheim, asserted a distinction between cultural unities based on common sentiments and modern civilization based on reason and positive sciences.[12] The distinction between culture (*hars*) and civilization (*medeniyyet*) corresponds to the difference between the particular and the universal. In Gokalp's image, there is a unified western civilization that supersedes the particular autonomous spheres of national cultures of Englishness, Frenchness, Germanness, etc.[13] The formation of Turkish identity should therefore go hand in hand with the task of modernization, which meant the integration of Turkishness as an autonomous cultural sphere into the universal western civilization as one of the particular components of it.

Gokalp asserts two theses in order to present westernization as a necessity. The first thesis is that there is in essence only one civilization and it is what we call western civilization. According to Gokalp's narrative on the history of civilizations, there has never been in history an eastern civilization and what we call eastern civilization is somehow a 'degenerated' form or a 'backward' version of western civilization:

> Mediterranean civilization was established in Antiquity through the efforts of Egyptian, Assyrian, Phoenician, etc., people. This civilization, after being matured in ancient Greece, passed to the Romans. Romans, after inoculating this civilization to hundreds of nations, split into the two independent states of Eastern Rome and Western Rome. This political split was, in effect, the split of the Mediterranean civilization into Eastern and Western civilizations. Europeans inherited and improved the Western Roman civilization, while the Muslim Arabs adopted not only the political institutions but the whole civilization of the Eastern Rome. Eastern Roman civilization thus acquired the name Eastern Civilization after being adopted by Muslims.[14]

This argument implies not only that there is only one essential civilization but also that there is an essential difference between the east and west which lies in the absence or presence of an essence capable of creating civilizations – an essence which Hegel called 'Spirit'. For Gokalp, as for orientalist thinkers from Montesquieu to

Max Weber, this essential difference is evident in the absence of 'dynamism' in the east:

> Eastern nations were not able to develop their civilization any further than its level in the Medieval Ages, because, according to the law of *stagnation*, unless an *agent* comes to change it, everything remains as it is.[15]

This 'agent', which he is careful to place outside the eastern society, is, for Gokalp, the graduates of the new imperial schools of engineering, medicine and administration, since they received exclusively western-style education. Gokalp asserts that these western institutions were the examples according to which the whole society should be institutionalized by the agents of change, while abolishing all the eastern institutions which Gokalp calls 'the ghosts of the Medieval Age'.[16]

The second thesis that Gokalp asserted was to claim that what was Ottoman, and what, therefore, belonged to the eastern civilization, was in fact alien to the Turks' essence. Gokalp argued that Turks have a glorified pre-Islamic past and that under Ottoman rule, Turkish identity was oppressed by a cosmopolitan elite. Leaving the eastern civilization therefore became an act of national liberation, since it was associated with emancipation of a nation from the culture of the oppressor, in its search for self-identity.[17]

Kemalist discourse inherited both of these theses of Turkist thought with some necessary amendments and it attempted to realise the Turkist end of creating a Turkish nation whose ideal was to modernize. The ultimate goal of the republican Turkey that was founded after the abolition of the Throne and the Khalifate in the wake of the 'National Struggle' in 1923, was formulated by the Kemalists so as to 'rise to the level of civilized nations'. The Kemalist 'revolutions' that followed, including the adoption of the Latin script, the reform in head-gear ('hat revolution'), the right to vote for women and the adoption of a modern Civil Code based on that of the Swiss, went beyond even Gokalp's proposals for the adoption of western institutions. Kemalists breached Gokalp's distinctions between culture and civilization with their reforms which amounted to 'force to civilize' a cultural entity that was reduced in their discourse to the status of an 'object' to be civilized. From this point onwards, the Kemalist 'will to civilization' went beyond even Orientalism as defined by Edward Said; 'a kind of western projection onto and a will to govern over the Orient'.[18]

The Kemalist grand-narrative: 'Turkish historical thesis'

'God can change the future, but only the Tsar can change the past'

Marquis de Custine

113

The eventual negation of the Orient depended on the west's recognition of Turkish society as being part of the west. Consequently, being a modern Turk meant, from its outset, to enter a 'battle of recognition' against the west in terms of Hegelian master-slave dialectics, which Kemalists hoped would end with recognition when the Turks eventually rose 'to the level of civilized nations'. This was a difficult task given the built-in racism and Orientalist prejudices of the modern western discourse. This difficult battle of recognition was in fact the primary reason behind the formulation of the Kemalist grand-narrative of Turkish history in the 'Turkish historical thesis'. Afet Inan, a close associate of Mustafa Kemal, recalls showing a French anthropology book to Mustafa Kemal in 1928, in which it is said that Turks belonged to the yellow race and are, therefore, inferior people, to which Kemal reacted angrily and commanded the teachers and important members of the new state apparatus to begin historical researches to prove that it is not so.[19] Consequently, the first assertion of the resulting 'Turkish historical thesis' reads:

> The Turkish race ... is not yellow. The Turks are white men and brachycephalic. Today, masters of our Homeland and founders of the oldest culture, we are their children acknowledging the same name.[20]

This 'thesis' is based on a crude articulation, in racial terms, of the Orientalist *a priori* that the east is 'an otherness of an essentialist character'[21] and it thus hoped to prove that in their essence, Turks were not different from the west. This *a priori* would in fact continue to constitute the primary dilemma of the Turks' search for identity: if we assume an essential difference between the Orient and Occident, Turks are located at the very interval separating the two. Turkish identity remains partially Oriental and partially Occidental, or, to rephrase in terms of the 'historical thesis', the Turkish race is partially yellow and partially white. Speaking psychoanalytically, it is the Kemalist elites' attempt to repress the divided and ambiguous nature of Turkishness that is reflected in the Kemalist discourse as a neurotic syndrome of racial superiority.

To constitute themselves as western, the Kemalists had to deny and repress any traces of the Oriental dimension of Turkishness. In doing this they placed themselves clearly 'outside' of this 'object' out of which the modern 'subjects' were to be made. They were 'outside' for they imagined themselves within the horizon of modernity, as the 'agents' whose mission was to inoculate modernity into a traditional structure as Gokalp had asserted; Kemalists were the 'modernizers'. But when looked at from the west, Kemalists also belonged to the Orient, as the modernizers of the Orient, since the very term 'modernization' is situated, by definition, at the spatial and temporal interval separating the traditional from the modern, the east from the west. As much as the Kemalists imagined themselves outside the Oriental object, they would be recognized by the 'big Other' (the west) only as being at the margins of the west rather than being part of it. Therefore, to be western, one had to reject more than the Orient; the rejection had to be 'superhard' as it involved a certain metaphorical surplus: the rejection of the impossibility of being the Other.[22] This is the junction at which a 'master race' fantasy is formulated, in two more assertions of the 'Turkish historical thesis'.

The alliance between the Muslim 'notables' of Anatolia and the Kemalist leadership had experienced a decisive split with the implementation of Kemalist 'revolutions' because the reduction of the Muslim population of Anatolia to the status of an *object* to be governed and transformed into modern subjects implied the denial and repression of the existing popular-Islamic subjectivity. The nationalist resonance between the reformist bureaucracy and the Muslim population of Anatolia, upon which Anatolian patriotism was built and the 'National Struggle' was carried out, no longer existed following the Kemalist attempt to secularize and 'civilize' the cultural domain of the *nation* which had always kept its relative autonomy *vis-a-vis* political authority under Ottoman rule. This split in identity alienated the Kemalists from the Anatolian population as an isolated force outside and above society. Kemalists were the dominant political force, but were lacking hegemony, which required the integration of force with legitimization, that is, in Gramsci's terms, moral and intellectual leadership.

The Kemalist imaginary would therefore be determined with the necessity of the legitimization of the Kemalist will to civilization, or, to put it in a different way, with the necessity to answer the question; 'if the Turks should be part of western civilization, what is then outside of the Turkish nation against which the Turkish identity could be defined?'. The Kemalist import of western values did not only bring about social disturbance but also ambiguity regarding the boundaries of the new discursive territory parallel to the changing meaning of the encounter with the west. The search for a satisfactory answer to this problem led the Kemalist leadership to elaborate a grand-narrative of Turkish history. The 'Turkish historical thesis' was thus produced by official historians and proclaimed in 1932, and despite all the 'rational' modifications that it has been through, this 'thesis' constituted, for seven decades, the backbone of the official historiography around which history teaching in school curricula and official arguments against political threats are formed. Two primary master-race assertions of the 'thesis' are as follows:

- The history of the Turkish nation as it has, up until today, been known, does not consist merely of Ottoman history. Turkish history is much older, and the nation which dispersed culture to all nations is the Turkish nation.

- The Turks, bringing civilization to the places in which they settled and first founded the civilizations of Mesopotamia, Anatolia, Egypt and the Aegean, are from Central Asia. We, today's Turks, are the offspring of the Central Asiatics.[23]

115

There are two problems that are tackled with these assertions. Firstly, the claim that Turkish history is much older than Ottoman history, which is traced back to a 'golden age' in Central Asia, refers to the second thesis of Gokalp – that what is *Ottoman* is, in fact, alien to the Turks' essence, and that leaving the Ottoman legacy meant the emancipation of Turkish nation from the culture of the oppressor, in search of self-identity. Kemalist discourse was thus critically formed upon the basis of a denial of the Islamic-Ottoman past, in fact, its re-articulation as a 'negativity' to become the modern republic's constitutive outside. The Ottoman past of the new nation-state should not only be excluded but also be redefined as a negativity that had prevented and was still preventing the achievement of full Turkish identity. The *Other* of the Turkish identity was thus constituted, which both provided the discursive territory with the essential means of closure, and legitimated the official war against Islamic beliefs and practices at the popular cultural level, by presenting popular culture as the traces of the Other contaminating authentic Turkishness.

At the popular 'common sense' level, however, the real contamination remained to be understood as the forcible introduction of western cultural norms into a Muslim-Turkish society. The Kemalist response to this view was to present westernization as the claiming back of a lost essence which was not only the essence of authentic Turkishness but also of all civilization. So, the thesis reads:

> Only the Turks had the original power of creativity and power to create civilizations ... The other racial types could not create civilizations before they came into contact with *Father-Turks*.[24]

The Kemalist grand-narrative of Turkish history thus asserts that at an imaginary point in history, the Turks, when they left their homeland in Central Asia and encountered 'other racial types', transformed these 'other racial types' into civilized races, and this is how the first known civilizations of Mesopotamia, Ancient Greece, Anatolia and Egypt emerged. Turks were the founding-fathers of all civilizations and that was why they were called Father-Turks. The 'thesis' continues to imply that with the adoption of Islam, the Turks were alienated from their essence and their creative power was quilted with an alien, backward culture. The Islam-dominated 'dark ages' of Turkish history inevitably led to the decline of the Ottomans, casting them down into an inferior position relative to western civilization, which, in its essence and origins, was Turkish civilization. In other words, the Europeans were strong because they were not really western, and the Turks were weak because they were not really Turkish. In order to become proper Turks it was necessary to rid Turkishness of alien-Islamic accretions that corrupted the Turkish essence. Only then would it be possible to discover the original, pure Turkishness which was completely compatible with the modern scientific world.

The 'Turkish historical thesis' thus elaborated a master-race fantasy in order to respond adequately to the necessity of beating the Islamist criticism. A discourse of

116

modernity, based on science and progress and armed with this nationalist grandnarrative would, it was hoped, 'reoccupy' the space left by the removal of Islam from the cultural sphere of society via secularization. In this sense, Kemalism became a form of state religion combining modern scientific discourses with racist fantasies, that is, a synthesis of the Enlightenment's 'Religion of Reason' and Rousseau's project to replace Christianity with a 'popular religion'.

'Thesis' as supplement and as repression

> While Ataturk's inclusive nationalism allowed them to be Turks – even demanded that they think themselves as Turks – they definitely did not want to be Turks. They wanted to be Kurds.
>
> Robert D. Kaplan

The Kemalists' 'superhard' negation expounded by the 'Turkish historical thesis' of the existing social entity within the borders of modern Turkey was not merely an Orientalist symptom of the split Turkish identity between east and west. The narration of Turkish history through the 'Thesis' is a result of a number of other vital problems of Turkish identity-building and should therefore be understood as furnishing a foundation for the Kemalist will to 'Turkisize' as much as to 'modernize'. The deconstructive notion of the 'logic of presence', which will be referred to below, can be helpful in understanding the full implications of 'Turkisization'.

Jacques Derrida views modern philosophy as undermined by its impossible dream of attaining a foundation for knowledge, an absolute bedrock of Truth that could serve as a guarantee of philosophical systems.[25] He terms this foundationalist approach to language and knowledge a 'metaphysic of presence' and defines the task of deconstruction as showing this disingenuous 'dream' at work. Just as a dream seemingly satisfies desire by providing a substitute for the object of desire, thus creating an illusion that the fundamental impossibility of the satisfaction of desire can be overcome, so the metaphysics of presence is the substitute which has allowed western philosophy to deceive itself into believing it could overcome and fulfil its desire for presence. This illusion is generated, that is, presence is attained, *without* really attaining it, through the strange logic of *supplement*. The supplement is added to a text to make up for a deficiency, but as such it reveals a lack, for since it is in excess, the supplement can never be adequate for the lack. The Derridean deconstruction, therefore, consists in showing that the whole edifice of western philosophy rests on the possibility of compensating for a primordial non-presence by way of a supplement. And once it is proven that the supplement is an integral part of the metaphysical machinery, it becomes easy to show how, in every instance, the notion of supplement serves to demystify full presence.

The logic of presence is manifested in the 'Turkish historical thesis' in two interrelated ways. Firstly, the 'thesis' represents a supplement added to the three discourses of the late Ottoman vision and secondly, it signifies the non-presence of the Turkish 'nation' as an objective entity prior to its discursive articulation. Despite its nihilistic attitude towards tradition, Kemalism was not born into a void; it originated from certain elements of each of the 'three modes of politics', and inherited, in particular, its main body from Turkism, as discussed above. But the relationship between Kemalism and Turkism also involved tension, particularly in the definition of the Turks' Homeland.[26] The 'Turkish historical thesis' reiterates, to a large extent, the theses put forward by Turkist thinkers, when assuming a continuity of Turkishness from Central Asia to Caucasus, Anatolia, Balkans, Hungary, Finland and Estonia. This imagined continuity, however, had a logical consequence in Turkism, that is, the aim to liberate *Turan*, the Turkish Homeland in Central Asia, and to unite the 'greater Turkish nation' in this Homeland as in their 'Golden Age'. Kemalism had to abandon the *Turan* utopia in favour of the pragmatic motto of 'peace at home, peace in the world', by announcing Anatolia as the home of the new modern nation, while continuing to rely heavily on the main body of the Turkist vision. It thus initiated a 'short circuit' in the Turkist ideals, and by the same token, Kemalism was born with an inherent logical inadequacy.

In this context, the 'Turkish historical thesis' represents a supplement, which attempts to overcome this logical inconsistency. When Turks are endowed with the status of the originators of all civilizations, there remains no need to return to the original Homeland; hence the official claims that prior to the Greeks, civilizations of Turkish extraction existed in Anatolia.[27] Anatolia was justified as the Homeland of the modern Turkish nation, by way of a myth of racial superiority, which was added as a supplement to the original historical narrative of Turkism, with the expectation that it would compensate for the unfulfilled desire of the revival of the greater Turkish nation in its original Homeland.

A deconstructive reading of the 'Turkish historical thesis' as a grand-narrative on the myth of origins, history and the future of the Turks would further serve to read this narrative as an attempt to cope with a lack; a nonpresence. In the beginning, nationalism was only the discourse of the Kemalist elite, overruled by popular Islamic culture at the level of common sense. The peasant population of Anatolia never called themselves Turks, nor did they want to do so, since they were Muslims and 'had nothing to do with those infidel nomads on the mountains'.[28] At the 'high culture' level of state tradition the situation was even worse; the claim that Ottomans were Turks, which, until the emergence of nationalism within the context of 'three modes of politics', could only be found in European, Arabic and Persian discourses, had been made only to 'expose' the destructive and barbarian nature of this state and culture. Similarly the Ottoman 'high culture' had never called itself Turkish; on the contrary, in that discourse, the term 'Turk' only signified a series of negative meanings including barbarism and inferiority. Consequently, the emergent Turkish nationalism at the turn of the twentieth century had to face the impossibility of identifying with a 'Turkic' community within the ethnic heterogeneity of Anatolia which had not been 'alienated' by Islam or was willing to participate in the Kemalist venture of 'discovering its true self'. The Kemalist 'will to Turkisize' thus lacked any building blocks to begin the construction of modern Turkish identity. That the category of Turkish nation, far from being obvious and transparent, was based on an 'absence', led to the Kemalist 'dream of presence' in the form of a strong myth of master race.

Kemalists were faced with the traumatic results of this absence in the process of the discursive construction of Turkishness. Kemalist discourse, which clearly excluded the non-Muslim ethnicities that had been already 'cleansed' by the conclusion of the national struggle, viewed all the Muslim peoples of Anatolia as the objectivities that would form the modern Turkish identity. One consequence of this viewpoint was the attempt to end the de facto autonomy of the Kurdish tribes in east and southeast Anatolia. Resistance to this annexation attempt emerged immediately as a successive chain of Kurdish revolts that began with the 1921 Kocgiri and 1925 Sheikh Said rebellions and continued until the suppression of the Dersim Rebellion in the late 1930s.

The decades-long Kurdistan campaign of the Kemalist dictatorship was aiming to repress Kurdish identity down to a point where the Kurds would be assimilated to a larger pool of Turkish identity. Parallel to the suppression of the Kurdish revolts, with the enforcement of a 'Forced Residency Act' in 1930, the Kurds were forcibly dispersed in Anatolia, all Kurdish sources of reference were destroyed, the use of the words Kurd and Kurdistan and publications in Kurdish were banned and speaking Kurdish was penalized. It is not a coincidence that the 'Turkish historical thesis' was produced in the most intense phase of this process of repression. The myths and fantasies of the 'thesis' on the ancient history were also intended to serve the repression of Kurdish identity. Any Anatolian and Mesopotamian civilization that the Kurds may claim as originally theirs had been turned into originally Turkish civilizations since 'no civilization is possible without being contacted by the Turks' creative power'. Only on these grounds does it becomes possible to declare that the Kurds were originally Turks who, as a result of living on mountains, had become linguistically degenerated and alienated from their Turkish mothertongue and their real identity.[29] From the 1930s onwards, the history of the Kurdish people in Turkey, who constitute about 20 per cent of the Turkish 'nation', can only be written as, in Foucault's terms, 'an archaeology of silence'.

The form of repression of the Kurdish identity – cultural assimilation, rather than physical annihilation – indicates the necessity for Kemalists to utilize any Muslim ethnicity of Anatolia as the building blocks of a larger Turkish identity. In this regard, although blended with a master race myth, Kemalist nationalism cannot be defined merely as a racist or exclusivist nationalism. Kemalists wanted to 'make' a nation in their image out of the Muslim population of Anatolia. The will to

Turkisize was symbolized in Mustafa Kemal's (Ataturk – the Father-Turk) motto 'how happy he is who says I am Turkish' which emphasizes the primacy of voluntarism in nation-building. By the same token, this statement contradicts the racist assertions of the 'Turkish historical thesis' since in this case Turkishness is presented as an identity not defined by race or ethnicity but by *volunté* and is situated over and above racial or ethnic affiliations as an overriding identity. The repression of Kurdish identity was not an act to externalize the Kurds, on the contrary, it consisted of the suppression of an attempt of voluntary exclusion from the invented modern Turkish identity. The formation of Turkish national identity which began with the physical elimination of non-Muslim ethnicities of Anatolia thus continued not with racial or physical but with discursive externalization of Islamic and Kurdish identities. The inclusive feature of Kemalist nationalism towards the Muslim population of Anatolia however does not make any difference in that Turkish national identity was built as an aggregate of repressed identities. In fact, this inclusive drive is responsible for the discursive externalization, that is, repression of Muslimhood and Kurdishness.

Hegemonizing common sense: Kemalist populism

Kemalism as the ruling discourse of Turkish modernity cannot be solely understood in terms of its alienation from popular masses. It was a project of 'authentication through westernization' since the westernizing reforms were almost always justified on grounds of congruity with the essence of Turkishness. Hence, westernizing reforms and a populist discourse involving a good deal of peasantism went hand in hand. Populism formed a new nexus around which the regime and a section of the intelligentsia developed an interest in the people, the new ultimate basis of political legitimacy. Authentication at the ideological level can be depicted in policies of language, a rustic nationalist poetry, glorification of the idealized folk tradition in the official propaganda material, etc.

Kemalist populism was backed by populist social and economic measures such as the establishment of a political-cultural network of 'peoples houses' and 'village institutes', encouragement of limited political participation within the local organizations of the Republican Peoples' Party (CHP), state promotion in agricultural modernization, protectionist measures during the world economic depression of 1929, promotion of peasant co-operatives and a limited land reform, and so on. The formation of 'village institutes' for the education of peasant youth to be mobilized in economic and cultural development of their own locality, and a nation-wide education mobilization resulted in the creation of a new idealist generation of 'organic intellectuals' of the Kemalist regime. The successful attempt at industrialization through the etatist economic policies of the 1930s strengthened populist policies.

Kemalism, in its attempt to build a new political community based on universal citizenship, was thus forming its institutions for the basis of power and legitimacy under the discursive horizon of a collective will – a modern Turkish society at the level of 'civilized nations'. In Gramsci's terms, this process was a transition from a 'corporatist group' to a 'hegemonic group' which for Gramsci involves the 'universalization' of the demands of a particular group.[30] Kemalist hegemony consisted on the one hand in the definition of modern Turkish identity with reference to its outside, that is, the Islamic-Ottoman past and alienation to authenticity, and, on the other, the rearticulation of subject positions to present variations, not adversaries, of the modern Turkish subject. The Kemalist will to civilization was objectified in this subjectivity grounded upon the discursive territory of nationalism and the horizon of modernity. The final discursive marker of this territory was Mustafa Kemal's personality, with his new surname Ataturk (the Father-Turk), whose statues and busts decorated the main squares of even the remotest towns of the country and whose portraits hung in every classroom of every school and every workplace throughout Turkey. Thus was represented the 'social body' which for over seven decades has survived through a combination of force and consent. Ataturk's body as the *point de capiton* of modern Turkish *body politique*, proved to be capable not solely of 'exclusion, blockage and repression' but also of 'producing effects at the level of desire',[31] that is, using Gramsci's terms, of formulating its will to civilization as a 'national popular' goal at the common sense level and of accommodating and rearticulating a plurality of identities and meanings within its discursive territory.

The seven decades of Kemalist hegemony were not experienced under one party dictatorship of the Kemalist elites. In the first multi-party elections in 1950, the Democrat Party (DP) came to power with a liberal-conservative programme based on full integration with the capitalist bloc and less government intervention in religious affairs. Under a decade of DP rule, Islam-state relations came to an equilibrium where the Islamic cadres, rather than aspiring to political power, were satisfied with limited influence on state affairs and the lifting of state intervention in religious affairs. The relaxation of anti-clerical measures did not bring about a decisive weight of Islamism in politics; religious communities, which were organized under the names of various Islamic orders, such as *Nakshibendi* and *Nurcu*, preferred representation at the political level via their limited influence on centre-right political parties, rather than direct involvement in political affairs. With the growing weight of urban life and industry in Turkish political economy, Turkish political life had superseded the 1920s and 30s secularism/Islam dichotomy. The emergence of working class organizations and the proliferation of modern identities led to the emergence of new discourses based on the oppositions of labour/capital and independence/imperialism throughout the 1960s and 70s. All these discourses, including liberalism, conservatism and socialism were, however, sharing the horizon of modern Turkish identity formed by Kemalism; they developed as the pluralization of language games around the paradigm of Kemalism rather than presenting fundamental challenges to this paradigm itself. Kemalism whose genealogy is blended with Turkism, authoritarianism and the dictatorship of Reason over religion, could also mean in the process, liberalism, ethnic and religious tolerance, social democracy, socialism, feminism, etc. It has, in this sense, been an 'empty signifier' able to be filled in with diverse discursive meanings, forming in effect the 'universe'[32] of all these 'particular' discourses.[33] At its outset, Kemalism was the social imaginary of the elites of a pre-industrial society, with a vision of Turkey becoming a modern industrial society; and this is precisely what Turkey became by the mid-1970s; the goals of Kemalism were achieved and the time was ripe for imagining a late-Kemalist future, defined in terms of economic prosperity, welfare state and socialism.

III

The crack of doom: Turkish identity in crisis

Since the late 1980s, the conventional social imaginary of modern Turkey as formulated by Kemalism in terms of modernity and nationalism has been challenged by a diversity of new discourses particularly by political Islam and Kurdish nationalism. The novelty of these discourses lies in that both of them are the products of new dislocations which led to the emergence of a language of difference to dominate the discursive territory of post-1980 Turkey. But they are at the same time 'revivals' of the discursive challenges to Kemalist nationalism which were repressed and externalized in the formative years of republican Turkey. They therefore represent the 'return of the repressed', that is, the return of the Other of modern Turkish identity causing traumatic effects on the existing social order. What follows is an account of this process of (re)emergence with an attempt to analyse its implications.

Ataturk's generals and Islamist revival

On 12 September 1980, the Turkish army carried out a coup d'etat with the claim to put a decisive end to the social disintegration and political polarization of the late 1970s. On his first public appearance as new leader of army and nation, General Kenan Evren cited a number of reasons for the coup, including the 'anti-secularist threat against Kemalism'. The junta stated that 'depolitization' of society was necessary in order to end polarization. It revitalised the myth of Kemalism – now pronounced as Ataturkism, in order to avoid left-wing connotations of the term – which signified national unity and security indicating the boundaries of a new discursive territory of the 'nation' defined in its difference from a totality of terrorists, secessionists and anti-secularists. But the military regime would realize soon the shortcomings of their Ataturkism in filling the vacuum left from the physical liquidation of the socialist influence on social and political life of late-Kemalist Turkey. Their anti-socialist stance consequently led the generals to favour the religious right in their search for legitimization. The 'Turkish-Islamic synthesis' was produced by conservative-religious intellectuals organized in the 'hearth of intellectuals' with its emphasis on authoritarian politics and social control through the use of cultural and religious codes. It provided the junta's Ataturkism with a perfect content. A 1983 state planning institute document clearly enunciated the importance of religion in 'safeguarding the state and national unity' in the current period of 'rapid industrialization and social change'. In a political climate where any other political tendency was practically banned, the conservative-religious political elements were able to obtain key positions in the state bureaucracy and educational apparatus where the left had previously been influential.[34]

The junta's religious move was followed by the Turgut Ozal-led Motherland Party (ANAP) government. Under Ozal, the etatist discourse of 'national development' was gradually replaced with the logic of consumerism and *laissez-faire* integration with the west. In the logic of consumerism, religious communities who were conceptualized in the old mode as 'fetters of modernization' were able to claim an equal 'subject position' to other identities of the discursive territory. Muslim identity was thus rehabilitated within the discursive territory of an emerging consumerist society.

But the 'revival' of political Islam in Turkey cannot be fully understood through an analysis limited to internal politics for it is an indivisible part of a global 'revival' of political Islam as a mode of the politics of authenticity in the midst of fundamental changes in the international arena. This factor will be discussed later in terms of a larger context of erosion of the discursive horizon of modernity.

The consequences of the religious move at the centre of Turkish political life in the 1980s went beyond all expectations. For over a decade, Islamist publications and radical Islamist groups proliferated around the country elaborating a discourse of traditionalism and anti-secularism. The Welfare Party (RP) acting as an umbrella organization for various Islamist and conservative tendencies gained unprecedented strength through the articulation of not merely the demands of its traditional constituency, consisting of degraded provincial merchants and middle classes, but also the urban poor and to a certain extent the Kurds in a political imaginary of 'Just Order'. The RP's rise began to ring the alarm bells for the conventional Kemalist order with its success in the 1994 local elections. This success was crowned by a subsequent win in the December 1995 general elections which ultimately brought about an RP-led coalition government to Turkey.

Discourse of the repressed: Kurdish nationalism

Another primary target of the 1980s junta was 'secessionism' which the generals held largely responsible for late 1970s social disintegration. The consequent military terror in Turkish Kurdistan over ordinary people was aiming to punish the Kurds for breaching the Ataturkist principles, that is, for failing to overcome their alienation in six decades under the modern republic to discover their essence by realizing that they were in fact 'mountain Turks'. It was under these conditions that a guerrilla group, the Kurdistan Workers Party (PKK), launched an armed struggle against the Turkish forces in southeast Turkey in August 1984. Parallel to the increase in PKK activities throughout 1980s, the military presence in the region grew dramatically, intensifying state terror over Kurdish civilians. Kurdish people were forced to choose between joining the government militia or being labelled as PKK supporters. One clear consequence of these oppressive policies was the growth of the PKK's popularity, which the leader of the PKK, Abdullah Ocalan, admits owed more to government terror than to their own activities.[35] The PKK gained popular support not only from among the population of southeast Turkey, but also the Kurdish inhabitants of major cities who constitute the largest portion of the alienated urban-poor.

The PKK's discourse – which was originally a strictly Marxist one, but has changed considerably through the years – is based primarily on a self-criticism of the Kurds' alienation from their true identity by surrendering to Turkish assimilation. This politics of authenticity is backed by a criticism on modernist lines of the pre-modern cultural state of the Kurds and a consequent formulation of the primary aim of the PKK as to initiate an 'enlightenment' in Kurdish mentality.[36] An integral part of this identity-building through an 'enlightenment' is the elaboration of a national history which begins with a long-forgotten 'golden age' and continues with the Kurds' alienation from their national 'essence' due to their 'backwardness' all of which are tied to a project of national liberation and modernization.[37]

The popularity of Kurdish nationalism has also gone well beyond the official claim that the whole movement was simply the work of an isolated group of terrorists. In fact the government and the mainstream media would speak of 'Kurdish reality' for the first time in modern Turkish history and in 1991 the People's Labour Party (HEP) would be founded with the profile of a Kurdish party and Kurdish deputies would enter Parliament. However Kurdish representation has been continuously blocked with coercive methods by the government: the arrest of Kurdish deputies in Parliament in March 1994, the prevention of Kurdish representation by the imposition of a national threshold in December 1995 general elections and the recent arrest of the HADEP leadership following the 'flag affair' mentioned above, are the milestones of continous official attempts to push Kurdish politics out of the field of legitimacy. But despite all the obstacles to legitimate channels of representation the discourse of Kurdish nationalism won undeniable popularity among the Kurdish masses so much so that the government had recourse to a Kemalist war-trick by declaring the Kurdish New Year, *Newroz*, a traditional Turkish holiday to be officially celebrated with the name *Nevruz* from 21 March 1995 onwards.[38]

From the politics of difference to hegemony

It has been argued in this paper that Kemalist discourse, which built modern Turkish identity, was founded upon modernity, as a mode of modernization. Kemalist modernization meant carrying Turkish society as an autonomous national territory under the discursive horizon of modernity. It is not a coincidence that discourses of difference with the primary aim of dismantling the essential identity of Kemalist nationalism emerged at a time when the foundational status of the central categories of the discourses of modernity is put under question with what Lyotard termed 'incredulity towards metanarratives'. While whether the 'unfinished project' of modernity has collapsed and therefore the world is in transition to a post-modern age or not remains an open question the existence of such a discussion in itself is enough to indicate a weakening of the discursive horizon of modernity parallel to an erosion of its metanarratives – such as the metanarratives of progress and emancipation. This global tendency however did not automatically materialize in Turkey. The erosion of Kemalist discourse had its peculiar dynamics as a consequence of contemporary dislocations of its discursive territory, which need further consideration.

Until 1980, the territory of modern Turkey was marked with literal closure. The ultimate aims of the Republic were defined in terms of economic development and productivity, in which the state played a guiding role. This closure was further protected by economic policies of import substitution, state monopoly on cultural life, etc. Opening up to global markets with a shift in economic policies from import substitution to export promotion, the consequent shift from productivism to consumerism in the logic of political economy and the development in communications technology brought about a new conception of the state which was fundamentally contradictory with the Kemalist corporationist state. The state's leading role in all fields of social life from economy to culture was gradually weakened. A new role for the state as the engine of liberalization and privatization, as inventor of a new trade regime, and as actor of new modes of foreign policy in search of markets for export had to be defined. The end of economic closure through neo-liberal economic policies, accompanied by the invasion of cultural life by diverse images and traditions through the explosion in communications, meant that the Turks, for the first time, became aware of the existence of a world beyond Turkey in a real sense. The post-1980 erosion of Kemalist nationalist discourse with its will to civilization would reveal Kemalism's inability to limit the imagination of the political community within the horizon of modernity, which paradoxically began with the full integration with 'civilization', the contemporary horizon of which was marked by the New Right and neo-liberalism. The total exposure of Turkish society to global modernity was radically transforming identity conceptions and social configurations into ambivalence and uncertainty. The fashionable word used to define this process is 'globalization'.

Both the rise of Islamism and Kurdish nationalism appeared in this climate to change the terms of political discourse from grand strategies of modernization to identity politics. Their emergence has radically disturbed the established priorities of identity/difference through which subject positions are determined and social relations are organized. Kurdish nationalism thus seeks recognition of a new Kurdish identity defined in its difference from Turkish and, similarly, political Islam comes to demand a space for Islamic identity defined in its otherness to modern secular identity. The problem here is the absence of any possibility for the existing discursive territory of Turkish nationalism to accommodate the two new identities in new 'subject positions'. Because both the Kurdish and Islamic identities are not defined within this territory by their difference from certain identities of the social domain but by their difference from this discursive territory itself. They represent the 'return of the repressed' in the sense that they correspond to the very 'others' of modern Turkish identity which was built upon their repression. The place of the subject positions of an anti-secularist Islamic identity is 'outside' of Turkish nationalism. Similarly, a Kurdish subjectivity based on the refusal of being a component of a perception of embracing Turkishness, places itself outside the discursive territory of modern Turkey. Each challenging identity with its own perception of subjectivity outside the territory of Kemalist nationalism, claims to furnish the real grounds of political community. Consequently the present conjuncture of the Turkish political landscape is determined by clashes between essentialist identity claims as the primary reference-points of political discourse – between secular identity and Islamic identity and between Turkish identity and Kurdish identity.

The consequence of these challenges to national identity is the presence of ambivalence and uncertainty as the markers of contemporary Turkish identity. The Islamist challenge brings back the ambivalence of Turkish identity by reviving the repressed Orient inside, while the formation of the Kurdish identity represents the (partial) failure of the Kemalist project of creating a modern nation out of various ethnicities thus revealing the ambivalence of the Turkish nation as an objectivity.

Islamism and Kurdish nationalism emerged as a consequence of the weakening of the centre of the Turkish political field and they served to weaken further this centre which has been conventionally marked with the unifying vision of national identity, thus deepening the identity crisis. Since they are the Others of modern Turkish identity, their challenge revealed the possibility of thinking of political community outside the terrain of Kemalist nationalism. Their articulation to the hegemonic discourse would mean depriving the system of its 'constitutive outside' and lead to the necessity of a redescription of the boundaries of the social domain as an aggregate of social identities.

Both of these discourses are 'unrepresentable' by the available signifiers of the language of the imagined community of Turks. Their condition of enunciation is a redescription of the political community based on a turning upside down of the existing practices of inclusion/exclusion and the us/them distinction. This impossibility of representation, as well as leading to the antagonistic dominance of identity politics on the basis of a language of difference, led to the opening up of a mythical space dominated by the necessity of a new definition of the discursive territory which would be able to accommodate the emergent identities and to provide the system with new means of closure through a new description of its outside. The neo-liberal discourse of the late 1980s and early 1990s, known as 'Second Republicanism' and represented by a group of journalists and intellectuals close to the late President Turgut Ozal, has been one of the discourses of this space. For the Second Republicanists, Turkey was going through a transition similar to that in the Eastern European countries after the collapse of the Soviet Union. The era of the First Republic stamped by Kemalism – which was equal to a number of terms, namely, bureaucracy, state, dogmatism, central authority, territorial nationalism, etc. – has come to an end. A Second Republic should be formed on the bases of liberalism, market forces, freedom, tolerance, local authority and an 'imperial vision'.[39] Since the death of Ozal in 1993, the influence of Second Republicanists has considerably diminished and while Ozal's party ANAP changed its image from an umbrella organization of various tendencies to a centre right party of the conventional political spectrum, the New Democracy Movement (YDH) which was formed by the Second Republicanists could not survive the political competition particularly from the discourse of Kurdish nationalism and the RP's Islamist discourse both of which it originally hoped to articulate in a hegemonic discourse of neo-liberalism.

Most of the solutions that Second Republicanism had put forward though were inherited by a second hegemonic attempt by the pro-Islamist RP which would prove to be successful in universalizing the demands of different layers of society – from industrialists to the urban poor, from the Kurds to the provincial middle classes – in a coherent critique of the existing social order to form an alternative horizon of its social imaginary called 'Just Order'. RP's discourse of Just Order, blended with a discourse of political Islam, presented the restoration of the notion of community on the grounds of traditional values as the ultimate solution to the dislocated structure and began to rearticulate the discursive territory around a vision of Islamic unity which is clearly situated against the west and the western influence on Muslim community for which the 'alienated' Kemalist elites are held responsible. A solution to the Kurdish question is also pronounced in the RP's discourse in terms of a brotherhood of believers under the Just Order. The RP discourse thus seemed to be operating as a counter-hegemony striking serious blows to the already weakened central discourse of Kemalist nationalism through a 'war of position', which the RP, with its tens of thousands of militants, carried out at every level of state and society. It seemed as if the political frontiers were drawn once again in terms of a secularist/anti-secularist dichotomy when following the RP victory in 1994 local elections, a chain of Kemalist rallies were held around the country with the aim of 'stopping the anti-secularist threat'. But the RP, aware of its strength within civil society, ignored the challenge for a 'war of manoeuvre' from the enemy, who, the RP was aware, still enjoyed a certain amount of strength within the state, and set its target instead to win the December 1995 general elections.

Turkey is at present governed by a coalition of the RP and the centre-right True Path Party (DYP) which carried out its electoral campaign on the theme of 'stopping the reactionary threat'. The DYP slightly modified its propaganda later while justifying its decision to form a coalition with the RP on the grounds that it would guarantee the secularist principle. That the RP is now at the top of a power mechanism, which was structured in its origins against 'reactionary Islam' is a contradiction in itself which reflects even upon the statements of the coalition partners, revealing through and through the identity crisis of the Turkish state and 'nation'.

A definition of the RP as merely an Islamist movement breaching the settled conventions of national and international politics is possible though only by ignoring the nationalist dimension of the Islamist discourse in Turkey. In fact the RP narrates its history as a continuity of a movement called 'National Outlook' which was founded in the 1960s under the leadership of Necmettin Erbakan, the present leader of the RP and the current Prime Minister of Turkey. National Outlook forms the backbone of the RP discourse and proposes a vision of the restoration of the unity of the Muslim world in which Turkey would play a leading role. The hegemonic character of the RP discourse thus consists in its production of a conservative-nationalist social imaginary with an emphasis both on community and Islamic identity and on Turkish nationalism, based on a redefinition of the discursive territory beyond the terms of the secularism/anti-secularism axis by reformulating the east/west dichotomy in terms of a new axis of Turkish national identity versus western identity. For the RP, economic development and social modernization are necessary not to gain recognition as an integral part of the discursive horizon of western civilization but to become strong enough to challenge the west and to lead the formation of an alternative horizon of the international community of believers. Within this equivocal imagery of 'Just Order', ambivalence is equated with the west and certainty with nationalism and religion.

Epilogue: 'flag politics' in post-Kemalist Turkey revisited

> Give me back the burning wall
> Give me Stalin, give me Saint Paul
> 'cause I see the future brother, it is murder
> > Leonard Cohen

'Flag politics' has become a daily phenomenon in the Turkish political landscape as a variant of the gradual construction of the this new conservative-nationalist hegemony. The flag is therefore both the symbol of a search for a new hegemony, a metaphoric expression of the desire to solve the Turkish identity crisis and a traumatic symptom of this crisis and the accompanying structural dislocations. As a symptom of identity crisis, 'flag politics' symbolize a variant in Turkish politics which Tanil Bora describes as 'the dark spring of nationalism', led by languages of difference which provide each and every position with ideological dressings to speak of its identity as the foundational ground of political community.[40] Within the terms of the language of difference, the flag comes to symbolize Turkish identity against Kurdish identity and Turkish national identity against the European identity.[41] The symbol of the politics of difference though, the flag has become a symbol of the will to rearticulate the discursive territory around a conservative-national identity, based on a new subjectivity beyond the terrain of Kemalist nationalism, through the restoration of the genealogical link between Islam and national identity.

Both the flag and national anthem though are not new symbols; they were the symbols of Turkish nationalism even before the construction of Kemalist hegemony. But with the emergence of Ataturk's body as a metaphor of the 'social body' in the form of busts and statutes, the flag and national anthem gained a secondary and official character. They become the symbols of state to be remembered on national days while Ataturk was to become an integral part of the folk culture as a rescuing and emancipating hero. But this body became too narrow a symbol, that is, it lost its universal character as an empty signifier, by being tied to a fixed signified – secularism – in the climate of the flourishing identity politics of the recent two decades. The flag and national anthem thus replaced Ataturk's body as the new primary symbols of Turkish identity, serving to widen the conception of Turkishness to include both nationalist and Islamist connotations. 'Flag politics' indicate a shift in the final discursive marker to constitute the grounds for a new definition of Turkey's political community, drawing the boundaries of Turkish identity in its difference from Kurdish separatism and western imperialism, and providing the Turks with a new conception of subjectivity within a plurality of subject positions based on identification with community under an embracing conception of Turkishness. All these points have been summed up in a short statement by the Islamist poet and writer, Ismet Ozel:

> In Turkey a new society is being formed through gaining national existence via Islam. [...] Turkey is on the threshold of a new opening which would bring her to the point of being herself, and this is a positive thing.[42]

In short, Turkish identity is experiencing a process of intertwined disintegration and reformation parallel to the erosion of its final discursive marker, Kemalism, which in turn should be thought of within the context of a global crisis of the discourses of modernity. I have shown particularly in the final part of this paper that there are not many reasons to share the triumphalist optimism of commentators such as Fukuyama in relation to the current crisis of the dominant political imaginaries of modernity, given that this situation gives rise to new essentialist languages of difference, in many parts of the globe, and, as in Turkey's case, conservative attempts to achieve hegemony. The episode of identity crisis in Turkey, however, is yet far from being concluded with the decisive overdetermination of the mythical space of social imaginaries by a conservative-nationalist discourse of hegemony. It is, therefore, still too early to decree the last judgement on the consequences of Turkish identity crisis: the openness and ambivalence that currently rule the Turkish discursive territory are not merely the sources of an antagonistic process of social disintegration or conservatism, but of freedom at the same time – freedom to realize the restrictions and countless obligations that are imposed upon the self in the making of modern-nationalist subjectivity; freedom to think of the Turkish 'social body' beyond the modern discursive field of Kemalism and any essentialist discourses of modernity; and freedom to imagine a common future for the various cultures, identities and ethnicities of post-Kemalist Turkey. The possibility of the articulation of Turkey's discursive field with a post-Kemalist hegemony, that is, a hegemony defined in its difference from that essentialist and foundationalist logic characteristic of Kemalism, remains the sole source of optimism for the future of Turkey.

Notes

1   Connolly (1991).
2   Laclau and Mouffe (1985).
3   Foucault (1980), p. 55.
4   For the dissolution of the *millet* system alongside the traditional class positions see Karpat (1973).
5   Laclau (1990), pp. 60-8.
6   These three discourses were discussed thoroughly by Yusuf Akcura in an essay titled 'Uc Tarz-i Siyaset' (Three Modes of Politics) in 1904. See Akcura (1976).
7   In this parliament, there were 147 Turks, 60 Arabs, 27 Albanians, 26 Greeks, 14 Armenians, 10 Slavs and 4 Jews. Ender (1984), p. 67.
8   The essential characteristic of the Ottoman administration is its pragmatism. As was mentioned before, the main axis of the debate between the different wings of Ottoman bureaucracy and intelligentsia was the 'Salvation of the State'. Consequently the late Ottoman debates were not between different ideological, political or ethical positions but on the question of which ideological position would serve best the eternal purpose of salvation of the state. In fact, even one of the founding fathers of Turkish nationalism, Yusuf Akcura, argued for Turkism in his article 'Three Modes of Politics' on the basis that it was the most 'useful' ideology for the state. See Akcam (1993), pp. 117-8. When this utilitarian perspective in their approach to

ideologies is taken into account, it will be understood how the CUP began with Ottomanism and continued as Turkists or how they began with liberal and constitutional ideals and ended up with an authoritarian one party rule without many signs of discomfort.

9   For the link between ethnic cleansing and the construction of Turkish identity see Akcam (1993).

10   I borrow the term 'will to civilization' from de Ferro (1995).

11   Chatterjee (1986), p. 11.

12   Gokalp (1976), pp. 28-9.

13   Gokalp (1958), p. 25.

14   Ibid., pp. 50-1. (My translation.)

15   Ibid., p. 55.

16   Ibid., pp. 57-60.

17   Ibid., p. 32.

18   Said (1979), p. 3.

19   Karal (1946), p. 59.

20   Ibid., pp. 59-64. (My translation.)

21   Malek (1981), p. 107.

22   Sayyid (1994).

23   Karal (1946), p. 64.

24   Galip (1977).

25   Rorty (1991).

26   Landau (1981), pp. 72-107.

27   See, for example, Cemil (1977), pp. 199-210; Salisik (1968).

28   Karaosmanoglu (1960).

29   Besikci (1977), pp. 187-92 and 219-37.

30   See Gramsci's discussion on 'relations of force' in Gramsci (1971), pp. 180-2.

31   Foucault (1980), p. 59.

32   See Laclau (1996).

33   Socialists could create the myth of an anti-imperialist Mustafa Kemal, emphasizing the national struggle, populism and etatism; the founding party of the state, CHP, could claim overnight to have become a social democratic party in the early 1970s without even having to change its name; liberals could identify with Kemalism since liberalism was impossible under the *ancien regime* of the Ottoman Empire; women could praise Mustafa Kemal for he imposed reforms which guaranteed an equal status with men; even the pro-Islamist Refah Party (RP) claimed in its election campaign that if Ataturk were alive he would vote Refah, and so on.

34   Akin and Karasapan (1988), p. 18.

35   Ocalan (1991), p. 252.

36   Ibid., p. 232.

37   For an example of Kurdish nationalist grandnarrative see Bender (1991).

38   In March 1995, the then prime minister Tansu Ciller suddenly announced that Newroz — which she now called Nevruz — was in fact a Turkish festival and that the government would organize celebrations in Ankara and the Southeast for this 'national' day. The Kurdish national colours — red, yellow and green — for the wearing of which the Kurdish deputies at the Parliament were charged in 1994, are now declared to be the traditional Turkish colours. In the Kurdish provinces, poorly attended official ceremonies were held which emphasized how large and sublime the Turkish nation was. The Turkish government thus suddenly discovered that Nevruz had been celebrated for centuries by our 'outer Turk' cousins as the spring holiday and decided to celebrate it with the representatives of 'Turkic republics' to signify the 'sublime day of the nation'" On 21 March 1996, official 'Nevruz' was celebrated with military parades and official Nevruz fires around Turkey including the Kurdish provinces, while the police and the army were taking extra-ordinary measures against any attempts to celebrate Newroz.

39   Arikan (1991).

40   Bora (1995).

41   Flag politics symbolize the Turkish frustration towards Europe given that Turkey's continous demands to enter the European Union while keeping as it is her horrifying human rights record and authoritarian political structure has been continuously refused by the European Union. This was interpreted by many Turks as the ultimate failure of the 'Turkish will to civilization'.

42   An interview with Ismet Ozel, *Soz*, 24 August 1996.

References

Akcam, T. (1993), *Turk Ulusal Kimligi ve Ermeni Sorunu (Turkish National Identity and the Armenian Question)*, Iletisim: Istanbul.

Akcura, Y. (1976), *Uc Tarz-i Siyaset, (Three Modes of Politics)*, TTK: Ankara.

Akin, E. and Karasapan, O. (1988), 'The Turkish Islamic Synthesis', *Middle East Report*, No. 153, pp. 17- 21.

Arikan, E. B. (1991, *Second Republic Debates in Turkey*, Unpublished Masters Thesis, Bilkent University: Ankara.

Bender, C. (1991), *Kurt Tarihi ve Uygarligi (Kurdish History and Civilization)*, Kaynak: Istanbul.

Besikci, I. (1977), *Turk Tarih Tezi ve Kurt Sorunu (Turkish Historical Thesis and the Kurdish Question)*, Doz: Istanbul.

Bora, T. (1995), *Milliyetciligin Kara Bahari (The Dark Spring of Nationalism)*, Birikim: Istanbul.

Cemil, H. (1977), 'Ege Medeniyyetinin Menseine Umumi Bir Bakis' (A General Overview of the Origins of the Aegean Civilizations), in Turk Tarih Kurumu. First published 1932.

Chatterjee, P. (1986), *Nationalist Thought and The Colonial World: A Derivative Discourse*, Zed Books: London.

Connolly, W. (1991), 'Democracy and Territoriality', *Millennium*, Vol. 20, No. 3, pp. 52-64.

Ender, A. (1984), 'The Origins and Legacy of Kemalism', *Khamsin*, No. 11, pp. 47-69.

Ferro de, C. (1995), 'The Will to Civilization and its Encounter with Laissez-Faire', *Alternatives*, No. 27, pp. 89-103.

Foucault, M. (1980), 'Body/Power', *Power/Knowledge*, Gordon, C. (ed.), Harvester Wheatsheaf: Hemel Hempstead, Hertfordshire.

Galip, R. (1977), *'Turk Irk ve Medeniyyet Tarihine Umumi Bir Bakis'* ('*A General Outlook on the Turkish Race's History of Civilization'*), in Turk Tarih Kurumu. First published 1932.

Gokalp, Z. (1958), *Turkculugun Esaslari (Principles of Turkism)*, Varlik: Istanbul.

____ (1976), *Turklesmek, Islamlasmak, Muasirlasmak (To Turkisize, To Islamize, To Modernize)*, Inkilap ve Aka: Istanbul.

Gramsci, A. (1971), *Selections from Prison Notebooks*, Hoare, Q. & Nowell Smith, G. (eds. & trans.), Lawrence & Wishart: London.

Karal, E. Z. (1946), 'Ataturk'un Tarih Tezi' (Ataturk's Historical Thesis), in Inan, A. and Karal, E. Z. (eds.), *Ataturk Hakkinda Konferanslar (Conferences on Ataturk)*, TTK: Ankara.

Karaosmanoglu, Y. K. (1960), *Yaban* (The Stranger), Remzi: Istanbul.

Karpat, K. (1973), *An Inquiry into the Social Foundations of Nationalism in the Ottoman Empire: From Millets to Nations, from Estates to Social Classes*, Princeton University Press: Princeton, N.J.

Laclau, E. (1990), 'New Reflections on the Revolution of Our Time', in *New Reflections on the Revolution of Our Time*, Verso: London.

____ (1996), 'Why do Empty Signifiers Matter to Politics?', in *Emancipation(s)* Verso: London.

Laclau, E. and Mouffe, C. (1985), *Hegemony and Socialist Strategy*, Verso: London.

Landau, J. M. (1981), *Pan-Turkism in Turkey*, C. Hurst: London.

Malek, A. (1981), *Social Dialectics*, State University of New York Press: Albany, N.Y.

Ocalan, A. (1991), 'Kurdistan Workers Party (PKK): Interview with Abdullah Ocalan, in Balli, R. (1991) *Kurt Dosyasi (The Kurdish File)*, Cem: Istanbul.

Rorty, R. (1991), 'Deconstruction and Circumvention', in *Essays on Heidegger and*

Others, Cambridge University Press: Cambridge.

Said, E. (1979), *Orientalism*, Routledge and Kegan Paul: London..

Salisik, S. (1968), *Tarih Boyunca Turk-Yunan Iliskileri ve Etniki Eterya (Turkish Greek Relations Through History and Etniki Eterya)*, Kultur Bakanligi: Ankara.

Sayyid, B. (1994), 'Sign O' Times: Kaffirs and Infidels Fighting the Ninth Crusade', in Laclau, E. (ed.), *The Making of Political Identities*, Verso: London.

Soz, (1996), 24 August.

Turk Tarih Kurumu (Turkish History Institute) (1977), *Birinci Turk Tarih Kongresi (The First Turkish Historical Congress)*, TTK: Ankara.

5 Political identity in postwar Japan: the Hegelian turn

Tim Stringer

Imitation lies at the heart of modern Japan's achievements and contributes to the persistent identity crisis that is the subject of endless treatises.[1]

Johnson's ungenerous assessment of Japan's postwar revival begs an important question about the nature and course of political and economic development in non-Western societies. To what extent is the complex of modern life a Western cultural artefact, providing a model of liberal-capitalism which Japan and other late developing countries have more or less successfully copied?

An affirmative answer indicates that Japan's credentials as a modern state are confirmed by standards which, *ex hypothesi*, it cannot fully meet. The copy is never quite as fair and true as the original and the practice of imitation may itself be regarded as an act of bad faith.[2] It is the inescapability of this dilemma for Japan which is the source of the identity 'crisis' to which Johnson refers. But if we reject the easy equation of modernity with the West, or at least recognize the indeterminacy of the question, then it becomes possible to understand Japan's modern, democratic trajectory in less agonistic terms.

Japan's entry into the modern world did not begin with the catastrophic defeat in 1945 and the postwar economic and political reconstruction, nor were democratic politics implanted by General MacArthur in the period of occupation (1945-52). The history of democracy in Japan is longer and more complex than some commentators have allowed.[3] But the defeat and foreign occupation represent some kind of break (or interlude) in the life of the Japanese polity. Postwar the Japanese began to negotiate the limits of their political community from a position of cultural subjection and disorientation, bounded within the intellectual world of Western liberal and democratic thought. According to the policy of the American Occupation authorities the Japanese were to be afforded the opportunity to study and emulate the lives of Americans and other democratic nations.[4] Yet the terms of this study regime did not produce sterile debate; on the contrary the immediate postwar intellectual and political climate in Japan was vibrant and immensely fruitful.[5] Defeat in the war exposed in a fairly brutal way the gross incoherence of the 'Emperor system' (*tennosei*) ideology, the organizational axis of the wartime Japanese State, and its historical failure – a nationalism which had failed to protect, and indeed supervised the destruction of, the nation. The Emperor system and its associated traditional ways of behaviour lost the capacity to integrate and organize the Japanese people, and Japanese intellectuals began to imagine a new or radically reconstructed democratic political culture. An examination of these postwar attempts to rethink a political identity for Japan gives some indication of the problems faced by a community which is obliged to confront the contradictory conditions of political identity as such.

The ambiguity of the Japanese response to the ruin of the Emperor system is conveyed by the writer Oe Kenzaburo, who was ten years old in 1945.[6] He recalled listening with his friends to the Emperor's broadcast of surrender on 15 August 1945. It was a moment of disenchantment and disbelief to hear that the Emperor spoke with an ordinary human voice:

> One of my friends could even imitate it cleverly. We surrounded him – a 12 year old in grimy shorts who spoke in the Emperor's voice, and laughed .... An instant later anxiety tumbled out of the heavens and seized us impious children .... How could we believe that the august presence of such an awful power had become an ordinary human being on a designated summer's day?[7]

It was not just that the heavenly king had fallen to earth, and become an object of play, but the displacement of the Emperor as the centre of Japanese social consciousness had profoundly disturbed the sense of belonging of ordinary Japanese. The ties of duty and obedience had been cut. Elsewhere Oe remarked that he had been transformed on that day from a 'patriotic boy' (*aikoku shonen*), who was willing to die at the command of the Emperor, into a 'democratic boy' (*minshushugi shonen*)[8] – an immediate sign that patriotism and democracy could not coexist in productive combination in postwar Japan.

Oe's second boyhood was to be reckoned not just in years, but in terms of the condition he shared with all other Japanese after 1945 of being in cultural apprenticeship to the American Occupation forces. His new democratic identity was not freely chosen and lightly worn, but had been partly organized and delivered from above. Japan was to become, as the Cold War strategy developed, the bulwark for democracy in Asia.

Oe occupies a place in the second generation of postwar writers, and holds a certain nostalgia and respect for the pioneers of postwar intellectual life.[9] Although the American Occupation maintained a regime of censorship, intellectuals in the immediate postwar were given new freedoms and a prominent role in the legitimation of the new order. Some like Maruyama Masao, painfully aware of the irony of the situation, felt themselves still to be 'democratic children', being taught the ABC's of civilization by General MacArthur.[10] In this context the focus became the need for the Japanese to achieve by themselves full rationality, independence and maturity.

These ambivalent attitudes to the new Japan appeared in a many-sided discussion of the conditions for and principles of individual subjectivity and the model of 'democratic personality'. Could the Japanese become a sovereign, democratic people and satisfy the conditions of entry to the modern world? This debate was partly inspired by an imported and distinctively Hegelian understanding of political identity and the necessary features of a modern state. An attempt was made by Maruyama in particular to recruit a more open, dialectical side of Hegel to the task of binding the Japanese people to a democratic future, by taking seriously the political implications of Hegel's view that 'history is the progress towards the consciousness of freedom'.[11]

This task was made all the more difficult by the severed link between nationalism and democracy in Japan. Hegel, after all, had insisted that loyalty and patriotic duty must exist, as an idea, in the minds of the citizens of a modern state, in order that private interests be sacrificed for the common good.[12] Japanese intellectuals had to struggle to find a form of identification within the postwar Japanese polity which did not depend on nationalist sympathies.

Hegel's ideas of modern self-consciousness were explored in the intellectual debate within broadly leftist circles after the war in Japan around the concept of *shutaisei*, a term of art for which the most appropriate translation may be 'subjectivity' or individual autonomy and self-direction.[13] The origin of the Japanese term lies in the pre-war Kyoto school of philosophical idealism. Since the Meiji Restoration (1868) and the opening of Japan to new influences, Hegelian thought had become part of the intellectual currency of modern Japan, but the association had tended to demean both sides. The idea of the monolithic state, a moral whole which monopolized the right to determine values and thereby violated the requirements of individuality and personality was associated both with Hegel's writings and with the Japanese state in its Meiji reform and ultra-nationalist incarnations.[14] But postwar thinkers saw the need to resist this kind of simplistic thinking, in relation to both Hegel and Japan.

In what follows I give a brief sketch of Hegel's philosophy of state and his understanding of modern society, in order to explain its salience to theories of new democracy in postwar Japan.

Hegel and the modern state

Hegel was perhaps the first modern thinker to examine the implications of the paradox that identity is complete in and completed by its non-identity (the Other). In political terms this meant conceiving a 'fractured' unity between the poles of identity and alterity in the complex of ethical life (*sittlichkeit*). Perhaps the beauty and allure of Hegel's 'dialectic of modernity' consists in the fact that when we finally find our place in the world with others, we do so under conditions in which the horizon of individual consciousness and the scope for autonomous action are massively enhanced and expanded.

According to Hegel's account in the *Philosophy of Right*, ethical life has three dimensions in which the idea of human freedom is progressively realized: family, civil society and the state. The family is described as an ethical bond or union in which the members achieve an emotional unity based on love and trust and each develops a limited self-consciousness and personal identity – selfhood is achieved within the relation with the other family members but it is limited by a lack of independence from the other members and the unself-conscious feeling of belonging.

Civil society is a realm in which individuality asserts itself through the satisfaction of needs and preferences in an economic and legal order. In particular, personality finds expression in acts of property-creation in which the self objectifies itself. In civil society individuals' relations with each other are mediated by the impersonal system of law and contract, and they experience life both as a separation and isolation from others and as dependent upon others in the system of needs and exchange. Finally there is the completing superstructure of the state, an organic community of citizens who share in a common life, express their unity in political action and sentiment and live a 'universal life'. Here the individual achieves a positive and substantive freedom and a harmony between his/her duties towards others and personal satisfaction.

For Hegel the life of a citizen in a state with good laws is the attainment of objective freedom not least because it presupposes and completes the other two dimensions of ethical life, family and civil society. Indeed it is a necessary condition of a modern polity that it maintains as distinct the spheres of private welfare (family life), private interests (economic and associational life in civil society), and public freedom in an organized, constitutional state.[15]

The concept of 'ethical life' thus denotes a complex and articulated unity of various dimensions of free individuality: subjective and objective, private and public, abstract and situated in social institutions and practices. Here could be preserved the fact of the separateness of human existence in civil society and economic life, and the unity of our communal life lived in the organic state under political conditions. The achievement of this complex structure of the self was, for Hegel, the mark of a modern society.

Fukuzawa Yukichi, pre-eminent in the Meiji era as an interpreter of 'conditions in the West' and a passionate advocate of modernization, showed the early influence of the Hegelian interpretation. In 1875 Fukuzawa opened his account of the course of progress and civilization as determined not by the level of material culture, but rather by the 'development of the human spirit' (or the 'common mind of the people').[16] This was something like a direct challenge to the traditional, Confucian principle of an enduring hierarchy in nature and in social relations. To assert the equality and independence of the common people (of the human spirit) drew attention within the Meiji period to what Fukuzawa called the 'imbalances of power' in all aspects of political and private life and the arbitrary use of authority within the family, economy and in government. Good government depended not on the private virtue of the rulers, but on the rational organization of public affairs and constitutional guarantees of the freedom to criticize authorities. And essentially for Fukuzawa, civilized progress required a multiplication of human needs and enterprises and more outlets to stimulate and invigorate the human spirit.[17]

Fukuzawa's influence on Maruyama Masao's understanding of the preconditions of a modern, democratic future for Japan will become evident.

The *shutaisei* debate and Maruyama Masao

In part the interest in postwar Japan in the category of the subject and the arguments for a more autonomous, self-assertive and responsible Japanese individual can be seen as a reaction to the forced diet of Americanization; as a suppressed desire that indigenous political forces must lead the work of democratic renewal, in order to co-ordinate the energies of the people who would otherwise be the passive victims or ciphers of the democratization of society.[18]

The concept of *shutaisei* also evoked a sense of personal responsibility and accountability for the self which fitted well with the guilt and contrition felt by some leftist intellectuals at their token or passive resistance to wartime ultranationalism. A lack of autonomous subjectivity seemed to explain the apparent ease with which some pre-war intellectuals had 'converted' from Marxist-Leninism to Japanese nationalism; for those engaged in the debate on subjectivity these type of beliefs demonstrated a slavish and dogmatic adherence to an external authority.

The debate on subjectivity thus spilled over into many arenas – in Marxist debate about revolutionary activism and the emancipatory theories of early Marxian thought, in literary works which focused upon universal values and the 'construction of a new human subject', and in political discussion about the requirements of democratic individuality.[19] Some of these arguments were humanistic and romantic in tone. Otsuka Hisao argued that institutional reform alone was not enough, Japan needed to create a democratic citizen body and to transform the 'general value orientation of the Japanese'.[20] In Otsuka's explicitly Weberian framework a Western inner-directed ethos of conscience, and the Christian principles of absolute good and evil were contrasted to an Eastern concern with form and appearance and the context-dependency of value-judgements. The Japanese cling to old personalistic ties of loyalty, show unreserved respect for group-leaders, and demonstrate a contempt for strangers and their problems. Otsuka believed the Japanese had suffered 'a long spiritual entombment in the ritual and values of communal living' with the effect that the existing mentality was premodern and undemocratic. Democracy is identified here with the ethos of inner spontaneity, the love of justice, and an impersonal respect for the common people.

But perhaps the most influential and important voice in this debate about subjectivity was Maruyama Masao's, a political scientist and intellectual historian at the University of Tokyo following his demobilization from the army. Maruyama at this time furnished an ideological critique of the cultural roots of wartime ultranationalism that implicated not the 'militarists' but the mental structure of Japanese society at its base – in the local neighbourhoods, villages and communities (*kyodotai*). Like Otsuka, Maruyama called for an inner, spiritual revolution of the mentality of the Japanese as a precondition for peaceful democratization, but on the basis of completing the Hegelian structure by creating in Japan the 'missing middle' – a plural and diverse civil society.

Maruyama's account of the development of Japanese ultranationalism as the illicit union between family and state bears comparison with Hannah Arendt's account of the origins of German Fascism. Arendt argued that fascist rule systematically destroyed the public realm of politics and atomized the people into a society of 'organized loneliness', which was then ripe for ideological incorporation.[21] For Maruyama too, the Japanese had become good, compliant Imperial subjects through a process of depoliticization and homogenization, based on an extended myth of the harmonious community capable of overcoming all social antagonisms. The origins of the myth were planted deep in the normative structure of Meiji Japan (and therefore not limited to the period of wartime ultranationalism) and involved a comprehensive mobilization of 'traditional' values, the core of which became loyalty to the Emperor (as father of the nation) and to the national polity (*kokutai*).[22] The idea of the *kokutai*, or the body of the nation, was sufficiently opaque and ill-defined to allow many interpretations but it became associated (and exclusively so by 1945) with the Emperor as the political and moral author of Japan. The Meiji Constitution of 1889 was itself authorized by the young Emperor 'to exhibit the principles, by which We are to be guided in Our conduct, and to point out to what Our descendents and Our subjects and their descendents are forever to conform'.[23]

In what has become a familiar argument, Maruyama claimed that conceiving the Meiji State as a moralized order tended to erase all differences and distinctions between the public and private realms, (a distinction in any case difficult to make in traditional Japanese thought), and was corrosive of the concepts of legality and constitutionality. Within the Meiji constitutional order there was created a dual structure of legally-defined institutions (although hedged in by the imperial prerogative) and an informal system of rule dominated by the Imperial Household, Privy Council and the oligarchs (*genro*).[24]

These structural conditions created what Maruyama described as a 'massive system of irresponsibilities' in which power, authority and ethical value were defined in terms of proximity to the Emperor as the ultimate moral entity. Moral judgement depended upon one's situation and proximity in relation to the centre, and political judgement was reduced to 'clarifying the national polity' – an empty formula which licensed any action, including the seditious and murderous acts of the young officers and other 'incidents' in the 1930s.[25] Under these conditions moral and political authority had no substantive meaning, and there were no moral agents or free subjects, not even at the very apex of power, since the Emperor himself ruled only by virtue of the final injunction of his imperial ancestors.[26] The chain of command and responsibility in government became impossibly convoluted, leading to and exemplified in the uncertainty and confusion involved in the decision to bomb Pearl Harbour.[27]

Below, at the level of the ordinary Japanese subject, Maruyama argued the self-consciousness of the people was displaced by a familial and nationalist ideology which exalted an unthinking loyalty to seniors and a kamikaze spirit of self-sacrifice. In Hegelian terms, dependencies created within family relations were projected directly (that is to say, not refracted through the intermediate organizations of civil society) onto political relations in the 'family state' (*kazoku kokka*). These ties, formed through a process of slow sedimentation, were crystallized in an official text produced in 1937 which gave doctrinal expression to the loss of self in a greater communal whole and the affective fusion of the family and state. This document, *Fundamentals of the National Polity*,[28] was issued by the Ministry of Education as an ideological aide-memoire to teachers and other subjects concerning the organizing principles of the Emperor-system and reportedly sold over two million copies. It created what might be termed a feudal and martial fantasy, in which a traditional social consciousness is harnessed to the mission of the Japanese to 'overcome modernity'. Some themes may be isolated:

• The significance of the historical community and its mystical role in forming the individual subject: 'An individual is an existence belonging to a state and its history which forms the basis of his origin and is fundamentally one body with it'.[29]

• A disavowal of the one-sided, narrow egotism of the Western Enlightenment tradition. Western rationalism is anti-historical and undermines the enduring character and purpose of the Japanese community. Social progress and the mission of the Japanese is tied to a notion of harmony, order and the non-antagonistic character of the social body. Western individualism is seen as a threat to the integrity of the nation, to the idea of society based upon spontaneous service, and to the 'pure manners and beautiful customs' of village life.

• Imperial subjects are given life and identity in an affective union with the Emperor as an 'ultimate entity' and head of the unbroken line of imperial succession stretching back to the goddess Amaterasu, creator of the Japanese archipelago. The subjects' duty is to obey and serve the Emperor intently: 'To walk the Way of loyalty is the sole Way in which we subjects may "live" and the fountainhead of all energy'.[30] In concrete terms subjects demonstrate their loyalty to the 'family-state' by exercising the confucian virtue of filial piety, a spirit of respect, love and indebtedness towards parents and the house (*ie*). The power of the Emperor is here relayed through the patriarchal head of the household, and by virtue of a sentimental unity of each member with the Emperor himself.

The obscurity of this official piece of propaganda with its eclectic mix of myths and traditions (bushido, shinto, zen, confucianism) no doubt contributed the desired romantic and anti-positivist effect, and was only part of the state's efforts to bind ordinary Japanese to the *kokutai*, but it is worth considering how seriously this text was received by the subjects who studied it. Carol Gluck comments that the transmission of the text is in itself some indication of the ideological effort the state exerted to 'rule the opinions' of the people.[31] And in the case of ideological indoctrination less is more: 'It is when hegemonic ideology is also the product of shared consent that it has its greatest impact'.[32] Certainly the overwhelming emphasis on unthinking loyalty suggests that the 'Emperor system' was an incoherent set of beliefs which never generated a spontaneous sense of affection between Emperor and subjects. In the early Meiji period, when Japanese imperialism was beginning to evolve, Fukuzawa Yukichi had claimed that there never had been any really close bond of feeling between the remote, semi-divine Imperial family and the people.[33] Had he written this in 1937 this would have been a 'dangerous thought', but true nonetheless. Equally by the 1930s the mass of the people were sufficiently de-politicized, disciplined and quiescent to need little mobilization.

This is where Maruyama's explanation of the phenomenon of the Emperor system, although contested by later historical work[34], is compelling: in its claim that Japan was structurally vulnerable to absolutist ideological forms, in the patriarchal family system; in the agrarian economic organization which encouraged an apolitical rusticity and heightened the importance of the local microcosm governed by the elders or local bosses; and in the continuity of feudal-bureaucratic forms of government which frustrated attempts to deconcentrate power and give people a political voice (most notably the failure of the mass campaigns of the 1870s and 80s called the Freedom and Popular Rights Movement).[35]

For Maruyama, Japan had achieved in the Meiji period the state structure envisaged by Hegel (albeit without true constitutionality) but it crucially lacked the intermediate moment in ethical life – a civil society. Civil society encompassed the social, economic and cultural structures where individuality would launch forth and flourish in all directions. In practical terms it included interest groups, cultural societies and clubs, economic institutions and all the intermediate organizations that could limit the reach of the family-system (*ie*) on the one side, and the state apparatuses on the other, in the day-to-day lives of the people. But because of the deformations Japan had experienced in its accelerated and managed modernization effort, a differentiated and plural social order, an associational life for the citizens, remained undeveloped, and Japan became a 'vast arena where social co-ordination

takes place without ever going through the channel of organ
disorganization of the State, characterized as the 'family State', allo
required, the State to swallow individual identities and create a fo
dependence in which the autonomy and independence of individua
The modern Japanese character, polite, self-effacing and uncritical,
time (de-)formed in this experience.[37]

The vigour and freshness of Maruyama's approach in the imr
period is unmistakable and his work represents a genuine attempt
critical uncertainty of the political future of the Japanese. Defeat in
was the beginning for Maruyama of a new and unprecedented stal
Japan. The people were free to reconstruct the national polity on de
But this would involve not just political reform at the centre, but
critically re-forming the primary groups and social structure of Japan
the family-system, the village organization and the community accorc
principles.

Maruyama looked towards a depersonalization of political relz
politics were conducted in a regular and ordered way and not by mean
associations. He described as typically Japanese a form of 'carnal polit
face (*haji, tatemae*, etc.) and guts (*haragei*):

> the things that go on in this arena are everything from naked violen
> intimidation to the more subtle pressures exerted by the *oyabun* an
> of bosses. I suppose we can say that these are methods of solving
> by means of direct human relations.[38]

Politics required more refracted and impersonal relations and i
organizations in which conduct could be regulated and rule-governe
envisaged a politicization of social life in the specific sense of introd
democratic, open and self-critical relations within the social envirc
constitutional terms this meant ordinary Japanese being prepared to assert
against the State. Maruyama believed that free subjectivity was essential t
kind of role-distance from which to reflect upon social arrangements and
these according to objective and universal rules.

Assessment after the postwar

The postwar era in Japan has taken on a rather limited and specific meaning
to the first wave of reform and democratization undertaken by the O(
authorities between August 1945 and about 1950. It encompasses the
enacting the egalitarian and pacifist Constitution (1947), land reform which
wiped out the landlords (as a class) and created a new, independent stratum

mers, reform of the civil and family codes in the direction of gender equality and ividual rights and the dissolution of the huge economic combines (*zaibatsu*) which 1 bankrolled Japan's wartime expansion. However with the onset of the Cold War, : Korean conflict and MacArthur's drive against new communist trade unions and .ivists there began a period known as the 'reverse course' in which the powers of blic order were tightened and political reform was essentially halted. This period minated in the internal struggle over the renegotiation of the Security Treaty with e US in 1960. The failure of Maruyama's project of imaginative reconstruction 's somewhere in this complex history and can be ascribed partly to its implication the now obsolete and discredited modernization thesis.

The high water mark of the modernization debate in relation to Japan took place 1960 at the Conference on Modern Japan held at Hakone.[39] The object of the onference seems to have been, at least from the American participants' point of ew, to certify Japan as having attained the full condition of modernity, according to ertain 'indices' or objective criteria: industrial output, urban concentration rates, chnological progress and so on. One effect of discussion in these dreary terms was terminate mainstream academic debate about the subjective and psychological imensions of modernization, and to invite the Japanese to end their agonism about feudal remnants' or inappropriate traditional forms of behaviour. Another effect was undermine in the eyes of the Japanese participants the coherence of any discussion f Japan in terms of modernity. The certification of Japan's modern status took place gainst a background of unprecedented civil disturbance connected to the renewal of he US-Japan Security Treaty, and therefore intellectuals like Maruyama who argued or Japan to continue and deepen the modernization process were seen as capitulating to American interests (disregard for the moment the vast intellectual space which separated Maruyama and figures like Edwin Reischauer and the other American participants in the 1960 Conference, and Maruyama's own active political opposition to renewal of the Security Treaty).

Some Japanese critics now claimed that the uncritical pursuit of subjectivity (*shutaisei*) in the early postwar represented another (failed) gesture by the Japanese towards Westernization, which of itself confirmed the lack of a truly Japanese principle of self-determination. *Shutaisei* was like 'a fictional version of one's own identity in terms of the other's desire', a gesture typical of colonized and subject peoples.[40] This criticism could (and did) easily turn, for want of a coherent alternative, into a reminder of the value and importance to Japan of the historical community and other traditional social structures, and indeed this period saw the re-emergence of an unapologetic cultural and economic nationalism.

Others pointed to the ambiguity of the concept itself, as it encompassed not only democratic self-management and a reflective attitude towards politics, but also a pattern of individuation which could slide into an atomized, consumerist individualism (civil society as market society). Something like this emerged in the 1960s with a new sense of private enjoyment – this was the era of Prime Minister

Ikeda's 'income-doubling' plan and the popular dreams of 'myhome-ism' and 'mycar-ism' – but it is prefigured certainly in Otsuka Hisao's delineation of the conditions for the development of a Japanese individuality, which included the development of 'the consumer powers of our people to create a vigorous domestic market'.[41]

Still others thought that somewhere in the 1970s Japan had finally 'overcome modernity' (by non-violent means) and solved the paradox of technological rationality and the loss of a community culture. Now the very conditions that had purportedly mired Japan in a feudalistic idiocy were seen as the keystone to Japan's economic miracle – the Emperor system ideology had shifted its focus from an imperialist to an economic nationalism, the company had become the new family-deity, but the values were the thing. They had searched for the lost soul of Japan and found it in its managerial culture. Criticism of traditional values seemed out of place when Western commentators and Wall Street analysts were studying the secrets of the samurai.

Some of these factors may certainly explain why the discussion of freedom and subjectivity have disappeared from the intellectual horizon (or appear only in *very* attenuated and ambiguous forms).[42] However they obscure the real reasons for the inadequacy of Maruyama's project, and at the same time the continuing importance and salience of the internal critique of modernity to contemporary Japanese politics. I will pursue these two points separately.

The first point returns me to Hegel. The postwar debate on subjectivity failed to create a pluralistic civil society and an active citizen body. The 1960s did witness the rise of new mass religious organizations such as the Buddhist *Sokka Gakkai* (which developed a powerful political wing the *Komeito*), but the 'new religions' in Japan were seen as replacing traditional communal associations (the family, village or neighbourhood) for economic migrants to the cities. It is doubtful whether commercialization and urbanization made Japan a more diverse and heterogeneous society, although there is scope for argument about this.[43] In the political arenas, ordinary Japanese were and still are notoriously disaffected and depoliticized. Participation rates are low and democratic activity, as in many other advanced countries, is vibrant only in the minority citizens' movements which organize on quality of life issues, anti-pollution, feminism and so on. The postwar peace and anti-nuclear weapons campaigns were genuine mass participation movements but these could be safely ignored or co-opted by the bureaucratic state, since it was in the interests of all postwar Japanese and US governments to keep Japan unarmed. (Things might have been fundamentally different had the Japanese government in 1960 not managed to resolve, by co-option and compromise, the Security Treaty crisis.)

The failure here is not purely intellectual of course, it involves the entire course and direction of Japan's postwar social and political development, Japan's dependency relation with America in the Cold War, and all the other domestic and international conditions which have shaped Japan's democratic trajectory. As John Dunn suggests, the causal properties of ideological thought are in any case indeterminate.[44]

There is nevertheless an one-sided and partial appreciation of the requirements of (a Hegelian) political identity in Maruyama's work which may have contributed to its practical failure. Maruyama argued that prewar Japan did not produce citizens able to bear the burden of political responsibility in a modern nation-state but he chiefly located this as a failure of civil society, or of the overburdening of civil society by the State, by the 'patriotism of national emergency' and by the tenacious family structure of Japanese society.[45]

However, the formation of a citizen body in the Hegelian scheme happens in the state itself, within the political associations, and not in civil society which is the realm of private individuals pursuing their own private interests. Maruyama and others, overawed by the power and penetration of the state believed that Japan should be democratized from the base upwards, but this is to commit something like a category error in Hegelian terms. Political life is lived in the state insofar as it is a public endeavour, as it represents us in our duties towards fellow citizens (rights, on the other hand, are claimed against others in civil society). The object of politics is to create a shared world in which we can act together, for collective reasons, for reasons of the good of the community itself.

Hannah Arendt had learnt this lesson from Hegel and others. Above all her account of political freedom stresses the need for public activity and mutual recognition in the fora of public life. In the presence of others we confirm our own identity as partly shared, and acquire a self-understanding as members of a unified community co-responsible for the public realm of the state. In our political existence we act together as equals, argue on the basis of the common good (which is not somehow produced out of the mystical 'community') and there with our fellow citizens live a universal life which surpasses the possibilities of economic life, which remains only a sphere of necessity. For Arendt, politics is a house where freedom can dwell. Totalitarian, and liberal-capitalist, regimes on the other hand destroy the political stage of appearance, the space where people can act together democratically to create their own world.

Some signs of a recognition of this argument, of the centrality of politics, are evident in Maruyama's thought, in an article published in 1947 called 'Politics as a science in Japan'. He writes:

On 15 August 1945 an unprecedented reform began .... It is true that this reform, usually called the 'democratic revolution', is not confined to narrow political changes. It includes fundamental transformations in every sphere of Japanese life, social, cultural, economic. Yet the point of departure for such enormous changes is undeniably *political* reform and the main agent is *political* power.[46]

But given the unprecedented state of affairs in postwar Japan, where there had been few traditional means of acting in public for the common good, almost no experience in living memory among the citizens of concerted political activity, the materials for creating the open arenas where political argument could be carried on were not to hand. And certainly the exigencies of the Occupation with its careful censorship of public discussion on such 'sensitive' issues as the atomic bombing of Hiroshima and Nagasaki, and the increasing nervousness of the American authorities concerning leftwing activism, put a determined brake on the progress of the democratic revolution. Postwar Japanese politics soon switched to the old familiar channels – bureaucratic management, the importance of local bosses, personal support networks and all the trappings of distributive politics in the so-called '1955 system' (single party dominance by the Liberal Democratic Party, the Socialist Party in permanent opposition). The 1955 system and the national aim of economic 'catch-up' before all else settled and entrenched an explicitly communitarian and atavistic Japanese political identity.

Ironically with the recent partial collapse of this one-party dominant party system in the 1990s there have been some echoes of Maruyama's concerns, but now in a liberal/conservative direction. Ozawa Ichiro, defector from the Liberal Democratic Party in 1993 and craftsman of the new opposition party *Shinshinto* has appealed for a reform in the politics, economics and consciousness of the Japanese. Ozawa criticizes Japanese politics for its 'excessive pursuit of consensus', over-centralization and bureaucratic regulation and the lack of political leadership and local autonomy. His vision of a new Japan takes in educational reform, reforms in the methods of political decision-making to strengthen the hand of elected politicians, and deregulation proposals to reduce the power of corporate Japan and to create regional and local independence. The ultimate goal of reform, he argues however, must be 'the autonomy of the individual. Real democracy begins with this autonomy'.[47] The autonomy of the individual is here imagined in terms of the opportunities for each person to express his/her individuality – the Japanese equivalent of the 'American dream', a society which truly values the individual and lets diversity flourish: 'Japan must become a society in which individuals can act freely, based on their own judgement'.[48]

Ozawa's reform package, an apotheosis of civil society, does not however encompass a greater share for the ordinary Japanese citizen in building a common life, nor does he recognize that Japanese citizens should exercise their judgement in public and political matters. His vision of a dynamic politics involves chiefly strengthening the executive arm of the State, principally the Prime Minister's Official Residence (*kantei*), to create a 'centre of political accountability',[49] and the devolved, regional management of administrative matters.

It is clear, however, from within a Hegelian framework that individual freedom in civil society is a fragile thing which relies for its strength and preservation on political protection by the state. A balance must be struck between, for example, our duties toward the state and our rights against it.[50] In the context of the present arguments about democracy this means that the realm of private freedom can only be enhanced and expanded if the realm of public and political freedom is secured and participation becomes real and earnest.[51] On this view we need above all to take seriously our political responsibilities toward our fellow citizens and to be sensitive to the collective condition and shared predicaments of social life. This issue is especially pressing in Japan where a particularly strong shared cultural background has not by itself predisposed the people to act together as citizens. Ozawa's discussion of autonomous individuality evades this problem by ignoring the political life of ordinary citizens, or by dissolving it into a question of government accountability through the National Assembly.[52] In the Japanese context, this is not wholly beside the point, but it hardly touches on the issue of how democratic institutions can be made to embody more closely the political wisdom of the wider community.

In the light of the contemporary disturbances of Japanese politics, to which the average Japanese citizen is merely a bemused and cynical onlooker, there is considerable scope for the re-examination of the conditions of political life and democratic citizenship. It might surprise some that Hegel could be a guide here, but his philosophy of state may provide a reliable defence against the apolitical extremes of uncritical communitarianism and narrow, self-serving economic individualism. Hegel furnishes a model for self-conscious, free *and* concerted action, and a means of articulating society, economy and polity which provides a valuable counter-weight to those, in Japan and elsewhere, who anticipate the end of modernity and indeed an end to political struggle. In this respect Maruyama's thought, and its critical relation towards modernity as an 'unfinished project', represents a challenge to contemporary orthodoxies, the neo-liberal versus bureaucratic solutions to Japan's political and economic stagnation.

Interestingly in his more recent work, Maruyama has shifted his attention to the conditions of political life, and the scope and meaning of politics (*seiji/matsurigoto*, or 'things governmental') in ancient Japan.[53] In one respect this is a conscious retreat from the practical concerns that absorbed him in the 1950s and 60s, and an abandonment of a Hegelian approach premised on the idea that 'history is going reason's way'. But in sacrificing Hegel's logic Maruyama has re-affirmed a Hegelian insight into the importance of our political life and duties. Examining ancient Japanese texts Maruyama claims to have uncovered some recurring themes in Japanese political thought and practice. The details of his work do not concern us here but his conclusions are of interest. Politics in premodern Japan, Maruyama argues, had two distinctive features: joint rule and the separation of power and legitimacy. The Japanese term for political matters, *seiji*, involved the idea of rendering service, rather than ruling or governing. The subjects of politics were the lower officials who reported their actions to superiors, and their responsibility towards the common people was to ensure that service was rendered to the Emperor by labour and the paying of taxes. In Maruyama's words 'the governed and the governors were both looking upwards'.[54] The Emperor remained throughout this period in a passive position of hearing reports from subordinates. The Emperor did not govern, although he alone was able to legitimate governmental actions. Political institutions evolved which embodied these central themes.

In the feudal Tokugawa period (1603-1868) the distance between the powerholders and the centre of legitimacy can be seen most starkly. The Shogun, a military commander, and his 'camp government' in Edo (Tokyo) ruled, but the Shogun's power was legitimated by the (powerless) Imperial court in Kyoto. And at certain times the nominal Shogun shared or ceded power to the Shogunal regent, lower-ranked clan members, and even household stewards. Power devolved downwards and was exercised informally by a number of junior figures.

In the modern period too, whatever the ideological principles of the absolutist 'Emperor system' dictated, this was modified by the dominant mode of political behaviour. The modern Emperor also did not rule, indeed sometimes he was overpowered by subordinates (*gekokujo*) and it was therefore true that in wartime Japan the Emperor bore no direct responsibility for the government's decisions and actions and the atrocities committed by junior officers and soldiers. Because power in Japan tended to retreat into the shadows, the locus of ultimate responsibility was bound to be obscured.[55] The nominal servant actually wielded power and under these conditions public power became ever more informal and private.

Maruyama draws no practical conclusions from these observations, but some points suggest themselves. In the period of democratic transition after the Second World War Japan's democratic institutions have also undergone a process of modification according to underlying patterns of behaviour. This has had positive and negative effects, which need to be understood and accommodated.

The ultimate source of legitimacy under the new Constitution is the people, and the elected politicians see their role as rendering service to the people. Often this has been interpreted in a narrow way as 'constituency service' or the politics of compensation: the giving of favours to local electors in return for their vote.

There is also a tendency within governments and party structures for power to retreat away from the figureheads (Prime Minister and Cabinet). Powerholders are shadowy figures (ex-Prime Ministers and party bosses) who are not directly accountable to the public. From this perspective, Ozawa Ichiro's pledge to make the the process of government in Japan more transparent may be at best disingenuous and at worst deeply hypocritical. Ozawa himself has operated for most of his political career from 'behind the curtain'.

On the other hand, the separation of power and legitimacy is part of modern democracies – the people do not actually rule. And the idea of joint rule means that power may be deconcentrated in governing elites such as the Liberal Democratic Party away from paramount leaders. This is also compatible with the democratic ideal that power should be transmitted downwards and shared among different centres. However, the principle of democratic accountability will tend to be compromised by the confusion of public and private power and the Japanese practice of *insei* or 'cloister government'. (This may be mitigated to a degree by the Japanese practice of extensive consultation before decisions are made.)

Maruyama's work continues to be insightful because it subverts the idea that Japanese structures of power are necessarily monolithic, hierarchical and non-egalitarian. Japan's relatively smooth democratic transition in the postwar period, and the radical shifts in the direction of social and economic equality, indicate that democratic and pluralistic practices, the differentiation of power, and the common sense of politics are not entirely alien to the Japanese tradition.

Notes

1   Johnson (1990), p. 72. Johnson graciously denies that there is anything 'inherently imitative' about Japanese culture.

2   Cohen has explained how subaltern attempts at racial and cultural assimilation are necessarily self-defeating. See Cohen (1988), pp. 9-15. On Japan, here is one example of the oft-repeated allegation that Japan is essentially a mimetic culture. In a book dedicated to exposing the misunderstandings between Europe and Japan, Endymion Wilkinson sees nothing incongruous in writing about the 'extraordinary Japanese ability to learn all sorts of things from other peoples, often in the end surpassing their former teachers, yet remaining self-consciously nervous, performing a stylised ritual which sometimes come near to caricature'. See Wilkinson (1983), p. 89.

3   This is Samuel Huntingdon's hasty judgement: 'only two East Asian countries have sustained experience with democratic government. In these two countries, Japan and the Philippines, democracy was the product of US presence. It was not just imported from the West; it was imposed by the United States'. See Huntingdon (1992).

4   Supreme Commander of the Allied Powers, (1970), p. 424.

5   Oe (1989) comments on the explosive power of literature in the immediate postwar.

6   Japanese convention is followed here and Japanese names are given family name first (except for scholars who work and publish mainly in the West).

7   Quoted by John Nathan in translator's introduction to Oe (1977), pp. xiii-xiv.

8   Quoted by Napier, (1991), p. 5.

9   Oe (1989).

10   Maruyama quoted by Koschmann (1989), p. 126.

11   Hegel, (1956), p. 19; quoted by Maruyama in his Author's Introduction (1969), p. xvi.

12   Hampsher-Monk (1992), p. 463.

13   The postwar debate on the concept of subjectivity has been discussed by Matsumoto (1966), Koschmann (1981-2). See also Miyoshi (1991), ch. 4.

14   Maruyama (1969), For a caricature of Hegel's views in this vein see Popper (1966).

15   On the importance of constitutionality and the division of political powers as the 'guarantee of public freedom', see Hegel (1967), paras. 271-2. On the limits of the State in relation to, for example, freedom of conscience, see para. 270.

16   Fukuzawa (1973), p. 1.

17   Ibid., p. 20.

18   Otsuka (1970).

19   See 'Subjectivity and Historical Materialism' (1948) discussed in Koschmann (1981-2).

20   See Otsuka (1970).

21   Arendt (1966), ch. 13. Note however Arendt's disdain for the economic realm of civil society, which for her is a realm of necessity, not freedom.

22   For an account of the modernization of tradition in the period of Meiji state-building and its crystallization around the concept of the *kokutai* see Gluck (1985).

23   From the Preamble to the Constitution of the Empire of Japan (1889) reprinted in Borton (1970), Appendix II, p. 569.

24   On the Meiji Constitution and its role in legitimizing the pre-existing power structure see Najita (1974), pp. 78-86; Maruyama (1964).

25   See the discussion of these incidents in Maruyama (1969), pp. 51-7.

26   Ibid.

27   According to Maruyama's account of the Tokyo war crimes tribunal, none of the wartime leaders could recall the exact sequence of events and discussions that had led to the decision to go to war with the United States, nor were any of the accused prepared to accept, or assign, responsibility for that decision see ibid., pp. 84-8.

28   *Fundamentals of the National Polity* (1958), pp. 278-88.

29   Ibid., p. 281.

30   Ibid., p. 280.

31   Gluck (1985), p. 283.

32   Ibid., p. 246.

33   Fukuzawa (1973), p. 175. By the 1880s Fukuzawa had changed his views on the importance of the Imperial House to Japan's drive to preserve its national independence, and began to stress its 'unparalleled sacredness' and role in promoting 'habits of virtue and righteousness'. See Craig (1968).

34   In particular later historians have disputed Maruyama's view about the rootedness of the Emperor system in the Meiji period (1868-1912). Gluck

(1985) and Irokawa (1985) have denied the inevitability of ultranationalist ascendency and have emphasized the uncertainty and ambiguity of ideological currents and political trends, especially in the first two decades of the Meiji era.

35   This radical, oppositional movement is discussed in Irokawa (1967). See also Irokawa (1985). In this latter work Irokawa challenges Maruyama's arguments about the weakness and timidity of early Japanese liberalism and the Freedom and Popular Rights Movement (cf. Maruyama 1969), pp. 4-5, 229).

36   Maruyama (1969), p. 264.

37   See Kogawa (1981).

38   Maruyama (1969), p. 264.

39   For an account of the proceedings of the Hakone conference see Hall (1965). For a brief critical account from the Japanese perspective see the Editor's Preface, *Japan Interpreter* (1970), pp. v-vii.

40   I have borrowed this expression from Richard (1993).

41   Otsuka (1970), p. 4.

42   For the strange re-appearance of the language of autonomy refer to Ozawa (1994). This text is discussed briefly below.

43   Fukuyama (1995), claims that there is a rich and dense network of associations in Japanese society which have provided the opportunity for Japanese to develop impersonal relations based on mutual trust, rather than ascriptive ties.

44   See Dunn (1985).

45   Maruyama (1969), p. 146.

46   Ibid., pp. 225-6.

47   Ozawa (1994), p. 12.

48   Ibid., p. 157.

49   Ibid., ch. 4 on reforming the Prime Minister's Official Residence (*kantei*).

50   Hegel (1967), para. 261 (cf. para. 155).

51   This argument is made with great force in Miller (1989), 'the conditions for differentiation and privacy are never secure unless at least some people are willing to assume some public responsibility. A society without public life cannot be one in which individuality can flourish in safety' (p. 17); cf. the more sceptical and cautious arguments of Dunn (1990) for the 'democratization' of political prudence and wisdom within a community to spread the burden of responsible political judgment.

52   Ozawa (1994), chs. 5 and 6.

53   Maruyama (1988).

54   Ibid., p. 36

55   Ibid., p. 39

References

Arendt, H. (1966), *Origins of Totalitarianism*, 3rd edn., Allen and Unwin: London.

Borton, H. (1970), *Japan's Modern Century. From Perry to 1970*, 2nd. edn., Ronald Press: New York.

Cohen, P. (1988), 'The Perversions of Inheritance: Studies in the Making of Multi-racist Britain', in Cohen, P. and Bains, H.S. (eds.), *Multi-racist Britain*, Macmillan: London.

Craig, A. (1968), 'Fukuzawa Yukichi: the Philosophical Foundations of Meiji Nationalism', in Ward, R. (ed.), *Political Development in Modern Japan*, Princeton University Press: Princeton.

Dunn, J. (1985), 'Totalitarian Democracy and the Legacy of Modern Revolutions: Explanation or Indictment?', in *Rethinking Modern Political Theory. Essays 1973-83*, Cambridge University Press: Cambridge.

____ (1990), 'Reconceiving the Content and Character of Modern Political Community', in *Interpreting Political Responsibility*, Polity Press: Cambridge.

Fukuyama, F. (1995), *Trust: the Social Virtues and the Creation of Prosperity*, Hamish Hamilton: London.

Fukuzawa, Y. (1973), *An Outline of a Theory of Civilization*, Sophia University Press: Tokyo. First published 1875.

Fundamentals of the National Polity (Kokutai no hongi) (1958), abridged translation in Tsunoda, R., deBary, W.T. and Keene, D. (eds.), *Sources of Japanese Tradition*, Vol. II, Columbia University Press: Columbia.

Gluck, C. (1985), *Japan's Modern Myths. Ideology in the late Meiji period*, Princeton University Press: Princeton.

Hall, J.W. (1965), 'Changing Conceptions of the Modernization of Japan', in Jansen, M. (ed.), *Changing Japanese Attitudes Towards Modernization*, Princeton University Press: Princeton.

Hampsher-Monk, I. (1992), *A History of Modern Political Thought. Major Political Thinkers from Hobbes to Marx*, Blackwell: Oxford.

Hegel, G. (1956), *The Philosophy of History*, Dover Publications: New York.

____ (1967), *Philosophy of Right*, Oxford University Press: Oxford.

Huntingdon, S. (1992), 'Foreword', in Cheng tun-jen and Haggard, S. (eds.), *Political Change in Taiwan*, Lynne Reinner: Boulder, Co.

Irokawa, D. (1967), 'Freedom and the Concept of People's Rights', *Japan Quarterly*, Vol. 14, No. 2, pp. 175-83.

____ (1985), *The Culture of the Meiji Period*, Princeton University Press: Princeton.

Johnson, C. (1990), 'The People who Invented the Mechanical Nightingale', *Daedalus*, Vol. 119, No. 3, pp. 71-90.

Kogawa, T. (1981), 'Japan as Manipulated Society', *Telos*, No. 49, pp. 140-3.

Koschmann, J.V. (1981-2), 'The Debate on Subjectivity in Postwar Japan.

Foundations of Modernism as a Political Critique', *Pacific Affairs*, Vol. 54, No. 4, pp. 609-31.

_____ (1989), 'Maruyama Masao and the Incomplete Project of Modernity', in Miyoshi and Harootunian.

Maruyama, M. (1964), 'Japanese Thought', *Journal of Social and Political Ideas of Japan*, Vol. 2, pp. 41-8.

_____ (1969), *Thought and Behaviour in Modern Japanese Politics*, Oxford University Press: Oxford.

_____ (1988), 'The Structure of *Matsurigoto* the *basso ostinato* of Japanese Political Life', in Henny, S. and Lehmann, J.P. (eds.), *Themes and Theories of Modern Japanese History. Essays in Memory of Richard Storry*, Athlone: London.

Matsumoto, S. (1966), 'Editor's Introduction', in *Journal of Social and Political Ideas in Japan*, Vol. 4, pp. 2-19.

Miller, D. (1989), *Market, State and Community. Theoretical Foundations of Market Socialism*, Clarendon Press: Oxford.

Miyoshi, M. (1991), *Off Center. Power and Culture Relations Between Japan and the US*, Harvard University Press: Cambridge, Mass.

Miyoshi, M. and Harootunian, H. (eds.)(1989), *Postmodernism and Japan*, Duke University Press: Durham.

Najita, T. (1974), *The Intellectual Foundations of Modern Japanese Politics*, Chicago University Press: Chicago.

Napier, S. (1991), *Escape from the Wasteland. Romanticism and Realism in the Fiction of Mishima Yukio and Oe Kenzaburo*, Harvard University Press: Cambridge, Mass.

Oe, K. (1977), *Teach Us to Outgrow our Madness*, Grove Press: New York.

_____ (1989), 'Japan's Dual Identity: a Writer's Dilemma', in Miyoshi and Harootunian.

Otsuka, H. (1970), 'The Formation of Modern Man: the Popular Base for Democratization', *Japan Interpreter*, Vol. VI, No. 1, pp. 1-8.

Ozawa, I. (1994), *Blueprint for a New Japan. The Rethinking of a Nation*, Kodansha: Tokyo.

Popper, K. (1966), *The Open Society and its Enemies*, Vol. II, 5th edn., Routledge and Kegan Paul: London.

Richard, N. (1993), 'Postmodernism and Periphery', in Doherty, T. (ed.), *Postmodernism: a Reader*, Harvester Press: London.

'Subjectivity and Historical Materialism', (1948), Symposium, *Sekai*, February.

Supreme Commander of the Allied Powers (1970), 'US Initial Post-surrender Policy for Japan' (29 August 1945), in *Political Reorientation of Japan*, Vol. II.

Wilkinson, E. (1983), *Japan versus Europe. A History of Misunderstanding*, Penguin: Harmondsworth.

6 An 'Islamic economics'? problems in the imagined reappropriation of economic life

Charles Tripp

I

Introduction

The concerns of this paper centre on the attempt to devise an 'Islamic economics' as a means of developing a strategy which would transform and strengthen the power of Islamic societies whilst preserving a distinctively Islamic character for the principal forms of economic activity. Two particular fears have preoccupied many of the self-consciously Islamic writers in this regard. The first has been the general fear that economic transactions have their own logic, their own dynamic, even their own ethic, which are capable of creating a world sufficient unto itself, establishing internal criteria of excellence, efficiency and status. Disturbingly for the idea of a distinctively Islamic order, they have the power to attract human beings, inducing them to concentrate exclusively on the concerns of and advantages to be gained in this world, shaping the ways in which they relate both to each other and to God. The concern of many of these writers has therefore been to ensure that all economic transactions are restrained by the ethical system of Islam – to ensure, in other words, that people are continually reminded of their obligations to the divinity and of the relative insignificance of the transactions of this world when compared to the relationship with God in the next.

The more specific fear of these writers has been the part played by the economic power of the capitalist West in reinforcing a trend which elevates the economic above all other concerns. Whether they encountered capitalist ideas and organization, or the Marxist critique of capitalism, there seems to have been general agreement that the alleged materialism of Western power had given a new and dangerous impetus to a force in human nature which the Islamic revelation was specifically designed to keep in check. It was for this reason that many of the writers preoccupied with the seductions of capitalism became engaged in twin endeavours. Firstly, they sought to renew people's awareness of the prescriptions of the *shari'a* which should govern their material lives and their economic transactions in particular. Secondly, they sought ways in which the power of the capitalist economy could be counteracted by a greater power which would simultaneously restore the Islamic identity of their societies and insulate those societies from predatory economic systems seeking to expand through domination of others.

This led them to encounter a number of distinctive problems on two levels. Some are particular to Islamic epistemology and to the Islamic tradition. Others, however, seem to derive from the very imagination of a separate domain of the economy. In other words, it was not simply that the economy as a domain of material life had its own logic, its own dynamic and its own seductions, but that thinking about the economy as a distinct sphere of knowledge, of understanding and of explanation of human behaviour seemed to bring its own rules, reasoning and criteria. By entering into arguments about the economy as a particular realm of human activity, many of these writers appeared to accept – although often with various degrees of unease – that they were entering into a discourse not of their own making. The struggle to 'make it theirs' has been a problematic one.

It is the intention of this paper to examine this struggle in the writings of one man, Muhammad Baqir al-Sadr (1935-1980), focusing in particular on his book *Iqtisaduna (Our Economy,* first published in 1961).[1] The problem as he formulated it, as well as the problems which he encountered in trying to think through his chosen, distinctively Islamic solution, find echoes elsewhere in the writings of other consciously Islamic writers. He is not being taken as a representative of all writers on the 'Islamic economy', nor is it suggested that his writing should be privileged above all others. Nevertheless, he is an interesting and original writer whose influence has been felt in a number of ways. More importantly for the purposes of this paper, his writings exhibit some of the distinctive characteristics and problems of many who have sought to construct an 'Islamic economics' as a viable programme for Muslims, seeking both to preserve their identity and to protect themselves and their values from the many seductions of materially sucessful economic systems not of their own making. He consciously sought, in other words, to reappropriate economic life in the service of an Islamic ideal. In doing so, however, he came face to face with the logic of an economic discourse which, in turn, significantly shaped his methodology and his prescriptions. In both areas, there are many who have either followed him or have come to very similar conclusions on their own. The distinctive writings which this process has engendered presently constitute the ambivalent, troubled discourse of 'Islamic economics'.

The paper will be divided into three parts. The first will concern the understanding of economics as a distinctive discursive realm and the categories of thought, as well as the principles which it imposes on those who would enter into it. Baqir al-Sadr's identification of a distinctively economic realm of thought and of prescription through the examination of much of the literature of the Islamic jurisprudential tradition *(fiqh),* as well as of its basic sources – the Qur'an and the Sunna of the Prophet Muhammad – inexorably draws him into the categories and criteria associated with the discourse of economics itself. This has significant implications both for his methodology and for the substance of his study, inevitably colouring the 'Islamic economics' which results.

The second part will examine one of the particular consequences of this endeavour. With the isolation and identification of a realm of the economy, came a related reformulation of the human environment to which it applied. Intertwined with and, in terms of intellectual pedigree, closely related to the idea of the 'economy' is the idea of 'society'. In terms of an understanding of a distinctively Islamic social realm, this required a rethinking of the nature of the community itself. Hitherto defined as an *umma,* or community of the faithful, an ideological community defined by its members' adherence to a common faith, Muslims were in this context represented as a *mujtama'* or society (lit. grouping of things). This had, in turn, a significant and not easily foreseen – or acknowledged – effect on Baqir al-Sadr's understanding of the identity and interests of that community. In some respects, it changed the nature of the community itself, transforming it into a community of individuals linked by common economic interests, giving substance to the fear that the evocation of economic interests began to create an identity and a dynamic that owed little if anything to any distinctively Islamic tradition.

This gives rise to the third part of the paper which deals with the ways in which Baqir al-Sadr came to examine the individuals who constituted the society which he had imagined, bound together by ties of economic interest and linked through their economic transactions. In common with many later Islamic writers, al-Sadr sought to repair the possibly corrosive effects of the conjuring up of 'homo economicus' on the idea of an Islamic community, by positing instead the ideal construct of the 'homo Islamicus', the basic building block, or imagined cluster of interests at the heart of the 'Islamic economy'. As will be made clear, this also led him into difficulties since he had by that stage taken on board so many of the assumptions and criteria of worth associated with a distinctive form of economic discourse that he sometimes seemed to be suggesting that 'homo economicus' was indeed a natural occurrence, that the qualities attached to this fictional construct did indeed correspond to the reality of a universal human nature. From this perspective, 'homo Islamicus' was to be the ideal form, the ethical mould into which raw human nature was to be squeezed – if necessary by coercive means.

The implications of this conclusion, which also emanate from al-Sadr's understanding of power and of the realistic framework for the establishment of an Islamic economy, are the themes reflected upon in the concluding section. This deals briefly with some of the consequences of al-Sadr's reasoning and the particular difficulties it encountered. In particular, it touches on two prescriptions for the future towards which he was led and on which he was to elaborate in his later writings: the call for the establishment of an 'Islamic bank' (an interest-free bank) and for the institution of an Islamic state as the means whereby an 'Islamic economy', an 'Islamic society' and an 'Islamic individual' could be realised. These seemed to represent for him solutions to the problems of reconciling power and identity or authenticity – problems which became ever sharper in the course of his outlining of the 'Islamic economy' and the logic of the argument and of the categories used as it unfolded.

II

The understanding of economics and of 'Islamic economics'

The emergence of a distinct discourse concerned with the delineation, understanding, explanation and prediction of a sphere of human activity known as economics was associated both with the intellectual trends of the seventeenth and eighteenth century European enlightenment and with the European industrial, capitalist revolution. There are four particular, obviously interconnected aspects of this discourse which, although they do not exhaustively define it, nevertheless could be said to be characteristic of economics as a distinct discursive field. More importantly, in this context, they are aspects of economics with which those wishing to devise an 'Islamic economics' have had perforce to engage – with unforeseen and often problematic results.

Two of the most characteristic features of economics as it has developed since the eighteenth century has been the attention paid to acquisitiveness on the one hand and to commodities as the objects of acquisition on the other. The former constitutes the basis of the assumptions about human nature and the distinctively economic order which form the foundation of this particular sphere of knowledge. In the human drive to acquire material goods a succession of authors claimed to find the basic impulse of mankind, the hedonistic drive of human nature which, in searching for complete fulfilment, would provide the dynamic for a thriving economy.[2]

The antecedents of this notion can, of course, be seen in earlier thought about politics, human society and the individual. Nevertheless, when linked to the acquisition and creation of material wealth it was seen as particularly disturbing by those who had hitherto regarded the acquisitive drive as a corrupting influence, a passion and vice which must be checked if the individual was not to be destroyed morally and the social order disrupted. In the newly emerging sphere of economic thought it was predicated as a fact of nature which was to be the driving force behind a successful economic order. Equally, and not coincidentally, it was increasingly held up as a steadying interest, rather than a disruptive passion. The pursuit of this interest and the creation of the social framework which would allow its successful pursuit were now portrayed as both the highest form of rationality and the secure foundation of a new, transparently rational social order. Some went on to argue that unlimited acquisition would benefit all since it would vastly increase the productive wealth of a society. The effect on the acquisitive individual might be morally deleterious, but this should be set against the great benefit which his actions – the pursuit of his private vices – might achieve for the generality of the society which he inhabited. The theme of private vice producing public good was, of course, one which was developed more systematically in the writings of the classical economists.[3]

The fact that it could be so developed was due to the emphasis placed simultaneously on commodification. It was this imaginative effort to transform all objects – all beings and all qualities – into objects capable of being alienated and acquired which allowed the emergence of the discursive formations of capital and labour which in turn constituted the economic agents at the heart of the imagined economy. If everything could be transformed into a commodity, everything could be quantified and its relative worth precisely calculated. In this way not only was a calculus of the good established, but the definition of rationality was increasingly associated with the capacity to make the kinds of calculation which allowed 'more' to equal 'better'. In some senses, therefore, this was the logical consequence of the elevation of acquisitiveness. Where such a calculus existed, it was patently in the interests of all to work out what their benefit would be and, theoretically, it was also in their capacity to do so.

This gave rise to a third distinctive feature or claim of economic discourse: the claim that the economic sphere has its own quantifiable values, free from moral or aesthetic – or indeed religious – criteria. The economy was argued to be a separable sphere of human activity – for some the epitome of human rationality – which could be measured, calculated, explained and on the basis of which predictions could be made which would measure the relative success of any endeavour by the 'de-moralized' criteria of economic efficiency. Indeed the discursive formations of capital and labour lent themselves to this claim, since they were constructs deriving from this imagined system and, in turn, gave rise to the discursively constructed economic agents who would, it was claimed, act in the 'perfect' conditions of the ideally constructed economic model.[4]

The notion of the imagined model of the economy and the strategies whereby it was divorced from values which might in some way 'interfere' with the perfect rationality of the economic agents, gave rise to the fourth distinctive idea: the notion that the economy could be imagined as a self-operating, independent sphere, crucially separated from the milieu in which it operated, and yet, paradoxically, highly effective within that milieu.[5] This was associated therefore with the idea of economics as above all the science of the technique of acquisition and wealth creation, theoretically transferable and applicable to all societies. Discursively, it had after all created its own universe in which the participants as economic agents were to behave as prescribed since they could do no other, constructs as they were of other discursive formations. Furthermore, it was in such a setting that they could be assumed to act in accordance with their economic interests, divorced in most important respects from other affective dispositions. Where the ideal construction of 'homo economicus' and his perfect rationality was associated with complete commodification and the quantifiability of all things divorced from all other criteria, then clearly the ambient culture and its values were simply irrelevant. And yet, of course, it was not simply an ideal construct, but also one which was seeking to prescribe how real people, living in given historical and cultural settings both would and should conduct their economic relationships.[6]

The power of the systems associated with these understandings of human nature and of social formations was a radical and transformative power that began to colonize and to change economic relations across the globe. In doing so, it inexorably caught up diverse populations and cultures in its momentum, facing them with challenges on two different levels. In the first place, the kinds of behaviour and calculation demanded by the forces of capitalism threw into question the values and identities of non-capitalist societies, whilst at the same time undermining the material, productive bases which had hitherto sustained them. New social formations began to emerge, engendered by capitalism and ostensibly designed to reproduce the system itself. This process may not have been as straightforward as it was once believed to be, both by its advocates and by its critics. Nevertheless, the rewards of the dominant systems of the global economy ensured that many thrived in the new circumstances, giving weight and plausibility to the values by which their success was now to be judged.

Quite apart from the disruption of social orders which these processes entailed, they also represented an intellectual challenge. The introduction of new vocabularies and epistemologies, as well as the power which these forms of knowledge appeared to confer upon those who could master them in their handling of the material and social worlds, suggested new ways of apprehending those worlds. It also suggested a certain urgency for those who wished to match the effectiveness of these systems of power in order to preserve an otherwise vulnerable set of values and of identities. In this way, the political economy of capitalism brought with it terminologies and ideas which were radically to alter the ways in which people saw their own societies and interpreted their own experiences. It also brought in its wake its own critique in the form of Marxist analyses and dissections of capitalism, its underlying processes and its many rationales.

It is in this context that Muhammad Baqir al-Sadr began to reflect upon and to map out his prescriptions for a distinctively 'Islamic economics'. As an Iraqi, but also as a Shi'i cleric, Baqir al-Sadr was responding to the predicament of the Iraqis as Muslims at a time when, in his view, their religious faith, their cultural identities and their spiritual well-being were being threatened by the twin dangers of capitalism and communism. Because of his situation and the circumstances of the time, he tended to see Marxism chiefly as an intellectual danger, whereas he represented capitalism as a material threat which brought in its train its own, inimical rationales and values.

Based in the Iraqi city of Najaf, al-Sadr was well aware of the growing strength in the city of the underground Communist Party of Iraq during the 1950s. Quite apart from the other appeals which the communist party had for young Iraqis during this period, its message contained a distinct element of anti-clericalism, as well as a forceful advocacy of modernism. This made the party and its critique of society and ideology an attractive organization for those educated Iraqis who had long resented the influence of highly conservative Shi'i clerics in such seats of learning as the seminaries of Najaf. The fact that the party was vigorously suppressed by the security forces of the Hashemite regime in Iraq weakened it as a political organization, but did nothing to dim the lustre of its critical, subversive and modernist message.[7] As a Shi'i cleric, al-Sadr responded to the threat as he saw it, by publishing his views on Marxism, his considered rejection of historical materialism and his advocacy of a distinct Islamic alternative that he believed would provide a more valid path out of Iraq's 'backward' predicament.[8]

This intellectual riposte took shape first in his book *Falsafatuna* (*Our Philosophy*, written in 1959). The subtitle of the book made its purpose clear: 'An objective study in the present ideational battle between different philosophical tendencies and in particular between Islamic philosophy and dialectical materialism (Marxism)'.[9] The revolution in Iraq in 1958 which brought to power a junta dominated by Colonel Abd al-Karim Qasim was seen by many within Iraq and beyond to favour the Communist Party of Iraq which was now permitted to organize openly and to publish. Although the relationship between Qasim and the Communist Party was a complex one which kept it some distance from effective power, this did not diminish the perception by many that the Communist Party was on the verge of taking over the country. For such people it became doubly urgent to counter the 'communist threat'.

It is against this background that al-Sadr wrote and published his book *Iqtisaduna* (*Our Economy*) in 1961. Again, the subtitle captures the intention of the work: 'An objective study comprising a critique of and research into the ideational foundations and the particulars of the economic doctrines of Marxism, Capitalism and Islam'.[10] The book opens with a section entitled 'With Marxism' which takes up 198 of its 700 or so pages. A second, much shorter section of only 40 pages is entitled 'With Capitalism' and the remaining 462 pages are devoted to a detailed examination of the 'Islamic economy'. The brief, but critical section on capitalism seems to have been inserted primarily as an answer to those who accused all critics of Marxism of being necessarily in favour of a capitalist alternative. However, it is in the extensive section on the 'Islamic economy' that al-Sadr fully develops his critique of capitalism, by repeatedly holding it up as the antithesis of that which an Islamic economy is seeking to achieve in terms of a social and ethical order. In doing so, he reinforces the notion that, for him Marxism was chiefly an intellectual danger, threatening to turn Muslims away from the path laid down by the *shari'a* and interpreted by the clerics. Capitalism, on the other hand, he seems to see as a powerful material force which can also succeed in turning people away from the fulfilment of their obligations as Muslims by virtue of its plausibility, effectiveness and seduction as a wealth creating system.

It was his understanding of the nature of these threats which led him to believe that there was an urgent need for the formulation, or, as he was to put it, the 'discovery' of an Islamic economics.[11] It was a need which was imposed externally, in the sense that the transformations of the world in the nineteenth and twentieth centuries had inexorably impinged upon the Islamic world. However, it was also in his opinion a need born of the gaps in the *fiqh*. These gaps created areas where, in the absence of any specifically Islamic guidance, the power of the material culture of capitalism, or the intellectual attractions of Marxism threatened to insert themselves.[12] As was the case with many of the consciously Islamic writers of those years, whether from the clerical elite or not, he was responding to an expressed or implied reproach about the silence of the Islamic authorities on pressing questions of the day, most notably political and economic questions arising from the predicament of Iraqi society.

At the outset of his work, al-Sadr is insistent on seeking to differentiate between 'economics' as a science and 'economics' as an ideological doctrine. The former he acknowledges is a discipline of relatively recent vintage, emerging simultaneously with the emergence of capitalism and aimed at understanding the processes by which capitalism works. The science of the economy, as he puts it, takes as given the ambient society and simply tries to explain it, to generalize from the particular, to formulate general rules which help both to explain causality and which have predictive power. In other words, he appears to be saying that economics, in this meaning of the term, can be a neutral instrument for the analysis of economic behaviour in whatever society or cultural setting it is used.[13] However, in his references to the relationship between the emergence of capitalism and the emergence of a science of economics a certain ambiguity about its neutral, 'scientific' status creeps in – an ambiguity which is to become more marked as his exposition proceeds.

Interestingly, he is not unaware of the power of economics as a discourse, since he is insistent on claiming that 'Islamic economics' is not a science so much as a doctrine or an ideological orientation in economics. In this manner, he hopes to keep the two spheres quite separate. (He reverts to this theme later in his study, when discussing some of the methodological pitfalls of the whole endeavour, but from which he himself cannot easily escape.) Thus, his understanding of 'Islamic economics' is the economic doctrine of Islam, the prescriptions of Islam on how to conduct a full economic life within the framework of an Islamic system, based on the ethical ideas of Islam. It would seem therefore that from the very outset he is conscious of the need for demarcation. He is, after all, delineating a discursive field which is to be distinctively and identifiably Islamic with the express purpose of preventing the kind of erosion of Islamic identities and values which he believes has occurred throughout the Islamic world as a result of the overwhelming power, easy seductions and thoughtless adoption of economic doctrines founded on beliefs and ideas quite distinct from those of the Islamic tradition.

However, despite his intention of keeping the two understandings and thus the two fields of economics separate, Baqir al-Sadr runs into a number of problems which are to have an impact on his identification of a field of distinctively 'Islamic economics' in a number of ways. Firstly, it is not long before he claims that all 'economics', whatever its scientific claims, has an ideology or philosophy at its back, a set of fundamental assumptions about human nature, about how the world should operate as much as about how it does operate. This would conform with his earlier assertion that the discourse of economics emerged simultaneously with and connected to the emergence of capitalism, but would seem to dilute his assertion that there is a clear distinction to be made between the 'science' of economics and economic 'doctrine'. As a consequence, it becomes harder for him to maintain the boundaries between 'economics' as he has understood it to have developed in relation to capitalism and 'Islamic economics' as separate discursive fields.[14]

Similarly, and relatedly, in demarcating a field as that of 'economics', even if qualified by the epithet 'Islamic', in order to give it its own identity and to maintain its separation from non-Islamic forms of knowledge, he is obliged to some degree to conform to the criteria established through the discourse of economics more generally as to what counts as an activity within that field. As soon as a particular area of social life is identified in this way, it would seem difficult – perhaps impossible – to avoid accepting some of the dominant criteria of that field, as defined by others. By accepting criteria of significance, of what counts and what does not, there is the strong possibility that a certain elision into the value system will take place, however adamantly al-Sadr insists on the ethical distinctiveness of 'Islamic economics'. Indeed, his insistence that 'economics' is in some senses a value-neutral science of 'how things work' would seem to prepare the ground for a certain ambivalence in this sphere.

This manifests itself in a number of ways in his writings. The first is visible relatively early on and takes on a 'developmentalist' coloration. One of his reasons for elaborating a distinctively 'Islamic economics' is, he claims, that economic programmes and development plans devised in other cultural settings and for other societies will not be appropriate if applied to a society whose fundamental values differ from those from which the economic programme and ideas of development derive. Thus, programmes of economic development, he argues, formulated in the West or indeed in the Communist world will not succeed unless they are in harmony with the values and culture of the *umma* - the Islamic community. This has a certain sociological sense to it and could be said to foreshadow debates about culturally appropriate growth strategies.[15]

However, the significance of this claimed need, as outlined by al-Sadr, is that it has already moved away from the ethical imperative which he originally claimed as the driving reason for the formulation of a distinctively Islamic economics. On the contrary, what he seems to be doing now is justifying the devising of a development strategy that will be effective in Islamic societies. Significantly, the target of such a strategy and the measure of its effectiveness is defined by him as the elimination of the 'backwardness' of Islamic societies. The comparison is, of course, with the 'advanced' societies of the industrialized world and the criteria would appear to be wholly material. It is apparent that his understanding of a distinctively economic arena has been heavily influenced by the dominant discourse of economics and his notion of 'development' follows closely the patterns of economic development suggested by the historical trajectory of the countries of the industrialized West.

Upon reflection, al-Sadr seems to have become aware of this difficulty and, having made this claim about the nature of 'backwardness', he seeks to recapture the ethical impulse of development for the Islamic system of values. He therefore makes an empirical claim about the developmental project – namely that 'there is no framework, other than the framework of the economic system of Islam, in which solutions to the problems of economic backwardness can be found'.[16] It is evident, however, that this 'recapture' will not be straightforward since, quite apart from the validity of the claim, two different kinds of order and objective are being invoked here.

In this section he seemed to be merely making a claim about what will be effective (although the question remains about the nature of the intended achievement that is to be the goal of 'development'). Nevertheless, he is rapidly drawn into making larger claims about the benefits of a distinctively 'Islamic economics'. Matching, or perhaps following mainstream economic arguments, these claims take on a markedly universal character. In doing so, al-Sadr appears to be making an explicit comparison between 'Islamic economics' and 'economics' on terrain defined by the latter. He does not simply make a case for the ethical superiority of an Islamic economic doctrine, but asserts that the 'Islamic economy' is superior to all other economic systems in two important ways.

In the first place, he argues that the Islamic economy provides a better and empirically more valid set of precepts for the organization of economic life because it is based on a more accurate understanding of human nature.[17] He is intending thereby to assert that the distinctively Islamic economic programme is a superior instrument for the organization of the economic life of society. Ironically, however, he runs the risk of compromising the distinctiveness of the Islamic economy, since his claim about its superiority is based not on some quality that is peculiarly Islamic, but rather on the universal category of 'human nature'. Empirically, his claim is hypothetically verifiable. In this sense, therefore, he has opened the field up to the possibility of refutation. Furthermore, his formulation of the argument bears a strong resemblance to those of the classical economists. They too tended to base the defence of their own economic models and prescriptions on the claim that these were superior to all others because they were founded on a true understanding of 'human nature'. In many ways, this similarity, even convergence of views seems to be a logical consequence of al-Sadr's earlier ambiguity about the claims of Islamic economics. It suggests that as soon as a distinctive field or discourse of economics is identified, it obliges those who enter into it to use the categories – even the criteria – associated with its own discursive logic.

Al-Sadr is tempted by this logic to go further. He makes a related set of claims about the capacity of an Islamic economy to provide a model that is more stable and less prone to wild fluctuations than any capitalist economy. Consequently, he argues, it would be demonstrably more efficient, according to the criteria established by capitalist economics itself.[18] Once again, he has made a claim that can be empirically verified and which equates the 'Islamic economy' with the capitalist economy in a number of important ways. Most significantly, he has made an explicit comparison between them, in order to assert the superiority of the Islamic variant, but in doing so he has suggested that they are competing on the same terrain. The problem here for the original intention behind his argument is that this terrain was not marked out by al-Sadr or by a distinctively Islamic tradition. On the contrary, it is defined by the dominant discourse of the discipline of economics as it emerged in the West. It is against this that he is seeking to assert the singularity and superiority of the Islamic economy. Regardless of the theoretically possible quantifiable comparisons that may not necessarily favour the Islamic alternative, this argumentative strategy runs the danger once again of dissolving the specificity of 'Islamic economics'.

If it is to compete on the same ground as capitalism and if it is to be judged by the same criteria as those which are applied to measure the success and efficiency of capitalist economies, then its role as the protector and reinforcer of a distinctively Islamic ethos and identity would seem to dissolve. Once again, thinking about economics appears to have led to the inexorable assertion of the ostensibly quantitative concerns of economic discourse. This would seem to suggest that in imagining economics as a distinct sphere, whether as 'science' or 'ideology', al-Sadr has been obliged to think in the existing categories of the discipline. Furthermore, it clearly brings with it two further categories which are associated with – some would say built into – the discursive formations of economics: the imagination of 'society' and the imagination of the individual. In both of these areas al-Sadr's attempts to imagine a distinctively Islamic equivalent – the *umma* and 'homo islamicus', respectively – are complicated and possibly fatally flawed by the new forms of imagining that are associated with the economic discourse.

III

Imagining society and community

In common with many other Islamic thinkers and writers of the twentieth century,

Muhammad Baqir al-Sadr was obliged to think of his community and its identity in new ways. Most important, in the context of this paper, was the transition from thinking about the *umma*, the community of the Islamic faithful, defined by its members' adherence to a common faith, to thinking about it as a *mujtama'*, a grouping of individual things or people. Given the history of the Islamic world, the notion of the *umma* had always been a fictional or imaginative construct, based on the assumed existence of ideological consensus and shared interests, belied in reality by the schisms and real differences which had separated one group of Muslims from others. Nevertheless, it was a powerful imaginative construct in the political, jurisprudential and philosophical discourses of the Islamic world. Indeed, al-Sadr's work and the whole edifice of 'Islamic economics' is testimony to the enduring power of this construct, since the enterprise is justified on the grounds that the *umma* has a special, distinctive character and moral system which demands an appropriate economic system to allow it to preserve its Islamic character and thus stay true to its Islamic mission.

However, as the previous section indicated, the same logic which began to apply when an 'economy' was identified and singled out as a distinct zone of human conduct began to affect and to transform understandings of the society associated with it. Al-Sadr's notion of development and of the Islamic economy that will be its most effective vehicle implies a certain understanding of the society that is to be the target of development. On one level, there can be no doubt that al-Sadr believed that the principal objective should be the construction of an ideal Islamic society, the *umma* revived and re-invigorated. However, the more he suggests that the principal means of reviving the *umma* is by the adoption of economic programmes intended to match and to counter the capitalist model of development on its own terms, the more questions arise concerning the nature of the society that will result from this process. The suspicion is that, in place of the desired distinctively Islamic society, a society will emerge shaped by the dominant paradigms of capitalism and geared, therefore, to the reproduction of a society more easily recognizable as capitalist than as Islamic.

Al-Sadr remains ambiguous on this point: not wishing to lose the distinctiveness – and moral superiority – of the *umma*, he nevertheless wishes it to thrive in the world under conditions which may erode that distinctiveness. At the very outset, his ambiguity is well captured in the following assertion: 'the feelings of the *umma* are that Islam is an expression of itself, the marker of its historical personality, the key to its former glories and is considered to be highly effective in winning the struggle against backwardness and in the furthering of development'.[19] In order to overcome, imaginatively, the possible divergence between the goal of retaining a distinctively Islamic identity and the development of economic programmes aimed at removing the causes of backwardness (in comparison with advanced capitalist economies), al-Sadr asserts that conscientious adherence to Islam will itself be a factor in the bringing about of these substantive material improvements. As his account progresses, it becomes clear that the logic of the introduction of the notion of society and the developmentalist paradigm means that a distinctively Islamic outcome can only be ensured within a very particular framework – that of an Islamic state.

In other respects, 'Islamic society' begins to look like any society. Indeed, it is not long before al-Sadr changes from talking about the problems specific to the *umma* to discussing problems common to 'Islamic society' (*al-mujtama' al-islami*). In reflecting upon this phenomenon he is tempted to single out those aspects of 'society' which all human societies have in common, seeking to understand what binds them together and what kinds of needs emanate from them. In doing so, of course, he is brought ever more closely into thinking about the members of the society, their characteristics and their needs. In the course of this speculation, the idea of the *umma* seems to recede, giving way to a general designation of 'human society' on the one hand, and to the more particular designation of a society made up of individuals given spatial definition, on the other.[20]

Unsurprisingly, this is associated in his writings with the increasingly universal categories and naturalistic reasoning (ie, human nature everywhere is much the same, human societies thus have similar things in common wherever they are etc.) which come to characterize his analysis of the character of economic relations. This, in turn, is associated with a functionalist view of society, marked by recourse to an organicist analogy. Rather than a community of the faithful, a picture emerges of society as a general, human category, constituted by individuals linked to one another in a multitude of ways, of which a common set of religious beliefs or a common moral code may simply be two ways among many. In the context of a discussion of their members' economic well-being, the suspicion emerges that such links might indeed be less relevant than those of material self-interest and self-definition. Given al-Sadr's preoccupations, this cannot be stated outright, but it becomes apparent in the logic of his reasoning. He is seemingly aware of some of the erosion of a distinctively Islamic logic that appears to be taking place since he tries from time to time to return to the binding nature of the Islamic imperative that will lend to the discussion its distinctiveness. Nevertheless, it is frequently a thinned out imperative, rather external to the debate and requiring increasingly some kind of powerful outside intervention to prevent the logic or dynamic of society thus conceived from developing on its own, free from specifically Islamic restraints.

In two areas this becomes particularly evident. The first lies in his understanding of the nature of social solidarity.[21] According to him this is something which all human societies aspire to, a fundamental feature of social cohesion without which life in society would be impossible and social order would disintegrate into the competition of atomized individuals. In his view, this can only be satisfactorily achieved – to meet this universal human need – in the context of an Islamic society, built upon an Islamic economy. Only then, he argues, will the ideals of social balance and social justice be fully realised since it is his contention that only Islamic prescriptions can bring this about in a way which he suggests is not simply pleasing to God, but which meets fully the universal human need for such justice. This social balance, as he calls it, eschews the ruthless competition of capitalism and gives each member of society a proper understanding of their social obligations.

The difficulty encountered by his argument, however, lies in the fact that in making a theoretically verifiable claim about the processes and needs of human society universally he is relegating the 'Islamic solution' to one among many designed as the solution to a problem of a largely secular nature. From this perspective, the Islamic programme for the construction of social solidarity, just as for a dynamic and efficient economy, can be judged by criteria which put it on a par with all other forms of social organization. Theoretically, it will be possible to verify empirically whether or not the 'Islamic economy' performs this universal function. Once again, therefore, the specificity of Islam has been eroded since it is being viewed from the perspective of the functioning of human 'society', as just another device among many. Ironically, by concentrating on the problems of 'society' al-Sadr seems to have done that which he accuses 'Western man' of doing: fixing his eyes on the mundane, rather than the otherworldly.[22] Indeed, this would seem to be the logical outcome of imagining the mundane concept of 'human society', allied to and part of the same logic associated with the imagination of the 'economy'.

The second area where this logic seems to shape his discussion and his construction of an Islamic economy in relation to the society of Muslims, lies in the use he makes of the equally universal notion of 'social welfare'. His writings here indicate that he intends by this not simply the welfare of a distinctively Islamic society, but that of a society made up of individuals who share a set of broadly similar needs by virtue of their common humanity. In connection with his outlining of a distinctive 'Islamic economic doctrine', he makes the point that some kinds of behaviour may be regarded as 'harmful to society' in certain epochs, but may be regarded with equanimity in others. Two features are striking about this discussion. In the first place, he seems to be arguing that economic arrangements should be judged to be desirable insofar as they contribute to the sum of 'social welfare', defined in humanist, rather than specifically Islamic terms. Secondly, he appears to suggest a degree of historical relativism in the determination of values. On the face of it, this is a surprising suggestion for an Islamic cleric to make.[23]

The importance of this line of argument is that it appears to elevate 'society' and 'social needs' above all else, making them the arbiter of that which is desirable and the ultimate justification for the adoption of any particular set of economic arrangements. In a secular context this might be unremarkable, even if controversy would be bound to rage about how to determine the nature of 'social needs'. In a self-consciously Islamic context in which the case is being made for a distinctively Islamic programme, the logic of this argument holds considerable dangers. Principally, the idea that the economy should be based on 'social needs' and that these should be equated with the idea of 'social welfare' (a mixture of social justice and a certain level of material well-being), tends to overshadow the specifically Islamic character of the arrangements. Under the terms of this argument it is theoretically conceivable that the Islamic features of the economy might have to give way before more pressing demands for greater social utility. It becomes apparent to al-Sadr, as to others, that the logic of society and the economy, a logic of secular colour at the very least, must be restrained. The Islamic character of the enterprise must be reasserted. One way in which he seeks to do so is through the imagination of the individual at the centre of 'society' and 'economy' as somehow inalienably 'Muslim'. Given the fact that this individual is equally a construct of the imagined economy and its associated society, it is not surprising that this endeavour also runs into certain conceptual and practical difficulties.

IV

Imagining the individual

To imagine society is also to imagine the individuals who are taken to constitute the members of that society. For al-Sadr, the *umma* was by definition composed of Muslim believers since their common adherence to the principles of Islamic belief was that which distinguished them from all others and made of them a specific community. The picture became slightly hazier when he moved on to think about society. In this, the individuals had a rather different identity. They may be Muslims, but that would be only one identity among many and, for the purposes of economic or even sociological analysis, these other identities, constituted of common interests, seemed to be of greater importance. These, after all, were to be the interests which determined the nature of social need, which gave rise to the demands for social justice and which formed the ultimate dynamic of the development of the economy. In other words, the individuals constructed from the imagined economy and society seemed to have nothing distinctively Islamic about them. If they did, it would only be contingent and might merely be one element among many in the constitution of their identities.

As an antidote to these tendencies and as a control mechanism for the society and the economy, al-Sadr developed the idea of the distinctively 'Islamic individual' – or the 'Islamic personality' (*al-shakhsiyya al-islamiyya*).[24] This is the 'homo Islamicus' on which the theory and the practice of the Islamic economy is to be based. Such individuals, through their understanding of and adherence to the rules of the *shari'a* have a key role to play in rescuing and maintaining the distinctively Islamic character of the society and the economy. If society is made up of such individuals, then 'social needs' and the demands of 'social welfare' cannot, by definition, contradict or overrule the requirements of Islamic obligation. Equally, an economy founded on the transactions of such individuals and the expression of their wants can become neither an instrument for unlimited acquisition or competition, nor the vehicle for social injustice. The 'Islamic personality' thereby becomes an ideal construct which will ensure the distinctively Islamic character of the economy and of the social order which that economy will develop. It is an internalization or an inner projection onto the abstracted individual of that order, its values and its characteristics. This makes it clear that it is a fictive device, the main characteristics of which derive from the discourse of Islamic jurisprudence and from the emerging discourse of 'Islamic economics'.

The problems arise in the uses al-Sadr makes of the concept. He occasionally suggests that, far from being a fictive construct, the 'Islamic personality' sums up the essence of what it is to be a Muslim in reality. He uses it to claim that these are the characteristics which make Muslims different from all other people.[25] Whilst trying to preserve something of the specificity of an Islamic identity, he goes on to claim that Muslims will always be protected by their faith and by the principles that constitute that faith from succumbing to the forces of capitalism, communism or Western influence in general. Yet his claim is belied by the very purpose and thrust of his writings. If Muslims had no doubts about the correct way of behaving, whatever the circumstances, then neither the material temptations of capitalism, nor the intellectual seductions of Marxism could shake their faith or their identity. Nor could the power of these systems prevent their transactions from being unfailingly Islamic. In such circumstances, the need for an 'Islamic economics', as delineated by al-Sadr, would be largely redundant. In fact, the notion of the 'Islamic personality' is an ideal construct, intended to serve as the basic building block of an imagined Islamic economic order and as an argumentative device to allow the reconciling of apparently contrary currents. As such, it was bound to reflect the principles underpinning that order and the preoccupations and priorities of al-Sadr. However, it cannot also serve as a sociological category with any real purchase upon the empirically verifiable world. In such a guise, it is too easy to refute.

However, al-Sadr suggests in other parts of his writings that, far from being a description of an actual social phenomenon, the 'Islamic personality' that is to be the cornerstone of the 'Islamic economy' is a model of ethical probity towards which all individuals must aspire. Its contours are being sketched out by al-Sadr to provide a model of Islamic identity and rectitude after which others can pattern their behaviour. Only once this is the case on a sufficiently large scale, it is suggested, can the prescriptions of an Islamic economic doctrine hope to be implemented.[26] In other words, if the basic building block of the Islamic economy is the Islamic personality, the most important task is the development of that personality. Indeed, this appears to be more in line with al-Sadr's concern about the ways in which the forces besetting Muslims in the twentieth century are undermining their identities and injuring their sensibilities. If the latter were really immune to erosion by the many seductions of materially successful, if morally reprehensible economic systems, then there would be few grounds for concern. However, these were the very fears which impelled al-Sadr to outline both the conditions in which the Islamic personality could be developed and the contours of the Islamic economy which was to be the outcome and framework of its development.

It is in these contexts that the question of the status of the self-interested individual arises. At the outset of his book al-Sadr tends to suggest that 'economics' is effective within the capitalist West because this was the culture from which it sprang and it therefore represents an accurate description and analysis of the self-interested individuals of capitalism. This comes simultaneously with his assertion concerning the immunity of the – ideally constructed – Islamic personality. However, as he proceeds and this construct becomes more obviously the ideal towards which people should aspire, rather than a description of an already existing reality, a question arises concerning the precise nature of the individual who occupies the central place in the present scheme of the economy. It is here that the imagining of the 'economy' and of the 'society' have indeed produced something which looks like a category of universal validity in the self-interested, calculating and rational individual.

Having decried the portrayal of 'homo economicus' as thin and culturally determined, al-Sadr seems to be accepting that it does indeed constitute some kind of universal archetype. In fact, the ideal of the Islamic personality is supposed to be aimed at imposing eventually internalized restraints upon precisely such a dangerously self-centred character. Successful economic systems, al-Sadr suggests, do speak to something ineradicable in human nature. They develop these traits, reward them and encourage them to be the economic agents reproducing their respective economic systems. Reverting to his understanding of 'economics' as a science, he seems to be accepting the picture of the individual assumed to lie at its heart as a fair representation of reality – a reality without moral restraint. This is to be the function of Islam: to introduce restraints on the hedonistic individual. Only then can an orderly society and an 'Islamic economy' be instituted.

It is noteworthy that al-Sadr appears to accept the construct of the individual associated with 'economics' and 'society' as he has apprehended them. This could be said to be the final piece of the logic of imagining the economy working its way through his thought about society, economy and the individual. Although he clearly does not approve morally of the picture of the individual with which he is faced, he nevertheless appears to accept the criteria of rationality associated with this discursive construct. There is little to choose between his portrayal of the rational, calculating, hedonistic individual and that depicted so regularly by economists and utilitarians. As far as he is concerned, this is to be the target of specifically Islamic reform. However, the kind of reform which he has in mind suggests that it will be based primarily on unmistakably utilitarian criteria of interest and benefit calculation. In order to divert individuals from thinking only of their immediate gratification and to set their mind on higher things, obliging them to act more justly and considerately of

171

others in this world, the time-frame of the utilitarian calculus must be extended to eternity.

In other words, al-Sadr seems to accept both the construction of the individual associated with the imagination of 'society' and 'economy' and appears also to accept the notion of the utilitarian criteria of rationality. However, in order to give the whole a distinctively Islamic character, he brings in the idea of an 'Islamic calculus'. This retains the utilitarian idea of the calculation of pain and pleasure as the basis for moral action, but extends it beyond this world to the next. This means that an individual must take into account the consequences of his or her actions not simply in this world, but also in the hereafter, where God's punishment or his reward must be factored into the equation. It is through this longer term calculation that al-Sadr claims the 'social problem' can be solved.[27] He defines this problem as that of trying to ensure that people reach a proper balance between their own self-interest and the interests of society. In the absence of such a balance, the 'social problem' will remain, bringing with it the attendant ills of social disorder and instability. It is ironic, but perhaps significant that this section of his argument should end with the restatement of a recurring issue in Western political philosophy: the tension between the claims of the individual and the claims of society. Al-Sadr places an Islamic gloss on the argument, in the sense of bringing in a distinctively Islamic interpretation of the divine will which the individual should use to guide his or her actions. However, this cannot disguise the centrality of the relationship between the constructs of 'individual' and 'society' that owe little or nothing to any specifically Islamic tradition.

V

Conclusions: the need for an Islamic state and for Islamic banks

Al-Sadr was increasingly drawn into an argument, the premises of which owed more to an already imagined economy and society, deriving from Western, liberal thought than from any distinctively Islamic tradition. Nevertheless, his concern was to ensure that the revival of the *umma* should be on the basis of a social organization and of cultural particularities 'which are not related in origin to the countries of the colonialists'.[28]   Given the problem he faces of trying to derive such a solution within the discourse of economics itself, he sought to develop two strategies, or strategic exits, in order to meet this difficulty. In *Iqtisaduna*, this manifests itself principally in the role he assigns to the Islamic state, or to the ruler, *wali al-amr*.[29] In terms of interpretative authority, legislative authority and finally in terms of ensuring that both the conditions for the nurturing of 'homo Islamicus' and for the subsequent proper functioning of the Islamic economy exist, he makes clear that the final repository of power is to be the state.

In this way, he possibly hoped to escape from the secular, universal logic of his arguments about the economy and society, using the imagined construct of the Islamic state as the final guarantor of the authentically Islamic nature of the economy. It was to be the duty of the ruler of the Islamic state to ensure both that the framework of economic activity was in accord with the spirit and letter of the *shari'a* and that the individual members of the associated society would keep God's commands at the forefront of their minds in all their calculations of material advantage. If necessary, the ruler was to use coercive force to ensure that individuals bore in mind the primacy of the Islamic ethic in all their transactions.

In fact, as his writing on the state here and in subsequent works was to indicate, this was not such a straightforward escape as he had perhaps imagined. He built into the calculations which the ruler should take into account in constructing his Islamic society or economy, criteria and principles which could be said to compromise the whole enterprise since they incorporated notions of 'social welfare' and 'social justice' which were intended to fill in the many 'gaps' of existing Islamic jurisprudence. By urging the ruler both to interpret Islamic obligations and to 'develop' his society along lines suggested by the dominant discourse of Western political economy, al-Sadr could be said to have significantly diluted the distinctively 'Islamic' character of this supposed ultimate guarantor of the state's authentically Islamic identity and economy.

Al-Sadr proposed a second, more modestly framed and individually oriented solution to the question of how to preserve a distinctive Islamic identity whilst at the same time taking part meaningfully and effectively in economic life. This took the form of the proposed 'Islamic bank', an idea elaborated by al-Sadr in his later writings, specifically in his book *Al-bank al-la-ribawi fi al-Islam* (*The Interest Free Bank in Islam*).[30] The intention of such a bank was to create a space for the economic transactions of individuals which would be strictly governed by the rules of the Islamic *shari'a*. In this way the individual would be able to ensure that his or her economic or financial life could be conducted effectively, but without fear that it would in some way compromise his or her Islamic identity or desire to conform with the rules of proper Islamic conduct.

The pragmatic advantage of such a scheme lay in the fact that it was not dependent upon the successful completion of the much more ambitious, but uncertain enterprise of the creation of an Islamic state or an Islamic economy. The emphasis on individual salvation is, of course, quite different in scale to the grander designs for the reform of economy and society. Nevertheless, as al-Sadr makes clear in *Iqtisaduna*, the foundation of the Islamic economy must be the individual Muslim, in his or her capacity as both a moral and an economic agent. He had hoped that the Islamic state or ruler would create these agents by the deployment of moral exhortation and the exercise of sanctions of one kind or another. Whilst waiting for this to happen, the Islamic bank was intended to help in the formation of the 'Islamic personality'. Ideally, individuals shaped in this way would be drawn towards properly Islamic economic behaviour and would, through the sum of their individual transactions, create the basis for an Islamic economy. It was to be a case of private virtue leading to public virtue.

Nevertheless, al-Sadr was fully aware of the fact that the Islamic bank, in order to survive as a financial institution, would be obliged to offer more than simply an opportunity to act virtuously. It would have to appeal to certain material interests, since it was intended to be a profitable institution, as well as a voluntary one – at least until the formation of an Islamic state. Al-Sadr was not unaware, however, of the pitfalls inherent in seeking to ensure that an apparently Islamic institution should serve a purpose that was not specifically Islamic. The danger was two-fold. In the first place, it was possible that the logic of efficiency, be it in the acquisition of political power or the achievement of economic success, would gradually displace the Islamic ethical imperative.

Secondly, in order to justify such a proceeding he realised that people might be tempted to adapt the authoritative Islamic text (*nass*) of the Qur'an or the Hadith to the dominant worldly reality, weakening their resolve to change that reality in accordance with the commands specified in the text. This, he believed, was already visible in the way in which Muslims had already begun to select or to ignore specific textual injunctions in accordance with the spirit of the times or according to purposes that were not specifically Islamic.[31] In the light of the arguments advanced in this paper, it seems clear that al-Sadr himself could not escape from this trap, insofar as his particular purpose involved him in forms of argumentation suggested by his subject, rather than by some unchanging Islamic 'tradition'. As far as the problems of Islamic banking are concerned, the experiences of the past few decades have tended to confirm al-Sadr's suspicions. Specifically Islamic obligations have been correctly observed for the most part, but their interpretation has tended to be governed by considerations of financial success in a capital market dominated by non-Islamic institutions.[32]

In seeking to imagine an 'Islamic economics', Baqir al-Sadr was trying both to protect a distinctive Islamic identity and the set of values associated with it, as well as to attach power to the project through the imagination of successful economic systems which would both deliver the material goods and conform with the values which gave Islamic identity its particularity and worth. The problem he faced derived from the fact that in imagining an economic system – even an 'Islamic' one – he appeared to be obliged to rely increasingly on the already imagined domain of economics as it had developed independently of any distinctively Islamic criteria or sensibilities. Imagining the economy as a distinct sphere of human activity, brought with it categories of thought (such as 'society' and the 'individual'), as well as a logic and criteria of worth which had a significant and troubling effect on the imagined goal of economic activity, if that was to be the preservation or restoration of a distinctively Islamic order.

Notes

1	The edition used for references throughout this paper is that published by the Dar al-Kitab al-Lubnani, in Beirut, 1982.
2	Hunt (1990), pp. 40-7.
3	Myers (1983), pp. 57-60.
4	Tribe (1978), p. 145.
5	Heilbronner (1985), pp. 53-69.
6	Macfarlane (1987), pp. 223-4.
7	Batatu (1978), pp. 465-82, 752-4.
8	Mallat (1993), pp. 7-14.
9	al-Sadr (1982b).
10	al-Sadr (1982a).
11	Ibid., pp. 346-9.
12	Ibid., pp. 356-8.
13	Ibid., pp. 6-7.
14	Ibid., pp. 290-4, 335-41.
15	Ibid., pp. *dal* & *ha*. [In the 1982 edition, the pages of the Preface to the 2nd edition are designated not by numbers, but by the letters of the Arabic alphabet.]
16	Ibid., pp. *alif* & *ba*.
17	Ibid., pp. 264-8.
18	Ibid., p. 293.
19	Ibid., p. *ta*.
20	Ibid., pp. 629-37.
21	Ibid., pp. 638-42.
22	Ibid., pp. *mim, nun* & *sad*.
23	Ibid., pp. 260-4.
24	Ibid., p. 260.
25	Ibid., pp. *nun* & *sad*.
26	Ibid., pp. 652-8.
27	Ibid., pp. 281-9.
28	Ibid., p. *ta*.
29	Ibid., pp. 628-37.
30	al-Sadr (1970).
31	al-Sadr (1982a), pp. 358-60.
32	Nomani and Rahnema (1994) pp. 162-86; see also Beaugé (1990).

References

al-Sadr, Muhammad Baqir (1970), *Al-bank al-la-ribawi fi al-Islam,* Jami' al-Naqi: Kuwait.
____ (1982a), *Iqtisaduna,* Dar al-Kitab al-Lubnani: Beirut.
____ (1982b), *Falsafatuna,* Dar al-Ta'araf li-l-Matbu'at: Beirut.
Batatu, H. (1978), *The Old Social Classes and the Revolutionary Movements of Iraq,* Princeton University Press: Princeton.
Beaugé, G. (ed.)(1990), *Les Capitaux de l'Islam,* Presses du CNRS: Paris.
Heilbronner, R.L. (1985), *The Nature and Logic of Capitalism,* W.W. Norton & Co.: New York.
Hunt, E.K. (1990), *Property and Prophets - the evolution of economic institutions and ideologies,* Harper and Row: New York.
Macfarlane, A. (1987), *The Culture of Capitalism,* Basil Blackwell: Oxford.
Mallat, C. (1993), *The Renewal of Islamic Law - Muhammad Baqer as-Sadr, Najaf and the Shi'i international,* Cambridge University Press: Cambridge.
Myers, M.L. (1983), *The Soul of Modern Economic Man,* University of Chicago Press: Chicago.
Nomani, F. and Rahnema, A. (1994), *Islamic Economic Systems,* Zed Press: London.
Tribe, K. (1978), *Land, Labour and Economic Discourse,* Routledge and Kegan Paul: London.

7　Tensions of selfhood in republican political theory

Luis Castro Leiva

I

The soul of man (whose life or motion is perpetual contemplation or thought) is the Mistris of two potent revalls, the one Reason, the other Passion, that are in continuall fuit; and according as she gives up her will to these or either of them, is the felicity or misery which man partakes in this mortall life.　For as whatever passion in the contemplation of man, being brought forth by his will into action, is vice and the bondage of sin; so that ever was reason in the contemplation of man, being brought forth by his will into action, is virtue and the freedom of soul .... Again, as those actions of a man that were sin, acquire unto himself repentance or shame, and afect others with scorn or pity; so those actions of a man are virtue, acquire unto himself Honour, and upon others Authority.[1]

Recent developments in political theory speak of a revival of republicanism.　Those interested in recapturing the intellectual relevance of republicanism for political theory have significantly related it to the present state of moral philosophy.[2]　Moral philosophy for its part is not in good shape;[3] hence the need for a suitable conceptual strategy to meet its current difficulties.　The strategy consists in refurbishing the classical tradition as a way of overcoming the present limitations of a stifling moral tradition.[4] I take this mainly to be a current Anglo-Saxon intellectual trend in moral philosophy and political theory; yet such is its cultural purchase that it has spread across to other philosophical, moral and political cultures until recently quite immune to this influence.[5] In what follows I want to focus on a different tradition, on what I shall call, paraphrasing J.G.A. Pocock, the South-Atlantic republican tradition.[6] In this pursuit I will take up a suggestion put forward by R. Morse on the possibility of a Spanish American political theory of government.　Morse suggested that the key to the understanding of Spanish American 'centrifugal separatism', as he termed it, lay in the consideration of the following historical thesis:

The answer this essay proposes is that at the moment when the Thomistic component became 'recessive', the Machiavellian component, latent since the sixteenth century, became dominant.[7]

Latin American republics were to him understandable in the terms of a political and moral mimesis of either a Florentine republic or of a renaissance principality. I would like to examine those tensions – both the old and the new. I wish to do so as they bear upon the issue of selfhood and the theory and practice of citizenship. This is how I shall proceed: I shall begin with a brief reconstruction of Spanish American republicanism and then consider its tensions of selfhood. Finally, I will say something about the role of those tensions in the clash between republicanism and liberalism in the process of economic modernization of Latin America today.

II

After a brief period following a pattern quite similar to the events produced in Spain by Napoleon's invasion, almost all the Spanish provinces of the Spanish Empire in the New World became republics.[8] At first the provinces following Spain tried to preserve their attachment to the crown. However, shortly after the first attempts at popular government proved themselves catastrophic failures, the idea of monarchical rule was again thought by some as a possible remedy to the combined evils of political anarchy and moral licentiousness.[9] Monarchical inclinations, however exotic and ill fated, had roots in the patriarchal languor and inertia of the Empire's past and in the increasing awareness of the difficulties involved in a republican conception of political and moral freedom.

The imperial past had at least two kinds of monarchical traditions to offer. On the one hand, the more or less extended idea of a *res publica christiana*, founded on the benevolent governance of a strong corporate idea of late medieval kingship, torn between Machiavellian recession and Thomistic or neo-Aristotelian dominance, and lasting over at least two and a half centuries; on the other hand, the enlightened conception of the realm's modernization attributed to the reforming zest of the Bourbon King Charles III during the course of the second half of the eighteenth century.[10] It has been convincingly argued that the concepts of nature, human nature, law, morals, politics, and above all theology and philosophy, were so radically challenged by the demands placed upon them by the enlightened Neapolitan and reforming spirit of Charles III's modernizing ideas, that by the middle of the eighteenth century the language of commercial society – what Franco Venturi has aptly called *l'era Genovesiana*[11] – had considerably sapped the Thomistic or neo-Aristotelian foundations of the Empire. Yet such was the force of the patriarchal conception of a *res publica christiana* that a decided reaction to enlightened modernization took place in the realm, especially in the New World. Consequently, republicanism in Spanish America had to counter at least two opposing intellectual strategies: first, the patriarchal intentions of a theology of reaction that opposed the Enlightenment's priority of philosophy over theology; second, the failure of the Burkean road towards an English constitution exemplified in G.M. de Jovellanos' moderate *whiggish* view of liberty.

What then is the nature of the resulting cast of Spanish American republicanism? Some of the earliest republican examples may illustrate its contents.

Addressing a convinced republican audience and wishing to rouse patriotic passion to a conveniently sublime pitch, *El Patriota de Venezuela* – a jacobin periodical circa 1811 – gives a sense of the transition from commercial liberal expectations to Roman martial virtues as the substance of republicanism. After having commended the specificity of the love of the fatherland (*amor a la patria*) as the source for the concurrent respect of the law and equality as the contents of political obedience, the periodical considers the causal efficacy of legal compliance as a unique source of republicanism:

> It produces that set of qualities that we call custom .... Republics cannot exist in the absence of virtue, and virtue cannot do without custom. Amongst all the virtues that flow from patriotism, the latter breeds a singular moral attribute – a human quality – in republics, the Sovereign princess of all public virtues, which in and by itself establishes the consistency of the republican character. It consists in a certain force of spirit (fuerza de ánimo) with which man not only awaits, resists, not only renders, but above all defies and urges upon himself the greatest and most imminent dangers for the sake of common liberty and civic health.[12]

It should come as no surprise to discover that the oration is an elegy. The lines mourn the glory of a recently deceased patriot. And quite appropriately Cicero's authority is invoked to explicate the virtuous demeanour of *quae magno animo*. Finally, in a rhetorical inflexion of retirement beseeching the intimacy of the fellow members of la *Sociedad Patriótica*, the discourse ends along stern Plutarchian lines:

> It weeps this loss, that of this young officer who ought to have been for the Venezuelan state what Leonidas was for Sparta, Epaminondas for Thebes, Temistochles and Aristides for Athens, what Fabius, Scipio and Marcellus were for Rome.[13]

This kind of ancient Roman countenance was not republicanism's only form; its history was guided in the Spanish American political imagination by the availability of a number of other republican paradigms. Three types of model republics were then acknowledged: the ancient, the modern and the nascent. The emerging discursive complexity is in this respect as intricate and puzzling as the case of the Scottish

Enlightenment or the appraisal of North American republicanism.[14] Natural jurisprudence and republicanism coalesced rather than opposed each other.

These allying attempts to combine different conceptions of liberty within republicanism faltered. The martial attributes of self abnegation and self renunciation, the Roman substance of public virtues, eventually overcame the prospects of self interested individualism and contractualism.

The accommodation of natural jurisprudence, civic humanism and commercial expansiveness into one polity became a practical impossibility. Republicanism was gradually reduced to holistic moral emotivism.[15] It became an extreme passionate *affaire du coeur*: the ethical sentimentalism of *patriotism*. No philosophical matrix was found capable of sustaining an enduring project for political stability amidst such a diversity of political languages and idioms, at least not in all the new republics. A discursive diaspora followed. Each moral, jurisprudential and political discourse was cut loose and left adrift to find for itself in the imagination its practical or theoretical status. A characteristic chasm was thus created reciprocally linking utopian republicanism to dire political reality. Natural jurisprudence, for example, found its formalistic resting place, its utopian abode in constitutionalism. This abstract heaven subsequently was to house a bizarre assortment of different jurisprudential and legislative idioms, some late humanist, some the enlightened criticisms of the latter, some overtly modern reversals of them all.[16] But considered as sheer power struggle, the art of politics became warfare: the general concern of *le citoyen soldat*. This militaristic ethos flaunted a Rousseaunian pathos[17] and stirred the passions of the political imagination into the revival of the ancient lives and characters of Romans, Spartans, and other Plutarchian heroes.

General Simon Bolívar – the Liberator of Venezuela, Colombia, Ecuador and Peru – perhaps captures at its best this political ethos and pathos. Similar ideas were expressed by Mariano Moreno in 1810 and much later by José Martí towards the end of the century. This ethos was rendered in some of Bolívar's trenchant formulations on the value of ancient virtues and his appeal to republican unity.[18] On the basis of a unique interpretation of civic republicanism in nascent republics, where power, *fortuna* and glory were rhetorically said to be elided in the sole pursuit of liberty, Bolívar in Angostura, perhaps then at the height of his constitutional innocence, admonishes over the kind of wholeness that a nascent *res publica* requires:

> In order to save our nascent republics from chaos all our moral faculties will fail if we do not fuse the mass of the peoples into a whole; we must make the composition of government into one whole; we must draft legislation into one whole; and build the national spirit into one whole. Unity, unity, unity this must be our motto.[19]

These neo-classical republican beliefs since then have become popular and widespread in Latin America, Fidel Castro's last stand in Cuba being the expression of their legacy. Ancient liberties, in a combination of pseudo Machiavellian republicanism and political romanticism, are the expression of their extended continuity.

What then are we to conclude from this presentation of republicanism? Three things, I suggest. First, that the civic humanist conception of a *res publica* and its ancient Roman mimesis dominated the political imagination of the political elites and eventually of the masses whilst attachment to a *res publica christiana* receded. Regardless of the heroic efforts of some Catholic thinkers to modernize the metaphysical and theological foundations of Catholicism, e.g. Domingo Muriel, J.G. Roscio, Benito Juarez, the *popolo basso*, i.e. Indians, Africans, mestizos, slaves, did not at first follow these abstract ideological republican or liberal innovations. They remained bound in their peculiar ways to Catholicism and its idea of a *res publica christiana*. Second, that the social practices of the *Ancien Regime*, however shaken, appear to have resisted modernization in politics, in morals and economics. Yet the succeeding deprivation masterminded by ancient republicanism paradoxically extended and reinforced the discourse of civic virtues substituting the glory of Christian virtues with the *virtú* reaped from the practice of civil discord and *il vivere pericoloso*.[20] Third, that the extension of republicanism and the levelling effect of militarism engendered a democratization of *virtu*. This took a popular Machiavellian, Rousseaunian and eventually romantic form.

In this format it has had a profound impact in Spanish American and Latin American political cultures. And quite characteristically what this public spirit hails as its most distinctive feature of moral and political identification is that men – especially men – are the exclusive protagonists of a positive programme of liberty and independence, i.e. of nationalism. Hence, the principal characteristic of selfhood that follows from all this is *singularity of character* and not rational individualism. Unlike Constant's *commercants*, or indeed Harrington's virtuous republicans, the heroes of Spanish American and Latin American republics are passionate men of fortune, unique individuals that have hitherto and in some places still are carving out their singularity for themselves in agency as a source for tragedy or comedy in political irony. Republican selfdom is notoriously immune to the prospects of self interested individualism. Yet for all its disposition to singularity this republican idea of selfhood is consistently obsessed by altruism and its effects. At the same time, such altruism only seems to thrive in the backwaters of political romanticism and collective suicide.

Morally the effects of republicanism are no less significant. Moral consequentialism, normative Kantian reflexivity or a natural law *conscientia*, either secular or not, have never succeeded in controlling the powers of Spanish American patriotism. This ethical sentimentalism, in Machiavellian disguise, seems to be the favourite invented narrative of republican selfdom in Spanish America. However, there are signs of its growing strains. The old communitarian self of the receding *res publica christiana* and its Machiavellian successor have had to join forces in selfdom in order to resist, where possible, the attack of libertarian ideas of selfhood and more generally of liberalism in the shape of the global causalities of economic modernization.

III

There are two general modes of selfhood and two corresponding processes of identification at the source of Spanish American republican consciousness. The first corresponds to the kind of self that leads the life of a member of a *res publica christiana* . For reasons of historical convenience I shall call this the neo-Aristotelian conception of selfhood and not, as Morse, the Thomistic.[21] The second I shall call the civic humanist conception of selfhood.

The first mode of selfhood is dependent on a teleological conception of nature and human nature. It requires a protean, articulated and strong conception of identity and a strong particularistic sense of selfhood. One, that is, that can account for the existence of the human animal's actions and passions, that is to say its practice, such practice being conditioned by the categories, i.e. place, time, position, relation, etc. It also has to account – indeed pretends to – for the peculiar force with which the human animal is drawn into the process of practice – slanted by dispositions and virtues – towards the achievement of the *Summum Bonum* both for itself and the city, which is the holistic sense that is morally and ontologically implied in the concept of felicity as well-being:

> If we are right in our view, and felicity should be held to consist in 'well-doing', it follows that the life of action is best, alike for every state as a whole and for each individual in his own conduct.[22]

Accordingly, a life read along such lines requires the concourse of vision and knowledge of the self and of its actions and passions, an impetus of the self, a peculiar mode of reason contingently conducive to self-control and a corresponding agonistic feasibility tied to the possible realization of ends pre-established by nature and its process of becoming. To these ends we are either drawn or disposed. According to these ends actions and passions are appraised.

Such views of identity give sense, purpose and fulfilment to the agent and makes such an agent the object of aesthetic moral appraisal by way of the expression and quality of its performances. In the process of acting out the agony of agency or of enduring its qualitative pathos, the self and its ensuing actions or passions are mirrored or made transparent by shared standards of practice. Human happiness evolves out of and is expressed in the practices of such actions and passions. This is the world of prudence, habits, custom and the search for a *Finis Ultimus*. Eudaimonic fulfilment rests on the practical acknowledgement of socially shared teleological correspondence between the way the world is and is conceived to be, and the way the agents live its practices as a result of their reflexive, normative consciousness of it. Vice and virtue are then the dispositions of one's character to act or forbear – to be identifiable – in certain more or less pre-established ways commonly shared by the city. One is then the character that through one's practices one carves for oneself before the eyes of the polity that beholds us and to which we are beholden.

The second mode of selfhood, which I shall call the civic-humanist conception of selfhood, seems to circumvent teleology. By means of this elision it captures for itself, as a prize for identity, a picture of nature and human nature – and of its doing and undoing – that is different from the former though retaining from it a similarity of language.[23]

Nature here is animated by a substantial amount of luck and by the constraints of fate. It is also riddled with divinatory signs perhaps expressive of the governance of humanly transcendent forces which defy and invite the agony of human agency. Human identity then seems tragically founded only on human agency. It is an idea of selfhood destitute of immanent supernatural assistance and devoid of teleology and of any form of providential assistance. Its dignity, as it were, is this very same metaphysical dereliction. It confers upon the identity of what is human a distinctive consciousness: the knowledge of an exposure to the phenomenal odds of *natura rerum*.

Yet this self and its idea of *humana natura* are also universal. The human condition is in respect to its natural dereliction everywhere and always the same. Accordingly, the moral and political ideas of agency that issue from this sense of identity are grounded on the need for universal accomplishments; on the need to invent or re-invent morality as the expression of the universal will to power in politics by imitating the exploits of human deeds in history.

Here, once again, not unlike in neo-Aristotelian selfhood, a strong sense of selfhood is required in selfdom. In order to acquiesce in one's existence, as an existence divested of any substantive teleological underpinnings, or transcendental subjection to Providence, the self, which becomes aware of itself in this way, must immediately prove itself capable of withstanding the sight of such dignity. It must also prove itself able to act upon it. But this show of initial strength is tried further. The ideals of an active life as a public undertaking requires the unflinching life commitment to the total demands of the freedom of the *res publica*. Patriotism, as we shall see, is suicide prone, especially if it be performed in the name of altruism, i.e. the republic.

These two kinds of republican selfhood and the process of identification that is comprehensive of both, are tied to a certain logic of social individuation. From its inception through to its termination, the identity that occurs in the personal process of political and moral identification – the enduring self, the *character* – is indeed identifiable as the identity of a persona and its authorship. This continuing identity of the particular and embodied inhabitant of the civic or purposive role, secular or not, which provides the object of social condemnation or approval, is a substance, i.e. an '*it*' that endures or sustains the contrary changes of status, place, time condition, relation, and the rest of the categories.

The peculiar effort of trying to be such a substance or of enduring through its becoming either in a mode of activity or passivity is in this sense what constitutes the personal animus in republicanism. To this animus belong the effort or agony of acquiring property or dominion over its circumstantial roles and thereby extended to things, e.g. goods, children, slaves, land, etc. It might significantly be noted here that in both modes of republican selfhood the personal identification peculiarly involved engages the question of gender individuation. Quite significantly only *virility* exclusively possesses selfdom as its universal political and moral dominion.

Paradoxically, and irrespective of the metaphysical significance of the idea of substance and its fathomless relation to a personal self, this intimacy seems in a way to be the more jejune aspect of republican identification. What ethically counts in its practice is how far and how consciously, and to what holistic extent, this is done for the sake of the City and not for the self. The flawlessness of one's civic or purposive role, of one's moral and political *telos*, seems to override the concerns of our individual sense of intimacy, which is not to say that there is no scope for an individual self to appear and bear witness to the singularity of a republican tragedy or comedy in political irony.[24]

These then appear to me as some of the converging features of both conceptions of republican self-hood. Yet between them there are also some significant divergences. For example, the neo-Aristotelian republican self – in whatever form of government – requires that the logic of social individuation contained in the process of political and moral identification should commit itself to self-renunciation whilst holding on to the intelligibility of its dispositions and realizations. It must prudentially endure as a character through Socratic self-affirmation and must be able to know and be recognizable as such.

The civic humanist republican self appears to contend with what looks like a wholly different universe and character strategy. It must also engage in self-renunciation and self-affirmation in role performance, but it appears to do so starting from the poles of somewhat different identities and a different relation to practical knowledge. To begin with, the self of a Florentine republican must know that it alone is responsible for what it attempts or dares to do, whatever the odds of *fortuna*. The republican life it leads is exposed to the dangers of being fortuitously cut adrift, severed from any transcendental or teleological dependency of agency. It must then make a self for itself; it must assume the romantic task of being a strong character in order to realise its fated condition and then to dare to act upon it. Actions and passions are at once more demanding and for the same reason much more defining, if only at the expense of their intelligibility. What counts is how uniquely spectacular or bold they may be. Their measure seems to be how strong willed they are: 'If lacking in force, audacity shall become glory; in things great to have willed is enough'.[25]

Unlike its neo-Aristotelian counterpart this kind of self draws no lessons from an animated nature. There are no lessons to be drawn other than those drawn from the considered reflection of human nature's plight in the search for power in history.[26] What men do or forbear to do – their history – is how men are and how they can and shall always and everywhere be. Experience of the secularized human condition is the only source of experience for moral and political experience. Memory requires a continuity of identity. The civic humanist self finds it in the annals of republican experience. The passions, actions and the prowess of the ancients – preferably the Romans – provide the *exempla* from which the exploits of greatness can be reproduced and willed in their new settings. These then are the divergences.

Notice now that I have said that each one of those two modes of selfhood involves a corresponding process of self-loss or self-renunciation. This is to say that in so far as they are meant to represent selves that are conceived and appraised as the virtuous embodiment of social dependency they are selves that share a common life.This commonalty is what lends personal ethical meaning to any life wishing to lead such a kind of life. In different ways such ideas of selfhood both require from the individuals who wish to lead the good republican life the consistent performance of abnegation. Self-denial in some crucial sense is its very sense and purpose, the measure of identity and identification in altruism.

To bear witness to the sense of consciousness of one's civic duties, regardless of the particular obstacles that might obstruct or make for its *denouement,* is the highest form of human flourishing in the conduct of a civic life, the attainment of virtue. This explains, I suggest, why and how death in republicanism can give such dense cultural and moral meaning to civic glory as a form of self-assertion conducive to self-loss. Hume very aptly expresses the thoughts I have in mind by appealing to a Florentine episode quite pertinent to my general purposes:

> A man is engaged in a conspiracy for the public interest; is seized upon suspicion; is threatened with the rack; and knows from his own weakness, that the secret will be extorted from him: Could such a one consult the public interest better than by putting a quick period to a miserable life? This was the case of the famous and brave Strozzi of Florence.[27]

For such a form of self-assertion and concomitant self-loss to move into action and be passionately endured, the practice of citizenship has to be embedded in certainty. The republican practice must be that of a polity that is able to understand and praise the kind of epistemic knowledge involved in the intellectual and affective process that this particular tension develops as part of the process living a life of this kind of republicanism.

A republican self ethically achieves human integrity and heroic anonymity through patriotic sacrifice. What happens, then, when the belief system of such a polity is shaken by the sudden entry of a fundamentally self-interested idea of selfhood? Put in another way what happens to a belief system that has a communitarian conception of selfhood when constrained into a conception of selfhood that is contractually self-interested?

IV

In this essay I have suggested that the modernization of Latin American economies has politically and morally challenged republicanism and its communitarian identities. This is a general effect of liberalism. Since liberalism is historically acknowledged as the political and jurisprudential outcome of modern individualism, the narratives of republican selfhood have been correspondingly reacting to this resurgence of economic individualism. What is the nature of this challenge?

In its usual presentations the history of liberalism in Spanish America follows the standard Mainian transition from *status* to *contract* . Spanish American republics are said to have evolved into somewhat surreal *Rechtstaaten* expressive of the alleged interests of bourgeois societies. In fact, history is something slightly more complicated than Marxism or libertarianism have made it out to be. In this respect I take it that the current processes of economic modernization of Latin America have favoured one general strategy of moral and political identification, namely a conscious move towards the advancement of 'rational choice' theories of agency and identity. Hence, rationality and universality are inferred from the structure and functions of the individual's economic wants and desires.[28]

Individuals thus become the centres of abstract imputation, bundles of quantifiable and measurable desires, purchasors of utilitarian identification. These unstable, disconnected and yet reflexive and desirous appetites, which intermittently are taken as the units of choice of neo-liberal adjustments, dissolve and paradoxically multiply identities. They do so in proportion to the expansion or contraction of the limited existing supply of resources to satisfy a limitless supply of desires, both private and public. Accordingly, moral and political identity and identification need a special narrative; one that may justify the purpose and value of these points of causal discontinuity in their quest for what used to be republican felicity. This is where the concept of economic modernization provides a suitable setting for the understanding of the conflicting tensions of selfhood induced by the sudden and recent expansion of neo-liberalism in Latin America today.[29]

Accelerated economic modernization is considered to have an inbuilt tendency to disrupt the state of consciousness of social and political bodies. It upsets the relation between individual wants and desires and the hope of their satisfaction. When by means of a sudden reversal of fortune societies are submitted to abrupt changes in the scope and scale of their members' cravings, in the structuring of their desires – either for the better or the worse - individual consciousness of social expectations, hopes and illusions, bear the brunt of these changes. When, for example, a state of affluence socially endures through time, desires tend to multiply in a most Hobbesian manner.[30] Human beings unleash their insatiable desires and submit their hopes and illusions to the expansiveness of their well-being. Should this state of things suddenly come to a halt, changes of fortune usually cause states of perplexity and anxiety. This is likely to be followed by a comparison as times past and times present are confronted. From this individuals extort the conscious social measure of their predicament. Quite frequently this results in a crisis of identification and social disaffection. Some may even find that life is no longer worth living – they may resort to suicide or exile. Others, perhaps more adept at survival, can rise in anger and seek to avenge the injustice of their misfortunes.[31]

Setting aside anger or justice as a response to this predicament, suicide – whatever its individual causes – in this sense provides information on the ideas or beliefs of selfhood available in the history of societies. In societies where the collective representations – the background political culture – are imbued with republican ideals, the prevailing suicidogenic tendencies tend to be altruistic in character. The Roman conceptions of civic patriotism and self-immolation as expressed in Horace's famous lines are characteristic of this social addiction to suicide and sacrifice: that of the value attached to the glorious discovery of virtue in wilful death.[32] A quite similar if not identical emphasis is found in Machiavelli's praise of patriotic devotion to the price of liberty in a republic. This kind of civic devotion to altruistic death is found in a host of prominent contemporary Latin American examples: Allende's death in Chile, Che Guevara's in Bolivia, Camilo Torres' in Colombia, Monsignor A. Romero's in Guatemala, José Martí's in Cuba, and in the chorus of revolutionary rhetoric of the political idioms of *Maderismo, Sandinismo, Allendismo, Guevarismo, Fidelismo, Peronismo,* et alia.

In other societies, where liberalism and individualism have attained prominence, suicidogenic tendencies by nature appear to be egoistic. The tragedies and the characters that represent in them these wilful acts of self-immolation are centred on the loss of meaning or purpose in selfdom. The suicidal antics of self-interested individuals are as much self-centred as they are self-driven. They seem to possess Ibsen's gloomy, despairing motivations, perhaps Camus's inclination to the absurd.

Egoistic and altruistic tensions of selfhood may find themselves in a state of equilibrium. However, where no accommodation is found for their diverging *egoistic* and *altruistic* identities to cancel out their contending pulls, a change of fortune may polarize these respective logics of social individuation with the result that political and moral consciousness becomes strained. Crisis and conflicts of identity, individual or collective, are then likely to occur. As a result the stability of the *res publica* may be jeopardized.

The question of whether the instability thus created results in social explosion or not is a deeply historical matter. In some cases, social explosions, by consistently violent means, may enhance and not reduce the pre-existing value of death in the political culture, thus invigorating ostensive altruism and thereby overpowering rival egoistic centrifugal forces. Alternatively, other societies may explode their polities into centrifugal anarchy, as altruism becomes disjointed and anomie spreads the splitting of political and moral identities. This kind of explosion, however, is perhaps best seen at the level of individuation and, as it were, individual implosion.

The self that has distanced itself from itself by reflexively considering a different prospect for its identity and identification, one different from that which is socially available, may or may not be able to cope with what such self knowledge reveals: exile, suicide or madness appear as a choice of possibilities in this particular predicament. My point, however, is that in both cases – in social explosion or individual disruption – the tensions of republican selfhood have a disposition to court anomie and anarchy in singularly acute and chaotic ways; specially civic humanist republicanism.

Now the prevailing conceptions of republicanism in Latin America are and have been variously threatened by the growing importance of libertarian liberalism. Libertarianism is the most commonly extended answer to populism in the wake of current economic modernization. Its main contention is the claim of extreme economic individualism. Usually, though not always, this is underwritten in the terms of an aggressive negative conception of liberty. The kind of selfhood involved in this mode of thought is thus obsessively opposed to republicanism just as much as to its more recently defeated arch-rival, Marxism. However, viewed in this light and conceived along such lines, neo-liberalism itself offers its own set of tensions for political and moral identification in its age old battle with republicanism.

First, it confronts the tension between a self that is expressively self-asserting in desire and is yet incapable of accounting for or justifying the continuity of its own identity through the very same stream of desires that consciously and unconsciously so constitute it. Each individual wills as much of its desires as it is possible for it to will and to satisfy, but since this involves the possible disruption of the same kind of motivation in all others, an external agency is needed to curtail potentially inconvenient infringements – Leviathan is thus the much needed and imagined universal other. Consequently, the question of justice and utility first precedes and then follows as the contractualist solution to the problem of a self born unto itself seeks to govern itself. Unless some potent super self – a Kantian one – is imagined, invented or constituted, sceptical utilitarian diffidence, pragmatist robustness or voluntaristic romanticism seem the only energetic and realistic ways out of this brutish trap. But since less advanced societies – as Durkheim thought – are the victims of 'insufficient individuation', neo-utilitarianism, neo-Kantianism and pragmatism would only seem to be viable philosophical strategies north of the Río Bravo.

Second, it confronts the tension between self-expansion and self-reliance, which issues into the practical dilemma of political liberty as the expression of the need for order and security and the corresponding need for deviance and toleration. Each individual is free to invent for itself whatever its chain of desires wills for itself as its liberty, and yet, at the same time, the possibility of this enjoyment of freedom requires an idea of Law to coerce hindrance or infringement of that very same sense of liberty. The Law must stand outside the self and its doings to be capable of coercing. Insatiably willed by impetus, coercible by fiction, the self of individualism serves two masters: one inside, the other imagined to be outside, both quite fragile betrayable inventions.

Yet the fiction of an outside universal self and its point of view out of necessity is and ought to be made mightier than reality, but it cannot be so. Fear of the inside, as the threshold of liberty, is indeed a source for the powerful constructive emergence of a political and moral scaffolding destined to serve the purpose of grounding the ethical constituency of self-interest; yet fear can be expressed in more than one way and can have more than one object as its purpose. The loss of self-expansion after times of affluence or the loss of self in its excitement of accelerated affluence, may both lead to chaos in selfdom: to the flight of self-control, to individual and/or social dissolution. These, then, are some of the internal problems that the libertarian tensions of selfhood find unresolved as they make their late-modern entry into Latin American republicanism defying the power of ancient virtues.

It is at this point, and in view of these tensions that I shall introduce Durkheim's account of anomic economic derangement. This idea will help us to understand the kinds of confusion over political and moral identification that these libertarian interpretations bring to those of republicanism in Latin America today. Durkheim argued, as I have suggested above, that a sudden breakdown of social expectations and the corresponding breakdown in the structuring of desires leads to a *déclassement*, thereby affecting the moral and political consciousness of individuals. Likewise, abrupt periods of prosperity induce societies and individuals to loose their grasp on the scope of what is and is not possible, with the added disadvantage – claimed Durkheim – that the frenzied excitability of such crises merely fuels blazing appetites.

The Hobbesian lines of Durkheim's understanding of capitalist development, something quite like the present sense of economic globalization, fatefully challenge republicanism's conception of selfhood. The contest takes place at the combined levels of collective and individual representation. It has a certain law-like character.

If and when the practice of political corruption has eroded both ideas of republican selfhood (an internal, patriotic affair), resistance might prove more anomic prone, and a centrifugal flight into anarchy is in order. If and when republics summon the moral resources of their *mores* and find practical comfort in their regenerative energy, resistance to individualism becomes stiffer and individualism may be beaten back. Contrariwise if and where individualism compromises in the name of justice – something which libertarianism finds difficult if not impossible to do – and negotiates the moral and political division of labour with republicanism, the prospects of coexistence between republicanism and liberalism look more promising. In this respect the *sprit de conquête* which Constant so sharply denounced as opposed to commercial society is today to be read in Latin America as the victory of a *Pax Americana*:

> War is a gift prior to commerce: the first is borne out by impulse from desire without experience; the second is a reckoning brought about by enlightened desire. Commerce must therefore replace war; but in so doing it will discredit it, it shall render war odious to all nations.[33]

The Empire is extending its *imperium* offering its commercial citizenship to Mexico and circling Cuba and Haiti. It remains to be seen at what point in the history of the decline or fall, or indeed rise, of this new Roman Empire we are currently living. In the meantime Latin American republicanism has once again met modern individualism and its fate.

V

I must now try to sum up my argument and conclude. I began with a succinct picture of Spanish American republicanism. I stressed the dominance of a romantic version of civic republicanism over its neo-Aristotelian counterpart. I then examined some of the tensions of those two conceptions of selfhood. Subsequently I presented the challenge to republican conceptions of selfhood via the economic liberalization of Latin America. In this context the concept of anomic economic derangement was introduced. I saw it as the setting for the understanding of the resulting conflict of political and moral identification in Latin America today.

The cultural density of this South Atlantic republican tradition in Latin America today historically exhibits both its weaknesses and strengths, the state of its moral and political emplacement. Political romanticism and the language of *virtú* have apparently tamed the classical virtues and its neo-Aristotelian ideas of selfhood. This conflict over the political secularization of consciousness has elided Kantian and utilitarian alternatives. However, today, faced with a common enemy both forms of republicanism are reacting to the extension of specific forms of quite belligerent libertarianism. In a *fin de siècle* governed by postmodern alacrity it would seem fruitless to go back in time. Nevertheless, sometimes the past is the present. The present state of moral and political identification in Latin America is still substantially this torn past. Part of the drama of its seemingly emblematic 'endism' is poignantly illustrated by the stark moral and political contrast which holds between the latest society to have turned republican and one of the earliest to have braved it: Cuba and Haiti. Both republics are in their own quite separate ways pitiful failures. In its more ancient, romantic scores, the present fate of republicanism was curtly put by Cabrera Infante thus: 'The practice of suicide is the only and of course, definitive Cuban ideology. A rebel ideology – the permanent rebellion of a perennial suicide'.[34]

Notes

1   Harrington (1656), p. 10.
2   Skinner (1990).
3   This is the claim made by Williams (1985).
4   This is the argument developed by MacIntyre (1981). It is also developed along different lines and for a different purpose by Williams, ibid.
5   See for example, *Revista Internacional de Filosofía Política* (1993), p. 189.
6   See Pocock (1975). On my use of the South-Atlantic republican tradition see Botana (1984).
7   Morse (1954) p. 79.
8   On this whole process see Guerra (1992). On the constitutional strategy of monarchical liberalism in Spain see the *Cadiz Constitution of 1812*. For a good example of the effect or monarchical constitutionalism see Canon Larrazabal's instructions to the Cortes of Cadiz according to a tract '*Proyecto de constitutcion fundamental Española y su gobierno*' part of the Ayuntamiento's guidelines to its representative Romero (1969), pp. 35 et seq.
9   See for example, Burke (1807). The University of Cambridge Library copy contains a bound set of tracts, three belonging to Burke and the rest corresponding to other authors dealing with the same question, e.g. Abate Viscardo y Guzman, F. de Miranda and perhaps Andrés Bello.
10   On the Bourbon reform there is a steady flow of literature following Sarraihl's classical work (1957). Since then discussion has flared on the depth of the eroding effects of this reform in terms that recall Tocqueville's assessment of the centralizing tendency of the *Ancien Regime*. On its Spanish American significance see Halperin Donghi (1985). For a recent general assessment see Brading (1991), pp. 465 et seq.
11   See Venturi (1969a). More particularly see Venturi (1969b), pp. 882-902. On Spanish America and the Enlightenment see Chiaramonte (1979).
12   *El Patriota de Venezuela* (1950). I am grateful to Carole Leal for having drawn my attention to this piece and to the *jacobin* significance of the *Sociedad Patriotica* in Venezuela.
13   Ibid.
14   On the question of natural jurisprudence and the Scottish Enlightenment see Haakonssen (1989). For the debate over North American republicanism and its relation to liberalism see Appleby (1992), chs. 4 and 5; Wood (1992). For a recent general discussion of the problems and the diverging positions

see Ben-Atar (1992). This is a review of the works of Appleby and Wood.

15   I use this expression as an analogy extracted from its philosophical context to express the evincing functions that republican patriotism through its emotive descriptions of actions and passions rhetorically produces as condemnation, reprobation and other speech acts. I further associate it with ethical sentimentalism as a more enlightened Humean-Rousseaunian way of conceiving the morality of patriotism.

16   For example, here are some idioms: the idiom of *ius commune*, as seen in the lineage of G.V. Gravinas to L. Muratori and reversed in G. Filangieri, a Neapolitan influence in the jurisprudential conception of Spanish and Spanish American Enlightenments: the idiom of *Painian republicanism* as translated and expressed in Venezuela at the beginning of independence; the *Burkean idiom* of liberty; the constitutionalism of the Federalist; the idiom of *'sensualisme'* as introduced by Condillac, etc.

17   On the influence of Rousseau see Rea Spell (1938).

18   Bolivar (1976), p. 125.

19   Ibid., p. 121.

20   On the sense of Machiavelli's departure from a classical tradition in *The Prince* see Skinner, (1981), pp. 36 et seq. On the same topic but less explicitly see Garin (1993) where Garin also relates Machiavelli to Rousseau. Henceforth I shall have this last sense of *virtú* in mind and not its classical conception, either Ciceronian or Aristotelian.

21   I refrain from the use of Thomistic, as Morse does, and use the vaguer term of neo-Aristotelianism instead for it seems to me to be less committed to what I take today is a secular invitation to a more easily anachronistic reading of Aquinas' Spanish American influence and with considerable blurring effects of the intellectual history of Spanish America.

22   Aristotle (1968) 1325 a 24-b 32, Book VII.iii 1-10, p. 289.

23   I realize that this is a thorny issue. The question is whether or not, as Harrington seems to suppose, Machiavelli does expound Aristotle's views. If he does, as some recently argue, then the continuity of language is telling and correspondingly ought to modify my account of the 'romantic' reading I make of *virtú*.

24   See on this issue of individualism and the self in Greek thought, running counter to established historiographically Kantian views, Williams (1993).

25   Quoted in Pico della Mirandola (1942), p. 58.

26   See for example Machiavelli's use of history. I have used here the French translation. Machiavelli (1952), pp. 377-8. As opposed to what has been called the moral point of view see Williams (1985), p. 6.

27   Hume (1987), p. 587. The editor's footnote on *Filippo Strozzi* at the

bottom of this page is even more central to my purposes: Filippo, a classical scholar of some attainments, modeled his suicide on that of Cato the Younger. He left behind an epitaph which read in part: 'Liberty, therefore, perceiving that together with him all her hopes had perished, having surrendered herself and cursed the light of day, demanded to be sealed up in his same tomb. Thus, O Stranger, shed copious tears if the Florentine republic means anything at all to you, for Florence will ever see again so noble citizen ... whose highest command was: in dying for one's fatherland, any sort of death is sweet.' Quoted in Bullard (1980), pp. 176-7.

28 See for example, Buchanan and Tullock (1967), pp. 32 et seq., specially p. 34.

29 I refer, of course, to the general readjustment programmes sponsored by the IMF and World Bank that have affected almost all Latin American economies. On the general and quite erratic assessment of the historical meaning of these processes a favourite libertarian locus is, of course, Fukuyama's famous version of the end of history.

30 The standard version of this manner occurs early on in Hobbes (1966), Part I, ch. XI, Of the Difference of Manners, p. 85.

31 I have relied on Durkheim (1897) in my account of much of what follows, specially on the relations between anomie, suicide and modernization.

32 This is a difficult point. Should the search for Glory be considered as suicide only when and if the agent does no longer believe in such Glory through death? Is the loss of faith in beliefs what distinguishes the two? My point is the following: republicanism morally and politically praises abnegation – requires it indeed exacts it – and this is what makes death a sublime, admirable or terrible telos for patriotism in both encounters with self-loss.

33 Constant (1822), chap. IV, p. 23. (My translation.)

34 Cabrera Infante (1993), p. 236. Here is the text in full: 'Martí will thus prove to be our most certain suicide, the "felo de se" faithfully committed to the open tomb. To victory by the sepulchre! Death on death! We will perish! Cuban, die by your own hand: for to die for the fatherland is to die.' (My translation.)

References

Appleby, J. (1992), *Liberalism and Republicanism in the Historical Imagination*, Harvard University Press: Cambridge, Mass.

Aristotle (1968), *Politics*, Barker, E. (trans.), Oxford University Press: Oxford.

Ben-Atar, D.S. (1992), 'Republicanism, Liberalism and Radicalism in the American

Founding', *Intellectual History Newsletter*, Vol. 14.

Bolivar, S. (1976), *Doctrina del Libertador*, Mijares, A. (ed.), 'Discurso de Angostura', Vol. 1, Biblioteca Ayacucho: Caracas.

Botana, N. (1984), *La Tradicion Republicana*, Editorial Sudaamericana: Buenos Aires.

Brading, D. (1991), *The First America*, Part 3, Cambridge University Press: Cambridge.

Buchanan, J.M. and Tullock, G. (1967), *The Calculus of Consent*, The University of Michigan Press: Michigan.

Bullard, M.M. (1980), *Filippo Strozzi and the Medici*, Cambridge University Press: Cambridge.

Burke, W. (1807), *South American Independence or the Emancipation of South America, the Glory and Interest of England*, J. Ridgway Co.: London.

Cabrera Infante, G. (1993), 'Entre la Historia y la Nada', *Mea Cuba*, Vuelta: Mexico.

Chiaramonte, J.C. (1979), *Pensamiento de la Ilustracion, Economia y Sociedad Iberoamericanas en el Siglo XVII*, Biblioteca Ayacucho: Caracas.

Constant, B. (1822), *Commentaire sur l'Ouvrage de Filangieri*, Chez P. Dufart: Paris.

Durkheim, E. (1897), *Le Suicide*, Alcan: Paris.

El Patriota de Venezuela, (1950), No. 2, (1811), Tracts BNH: Caracas.

Garin, E. (1993), 'Aspetti del Pensiero di Machiavelli', in *Dall Rinascimento all' Illuminismo*, Le Lettere: Florence.

Guerra, F.X. (1992), *Modernidad e Independencia*, MAFPRE: Madrid.

Haakonssen, K. (1989), 'Natural Jurisprudence in the Scottish Enlightenment: Summary of an Interpretation', in MacCormick, N. and Bankowski, Z. (eds.), *Enlightenment, Rights and Revolution*, Aberdeen University Press: Aberdeen.

Halperin Donghi, H.T. (1985), *Reforma y Disolucion de los Imperios Ibericos, 1750-1850*, Alianza: Madrid.

Harrington, J. (1656), *The Commonwealth of Oceana*, London (Wren Library copy).

Hobbes, T. (1966), *Leviathan, The English Works, III*, 2nd reprint, Scientia Verlag Aachen: Germany.

Hume, D. (1987), 'Of Suicide', *Essays*, Miller, E.F. (ed.), Liberty Classics: Indianapolis.

MacIntyre, A. (1981), *After Virtue*, Notre Dame University Press: Chicago.

Machiavelli, N. (1952), 'Discourse sur la Premiere Décade de Tite Live, avant Propos', *Oeuvres Complètes*, Gallimard: Paris.

Morse, R. (1954), 'Towards a Spanish American Theory of Government', *Journal of the History of Ideas*, 1 (15:1), pp. 71-93.

Pico della Mirandola, G. (1942), *Dignita dell Uommo (De Hominis Dignitate)*, a cura Cocognani, B. (ed. and trans.), Vallecchi: Florence.

Pocock, J.G.A. (1975), *The Machiavellian Moment: Florentine Political Thought and the Atlantic Republican Tradition*, Princeton University Press: Princeton, NJ.

Rea Spell, J. (1938), *Rousseau in the Spanish World Before 1833*, The University of Texas Press: Austin.

Revista Internacional de Filosofia Politica (1993), Madrid, No. 2, November.

Romero, J.K. (ed.) (1969), *Pensamiento Politico de la Emancipacion*, Vol. 24, Biblioteca Ayacucho: Caracas.

Sarraihl, J. (1957), *La España Ilustrada*, FCE: Mexico.

Skinner, Q. (1981), *Machiavelli*, Oxford University Press: Oxford.

____ (1990), 'The Republican Ideal of Political Liberty', in Bock, G., Skinner, Q., Viroli, M. (eds.), *Machiavelli and Republicanism*, Cambridge University Press: Cambridge.

Venturi, F. (1969a), *Settecento Riformatore, da Muratori a Becarria*, cap. VIII, 'La Napoli di Antonio Genovesi', Einaudi: Torino.

____ (1969b), 'Un Bilancio Della Politica Economica di Carlo Borbone', *Rivista Storica Italiana*, Anno LXXI – Fascicolo IV, Napoli.

Williams, B. (1985), *Ethics and the Limits of Philosophy*, Fontana: London.

____ (1993), *Shame and Necessity*, University of California Press: California.

Wood, G. (1992), *The Radicalism of the American Revolution*, A.A. Knopf: New York.

8　Beyond satisfaction: desire, consumption, and the future of socialism

Robert Meister

I

In the second half of this century the moderation of consumer demand became an increasingly central goal for many socialists – both in and out of power – who saw the perpetual dissatisfaction of consumers as a major defect of capitalism and the unquenchable desire for new products as a major obstacle to socialism. Their anti-capitalist 'alternative' was to be a society in which people would be satisfied in their material culture without desiring anything new. Theoretically, this might have come about through ending alienation, expanding human potential, creating an egalitarian community, and achieving abundance. The day-to-day reality behind the socialist 'alternative' however, is well-described by the Croatian feminist Slavenka Drakulić. When asked, '[H]ow do you think we survived communism?' she responds, 'Certainly not by throwing away useful things.' In her account the 'communist household' is 'almost the perfect example of an ecological unit, except that its ecology ... doesn't stem from a concern for nature, but from a specific kind of fear for the future.' Everyday survival thus became a matter of '... collecting and recycling ... redefining an object (pantyhose for example) ... by ... giving it one function after another.... [Y]ou throw it away only when you have made absolutely sure (by experiment of course) that it can't be used anymore....' Drakulić continues, 'While leaders were accumulating words about a bright future, people were accumulating flour and sugar, jars, cups, pantyhose, old bread, corks, rope, nails, plastic bags.'[1]

Socialism and consumption

The socialism of consumer restraint has surely lost most of its moral intelligibility over the past fifty years. Socialists who still believe that capitalism keeps consumers, like addicts, in a state of perpetual dissatisfaction must now face a serious counter-claim: that the 'satisfaction' promised by socialism is a form of living death – a collective tomb in which whole peoples would be surrounded, like dead Pharaohs, by the material things that will serve them forever. 'What communism instilled in

196

us,' says Drakulić, 'was precisely this immobility, this absence of a future ... of the possibility of imagining our lives differently .... [W]e learned to think: This will go on forever....'[2] It did not go on forever, and the mantle of historical inevitability that socialism once claimed seems to have fallen on capitalism instead.[3] Capitalism today owes much of its appeal to the relative inefficiency and authoritarianism of twentieth century socialist responses to the desire and need for consumer goods.

But to say this is not the same as saying that *what* won out in the ideological struggle between capitalism and socialism was merely the *principle* of market efficiency, leaving the socialist critique of consumption under capitalism otherwise untouched. That critique began to lose its moral force for reasons that were relatively independent of the collapse of the socialist economies. The problem, put crudely, was that the Walkman, the compact disc, and the personal computer were replacing addictive drugs, cigarettes, and chewing gum as the new paradigms of artificial needs produced by capitalism. How could socialist leaders continue to argue that consumers must be saved from enslavement to artificial needs that seemed highly desirable, especially when those same regimes were attempting to satisfy consumer demand by producing cheap cigarettes and liquor? Perhaps the inefficiency of socialist regimes is not the only reason socialism lost its democratic appeal. Perhaps that inefficiency became less tolerable when the traditional socialist critique of the capitalist ideal began to lose its moral force.

Suppose, for example, that the East Germans *had* finally succeeded in making a good Trabant – a low-cost, serviceable, efficient car lasting a lifetime and available to anyone who needed it. Would the citizens of the former DDR have felt better off (in this respect at least) than the West Germans who are inundated each year with advertisements designed to make their present cars seem obsolete?[4] Or would such an achievement have meant little to a working class for whom the distinction between real and artificial needs was no longer morally significant? Even if Eastern European socialism had succeeded in providing sufficiently for mass consumption according to distinctively socialist principles, it would still have been worth asking whether capitalism gained in democratic appeal when *its* rationale shifted from the satisfaction of existing needs to the creation of new wants.[5] The evident failures of socialist regimes in this century to deliver the goods should not distract us from such questions today.

Equality or abundance

This paper starts with the premise that socialism lost a central part of its democratic appeal as it became committed to a theory of virtue based on the moderation of consumer demand – thereby leaving the promise of renewal through abundance to capitalism.[6] Capitalist parties did not always have this political advantage. Traditionally, *they* were the parties of moderation, while socialist parties promised that abundance would result from greater social equality. For socialists through the 1930s it was capitalism that had failed to deliver the goods. Although they strongly advocated limiting luxury consumption in the interest of greater equality, they had no hostility to mass consumption as such. As we near century's end, however, the moral focus of the mainline socialist parties has been largely reduced to a puritanical disdain for the consumer society which they remained committed to achieving in the increasingly distant future.[7] Their socialism – which long-ago abandoned its grounding in any emancipatory vision – came to be a *defense* of the austerity, scarcity, and self-sacrifice that many critics of socialism see as the inevitable consequence of attempting to achieve greater equality than the market allows.

The New Left of the 1960s generation – at least in North America and Europe – acknowledged the unprecedented material abundance of post-war capitalism, but argued that even its apparent beneficiaries were destined to remain unhappy. Late capitalism was based, according to this view, on the creation of new and artificial desires on the part of ordinary people – desires that could never be satisfied. The New Left compared these artificial desires to the continuing need of an addict for drugs and suggested that the maintenance of an adequate level of consumer demand in an economy already glutted with goods was a pathological need of the capitalist system itself. To the traditional socialist demands for equality and abundance was added a new, and potentially incompatible, call for the moderation of material desire.

Today, the hope that moderation would allow us to reconcile equality and abundance has all but vanished from the political scene. Capitalist parties are the rising mass parties of abundance and deficit spending, openly avowing that the relentless superannuation of products and desires is a strength, not a weakness, of market systems; socialist parties (where they still exist) are the declining mass parties of an equality without abundance. The New Left's claim that the moderation of consumer demand is desirable in itself is now defended mainly by the Greens. For them, however, abundance has ceased to be a goal that is compatible with greater equality. At the global level, Greens argue that the conspicuous consumption of wealthier countries will have to be curbed in order to make self-restraint more acceptable to poorer countries in a more egalitarian world. Domestically, material equality remains on the Green political agenda, but only to the extent that limiting luxury consumption is necessary to make self-restraint politically acceptable to the masses.[8] Ultimately, the political goal of the Greens is the limitation of mass consumption. We must *all* be satisfied with less, they say – moderation is the virtue that will save us from the environmental devastation that is likely if mass consumption continues to grow at its present rate.

Green politics claims to transcend both capitalism and socialism by suggesting that the ultimate goal of both systems should have been the *satisfaction* of each individual, rather than equality or abundance as ends in themselves.[9] The Green ideal is a society, whether socialist or capitalist, that would produce good 'Trabants' and people who would be satisfied with them. If satisfaction is truly our goal, say the

Greens, then consumption that stimulates new desire should be generally disfavoured – there is no moral difference between the market forces that addict us to narcotics and the market forces that addict us to gasoline, once the destructive consequences of both addictions are correctly understood.

Is it possible, however, that both the socialist parties and their Green successors have misunderstood the popular desire to consume? Implicitly or explicitly, these defenders of moderation believe that the ultimate goal of consumption is satisfaction – a state of wanting nothing more – and that wasting what we have is merely an undesirable side effect of getting what we want. But this ideal of satisfaction is at best incomplete; we may also consume in order to renew our desire – to stay *alive* – in which case waste is part of the point. Perhaps the object of our desire is not satisfaction at all, but desire itself.[10]

Celebrants of capitalism now argue that in the struggle between liberty and equality, liberty has won because it led to abundance. But what if the struggle was only between moderation and renewal? My earlier claim that socialism lost its majoritarian appeal when moderation became its paramount virtue is the beginning of an argument that the triumph of consumerism need not end the moral debate about capitalism, once we grasp the complexity of the human wish to spend.

What has triumphed?

The force of this claim may not be obvious to those on the Left for whom it is still a *prima facie* objection to capitalism that it creates new wants at a time when existing needs have not been satisfied. They still remember – still inhabit – the time when both socialism and capitalism put themselves forward as the legitimate heirs to Enlightenment utilitarianism – one basing human happiness on the satisfaction of true need; the other on the satisfaction of actual desire. Within this utilitarian framework the inherent tendency of capitalism to create new wants raised obvious questions that some capitalists felt bound to answer: does the expansion of capitalist markets raise the sum of human dissatisfaction by creating new wants faster than it can satisfy them? At what point do these created wants become artificial needs that increase the material dependency of persons who are subject to exploitation?

Sometime in the 1980s the terms of the debate changed. The Left, preoccupied as always with its own problems, failed to notice that capitalist ideology was becoming post-bourgeois and post-modern[11] – openly avowing that at the level of material desire there is no such thing as enough. Those on the Left who continued to use the notions of 'greed' and 'excess' to criticize contemporary capitalism found themselves increasingly driven into a politics of eco-Calvinism[12] – which, like earlier Calvinisms, is primarily aimed at limiting mass consumption. One irony in the present plight of the democratic Left is that by leaving the Protestant Ethic behind (at least on the issue of consumption) capitalist parties were able to put themselves forward successfully as the parties of the people.

A second irony is that capitalist parties accomplished this while abandoning the utilitarian conception of happiness as a fortunate correspondence between what we want (need?) and what we actually get.[13] While the Left was still debating which system could in principle best satisfy existing demand, capitalism was justifying itself through its ability to create new demand. While socialism was promising to keep on producing phonographs and LPs until everyone had them, capitalism offered up the CD and invited people to replace possessions that might have many years of useful life remaining.

By the end of the 1980s, the fact that capitalism creates desires faster than it satisfies them was no longer a self-evident objection. Most citizens of democracies do not believe that, after basic human needs are met, we might close the gap between desire and its fulfillment by moderating our desires rather than by producing more and better goods. Neither are they troubled by the prospect that pursuing more and better goods is likely to widen the gap again. Once the production of new needs is recognized as a potentially legitimate activity, the relentless superannuation of products can be seen as a strength, rather than a weakness, of capitalist economies.[14]

This change has blunted the force of most traditional critiques of capitalist abundance from the Left. We are not far from the day when capitalist ideology will have left utilitarian goals to the socialists (who were in any case failing to achieve them). The emerging ideology of global capitalism already makes room, as socialism did not, for the dark questions underlying utilitarian rationality: is desire a mere prediction of happiness – a state of satisfied sufficiency in which we would want nothing more? Or is happiness rather the multiplication of desire without end and satisfaction the mere memory of need?[15] Many of the standard arguments for socialism will lose their purchase when the arguments for capitalism are no longer utilitarian.

For those who would still be socialists the problem here is as serious at the level of theory as it is at the level of practice. Marx understood as early as 1844 that in creating new products capitalism must also produce the human needs that those products satisfy, and noted that the plasticity of human needs could be a basis for both oppression and liberation. These observations are no less true today. But if we drop the utilitarian project of reducing the gap between desire and satisfaction, then the burden is on the critic of capitalism to explain why a rise in the level of material dependency is objectionable.

Many such arguments are available, including arguments that point to adverse physiological and ecological side-effects of increased levels of consumption,[16] but one argument no longer available in a post-utilitarian world is that it is intrinsically painful to expand desires faster than they can be satisfied.

The Left needs to acknowledge, along with most of the world, that shedding one's old desires by acquiring new ones can be pleasurable in itself quite apart from satisfaction – and that satisfaction (seen as the elimination of desire) may be an incoherent goal, even in societies where there remains an acute memory of scarcity and need. Critics of capitalism can still insist that pleasure is not the only good, and that the pleasures of consumption are invariably mixed; but if capitalism has captured the imagination of much of the world because it recognizes a moral value in the expansion and supersession of desire, it is worth asking whether there *is* a moral value here that may have been missing from the socialist vision of the good life. Maybe the Trabant really wasn't very good; maybe genuine socialism has yet to be tried. But it also seems possible that socialists, and eudaemonists in general, have given too much weight to the desire for things that last as the major components of happiness and too little weight to those forms of consumption beyond need that create new desires. Is the happiness that socialism promises still intelligible for consumers who do not know the meaning of 'enough?' Is there something consumers want that lies beyond satisfaction with the commodities they buy?

II

One way of approaching this problem would be to focus on whether specific commodities are really material *goods* in an Aristotelian sense. Perhaps (the argument goes) we can include among the objects of rational desire those things that expand and transform our human potential, even if (unlike Aristotle) we can see no clear end-point at which our potential would be fully realized.[17] Marxists who stress the ways in which capitalist commodification alienates us from our social nature generally rely on some elements of this Aristotelian perspective.[18]

Without directly addressing the limitations of such a commodity-based approach to consumption beyond need, I want to move in the opposite direction and focus on the act of spending itself. Is there a moral point in the desire to *spend* that is separable from the desire to have what we need to function at our highest level?

Waste not, want not

Spending? It is practically by definition an instrumental or derivative good. We spend in order to get; get in order to have; have in order to use; use in order to enjoy; and to what end? It could only be our own satisfaction, or so the Aristotelians among us would say. No doubt they are partly right. One good of spending is the realization or discovery of capacities that were latent within us, the exercise of which will allow us to enhance the quality of our lives.

But we do not spend only in order to acquire; sometimes we acquire merely in order to spend. The desire to spend in this way would be the paradigm case of a desire beyond need – or more precisely of a desire that does not have satisfaction as its goal. Such a desire becomes conceivable if we recognize that to empty ourselves can be a form of renewal, and not merely a formula for dissatisfaction. In these instances we may actually spend in order to lose rather than gain.[19]

Without suggesting that all spending is reducible to a single dimension, this paper is a bet that there is something worth exploring in the connection between spending, loss, and renewal that can shed light on the moral appeal of capitalism and the apparent decline of socialism. There is, I am suggesting, a dimension to all spending that is orthogonal to the desire to get, have, and use which we normally associate with consumption: spending also necessarily involves the willingness to lose something, to let go, to separate oneself from a prior object of desire. In the phenomenology of consumer spending the precondition for renewal is, if not the experience of loss, the exercise of the ability to lose.[20]

This connection between loss and renewal has deep theological roots, as we shall see, but Freud was among the first to capture it in the non-religious language of science. His idea of instinctual ambivalence can help us to understand how our desire to consume goes beyond what is necessary for us to achieve satisfaction, and encompasses, also, a desire to *spend*.

In Freud's mature theory all life activity is a redirection outward of two instinctual tendencies originally focused on the body: the first is a 'narcissistic' attachment to the self which, when redirected, appears as a tendency toward union with objects in the world; the second is a, harder to perceive, 'masochistic' tendency to return to a quiescent state which, when directed outward, appears as a tendency toward separation. Extending normal usage, Freud called these two instincts 'love' and 'death' and regarded 'life' as an ambivalent and dialectical fusion of the two. He believed that in biological nature the instinctual tendencies to effusion and expiration are combined in the body of the individual organism – in nature coming to fruition is always a process of coming to death (ripe fruit falls). Human psychology and human civilization begin, Freud argues, when these two instincts are de-fused and consequently repressed.

My limited suggestion is that we think of spending as a form of 'life' that is a fusion of our need for gain and our need for loss – and thus recognize that both acquisition and expenditure (the purchase and the price) are essential to the project of consumption. Although this point does not directly depend on Freud's theory of instincts as such, his account of instinctual *ambivalence* can help to illustrate my claim: that both 'satisfaction' and 'excess' look different as a way of redirecting *two* repressed drives (love and death) than they do as a way of bringing a single drive (love) into better accord with the reality.

Instinctual ambivalence was not always central to Freud's theoretical position. His earlier work mostly supported the view that there was only *one* instinct, libido, that had to be repressed because it could not be satisfied in external reality. On the basis of this work Freudian socialists, such as Fromm and Marcuse, claimed that mankind suffers from a level of self-repression that is no longer socially or biologically necessary to adjust to external reality. They believed that primary narcissism – the original manifestation of the love instinct – must eventually find expression in sublimated social forms, and that the proper goal of both therapy and civilization is to reduce the amount of *unnecessary* frustration imposed on our sublimated self-enjoyment.[21] Marcuse took this view even after writing a seminal critique of 'neo-Freudian revisionists' who denied the death instinct.[22]

These efforts to reconcile Marx and Freud gave too little weight to the crucial transformation in Freud's thought that occurred when he ceased to view repression as rooted in the conflict between the 'pleasure principle' and the 'reality principle,' and began to see repression as rooted in an ambivalence internal to the human organism itself between love and death. On this basis Freud reconceived the 'pleasure principle' itself as an outgrowth of our 'instinctual' ambivalence between the arousal of mental energy that produces enjoyment (bonding) and the release of mental energy that leaves us fulfilled (separation). Once we give due weight to Freud's eventual acceptance of primary masochism, alongside primary narcissism, as a part of our bodily constitution, we can no longer simply equate increased happiness with the decreased repression of the love instinct. We must also ask how the death instinct is repressed and what becomes of it when our desires are purportedly satisfied.[23]

Within the framework of Freud's mature theory the Apollonian pursuit of permanent satisfaction is no more or less neurotic than the Faustian pursuit of perpetual dissatisfaction: happiness-as-satisfaction is ultimately a fantasy of consumption as the death of desire; happiness-as-dissatisfaction is merely a *different* fusion of the redirected aims of primary narcissism and primary masochism.[24] The production of waste is thus not an undesirable side-effect of Faustian consumption, but part of its unconscious aim. For this reason Freud saw our desire for novelty and stimulation as a repression and redirection of our compulsion to repeat which is a primary manifestation of the death instinct. As a desire for life in death, the revolt against boredom is as much an urge to destroy the old as to bring on the new. Freud (who was himself a long-time cocaine addict) eventually saw the goal of satisfaction as merely a sublimated denial of the ambivalence of all desire.

My point in expounding Freud's view of instinctual ambivalence is to capture the situational dilemma of the goal-seeking (desiring) organism – not to defend the controversial physiological assumptions on which his inchoate arguments for a death instinct provisionally rest.[25] Despite the complexity of Freud's theory, that dilemma is easy to state: how do we avoid being trapped by our goals? There is no answer if our goals are too simple, but to select goals that are inherently unattainable is also a trap.

Freud's enduring insight was to recognize the ambivalence of our desire for *attainable* goals. He saw that getting what we want must be self-destructive in order to be self-creative – that loss and gain are both involved in the fulfillment of every desire. If we were not continually spending ourselves to get what we want satisfaction would be the *end* of desire – in a sense death would be our *only* goal.

More deeply than other theorists, Freud saw that the implicit problem of social thought has always been to relate the biological determinants of our inner states – desire and satisfaction – to the objects that our material environment presents to consciousness. If his theory is plausible, then the ordinary satisfaction of desire may be closer to the substitution of methadone for heroin than to anything Aristotle had in mind. The obvious question – both physiological and environmental – is how long can we keep it up? There is no reason to suppose that the answer is, or should be, 'forever.'

Addiction and satisfaction

The foregoing account of Freud reopens the question of why addiction is presumed to be morally troubling in a way that satisfaction is not. Most of us believe that the behaviors we designate as addictive are also *dangerous* because they are ultimately unsustainable – biologically, psychologically, or environmentally. But what is the moral objection to a 'safely addictive' behavior – one that is sustainable without the undesirable side-effects?[26] Suppose that we set aside our beliefs about the dangerous side-effects, or perhaps (following Freud) that we bracket our moral assumptions that danger is intrinsically undesirable and that permanence is intrinsically desirable: addiction and satisfaction will then seem to mirror each other in ways that are morally dizzying.

They will 'mirror' each other in the sense that the remaining moral distinction between addiction and satisfaction is likely to begin with the claim that one is a mere 'simulation' of what the other is in reality. But which is which? Is opium addiction, for example, morally troubling because it *simulates* satisfaction by purely chemical means? Presumably, what is missing from this simulation is something cognitive (as well as something chemical). But why not say that *satisfaction* simulates by purely *cognitive* means whatever it is that really 'hooks' us – freedom, self-creation, danger, death – the *true* addictions? What would be missing from the 'simulation' here is presumably the reproduction of the desires that make the satisfaction meaningful.[27] Is *satisfaction* the opiate of the people insofar as it serves to dull or extinguish desire?[28]

The problems are equally serious if we try to distinguish between simulation and reality from the opposite direction. Suppose we say that the trouble with addiction is that it creates *real* dissatisfaction? How then do we characterize the moral discontents of the non-addict – the person who obsessively pursues truly desirable goods? Are these discontents merely illusory, when properly understood, perhaps because the pursuit of morally valuable goals ought itself to produce the kind of pleasurable stimulus, or even contentment, that opiates merely simulate? (Socrates is not really 'dissatisfied'; he is 'hooked' on The Good.) Do we rather say that the true discontents that come from pursuing morally unavoidable ends are in every sense superior to the false contentment that comes from satisfying artificially created needs?

Are moral obsessions better than addictions because the discontents they produce are *real*?[29] (Are the dissatisfactions of the 'pig' worse than those of Socrates?)

The difficulty of formulating a morally-relevant distinction between addiction and satisfaction is even more apparent at the level of social and political philosophy. Here it remains an open question whether (and when) it is better for a form of life, or a pattern of behavior, to reinforce the desires that led to it, rather than extinguishing them. When do we want individuals to be 'addicted' to a particular social practice, rather than merely satisfied by it? John Rawls has argued that just institutions should strengthen, rather than eliminate, the passion for justice.[30] (In a sense they make us 'justice-junkies'.) Why, then, should it be an objection to a market society that it reinforces, and does not moderate, the desire to consume – that it makes us 'mall-junkies'?

Clearly, the standard moral critique of consumer society needs to be reconsidered if the distinction between addiction and satisfaction is no longer obvious – and if we are compelled to recognize that satisfaction is not our only goal.[31] An analysis of capitalism that recognizes the ambivalence of consumer spending would go a long way toward explaining the failure of those forms of socialism that presuppose that the only rational goal of consumption is satisfaction, and that waste is always an undesirable side-effect. From such an analysis we might plausibly conclude that the connection between desire, loss, and renewal can be as important in our vision of the human good as the connection between desire, gain, and satisfaction.

Accumulation and waste

Is it possible to acknowledge the ambivalence of all desire, as Freud did, and still put forward a coherent *critique* of capitalist triumphalism? Marx, Nietzsche, and Weber each believed that accumulating without spending – the basis of capitalism – would be impossible to explain if satisfaction (utility) were our only goal. Despite their theoretical differences, each suggested that capitalism was an outlet for impulses and anxieties that would otherwise have found religious expression; and each believed that the critique of capitalism had much in common with the critique of religion. Freud allows us to deepen these claims. His account of the ambivalence of all desire helps to explain how the desire to accumulate the surplus could have originated out of an 'earlier' form of desire that did not have satisfaction as its aim.

Before the surplus was accumulated, according to Freud, it was sacrificed (spent, given away). Such sacrificial consumption was at its core a *useless* destruction of useful things.[32] Freud believed that the goal of sacrificial activity was the expiation or relief of guilt:[33] the archaic individual sought such relief by directing his self-aggression outward in the form of largesse that aimed to humiliate the other.[34]

This suggests that the act of accumulating surplus exchange values is not based on a simple desire for gain – it is rather a transformation of the impulse to sacrifice surplus *use* values. The individual who accumulates without spending has in effect transformed the ritual sacrifices that expiate guilt into a ritual of *self*-sacrifice – 'in accumulating possessions the individual shoulders the burden of his own guilt.' As N.O. Brown puts it, '[t]he modern psychology of taking is constructed, by a process of denial, out of its archaic opposite, giving.'[35]

The Freudian idea that in consuming we wish to lose as well as to gain, to spend as well as to have, helps explain how exploitation under capitalism can occur through a process of voluntary submission rather than overt domination and control. From a Freudian perspective the wasteful consumer of post-utilitarian capitalism goes one step beyond the Protestant Ethic – he unconsciously expiates and humiliates himself at the same time. Because continuing possession is no longer essential to his goal, he is able to achieve part of the aim of giving (loss) and part of the aim of taking (gain) in a fantasy of renewal that conceals his ambivalence about both aims. Part of the impulse to consume under capitalism fits the language that one Freudian feminist has used to describe sexual masochism: 'a wish to be penetrated, found, released – a wish that can be expressed in metaphors of violence as well as in metaphors of redemption.'[36]

The new element in this approach is the explicit recognition of our ambivalence about both possession and control. For Freud there could be no such thing as a single-minded desire for gain and no such thing as an unalloyed desire for dominance. When he argued that sadism is a redirection outward of primary masochism, he did not go on to conclude – as many have since – that sadism is justified when the victim is a masochist.[37] His point was rather that both sadistic domination and masochistic submission are already ambivalent on both the moral matrix of love/justice and the biological matrix of love/death.[38] It follows that the masochist will not be truly 'free to lose' unless both this moral and instinctual ambivalence is respected by a sadist whose conscious pleasure (gain) is rooted in an unconscious identification with the masochist's loss.[39]

For our purposes the central point in Freud's argument is that neither the desire to gain (Rational Choice) nor the urge to dominate (The Will to Power) are primary and self-explanatory. The desire to gain is rather a redirection of our (possibly unconscious) wish to lose, driven perhaps by our fear of those dimensions of freedom that require a capacity to lose. By parallel reasoning, our desire to dominate is a redirection of our (possibly unconscious) wish to submit, driven perhaps by our fear of those dimensions of freedom that require a capacity to submit.

Freud's theory suggests that there is a deep level in the psychology of capitalism at which the systemic tendency to sacrifice (waste) surplus use values as consumption is fused with the tendency to accumulate surplus exchange values as investment. This is the level at which political economy merges with social ecology. A critique of capitalism that looks at consumer waste and capital accumulation as the two sides of historical materialism could be fundamentally coherent with Freud's insight into the ambivalence of all desire.[40]

III

But before we reach this point, we will first have to consider why the recognition of this fundamental ambivalence does not directly appear within the broad tradition of thought about equality that culminated in the socialist critique of capitalism. The reasons for this avoidance are deeply rooted in a powerful conceptual framework that the Left has shared with the views that it opposes. Notwithstanding their insights into the psychology of gain and loss, not even Marx, Nietzsche and Weber were able to fully escape the power of this framework in their writings on social justice.

Domination and exploitation

Traditionally, socialist thought is an effort to reconcile two ways of looking at the politics of equality. The first is to focus on the politics of domination and subjection. (What makes some people submit to others – is it force, fear, love, identification?) The second way of looking at equality is to focus on the politics of gain and loss. (Who benefits at whose expense?) On the Left the second set of issues is usually referred to as the problem of exploitation.

The socialist tradition conceives exploitation and domination to be conceptually separate phenomena – distinct 'circuits' of power that are especially objectionable when they flow, as they usually do, in the same direction. By distinguishing in principle between these two circuits, socialists can stress the continuity of markets with preceding social forms, such as feudalism, in which those who are dominant clearly gain. Even in the market, socialists say, exploitation can be a means of domination, and domination a means of exploitation.[41] Historically, the Left has therefore focused on both dimensions of inequality – domination and exploitation – and on the connections between them in a given social order. The moral force of the critique of exploitation is almost always that gain has been used to achieve dominance; the moral force of the critique of domination is almost always that dominance has been used to reap gain.

Clearly, however, the effectiveness of such arguments rests on answers to more basic questions that are not confined to the Left. Are exploitation and domination independently objectionable? Could either one exist in the absence of the other? Is it the specific *relationship* between the two that makes each illegitimate in most historically existing societies? Might we imagine a different relationship between the politics of gain and loss and the politics of domination and subjection that could legitimate both unequal gain and unequal glory? We cannot identify the Left's presuppositions on these points without a broader understanding of the role that the distinction between domination and exploitation has played in the development of Western civilization.

Exploitation and domination – the two forms of inequality – are both of course circuits of *power*. But natural power – the production of heat – is an undifferentiated unity, at once creative and destructive. Biologically, too, creation is self-expenditure; gain and loss are generally fused in the same creative act.[42] In these examples of fused power ambivalence is clearly present. It is only when these powers are *de*-fused that the loss and gain sides of the creative act can be allocated to different individuals or classes, and that domination and exploitation appear to be separate.

How did this separation occur in the human consciousness? We can only speculate that it had something to do with the origins of religious belief – the first form of credit. Perhaps the origin of culture *is* the splitting of the creative and destructive aspects of natural power. How could any natural being believe *itself* to be a creature without also recognizing what it means to be a beneficiary of creation and a victim of destruction?

What does this separation mean? It means that theology must now cope with the ambivalence of divine power through the technique of reconciling the distinct accounts of dominance and gain.

Consider Western monotheism, which ascribes to God the power to create as much as possible (everything) out of as little as possible (nothing). Did He keep the gains while leaving us the power to choose? How then can we ever please Him, if we are always mere guests at His table? Or did He give up the gains, while still retaining control over us? How then can we ever thank Him, if we remain in His debt? Is it God or man who deserves the credit?

Instead of a self-consuming spendthrift God, the Old Testament describes two closed circuits of divine power: the circuit of domination/subjection ('the Lord is my Shepherd') and the circuit of gain/loss ('I shall not want'). As separate accounts (accountings) of the unequal and non-reciprocal relation of God and man, the issues of domination and exploitation are here always inseparable, but never easily reducible to each other.[43] They are, however, *fungible*. It is the fungibility of exploitation and domination that underlies the Christian effort to reconcile accounts with God.

Love and justice

The Christian theology of love and justice is an explicit attempt to reconcile domination and exploitation.[44] For the Christian theologian, such as Paul or Augustine, there is no question that God is *dominant*. The problem is to show that He is not also *exploitative*. Is God's creation truly a gift to His creatures, or does God dominate for the sake of gain, as the Devil charges?[45]

The theology of the cross is a direct response to this charge. To redeem mankind from the Devil, God must first demonstrate through Christ that His dominance is self-sacrificial.[46] This divine self-sacrifice is necessary in order to give mankind the choice of accepting God's dominance as an act of love. Rather than transcending justice, however, the Christian concept of God's love directly connects the justification of mankind's submission to the acceptance of gain and the justification of God's dominance to the capacity for loss. In the Christian view of God's love for man (*agape*) we have what purports to be a pure example of domination without the exploitation of those who submit. Justified power in this sense requires the voluntary self-expenditure (self-exploitation?)[47] of the dominator.

For Augustinian Christianity, the justification of power depends upon our ability to distinguish between the direction of gain and loss and the direction of domination and subjection. Paradise is lost when the two reinforce each other; regained when the two counteract each other. In important respects Christian ethics is based on the moral ideal of the Greatness of the Servant. This ideal implies that the only legitimate domination is self-sacrificial, and that humility without humiliation is an appropriate response to domination exercised in the spirit of love.

Inequality and legitimacy

Without detracting from its power as theology, we can generalize the logic of the Christian view of love and justice as a form of double-entry bookkeeping. We are asked to imagine that for each person separate accounts are kept of gain/loss and domination/subjection, and that for each transaction entries will be made in both ledgers. The books would be balanced when a credit in the one ledger is offset by a debit in the other. Thus, loss 'justifies' dominance over the gainer; gain 'justifies' submission to the loser. (We do not ask whether domination by losing is a form of submission – or whether winning by submitting is a form of losing.) Taken together, the crossed ledgers of Christian theology simultaneously accomplish the reconciliation of each person's ambivalence about gain/loss and dominance/ submission and the 'justification' of the inequality between God and man.

Broadening this framework brings out a crucial point: the intrapersonal project of reconciling ourselves to ambivalence is continuous with the interpersonal project of justifying inequality. In its Christian form that project is, as Milton said, 'to justify the ways of God to men'.[48] God's dominance is justified in part by the absence of exploitation by Him. His self-sacrificial love makes Him the perfect master for His creatures. Another Milton (Friedman) defends capitalism with a variant of the same logic. His task is to defend unequal gains in the market, and he does so by positing an absence of domination. The fact that we are free to choose, he says, makes the resulting inequality legitimate.[49] To the degree that the market gainer reaps rewards by meeting the needs of others, he, too, partakes of the Greatness of the Servant.[50]

Although most classical socialists believed that exploitation and domination were inseparable in human affairs, they nevertheless operated within the broad logic of the Christian theology of love and justice described above. Their socialism was based on the assumption that those who dominate (with the possible exception of God) will always tend to exploit, and that those who exploit will eventually come to dominate.

In its revolutionary moments classical socialism turned the Augustinian logic on its head: instead of ascribing non-exploitation to the dominators, socialists demanded the dominance of the exploited.[51] Socialists in power, whether revolutionary or reformist, tended to argue that both domination and exploitation can be avoided through the reciprocity of gain and the mutuality of respect.[52] They were in this respect purporting to give reality to the idealized self-description of the market.

Free to lose

Although there is no direct acknowledgment of psychological ambivalence in the classical critique of exploitation and domination, the will to lose and to submit are clearly present alongside the will to gain and to dominate. All four of these categories are formally necessary to the process of reconciling individual accounts described above. In this process of reconciliation 'loss' and 'submission' are, of course negative categories in the strictly formal sense in which 'debit' and 'liability' operate as negatives in ordinary accounting. But this does not mean that the human desires to lose or to submit are viewed as something intrinsically reprehensible or illegitimate – they may be virtuous (and in the case of loss, even godlike).

Properly understood, both sides of the traditional moral debate over the legitimacy of the market presuppose that gain and dominance are no more or less fundamental to the system than loss and submission. A standard moral justification of the market is that each participant in a trade benefits from the desire of the other to gain. All gains are therefore mutual, and the corresponding losses simply balance the accounts. We have already seen, however, that the implicit agenda of this argument is to justify whatever inequality may result from such transactions. Defenders of 'capitalist acts among consenting adults' believe that legitimate inequality can result from taking advantage of someone else's wish to gain.[53] Their favourite example is a fair lottery in which every participant is motivated to win – while knowing in advance that the prizes are very unequal. The underlying notion here is that the resulting inequality is non-exploitative if it comes about through taking advantage of another person's unalloyed desire for gain.

A standard moral critique of the market makes the correlative point: market inequality is exploitative if it comes about through taking advantage of the desire of another person to lose (or submit). Thus, the capitalist exploiter is, in one manifestation, someone who panders to an addictive desire that can never be satisfied, and that gives the panderer increasing power over the person whose desires are ostensibly being 'served'. The British creation of an opium market in China would be a classical example of exploitation in this sense. Selling drinks to a drunk would be another; so would enslaving a saint, or a lover. At the most general level critics of market exploitation share the perception that it is illegitimate to gain from taking advantage of someone else's wish to lose – unless the loser is also the dominant party in a relation of self-sacrificial love (perhaps lotteries, too, exploit the wish to lose).

The moral purchase of this critique of exploitation is not confined to socialists, who tend to see capitalist markets as inherently exploitative – it is built into the legal framework of market societies themselves. Within these societies there have generally been avenues in common law to protect potential losers from the detrimental effects of their own contracts, and to extend the liability of those who exploit the needs of the exceptionally vulnerable. Such pre-existing legal techniques have been reinforced by regulatory reform in partial response to specific criticisms of market inequities emanating from the Left. In many domains of market society we will no longer hear the gainer to argue that the consent of the victim is sufficient to legitimate his gain, or the power that results from it.

Until recently, the main dispute between critics and defenders of the free market was not over the relevance of the moral critique of exploitation, but rather over its domain. The strategy of most defenders of the market has generally been to minoritize the problem of addiction, and hence to marginalize the issue of exploitation. (We fight a 'war' on drugs, for example, and ban the sale of films that appeal to 'prurient' interests while at the same time exempting from the label of addiction most consumer needs that are created or stimulated by the market.)[54] At the other extreme, classical socialists were committed to showing that the problem of exploitation is a general characteristic of a market mode of production because the worker's consumption of the goods he can buy with his wages has the effect of reproducing and increasing the worker's dependence and powerlessness. (This is nowhere more apparent than in Marx's own writings.)

In a deep sense capitalism and traditional socialism – both grounded in the theology of love and justice – are driven by the wish to carve out of the domain of legitimate gain a domain in which we are legitimately free to lose. For defenders of the market the latter domain is, implicitly or explicitly, consumption, ideally defined as a realm in which domination is absent.[55] The power to *spend* is thus described as the kind of emancipation that markets provide; freedom is found in the ability to pay the price without having to justify the purchase. Critics of the market tend to locate our freedom to lose as a space in which exploitation is absent or impossible; in which no one can gain at another's expense. Thus, even the most intrusive socialist utopias contained spaces, such as sexual relations, in which free exchange would be encouraged. The moral impetus of classical socialism was to protect individuals from the exploitation of their agapistic need to lose so that generosity, kindness, and love would once again be possible at the level of collective life – an impetus forgotten, and sometimes reversed, by the puritanical socialists who came to power in our century. (The corresponding moral danger was that the domination of a vanguard party could be rationalized if it was defined as inherently non-exploitative – unlike the domination of a class.)

Neither market relations, nor the various alternatives to them, would be morally intelligible if the desires to lose and submit did not exist in the ledgers of each person as counterparts to the desires to gain and dominate. As we have seen, however, the tradition of debate over inequality between persons has been to cross the ledgers of different persons in a way that keeps from view the ambivalence of each about both gain and dominance. If with respect to any interpersonal transaction domination and loss are entered in one name, and submission and gain are entered in another, then the moral accounts are reconciled and the resulting inequality is deemed legitimate. Gain thus seems to be a fair trade for submission; dominance a fair trade for loss. (This is how the capitalist is supposed to view the dominance he gets by paying wages which can be tallied as a gain for the worker.) If, however, the dominance and gain appear in one account, and the submission and loss in another, the resulting inequality is deemed illegitimate. (This is how the capitalist's appropriation of the surplus is supposed to appear to the class-conscious worker who both submits and loses in the course of his relations with capitalists as a class.)

Until recently, this moral economy has made it possible to regard the motivation for dominance and gain in each account as self-explanatory, and to avoid confronting our fundamental ambivalence about each. For each person, as we have seen, exploitation (gain/loss) and domination (dominance/submission) are kept in separate ledgers in which offsetting entries are made. In the debate over inequality among persons the process of justification occurs between accounts kept in different names. (God is at the very least a *name* that can be used for accounting purposes: our gain can be balanced against His dominance; our submission can be balanced against His loss.) Through this process we are each, ideally, reconciled to our ambivalence about both gain and dominance, and justified in the unequal advantages we have and take.

Ironically, however, with the triumph of capitalism the process described above is breaking down before our eyes. Our ambivalence about gain and loss is now entering directly into the rationale of consumer spending itself. The significance of this fact, however, has yet to be absorbed by the socialist Left, which has not even begun to ask the necessary questions: will large areas of inequality seem increasingly unjustified if we are no longer reconciled to our ambivalence about gain and loss? why should people who acknowledge that ambivalence continue to accept the fungibility of gain and submission?

IV

Although traditional socialists, and their Green successors, still believe that the desire for gain is primary and self-explanatory, this assumption is not shared by other analysts of consumer society who tend to identify with the cultural Left. In recent years Nietzschean insights have been presented by post-modern thinkers, following Foucault, as empirical discoveries that discredit the assumptions of both Marxist and liberal theory about what people really want. These post-Nietzscheans can easily acknowledge that the goal of consumer spending is not reducible to satisfaction; to them it is obvious that spending itself is an act of personal sovereignty exercised through the capacity to lose.[56] Instead of recognizing our fundamental ambivalence about gain and loss, however, the Nietzscheans tend to see both of these desires as reducible to the desire for domination about which, they believe, we are fundamentally unambivalent. People *simply do* want dominance for its own sake, say the cultural Nietzscheans; only a Marxist (or perhaps an economist) would assume that beneath the apparent pursuit of dominance lies a desire for gain which is somehow a better explanation.

Consumption and sovereignty

Following the collapse of the communist 'alternative' to capitalism, this post-Nietzschean perspective has emerged as a new paradigm of Left political thought in which the critique of exploitation either disappears altogether or is folded into the critique of domination. On the Nietzschean Left there is no longer a direct concern with the illegitimacy of non-reciprocal gains. There is, instead, a debate about what it means to pander to an addictive desire if all that is at stake is power. In this debate the fundamental question posed by addiction is when and whether waste and dependency are essential to the human project of achieving sovereignty over need. Who is really being prostituted – the addict or the panderer? Is the panderer more like a master, or more like a slave? Is the addict made dependent by his desire – humiliated or enslaved by it? Or does the very pursuit of excess bespeak a liberation from the bonds of self-repression?

These have proven to be divisive questions in the post-Nietzschean politics of culture. Moderate Nietzscheans want us to distinguish between the problem of addiction and ordinary consumer behaviour in the market. There is a big difference they argue, between drugs and cars, between gambling and investing, between prurience and sublimation. Green Nietzscheans universalize the model of addiction-as-slavery to cover much of mass consumer behaviour in the marketplace. There is no difference, they argue, between drug addiction and our artificially created need for more and more gasoline. At another extreme are the Dionysian free marketeers, such as George Gilder, who universalize the model of addiction-as-freedom. They argue that the addictive component of all desire is part of our nature: to live is to die, ripe fruit falls.[57] Despite this range of diversity, however, there now seem to be two mainstream positions among Nietzscheans today – one on the Left, and the other on the Right.

For the post-Nietzschean Left, sexuality and colonialism have replaced the mode of material production as the main source of ideas about equality. In the area of sexual discourse the theory of inequality begins by recognizing the simultaneously coercive and consensual character of domination. The growing literature on sadomasochism – as a reality and a metaphor – focuses on the respects in which domination and submission may be based on bonds of love and knowledge that do not necessarily exclude the use of violence.[58] In the area of colonial discourse the paradigm of social injustice is the imposition of a foreign language on an indigenous culture: to oppress is to understand the other in your own terms; to be oppressed is to understand yourself in the language of the other. It follows that some form of sovereignty is the true aim of every expression of cultural difference. Fixated as it is on sexual and colonial domination, the post-Nietzschean Left is just beginning to acknowledge the joint paternity of the Marquis de Sade and Woodrow Wilson – strange bedfellows indeed.

This style of argument is equally attractive to many on the Nietzschean Right. In a post-Soviet world, they suggest, the free market no longer needs to be defended as a system in which all legitimate transactions are based on mutual gain; the legitimacy of the market no longer needs to be defended at all to those who lose. From a post-Nietzschean perspective trade is a form of war – not a relation of mutual advantage – and the relevant question in any transaction is who has dominated and who has been humiliated by the non-reciprocal aspects of the exchange. Recently, an entire literature has emerged about the geopolitics of trade that is based on extending the metaphor of cold war to the global economy. Within this literature a crucial issue is when (and whether) a trading nation achieves dominance through its ability to spend or through its ability to save.[59] Has Japan mastered the US through producing what we Americans consume; or has the US mastered Japan by consuming what the Japanese produce?

At the very moment when market liberalism seems to be globally ascendant, my sense is that the Nietzschean paradigm described above is now replacing utilitarian rationality as the ideological basis of post-Cold War capitalism and also of its critique – encompassing both the global integration of markets and the cultural fragmentation of states. From this perspective the apparent triumph of capitalism in the ex-Second and ex-Third worlds is really a revolt against the servility of consumption in those societies. The clear implication is that the demand for non-servile forms of consumption is ultimately based on a desire for personal sovereignty rather than gain.[60] Such a demand will not be satisfied by the creation and expansion of markets. It will rather find expression in other demands for sovereignty of various kinds – multiple excesses such as the 'million mutinies' described by V.S. Naipaul in his recent book on Indian democracy.[61]

Both the Left and Right versions of the Nietzschean perspective point us to a deep ideological connection between the consumer revolution that is creating one world, and the global outbreak of identity politics that is reducing the politics of existing states to a struggle for cultural dominance in the guise of asserting equality. In some respects the State Department strategist Fukuyama has seen the political implications of Nietzsche more fully than the radical Foucault:

Nietzsche's central concern ... might be said to be the future of *thymos* – man's ability to place value in things, and in himself.... While we do not, *for now*, [italics added] have to share Nietzsche's hatred of liberal democracy, we can make use of his insights concerning the uneasy relationship between democracy and the desire for recognition. ... [T]o the extent that liberal democracy is successful at purging *megalothymia* from life and substituting for it rational consumption ... human beings will rebel ... at the idea of being undifferentiated members of a universal and homogeneous state ... Liberal democracy could, in the long run, be subverted internally either by an excess of *megalothymia*, or by an excess of *isothymia* – that is, the fanatical desire for equal recognition.[62]

It would follow that those who feel threatened by demands for equality on the part of marginalized or oppressed groups are ultimately and deeply correct – the intrinsic point of such demands *is* to humiliate and demean the arrogant, not merely to get a bigger piece of the pie. Although Fukuyama clearly hopes that consumerism will protect liberal democracies from fanaticism, his words and his analysis have a different import: ultimately, the triumph of consumerism and the politics of identity are one.[63]

The Nietzscheans' basic claims are that self-sacrifice and self-assertion are inseparably linked, that a gift undistorted by the will to power is an illusion, and that the costliness of power is its sovereign aim.[64] This implies that liberalism and socialism are both impossible attempts to make power servile without thereby making it legitimate. Power can never be made legitimate – it can only be exposed.

For those interested in social reform the implications of this view are not promising. If identity politics is fundamentally about resentment and empowerment after all, then its demands can never be satisfied (or avoided) by economic redistribution. A Nietzschean might argue that one reason economic redistribution has never been successfully carried out is that socialists failed to answer the question, 'What comes after?' 'Nothing,' we must say, if satisfaction is our goal, or, perhaps to put it differently, 'Liberalism, at last!' But, if the post-Nietzscheans are right, what must follow material redistribution is an accentuation of the resentments and identity politics that preceded it.

The new, post-Nietzschean, paradigm suggests that Marx's effort to empower the working class was merely a special case of the phenomenon of resistance as reinterpretation – an attempt to redescribe the visible success of capitalism as though it were really a manifestation of the power of labour to transform the world. To post-Nietzscheans on the Left the New Social Movements of the 1970s and 80s were no different from the traditional labour movement thus understood. Rather than being heirs to the revolutionary potential of the proletariat, however, the New Social Movements are now described as recent bearers of the unsatisfiable will to power that once resided in the working class.

The gulf between this Nietzschean view and its Marxian precursors now seems to be unbridgeable from either side. For Nietzscheans the struggle against injustice is reducible in the final analysis to the critique of arrogance – a critique from which even liberalism is not immune.[65] Within this context Marxian materialism presents itself as an alternative to the Wilsonian implications of Nietzsche – both political and cultural – that view all assertions of legitimate difference as demands for self-determination, and that leave the economic basis of exploitation largely intact.[66] Considered purely as a response to the Nietzscheans, the main thrust of Marxism today would tell us to look for the real winners in any social system, and not be distracted by who gets the glory. Within this context Nietzschean radicalism presents itself as an alternative to the various forms of economism, both mainstream and Marxist, that take the desire for gain as the underlying explanation for everything. Considered purely as a response to Marxism, the Nietzschean perspective on capitalist post-modernity is that everything really is as it seems to be before we try to explain or justify it.

Exploitation and/or domination: a personal note

I believe that the Nietzschean perspective that seems to be supplanting Marxism today is not an empirical rebuff to the pretensions of 'grand theory' as such, including that of Marx. It is becoming, rather, *another* theory on a par with Marxism, replete with moral and methodological assumptions of its own. On the Left we now have *two* critical theories of modern society in the field, each with its own paradigmatic analysis of the relationship between exploitation and domination within institutional frameworks. In the real world of political struggle it may be necessary at crucial moments to choose between these two perspectives, and in such circumstances my own predilections would generally lie with Marx. As theorists, however, we have the opportunity to tease out what is right in each perspective, and to explore whether a fruitful synthesis is possible.

Until recently, I could not see the need for the synthesis suggested above. As someone who has taken Marxism as a model of social theory, I was guided by three premises: (1) that overt domination is costly and never self-explanatory; (2) that what explains domination is the preservation or extension of a system of exploitation; and (3) that exploitation *is* self-explanatory.

These premises served to shield me from the broad implications that the work of Foucault has acquired for what is now commonly called 'post-Marxist' theory. As a Marxist teaching Foucault, I always stressed its incompleteness. Foucault, I told my students, showed the *how* of domination, but not the *why*. I sometimes argued that, taken in itself, Foucault's theoretical framework is no more satisfactory than a Bugs Bunny cartoon: we get lots of unmotivated, costly domination, lots of spontaneous, exuberant resistance, but nothing ever changes and nothing is explained. (There was no political economy of the carrot patch.)

216

From my perspective Foucault's illustrations of the disciplinarity that accompanies exploitation seemed to be a useful adjunct to Marxism, reminding us of the friction that is necessarily produced by even the most smoothly-running machines. My Marxism taught me to analyze costly mechanisms of overt repression as a symptom of weakness rather than strength in the underlying system of exploitation: the more overt domination there is, the more likely that the mechanics of structural exploitation are breaking down. I therefore hoped and expected that the reading of Foucault would drive students and scholars to Marx for the rest of the story.

But the study of Foucault did not lead people back to Marx, at least in the West. Foucault instead became the spearhead of a movement to break the connection between the politics of domination and subjection and the politics of gain and loss that had been the primary concern of both the Judeo-Christian and the socialist traditions.

I did not understand the depth of Foucault's challenge to Marxism until I realized that Foucault's main ideas are not an extension of the French Marxism of Sartre and Merleau-Ponty, but are based rather on an understanding of Nietzsche derived from the French philosopher and pornographer Georges Bataille, whose major theoretical works have only recently been translated into English. Bataille's key point (a fusion of Freud, Mauss, and Nietzsche) is that the insult of domination is not essentially connected to taking: *one can also dominate by giving.* In this case the very costliness of domination may be intrinsic to its goal, which is not gain for the self but humiliation of the other.

The challenge to Marxism is direct and obvious if Foucault is read as carrying the work of Bataille forward at the level of concrete institutional analysis (while abandoning it in certain other respects.)[67] Once we recognize that both giving and taking can be equally oppressive and humiliating to the 'other,' it follows that the direction and amount of exploitation – surplus flow – has little bearing on the legitimacy of domination. The implicit assumption of most Foucauldians is that domination is illegitimate *per se*, and that resistance to domination is the only kind of legitimacy there is. (Is the persistence of domination necessary to legitimate resistance?)

Although Foucault himself avoided pronouncements about the legitimacy (or illegitimacy) of resistance, he clearly meant to argue that this question has no necessary relation to the distribution of gain and loss, as it does in both the Christian and socialist traditions. Even if we knew which way surplus was flowing, he assumed that we would still have to determine whether domination is being exercised by taking or by giving. Thus understood, domination is always an act of interpreting what is done with the surplus and resistance is always an act of counterinterpretation. One political implication of the Foucauldian perspective is that the essential evils of colonial domination could have occurred through either surplus extraction or largesse; it really doesn't matter which.[68] In effect both capitalism and colonialism are merely special cases of the broader, and all-pervasive, problem of hegemony.

From the perspective of Bataille and Foucault it is domination, not exploitation, that is self-explanatory and structural – domination is desired for its own sake regardless of, perhaps even because of, its cost. It follows that the Marxian analysis of surplus flows would show *how* exploitation was occurring but not *why*. Traditional Marxism would thus appear as a Ptolemaic exercise showing epicycles on an eternal human problem that has nothing ultimately to do with gain and loss. If the point of both taking and giving is to establish dominance, then there is no need for further explanations based on underlying class interest. When I described the implications of this view of colonialism to a Marxist colleague in Africa, he was astonished: 'Are you saying that people over there believe that things really are as they appear?' His perception was apt: from the post-Nietzschean perspective domination is exactly what it would seem to be before 'deeper' explanations, or moral justifications, try to turn it into something else.

The precise challenge that the post-Nietzschean analysis of capitalism poses for traditional socialists can now be stated: does the moral economy of gain and loss still matter at the level of social theory?

For many post-Marxists the answer will be *no*. Even if capitalism has prevailed at the level of economics, they seem to say, politics is ultimately a struggle for *cultural* dominance – and in the arena of culture the logic of class struggle still applies. That struggle, however, is here conceived to be over the question of who gets to interpret the meaning of whose oppression and whether alternative interpretations can prevail. Cultural Marxism has no difficulty accepting the Nietzschean critique of Marx because it relies mainly on the views of Gramsci and Lukacs who were, at best, highly skeptical of the desire for gain as a self-explanatory motive in the arena of cultural struggle.

For Rational Choice Marxists, however, the desire for gain is rational and self-explanatory, just as it appears to be in conventional market economics. The core thesis of Rational Choice Marxism is that, under certain plausible assumptions about the initial distribution of property, exploitation would occur in a perfect market – even in the absence of coercive domination.[69] From this perspective unmasking the 'micropolitics of domination' that underlies exchange would be, at best, superfluous. If Cultural Marxism explicitly accepts the Nietzschean challenge, Rational Choice Marxism implicitly ignores it.

But these are not our only choices on the Left. My own approach is to consider whether Freud's insight into the ambivalence of all desire can allow the Left to preserve the sense that it matters who wins and loses in material struggles without reducing everything to either Rational Choice or the Will to Power. This approach would begin by accepting the standard Marxian critique of Nietzsche which insists that the desire to dominate is not self-explanatory. But it would also recognize the validity of a Nietzschean critique of those versions of Marxism that share the economistic assumption that the desire to gain is self-explanatory. Although I am intellectually committed to developing a view of Marx that largely avoids this objection,[70] it seems fair to admit that on the whole both Marxians and Nietzscheans have been right in their suspicions of each other. In a sense my approach goes back to the Augustinian insight that the critique of domination and the critique of exploitation must be irreducible and inseparable dimensions of each other. New, however, is the recognition that the underlying unity of exploitation and domination between persons is grounded in the ambivalence about both gain and dominance that exists within each of us.

V

How might the type of synthesis sketched above expand our view of the relation between exploitation and domination in market societies? Despite the well-known danger of metaphors in political theory especially biological metaphors, the heuristic use of such a metaphor is the most efficient way to sketch the type of transformation I have in mind. Very tentatively, I would suggest that a full acknowledgment of our ambivalence about both gain and dominance would require a shift in the controlling paradigm of our critique of capitalism from the metaphor of predation (where the gainer and loser are clearly identifiable) to that of parasitism (where who gains and who loses – and exactly what is gained and lost – is much more complex).

Predators and parasites

A fear of predation lurks behind most existing critiques of both domination and exploitation. Does the predator eat in order to kill, or kill in order to eat? This is surely the foundational question dividing Nietzscheans from the classical Left, whether meliorist or Marxist. For those who live in fear of predation there is always reason to hope that the predator is merely hungry, and that predation is ultimately an expression of material need that the predator shares with the prey. Nietzsche comes to tell us that this wishful thinking is the basis of what we call 'morality.'

The kernel of truth in Nietzsche's argument is that the classical theories of love and justice, as outlined above, are responses to the fear of predation.[71] These responses are based on the recognition that pure predation can exist only at the individual level, where the predator has no interest in the survival or reproduction of an individual prey – and that no *species* can be purely predatory of another species and still survive.[72] The core thesis of traditional socialism (and modern environmentalism) is that human predation will cease when individuals acquire 'species consciousness'.

But the critique of predation has never been a strong enough foundation for a comprehensive social theory. Although instances of apparently predatory behaviour certainly exist in social life (theft, for example), predation is not the most usual and general form of non-reciprocal material dependency.[73] More typical, and much more varied, is the relation between a parasite and host. Expanding, for a moment, on the facts of biology can enrich this social metaphor. A parasite may be a symbiont, a disease, a developmental irritant, and even an offspring of the host. Some parasites become so specialized and simplified in their reliance on the host that they are virtually incapable of surviving outside. (In describing their relationship of mutual adaptation one might here say that the host dominates while the parasite gains.) Other parasites can be spurs to the host's efficiency, and ultimately to the evolutionary development of the host species. (Here, in a sense, the parasite dominates but the host gains.) Of course, there are also some parasites that infest and infect the host, and other near-parasites that scavenge on the host's carrion.

To begin social theory with the metaphor of parasitism is to acknowledge the interest of the individual parasite in preserving or reproducing the individual host off which (and on which) it will continue to live. We would thus presuppose that ideals of husbandry and mutuality are initially part of the problem, and not the obvious solutions they would seem to be if the problem were predation. Unlike the metaphor of predation, the metaphor of parasitism allows us to focus on the extent to which the parasite enjoys the confidence of the host, and the devices through which such confidence may be maintained or betrayed. Ideology lies at the core of social parasitism, which is why the classic fabulists, from Aesop to La Fontaine, have done their work by ascribing to natural predators – the fox, the lion – the social manners of parasites.[74] One mode of ideological critique is to unmask the ruses of parasitism, as if the parasite could thereby be recognized as a pure predator and then expelled. There is, however, very little advantage of a shift to the metaphor of parasitism if the fundamental task of social thought is to unmask the predator in every situation. But predation is not self-explanatory as an end-point of analysis if we are ambivalent about both gain and dominance.

Parasitism, as a metaphor, has the advantage of opening questions that tend to be crowded out by the fear of predation. Which is really dominant, the parasite or the host? Which party is the loser and which the gainer in a truly parasitical relationship? The metaphor of parasitism embraces the ambivalent meanings of social dominance and material gain in a way that the metaphor of predation does not.

In a sense parasitism is ambivalent predation, ambivalence about being either predator or prey. This is true even when parasitism appears to be predation from the inside out (rather than from the outside in) because even in such cases the successful parasite must change the host and/or be 'mistaken' for a part of the host.[75] A political theory based on the metaphor of parasitism would recognize that the successful parasite often begins as a foreign body capable of resisting, and even thriving on, the host's mechanisms of 'persecution'. To *get inside*, the parasite must often use itself as bait, first attracting or appeasing the host in some respect. *While present* in the host it functions as an infestation, an irritant, a stimulus and sometimes a master. Its *departure,* when this occurs, is a healed wound, the embodied memory of a host turned inside out.[76] Adopting parasitism as a heuristic metaphor of political and social theory has several important ramifications.

The first ramification is that, instead of directing our attention to the specific problem of *ingestion* (eat or be eaten), parasitism as a metaphor focuses our inquiry on the more general problem of *incorporation.* In the dynamics of parasitism the interpenetration of boundaries is the norm; organic self-sufficiency is the exception, itself the product of successful resistance and adaptation to the surrounding world of parasites (and only one, among many, definitions of health). In the general form of parasitism one organism typically functions as part of another, while also using the other as a habitat for itself.[77] Before cooperation, the question is always one of subversion: who is co-opting whom?

A second ramification of the metaphor of parasitism is thus to shift the focus of political theory from social cooperation to mutual *subversion.*[78] A political theory based on the metaphor of parasitism would focus on a dialectic between two forms of subversion: assimilation of the parasite into the host, or co-optation of the host to serve the needs of the parasite.[79] Each may also be seen as (or become) a form of adaptation between parasite and host, and ultimately of co-development. At what point does the parasitical organism function as an organ in the host? At what point does it share organs with the host?[80] Just as the logical sequel to predation is cooperation, the logical sequel to subversion is evolution.

A third ramification is that in parasitism dependency can be mutual, without necessarily being equal: both parasite and host can contribute asymmetrically to each other's individual survival, and differentially to each other's development as a species. Once again, the social metaphor of parasitism contrasts sharply in its implications with that of predation. In purely predatory relationships the gains flow entirely in one direction (a paradigm of injustice): the obvious antidote to predation is equal exchange, a vision of justice based on a full mutuality of advantage. The metaphor of parasitism, however, encompasses relationships of material dependency in a variety of forms. Equal reciprocity (based on exchange) and unilateral predation (based on violence) are merely limit cases.[81] There may also be, for example, retaliation, immunization, appeasement, anticipatory self-sacrifice, wasting, engorgement, and other form of uneven development. An awareness that reciprocity is not necessarily equal, and that inequality is not always predatory, would greatly enrich the vocabulary we use to criticize market relationships.

It follows, as a fourth ramification, that parasitism is the social and biological form that presupposes the existence of a natural surplus, as distinct from equilibrium, and thus allows for the development of something new. The French biologist Michel Serres points out that, where a surplus exists, there is always a parasite to spoil or preserve it. He describes the role of exchange in pre-capitalist modes of social reproduction as being similar to the role that fermentation plays in the making of wine, bread, and cheese in the respect that a natural process of decomposition is transformed into a technique of preservation: ('It might have become rotten, and now it is money'). In such contexts exchange is merely one alternative alongside largesse and putrefaction, and consumption following exchange is merely one variant of the process of natural decomposition.[82] But these are not the only patterns. Often, the parasite appropriates the surplus of the host directly without exchanging anything that is of equivalent value to the host.[83] To be sure, the parasite spends *itself* in the relationship; nevertheless, something is being taken 'for free.'[84] (Volumes II and III of Marx's *Capital* could be fruitfully reinterpreted along these lines.)

The path ahead

Although we have, rather too quickly, returned to the subject of political economy, the foregoing should begin to suggest how much rethinking will be needed to incorporate the best insights of both Marx and recent Nietzscheans into a critique of post-utilitarian capitalism. Once Marxism more fully acknowledges that satisfaction is not the whole point of consumption, it will be able to recognize that consumer spending under capitalism invariably reproduces our desires and may often stimulate them. Once the post-Nietzscheans admit that sovereignty alone is not the main point of consumption, they should be less reluctant to identify those who gain from the process by which our produced desires are ostensibly 'satisfied'. For theorists immersed in these respective approaches the path to these realizations may be hard and painful.

There is, however, promising raw material in both approaches that might fit better in the new synthesis than in its present theoretical home. Marx, for his part, learned from the classical political economists that consumer goods are in principle stripped of exchange value at the point of purchase, to consume something is economically indistinguishable from throwing it away.[85] From this he concluded that the worker would not reenter the labour force if most of the goods he purchased with his wage retained their value in use (or transferred their value to some other commodity). Although Marx recognized that from a material perspective the worker's consumption serves to reproduce his labour power, Marx also argued that under the capitalist system of accounting the consumer *needs to lose* – and loses in order to need once more. The 'waste' of exchange value in consumer spending lies at the basis of the domination of capital over wage labour. One moral criticism of the market mode of production is that the capitalist class exploits this relation between consumption and loss as a basic precondition of wage labour itself.[86] Another possible criticism lies in the well-known contradiction between the economic and ecological significance of consumer waste.

For their part Bataille, Foucault, and other post-Nietzscheans have clearly understood that the 'consumer sovereignty' that was missing from planned economies is the recognition that expenditure on consumer goods has two aspects; in satisfying our needs we are also getting something new. At various points, however, they suggest that the excitement of desire can itself function as a form of internalized discipline, alongside the regulation of desire through guilt, becoming yet another way in which capital invades the logic of our lives. Instead of being an exercise of power through loss, consumer spending might thus become merely another act of submission to market forces. If the socialist experiments of the century failed (in part) because consumption was often experienced as humiliating and servile, it may now be the case that capitalism has learned to exploit our need to humiliate ourselves whenever we shop. From this we might infer that the planned obsolescence (planned 'newness') of consumer markets could become as oppressive as various forms of centralized planning have been in the past.

The best insights of both the Marxian and Nietzschean approaches will be needed if we are to take on the major task facing the Left: a restatement of the underlying unity of exploitation and domination in capitalism as it exists today. As we saw earlier, the original critique of exploitation and domination was rooted in a system of double-entry accounting that had its roots in Christian theology. We need today, more than ever, a thoroughgoing critique of the system of double-entry accounting that is the skeleton of modern capitalism.[87] Is the consumer's exercise of his capacity to lose really credited to his own sovereignty? Or does the corresponding gain in sovereignty accrue to someone else?

Daunting as this task may be, it is also necessary. A moral critique of market society will not deserve a hearing until it can respond to the new Nietzschean rationale of capitalism in much the way that Marx responded to its utilitarian rationale in *Capital*. Only then can socialism locate itself in history as a desirable future for capitalism, rather than a lost illusion of the past.

A socialist politics of the future, however, must be more than an horizon on capitalism. Socialists must be able to argue that the system in which we live is already in transition to something else for which it is possible to hope. The need for a new, Nietzschean, rationale of global capitalism suggests that it may now be working to transcend its own limits as it strains toward a promise of renewal that is implicitly religious in character. It remains for us, the critics of capitalism, to understand those limits and to analyze the possible forms that their transcendence might take as evolutionary possibilities within our present world. If socialism is to have a future, it must be the future of capitalism as well.

Notes

1   She concludes, 'If the politicians had only had a chance to peek into our closets, cellars, cupboards, and drawers - looking not for forbidden books or anti-state material - they would have seen the future'. Drakulić (1993), pp. 181-9.

2   Drakulić (1993), p. 7.

3   For an extreme example see Fukuyama (1992).

4   I am indebted to Norman O. Brown for first posing this question to me.

5   This aspect of capitalism was identified and discussed by George Gilder at the outset of the Reagan-Thatcher era. See Gilder (1981).

6   See also Meister (1993).

7   George Fernandes, a socialist member of Parliament and a former Minister of Industry, spoke nostalgically about the time he threw Coca-Cola out of India. 'When I chucked out Coca-Cola in 1977, I made the point that 90 per cent of India's villages did not have safe drinking-water, whereas Coke had reached every village', he recalled. 'Do we really need Coke? Do we need Pepsi?' Now, to his great dismay, not only is Coke coming to India, but Pepsi is already back.' Gargan (1992).

8   This is clearly a politics of virtue, but Greens differ as to whether its basis is Kantian (What if everyone did this?) or Aristotelian (Will it really make you happy?)

9   The Green critique of capitalism is essentially that 'more' is not necessarily better than 'enough.' An implicit corollary would be a Green critique of socialism – the argument that there is no further justification for equality once sufficiency has been achieved.

10 For a related line of argument see Neu (1996).

11 See Goux, (1990). Cf. Gilder (1981), part III.

12 By this I mean a type of socially responsible puritanism that rejects the pleasures offered by this world in order to avoid the prospects of some future Hell, now conceived as a very bad environment indeed.

13 See Meister (1990), ch. 2.

14 See Brown (1991), pp. 190-3; cf. Schumpeter (1970), pp. 82-3. Brown correctly observes that capitalist ideology has finally embraced the inherent tendency of capitalist economies to engage in what Schumpeter called 'Creative Destruction'.

15 Some of these questions are raised in the modern literature on welfare economics. See e.g., Sen (1987), Scitovsky (1976), Das Gupta (1991).

16 The trouble with such arguments is that, as the economist Herbert Stein likes to observe, things that can't go on forever generally won't.

17 See e.g., Nussbaum (1992); Elster (1989).

18 In correspondence Bertell Ollman raises the provocative question of whether satisfaction might need to be redefined outside the alienated context of capitalist consumption.

19 Bataille (1985) pp. 118-20; Brown (1991).

20 Eudaemonists have difficulty appreciating the virtues connected with our pursuit of ephemeral goods. Why 'have' children when one knows that they

will leave? Why not devote oneself instead to the friends (or perhaps the students) whom one will 'keep'? Do we merely hope our children will be the kind of students who turn into lifelong friends? Must we idealize our children as our greatest 'creations' – a form of immortality. Or are we also looking for a new beginning in which the ultimate aim is to give without expectation of return? These questions would be difficult to answer, much less ask, if the aim of human activity – both individual and collective – were simply reduced to the satisfaction of desire.

21 This happy prospect is well-represented by Marcuse (1955), Fromm (1951, 1956). See also, Marcuse (1965, 1966), where the possibility of overcoming socially unnecessary repression appears as a liberatory theme.

22 See Marcuse (1955). Cf., e.g. p. 248ff. and p. 119 ff.

23 This account of Freud's mature theory is deeply indebted to Brown (1970). See also Benjamin (1988). The primary references to Freud's own mature work are Freud (1959, 1960, 1962a, 1962b). See also, 'Instincts and Their Vicissitudes', 'Mourning and Melancholia', 'The Economic Problem of Masochism', and 'Negation', reprinted in Freud (1963a), chapters 4, 8, 11, 14. Cf. 'Therapy, Terminable and Interminable', reprinted in Freud (1963b).

24 By 'primary masochism' in the text I refer to the phenomena that Freud associated with the 'Nirvana Principle' (i.e. the tendency toward a zero-state of energy) and the 'repetition compulsion.' See generally, Laplanche (1989).

25 M. Cunningham informs me that many of the phenomena Freud identified can be better-explained using the physiological insights of D. O. Hebb. See Hebb (1949). The plausibility of this claim must await the completion of Cunningham's own work on evolutionary psychobiology.

26 This is the question raised by those who wish to substitute methadone dependency for heroin dependency; and it is raised in a different form by those who wish to replace alcoholism itself with a lifestyle focused on what it means to *be* an alcoholic.

27 See Neu (1996).

28 M. Cunningham suggested this point to me.

29 Is 'religion the opiate of the people' because it is a false satisfaction of a real need, or a real satisfaction of a false need?

30 See Rawls (1971), ch. 8.

31 M. Cunningham helped me to elaborate this point.

32 See Bataille (1992b).

33 Guilt for Freud is essentially aggression toward a loved object that has been repressed, internalized as a superego, and redirected against the self.

34 This point is further developed in Mauss (1967). See n. 68, *infra*.

35 Brown (1970), pp. 278-9.

36 Benjamin (1988), p. 73.

37   Perhaps masochism would present fewer moral problems if there were not sadists around to exploit it.

38   J. Seery discusses the relation between justice and death in his forthcoming book on 'a plutonic theory of justice.' Seery (1996).

39   For a fascinating discussion see Benjamin (1988).

40   We will not, however, absorb Freud's lesson about ambivalence until we understand that waste is part of the aim of all human consumption. A central argument of this paper is that attacking the wastefulness of capitalism is not an adequate foundation for a morally viable socialist politics.

41   Socialists thus resist the optimistic assumption that (in the long run) the market eliminates both domination and exploitation. Typically, this resistance is based on the recognition that markets themselves are historically specific institutions that depend for their existence upon non-market forms of institutional and cultural power. From this it follows that, purchasing power is not the only form of social dominance exercised in market societies.

42   Cf. Brown (1970); Peirce (1992).

43   I owe the preceding paragraphs to the, rather different, responses of M. Cunningham and W. Brown to an earlier version of this essay.

44   I have in mind the view originating in the Epistles of St. Paul (especially *Romans* and *Hebrews*), developed in the works of St. Augustine, and given epic expression in *Paradise Lost*.

45   In Milton's *Paradise Lost*, for example, Satan persuades the fallen angels that Heaven is a regime in which God gains worshippers through His gifts, and that renouncing Heaven is better than allowing God to take advantage in this way of His omnipotence.

46   As *Paradise Lost* unfolds, God competes with Satan for the soul of mankind by demonstrating a capacity to *lose* through the sacrifice of His Son.

47   In ordinary usage 'exploitation' tends to be used in only those instances where we mean to imply that the advantage taken is unjustified. When a non-reciprocal gain is justified, we generally cease to call it exploitation. Domination, however, may be called 'domination' whether it is deemed to be justified or not.

48   Milton (1963), bk. I, l. 26.

49   See e.g., Friedman (1962, 1980).

50   This view is contradicted in its own terms by the self-described Rational Choice Marxists, such as John Roemer, who argues that unequal exchange, even in the absence of domination, is still objectionable as exploitation. See, e.g. Roemer (1982, 1988).

51   See e.g., Kautsky (1964). Cf. Balibar (1977) and Ehrenberg (1992).

52   See e.g., Tawney (1952); Terrill (1973).

53   See e.g., the general argument of Nozick (1974).

54   Could market mechanisms serve addictive desires without allowing the addict to be exploited? I do not know. In defining what is pathological in addiction, and other forms of compulsive consumption, the deepest problems lie in understanding the relation between repetitive activity, the renewal of desire, the loss of desire, and death. Neu (1996). In what way is death itself part of the aim of addictive consumption, and how does pandering to that consumption exploit in illegitimate ways the unconscious wish for death? An interesting Freudian question is whether, in the absence of social exploitation, the addict's instinctual ambivalence about self-destruction would be likely to activate a natural mechanism of self-protection. In addition to these Freudian concerns, there are also cognitive problems with addictive consumption of a sort familiar to Marxists: perhaps the addictive behavior constitutes an illusory escape from an oppressive reality; perhaps the addict conflates comfort and renewal, achieving neither while systematically misunderstanding the tensions between them. But to go on with this line of analysis we would need to consider what is wrong with such self-deception. And here the argument would carry us beyond the individual, and into claims about the underlying patterns of inequality and power in political institutions and social structure.

55   This consumption, however, occurs largely in the family where non-market forms of domination still prevail, and is influenced by marketing techniques that rely on unconscious mechanisms of identification. See e.g., Okin (1989) and Bowlby (1993).

56   See Bataille (1991), volume III.

57   These positions lend themselves to many further variants and combinations. Some of my more-or-less-Green friends purport to be sexual Dionysians and environmental puritans; and many environmental Dionysians profess, at least publicly, to be sexual puritans. Outside of their own preferred area of permissible excess, many moderate Nietzscheans tend to be (in William Connolly's phrase) 'agonistic' liberals most of the time. See Connolly (1991).

58   See e.g., Benjamin (1988).

59   For a recent review of strategic trade theory by a military historian, see Luttwak (1993b). See also Luttwak (1993a). For a thoughtful critique of this tendency see Krugman (1994).

60   In his major posthumous work, *The Accursed Share*, Bataille argued that both bourgeois and socialist revolutions were essentially attacks on the 'sovereignty' of consumption – the sumptuary freedoms of feudalism to dispose unproductively of the excess that human labour always creates. For him the only difference was that post-revolutionary capitalism makes the commitment to productive expenditure a matter of ethical discipline – the 'servility' of the bourgeoisie derives from the Protestant Ethic – whereas post-

revolutionary socialism makes the commitment to productivity a matter of political discipline as well (Bataille, 1991, vol. 3, pp. 277-99). Having identified capitalism with the servile consumption of the Protestant Ethic, Bataille did not anticipate that the celebration of newness beyond necessity could eventually give the idea of capitalism a mass political appeal in socialist societies where consumption had been merely servile. To replace both capitalism and socialism Bataille himself had sought a 'non-servile' interpretation of 'popular sovereignty' as a form of consumer sovereignty – sumptuary freedom – for the masses. This project, as he conceived it, would amount to nothing less than a Dionysian theory of justice based on Nietzsche rather than Marx. For an argument that brings Bataille up to date on this point see Goux (1990).

61 Naipaul (1990). See esp., pp. 517-8.

62 Fukuyama (1992), p. 314.

63 For a related argument connecting multiculturalism to the needs of global capitalism see Rieff (1993).

64 Here Bataille closely follows Nietzsche. See Bataille (1991, 1992a).

65 See e.g., Connolly (1993).

66 A critique of Wilsonianism, both political and cultural, appears in Meister (1995/6).

67 In essence Foucault absorbs Bataille's Nietzsche and ignores Bataille's Freud. But even this is not the whole story. Wendy Brown points out (commenting on this paper) that Foucault has thereby suppressed the ambivalence about domination/subjection that Freud himself may have derived from Nietzsche. In the end Foucault simply transposes the utilitarian logic of gain and loss to describe a parallel economy of domination and subjection.

68 Could western colonialism have been a form of potlach? Consider Mauss: 'To give is to show one's superiority, to show that one is something more and higher, that one is *magister*. To accept without returning or repaying more is to face subordination, to become a client and subservient, to become *minister*'. Mauss, (1967), p. 72.

69 '[D]omination at the point of production, so often a concern of Marxism, is quite distantly related to the concern with exploitation. I think the essential injustice of capitalism is located not in what happens at the point of production, but prior to that, in the property relations that determine class, income, and welfare.' Roemer (1988), p. 107.

70 See Meister (1990) for the basis of such an approach. In this earlier work I argue that Marx's political analysis begins with the premise that ordinary institutions divide us twice over, according to the politics of identity (domination and subjection) on the one had, and according to the politics of interest (gainers and losers) on the other. As a hypothetical illustration, I

consider the race between the tortoise and the hare in Aesop's fable and argue that the fable may be read as a legitimating ideology showing why the race must *actually* be run, despite the fact that we already know who is faster, and teaching both the tortoise and the hare alike that they must run in order to win (pp. 206-10).

I now see that both Nietzscheans and Marxists could offer pertinent critiques of such an ideology. A Nietzschean could say that the fable expresses the *ressentiment* of the presumptive losers against the arrogance of the hares, and would go on to ask whether the hare better expresses his superiority by running or by refusing to run. Which is more humiliating to the tortoise? In contrast a Marxist could say that the fable is a way of making the tortoises run as fast as they can in order to make the hares run fast enough to win. The Marxist would go on to ask why the running of the tortoises is necessary for the race. What cumulative gains does the race produce? Who receives those gains? What is the role of the gains and losses created by the race in the functioning of other social practices? The Nietzschean and the Marxian perspectives each have their point, but a deeper reading of the fable would connect the insights of Marx with those of Nietzsche. It might also stress the fundamental ambivalence of the tortoise and hare about dominance, gain, and the relation between them, and how the running of the race reconciles each to that ambivalence in ways that seem to justify whatever systemic inequality between tortoises and hares is produced as a result.

71 Nietzsche himself, however, seems to have been terrified of parasites.
72 Recent studies of artificial parasites, such as computer viruses, have underscored this point. For applications of research on artificial parasitism to problems in evolution and biodiversity, see Levy (1992) and Rennie (1992).
73 '[W]e began with hunting, but this first stage, like the first seconds of the universe, was so short, so limited, that it is not worth the trouble of talking about it. From the dawn of time there are no more prey.' Serres (1982), p. 10.
74 Ibid., p. 8.
75 From this perspective the predatory tyrant (or wolf in sheep's clothing) would not be a special case, but merely a point on a continuum of similar relations.
76 We would have no memory without our scars, no history without our parasites.
77 See Meister (1990), chs. 8-9,
78 Subversion has not been a core concept in mainstream political theory, which tends to focus on the choice between cooperation and competiton (as in the *Prisoner's Dilemma*). Social contract theory, for example, sees cooperation as a desirable alternative to forms of competition that are essentially predatory.
79 See Meister (1990).

229

80   What is the relation between disease and the inability to share one's organs, or to otherwise adapt to one's parasites?

81   For discussion of retaliatory violence, mutual exchange, and expiatory self-sacrifice as three forms of reciprocity, see Anspach (1992).

82   Serres (1982), p. 156.

83   The discussion above draws on the suggestive treatment of these themes in Serres (1982), esp. pp. 7-10. I am indebted to N.O. Brown for directing my attention to this book.

84   A friend, and houseguest, reminded me while I was writing this essay that 'the key to managing human labour is understanding how hard people will work to get something for free.'

85   It is interesting in this regard that expenditures on owner-occupied housing are not regarded as 'consumption' for the purpose of calculating GDP.

86   A further point, perhaps technical and certainly controversial, is that the degree of exploitation could arguably increase as wage goods make up a diminishing proportion of the total product. See Meister (1990), pp. 286-9.

87   Ibid., chs. 11-12.

References

Anspach, M. (1992), 'Vengeance in Reverse: Reconciliation Through Exchange', *Stanford French Review*, 16, No. 1, pp. 77-85.

Balibar, E. (1977), *On the Dictatorship of the Proletariat*, Humanities Press: Atlantic Highlands, N.J.

Bataille, G. (1985), 'The Notion of Expenditure', in Stoekl, A. (ed.), *Visions of Excess: Selected Writings 1927-1939*, Stoekl, A., Lovitt, C.R., and Leslie, D.M., Jr., (trans.), University of Minnesota Press: Minneapolis.

___ (1988), *The Accursed Share: An Essay on General Economy, Vol. I (Consumption)*, Hurley, R. (trans.), Zone Books: New York.

___ (1991), *The Accursed Share: Vol. II (The History of Eroticism), Vol. III (Sovereignty)*, Hurley, R., (trans.), Zone Books: New York.

___ (1992a), *On Nietzsche*, Boon, B. (trans.), Paragon House: New York.

___ (1992b), *Theory of Religion*, Hurley, R. (trans.), Zone Books: New York.

Benjamin, J. (1988), *The Bonds of Love: Psychoanalysis, Feminism, and the Problem of Domination*, Pantheon Books: New York.

Bowlby, R. (1993), *Shopping with Freud*, Routledge: New York.

Brown, N.O. (1970), *Life Against Death: The Psychoanalytical Meaning of History*, Wesleyan University Press: Middletown, Connecticut.

___ (1991), 'Dionysus in 1990', in *Apocalypse and/or Metamorphosis*, University of California Press: Berkeley.

Cohen, G.A. (1978), *Karl Marx's Theory of History: A Defence*, Princeton University Press: Princeton.

Connolly W.E. (1991), *Identity/Difference: Democratic Negotiations of Political Paradox*, Cornell University Press: Ithaca.

Connolly, W. (1993), 'Beyond Good and Evil: The Ethical Sensibility of Michel Foucault', *Political Theory*, 21 No. 3, pp. 365-90.

Das Gupta, P. (1991), *An Inquiry into Well-Being and Destitution*, Clarendon Press: Oxford.

Drakulic, S. (1993), *How We Survived Communism and Even Laughed*, Harper: New York.

Ehrenberg, J. (1992), *The Dictatorship of the Proletariat: Marxism's Theory of Socialist Democracy*, Routledge: New York.

Elster, J. (1989), 'Self-Realization in Work and Politics: The Marxist Conception of the Good Life', in Elster, J. and Moene, K.O. (eds.), *Alternatives to Capitalism*, Cambridge University Press: New York.

Freud, S. (1959), *Beyond the Pleasure Principle*, Strachey, J. (trans.), Bantam: New York.

___ (1960), *Group Psychology and the Analysis of the Ego*, Strachey, J. (trans.), Bantam: New York.

___ (1962a), *Civilization and its Discontents*, Strachey, J. (trans.), Norton: New York.

___ (1962b), *The Ego and the Id*, Riviere, J. (trans.), Norton: New York.

(1963a), *General Psychological Theory: Papers on Metapsychology*, Rieff, P. (ed.), Collier Books: New York.

___ (1963b), *Therapy and Technique*, Rieff, P. (ed.), Collier Books, New York.

Friedman, M. (1962), *Capitalism and Freedom*, University of Chicago Press: Chicago.

___ (1980), *Free to Choose: A Personal Statement*, Harcourt Brace Jovanovich: New York.

Fromm, E. (1951), *The Sane Society*, Rinehart: New York.

___ (1956), *The Art of Loving*, Harper: New York.

Fukuyama, F. (1992), *The End of History and the Last Man*, Free Press: New York.

Gargan, E.A. (1992), 'A Revolution Transforms India: Socialism's Out, Free Market In', *New York Times*, Sunday, 29 March.

Gilder, G.F. (1981), *Wealth and Poverty*, Basic Books: New York.

Goux, J.J. (1990) 'General Economics and Post-Modern Capitalism', *Yale French Studies* 78, pp. 206-24.

Hebb, D. O. (1949), *The Organization of Behavior: A Neuropsychological Theory*, Wiley: New York.

Kautsky, K. (1964), *The Dictatorship of the Proletariat*, University of Michigan Press: Ann Arbor.

Krugman, P. (1994), 'Competitiveness: A Dangerous Obsession', *Foreign Affairs* 73.2, pp. 28-45.

Laplanche, J. (1989), 'Why the Death Drive?', in Spurling, L. (ed.), *Sigmund Freud: Critical Assessments, Vol. 2*, Routledge: New York.

Levy, S. (1992), *Artificial Life: The Quest for a New Creation*, Pantheon Books: New York.

Luttwak, E. (1993a), *The Endangered American Dream: How to Stop the United States from Becoming a Third World Country and How to Win the Geo-Economic Struggle for Industrial Supremacy*, Simon & Schuster: New York.

___ (1993b), 'Who's Bashing Whom? Trade Conflict in High-Technology Industries', *Times Literary Supplement* 4691, pp. 7-9.

Marcuse, H. (1955), *Eros and Civilization: A Philosophical Inquiry into Freud*, Vintage Press: New York.

___ (1965), *Reason and Revolution: Hegel and the Rise of Social Theory*, Beacon Press: Boston.

___ (1966), *One Dimensional Man*, Beacon Press: Boston.

Mauss, M. (1967), *The Gift: The Forms and Functions Exchange in Archaic Societies*, Cunnsion, I. (trans.), Norton: New York.

Meister, R. (1990), *Political Identity: Thinking Through Marx*, Blackwell: Oxford.

___ (1993), 'Is Moderation a Virtue? Gregory Vlastos and the "Toxins of Eudaemonism"', *Apeiron* 26, No. 3-4, pp. 111-35.

___ (1995/6), 'Sojourners and Survivors: Two Logics of Constitutional Protection', *Studies in American Political Development* 9, No. 2 (1995), pp. 229-86; *University of Chicago Law School Roundtable*, 3, No. 1 (1996), pp. 1-64.

Milton, J. (1963), *Paradise Lost*, Holt, Rinehart, and Winston: New York.

Naipaul, V.S. (1990), *India: A Million Mutinies Now*, Viking Penguin: New York.

Neu, J. B. (1996), 'Boring from Within: Endogenous vs. Reactive Boredom', in Flack, F.W. Jr. and Laird, J.D. (eds.), *Emotions in Psychopathology: Theory and Research*, Oxford University Press: New York.

Nozick, R. (1974), *Anarchy, State, and Utopia*, Basic Books: New York.

Nussbaum, M.C. (1992), 'Human Functioning and Social Justice: In Defence of Aristotelian Essentialism', *Political Theory* 20, pp. 202-47.

Okin, S.M. (1989), *Justice, Gender, and the Family*, Basic Books: New York.

Osborne, K. B. (1990), *Reconciliation and Justification: The Sacrament and its Theology*, Paulist Press: New York.

Peirce, C.S. (1992), 'Evolutionary Love', in Houser, N. and Kloesel, C. (eds.), *The Essential Peirce: Selected Philosophical Writings, Volume I (1867-1893)*, Indiana University Press: Bloomington.

Rawls, J. (1971), *A Theory of Justice*, Belknap Press of Harvard University Press: Cambridge, Massachusetts.

Rennie, J. (1992), 'Living Together', *Scientific American*, 266.1, pp. 122-31.

Rieff, D. (1993), 'Multiculturalism's Silent Partner: It's the Newly Globalized Economy, Stupid', *Harper's Magazine* 287.1719, pp. 62-72.

Roemer, J.E. (1982), *A General Theory of Exploitation and Class*, Harvard University Press: Cambridge, Massachusetts.

___ (1988), *Free to Lose: An Introduction to Marxist Economic Philosophy*, Harvard University Press: Cambridge, Massachusetts.

Schumpeter, J.A. (1970), *Capitalism, Socialism, and Democracy*, Unwin University Books: London.

Scitovsky, T. (1976), *The Joyless Economy: An Inquiry Into Human Satisfaction and Consumer Dissatisfaction*, Oxford University Press: New York.

Seery, J. (1996), *Political Theory for Mortals: Shades of Justice, Images of Death*, Cornell University Press: Ithaca.

Sen, A. et al (1987), *The Standard of Living*, Cambridge University Press: New York.

Serres, M. (1982), *The Parasite*, Schehr, L.R. (trans.), Johns Hopkins University Press: Baltimore.

Tawney, R.H. (1952), *Equality*, Allen & Unwin: London.

Terrill, R. (1973), *R. H. Tawney and His Times: Socialism as Fellowship*, Harvard University Press: Cambridge, Massachusetts.

Acknowledgements

Earlier versions of this paper were delivered at a conference in memory of Professor Gregory Vlastos, Berkeley, California (1-3 May, 1992), Jawaharlal Nehru University (18 November, 1992), Stanford University (26 February, 1993), the Western Political Science Association (19 March, 1993), the Cultural Studies Colloquium, UC Santa Cruz (26 April, 1993), the Centre for Basic Research, Kampala Uganda (28 July, 1993), and the Conference on Identity, Modernity and Politics, SOAS, The University of London (14-15 September, 1994). I am grateful to A. Rai, R. Bhargava, J. Seery, M. Tunick, J. O'Connor, M. Mamdani, R. Hawkinson, T. Strong, P. Euben, R. Inden, A. Montefiore, W. Brown, B. Ollman, and P. Ollman for helpful comments on particular drafts. Throughout the gestation of this paper I have been deeply indebted to M. Cunningham for his role as a developmental irritant, and to N.O. Brown for pushing me to extremes. Were it not for them this paper would have turned out differently. An earlier version of this essay was published in *Topoi: An International Review of Philosophy* 15 No. 2 (September 1996), pp. 189-210.

9 Postmodernism and the politics of identity

Noël O'Sullivan

The central theme of postmodern political thought is the need to create a new politics of identity in place of the traditional liberal democratic politics of rights and toleration. Traditional liberal theory, it is said, has precluded any possibility of creating a genuinely emancipated community because it has equated identity with sameness, and has therefore inevitably excluded minorities. The essence of postmodern politics, by contrast, is a philosophy of identity that is intended to do justice to difference or diversity. Instead of equating fundamental identity with sameness, that is, the new politics celebrates difference and an open, non-exclusive form of democracy.

The aim of this paper is to explore the postmodern philosophical critique of the western tradition that underpins this politics of difference, on the one hand, and to consider, on the other, whether postmodern political theory has in fact succeeded in giving the new politics a coherent form.

It is necessary to consider at the outset, however, an objection calculated to abort an inquiry of this kind before it has even got off the ground. The main motivation behind postmodernism, the objection holds, is a critique of the Enlightenment dream of universal emancipation, but – the objection continues – the Enlightenment which postmodernism targets is in reality no more than an historical caricature. It is, as Knud Haakonssen recently put it in an eloquent attack upon postmodernism, merely a 'papiermaché' Enlightenment, fabricated by postmodern thinkers whose historical illiteracy conceals from them the hollowness of their victory when they subsequently demonize their papiermaché construction as 'foundationalist, rationalistic, abstract, universalistic, mechanistic, individualistic, obsessed with impartiality, rules, rights, institutional forms, and undoubtedly much else.'[1]

What actually existed, Haakonssen maintains, was an Enlightenment with a far more subtle and conservative moral philosophy than either its postmodern critics or its modernist defenders have appreciated. In this conservative Enlightenment, the emphasis was not on natural rights but on natural duties, which were not thought of in abstract, non-contextual terms but were always conceived of, on the contrary, in intimate connection with concrete, experientially defined offices, or social stations. Natural rights, far from being the abstract anchorage of Enlightenment thought, were

234

entirely derivative from these concrete natural duties.[2]

To pursue Haakonsson's portrait of the historical Enlightenment in further detail is not relevant here. What matters is that, even if the postmodern interpretation of the Enlightenment project is as historically defective as Haakonsson maintains, there is a major issue at stake which cannot be resolved within the framework of historical criticism. This issue, which is a philosophical one, concerns the postmodern critique of the whole western intellectual tradition as profoundly hostile to the concept of difference or otherness, in a way which (it is claimed) has had an extremely adverse impact on the modern liberal-democratic tradition. Since the more immediate origins of this philosophical critique lie in Heidegger's call for a creative *Destruktion* of the western intellectual tradition, a brief consideration of what this *Destruktion* entails provides the best way of setting the postmodern political programme in context.[3]

This is the concern of the first part of the paper. The aim, more precisely, is to trace the steps by which the postmodern goal of deconstruction emerged out of Heidegger's *Destruktion* project. After that, the second part of the paper reviews the attempts of continental thinkers to construct a new politics of difference on the basis of the deconstruction enterprise. It may be said in advance that these efforts are disappointing, being open to the charge of never getting much beyond a comprehensive debunking enterprise. This part of the paper is thus in many ways a ground clearing exercise preparing the way for the third, which identifies four Anglo-American versions of a postmodern politics of difference that, it will be suggested, deserve more sympathetic consideration. One of these in particular, focusing as it does on the concept of civil association, returns to the classical tradition of modern political thought inaugurated by Hobbes, with the ironical result that, at this point, the quest for a postmodern politics threatens to turn full circle. This, in a nutshell, is my conclusion – that postmodernism, in its most plausible form, takes us backwards rather than forwards.

For the moment, however, I want to begin by asking what Heidegger had in mind when he gave much of the original impetus to postmodernism by calling for the *Destruktion* of the western intellectual tradition.

Heidegger and the *Destruktion* project

In order to answer this question, it is necessary to begin by noticing a now familiar distinction between two Heideggers.[4] The first is the notorious Heidegger whose pessimistic vision of our age led him to sympathize with Nazism. This is the Heidegger whose characteristic concerns are with our supposed alienation from Being, with the spiritual decadence of our age, with nationalistic ideas about Germany's special redemptive mission, and with what Adorno called the 'jargon of authenticity'. This first Heidegger does not concern us at present. The relevant Heidegger is the second, earlier Heidegger, whose critique of the western tradition in *Being and Time*

(1927) had not yet led him to disastrous political conclusions. It is with this second Heidegger's project of *Destruktion* that we are concerned.

The reason why *Destruktion* is necessary, Heidegger maintains, is to overcome a disastrous tendency in the western tradition to impoverish human experience by marginalizing difference or diversity in so far as it does not fit in with dogmatically based definitions of what is real. To be more precise, various ways of distinguishing between subjective and objective areas of experience have all equated reality (or objectivity) with something beyond or 'out there', whether in the form of Plato's realm of ideas, or the medieval conception of God, or the modern conception of empirically validated facts. In every case, as was said, the result has been that diversity has been downgraded to a realm of mere appearance, or of worldly corruption, or of purely subjective experience. Only the *Destruktion* of this tradition, it follows, can bring about a more adequate acknowledgement of diversity.

More light is shed on the influence of Heidegger over postmodern thinkers, however, if we consider a little more closely why he considered that this *Destruktion* is not in fact destructive in a negative sense but is, on the contrary, a positive step towards human emancipation. It is positive, because it aims to free man from four crucial misunderstandings which the tradition has inculcated about the nature of human identity, on the one hand, and man's relation to the world, on the other.

In the first place, Heidegger maintains, from its earliest Greek roots the tradition has misunderstood human nature itself. The misunderstanding consists of applying a discourse modelled on *things or substances* to *self-conscious beings* to whom the language of thinghood does not apply. This is the great mistake of metaphysics in the classical sense – it speaks, that is, as if the language of substance can be applied to human beings. In a variety of more or less complicated forms, the western tradition has continued to replicate this initial error ever since. The result is that we have failed to understand that man is the only creature whose identity is eternally in question for him. So far as he can be described as having a nature at all, that is to say, it is marked by reflexivity.

In the second place, the tradition has also systematically misunderstood man's relation to the world by encouraging the belief that the knowing subject can occupy an absolute vantage point in relation to the universe. This conviction reinforces the anthropocentric assumption that man occupies a privileged place – indeed, the central place – in the order of existence. The result is that the tradition has concealed from him a fundamental feature of his existence, which is its contingency. The reality, as Heidegger puts it, is that we are 'flung' into being, with nothing except our own self-interpretation to give meaning to our existence. By encouraging a complacent anthropocentrism, moreover, the tradition has nurtured an instrumental, or technological, outlook that is completely insensitive to the environment, which is treated merely as a reserve of resources available for the gratification of human needs.

In the third place, the tradition has been unable to grasp the true nature of man's relationship to his fellows. This is because the technological outlook is not confined to nature but has also been extended to society. The result has been that, in the name of liberation, the tradition has defended forms of hierarchy that entail domination and exclusion.

Finally, the tradition has misunderstood man's relation to time. To be precise, we have been thought of as existing 'in' time, in a sense that implies that time is external to us. Time has been thought of, that is, as a sort of invisible fluid that flows round us. In fact, Heidegger insists, our existence is pervaded to its very core by historicity. This insistence on the relation between identity and historicity has been passed down to postmodern thought in the form of a critique of the idea that we can ever discover universal, absolute truths. From this aspect of Heidegger postmodernism derives, that is, the idea of the inescapably contextual (or 'situated', or perspectival) character of all experience. It is but a short step from this view of knowledge as always somebody's knowledge to the claim that knowledge and power are inseparable.

These then are the four themes that lead to Heidegger's demand for the *Destruktion* of the traditional western vocabulary of selfhood. His alternative concept of identity is contained in the term Dasein, or being-in-the-world.[5] The detailed interpretation of that concept is not relevant at present; what matters is the three main implications drawn from it by postmodern philosophers conscious of the revolutionary new view of man that it entailed.

The first implication is that all human experience is inevitably conditional, in the sense that it can never be based on an encounter with an absolute reality, whether conceived of as Being, God, or things as they are in themselves. One of the best known formulations of this proposition is by Lyotard, who expresses it in the claim that there cannot be any metanarratives, meaning by that term any uniquely privileged forms of discourse.

The second implication is that the 'quest for depth' which has characterized western philosophy ever since Plato is misconceived. To this latter feature of the western tradition, postmodernism opposes the view that everything lies on the surface. At the risk of oversimplification, this may be dramatized by reformulating it as the proposition that for postmodern philosophy, everything is essentially horizontal, by contrast with the vertical or hierarchical structure of earlier philosophy. This distinctively 'horizontal' postmodern perspective is evident, for example, in Deleuze's claim that the true nature of the postmodern intellectual revolution is well brought out by Lewis Carroll in the story of *Alice*, a story in which Deleuze sees the shift from depth to surface exemplified. In the first half of that story, Alice, Deleuze observes:

> still seeks the secret of events, and of the becoming unlimited which they imply, in the depths of the earth, in dug out shafts and holes which plunge beneath, and in the mixture of bodies which interpenetrate and coexist. As one advances in the story, however, the digging and hiding give way to a lateral sliding from

right to left and left to right. The animals below ground become secondary, giving way to card figures which have no thickness. One could say that the old depth having been spread out became width. The becoming unlimited is maintained entirely within this inverted width.[6]

Heidegger himself, it must be added, never quite abandoned the quest for depth. This, it will be seen shortly, is one of the main reasons why postmodern thinkers have maintained that he was not true to the logic of his own *Destruction* project.

The third implication of Heidegger's philosophy drawn by postmodernism is often dramatically referred to as the 'death of the subject'. Since this third implication is often considered to pose a radical challenge to the individualism on which the liberal democratic tradition has long prided itself, it is easily dismissed as a perverse and destructive rejection of all humanist values. As Levinas explains, however, the target is not really the individual as such, but a particular way of thinking about the self that first received modern formulation in Descartes' philosophy. What postmodernism in fact maintains, in opposition to this philosophy, is that 'Human experience is not some self-transparent substance of pure *cogito*; it is always ... tending towards something in the world which preoccupies it'. By 'tending towards', he explains, what is meant is that the object which seems to confront the (Cartesian) subject as something absolutely separate from it is not in fact wholly detached from it. Rather, 'consciousness is at once tied to the object of its experience and yet free to detach itself from this object in order to return upon itself, focusing on those *visées* of intentionality in which the object emerges as meaningful, as part of our lived experience.'[7] Derrida, the most enthusiastic postmodern deconstructionist, is even more reassuringly modest about the limited nature of the postmodern attack on the subject:

I have not said that the subject should be dispensed with. Only that it should be deconstructed. To deconstruct the subject does not mean to deny its existence. There are subjects, 'operations' or 'effects' (*effets*) of subjectivity. This is an incontrovertible fact. To acknowledge this does not mean, however, that the subject is what it *says* it is. The subject is not some meta-linguistic substance or identity, some pure *cogito* of self-presence; it is always inscribed in language. My work does not, therefore, destroy the subject; it simply tries to resituate it.[8]

Despite Derrida's modest disclaimer, however, the overall outcome of the Heideggerian *Destruktion* project, especially when extended into postmodern deconstruction, is a revolutionary change in the western conception of human identity. But what, it must now be asked, are the political implications of this change? For Heidegger himself, it pointed to a politics of redemption with strong nationalist overtones. Postmodern proponents of the *Destruktion* project, however, have tended to combine a sceptical, anti-redemptive politics with a radical ideal of liberation, in a mix that crystallizes in demands for the new politics of difference referred to at the outset. What this mix involves must now be examined more carefully.

The postmodern politics of difference

Postmodern philosophy maintains that although Heidegger was moving in the right direction, he did not in fact complete the deconstruction of the western philosophical tradition which he set out to undertake. As a result, he failed to create a philosophy that genuinely provides for diversity. The aim of postmodern thinkers is to make good this deficiency by going beyond Heidegger and developing a truly pluralist philosophy. Although the intellectual strategies they have deployed for this purpose have varied, those of Levinas and Derrida are especially suggestive. Consider first Levinas, since his thought illustrates with particular clarity some of the main reasons for postmodern dissatisfaction with Heidegger.

In spite of his philosophical brilliance, Levinas maintains, Heidegger himself ultimately displays the principal deficiency of the western intellectual tradition at large, which is a complete failure to acknowledge otherness, difference, or plurality adequately. In this tradition, Levinas claims, difference is sacrificed to a dominant obsession with totality and system. This obsession with totality means that the metaphysical tradition is fundamentally a tradition of violence, in the sense that war is relentlessly waged against otherness. As Levinas himself puts it, 'The visage of being that shows itself in war is fixed in the concept of totality, which dominates western philosophy. Individuals are reduced to being bearers of forces that command them unbeknown to themselves. The meaning of individuals (invisible outside of this totality) is derived from the totality.... For the ultimate meaning alone counts.'[9]

Levinas' aim follows naturally from what has been said: it is to expose the violence that underlies the western concept of being and, in the process, liberate difference through what he claims is the first authentic philosophy of freedom, which is necessarily a pluralist philosophy. This philosophy of freedom, Levinas stressed, must avoid merely standing the dominant cult of totality on its head by putting in its place an equally intolerant ideal of boundless self assertion, which he terms 'infinitization'. In this perspective, Levinas' thought may be seen as a quest for a third way that will avoid these two extremes, neither of which acknowledges the intrinsic value of difference. The aim of this quest, more specifically, is to create a vocabulary in which we can give expression to the originary, non-instrumental encounter with the face of the other on which morality is grounded.

Levinas's sympathy for Heidegger emerges clearly when he maintains that the true nature of the encounter with the other cannot be grasped from the standpoint of the modern philosophy of the subject. For this philosophy, identity is associated above all with consciousness. The truth of the matter, however, is that 'The world I live in is not simply the counterpart or the contemporary of thought and its constitutive freedom, but a conditioning and an antecedence.'[10] By terming the world I live in 'a conditioning and an antecedence', Levinas aims to break with the philosophy of the subject, in which the basic relation of man to the world is conceived of as a relationship between a self-sufficient thinking being, on the one hand, and a wholly external object, on the other. Such thinking is necessarily always representational, in the sense that it always postulates a gap or separation between subject and object and then sets out to bridge the gap by a representation of the object.

Once we have abandoned the philosophy of the subject we are in a position to grasp that the other does not have the total externality which perception misleadingly suggests. But what does Levinas consider to be the political implications of the reformulated relation to alterity? So far, Levinas maintains, the western tradition has destroyed the possibility of a direct, face to face relation with the other by putting in its place a side by side relationship, exemplified by the philosophy of the subject, in which the participants face outwards in a quest for union with some transcendental entity, rather than recognizing that only in confronting each other will they simultaneously discover transcendence:

> Beginning with Plato, the social ideal will be sought for in an ideal of fusion. It will be thought that, in its relationship with the other, the subject tends to be identified with the other, by being swallowed up in a collective representation, a common ideal. This collectivity naturally establishes itself around a third term, which serves as an intermediary .... Against this collectivity of the side by side, I have tried to oppose the 'I – you' collectivity .... [Here there is] not a participation in a third term, whether this term be a person, a truth, a work or a profession. It is a collectivity that is not a communion. It is the face to face without intermediary and is furnished for us in the eros where, in the other's proximity, distance is integrally maintained and whose pathos is made of both this proximity and this duality.[11]

The trouble is that, no matter how sympathetic one may be to this theory of alterity, its political implications appear, in fact, to be extremely anti-political. This is because any concrete social relationship is likely, from this point of view, to be experienced as a mask that conceals the pure, wholly unmediated relationship which Levinas seeks in the encounter with the face. Nevertheless, Levinas did consider his philosophy had profound political implications. What these were is evident, above all, from the theorizing in which he engaged after he became a leading spokesman for the new state of Israel.

What is instructive, in this connection, is that Levinas' politics of alterity did not lead him in a very novel direction. On the contrary, he began to speak of the Jewish state in a language that seemed all too familiar – the very same language, in fact, in which Marx had long before spoken of the universal mission of the proletariat, and

Heidegger of the special mission of the German nationalist movement.

Consider, for example, what Levinas had to say about the visit of the Egyptian President to Israel in 1977 to discuss the possibility of peace. He hailed this visit because, he said, it indicated that President Sadat of Egypt had penetrated the mask of power politics and Machiavellian calculation in a way that showed he appreciated the 'prophetic morality' which is the essence of the Zionist movement, raising it high above the humdrum world of nationalist politics and lending moral justification to such bloodshed as it might cause. In this respect, Levinas enthused, Sadat had demonstrated that his outlook was immeasurably superior to that of the western nations, most of which interpreted Israel's doings in the vulgar light of 'political book-keeping'. Unlike Sadat, they failed to recognize that Judaism has a universal significance because the suffering of the Jews, allied to the biblical tradition which enables them to reject the 'totalizing' rationalism of the western intellectual tradition, leaves them better placed to experience and affirm alterity than other nations are.[12]

Unfortunately for Levinas, his attempt to establish the special position of the Jews in relation to the politics of alterity suffered a severe setback five years later, when the Israeli government had to accept responsibility for collusion in a two-day massacre of suspected Arab infiltrators being held in Israeli supervised prison camps. Until 1948, Levinas held, the Jewish people had for two thousand years been the innocent, passive victim of history.[13] Now, however, this picture of the Jews as a principal victim of western exclusionism had to be qualified by recognition that they themselves might be just as good at a bit of alterity negating as the rest of mankind.

It was in the course of being interviewed about this on French radio that a major theoretical deficiency of Levinas' politics of alterity became apparent. Asked whether he felt the Jews could be held responsible for atrocities which it had once been thought they were only able to suffer, and never to inflict, Levinas replied without hesitation that the Jews were indeed responsible. But this responsibility, he immediately added, was only an instance of the universal responsibility we all have towards others. What he also made clear – and this is the relevant point at present – is that 'every man's responsibility towards all others ... has nothing to do with any acts one may have committed.' This, he stressed, is because ethical responsibility in his sense is an 'original responsibility', arising from the fact that 'Prior to any act, I am concerned with the Other.' Unfortunately, ethical responsibility in this sense amounts to a formula for political irresponsibility, in so far as it is completely indifferent to acts, agents, and contexts.[14] This is the striking thing about Levinas' response to the Jewish atrocity of 1982: what it reveals is the wholly abstract, totally *a priori* nature of his politics of alterity.

The politics of alterity, then, does not seem to be a new politics, nor a philosophically very coherent one. The most powerful critique of Levinas' version of the politics of difference comes, however, from a fellow postmodern philosopher. According to Derrida, Levinas' desire to affirm difference in unconditional terms exposes him to the charge of nihilism.[15] In order to feel the full weight of this criticism, it is necessary to consider first the considerations which led Derrida himself to be dissatisfied with Heidegger's execution of the *Destruktion* project.

Like Levinas, Derrida rejects Heidegger's quest for Being as a wild goose chase and seeks to put in its place a philosophy of diversity. His own version, however, is very different from that of Levinas. The essence of Derrida's position is his rejection of the possibility – indeed, of the very intelligibility – of an absolute or unconditional encounter with reality, either in the ontological form pursued by Heidegger or in the ethical one pursued by Levinas in his quest for a direct encounter with the face. In this respect, it may be observed, Derrida displays a deep sympathy for Hegel, whose dialectic stresses the inescapability (as well as the positive nature) of mediation in a way quite alien to both Heidegger and Levinas.

The impossible quest for unmediated experience Derrida terms the quest for *présence.* He rejects this on three grounds which, taken in conjunction, provide the rationale of the deconstructive project. The first is that what has passed as philosophy turns out on closer scrutiny to be inspired by metaphor. The second is that the western tradition has from the start been logocentric (or phonocentric), in the sense that it has arbitrarily privileged speech over writing. The result has been the creation of a series of asymmetrical dualisms, of which the male/female one is the most fundamental. The third is that there is no reality outside the text. All there is, is *différance,* which is the endless, and essentially inconclusive, constitution of meaning in an unending chain of internally related terms, a chain which by its very nature eternally defers the moment when *présence* will be achieved.

With this sketch of Derrida's deconstructive project in mind, it is easy to understand why he detects a potential nihilism in Levinas' unconditional and unmediated affirmation of otherness. The only way to achieve an unmediated contact with the other, Derrida maintains, is to destroy everything that makes a relationship (any relationship) possible at all, which ultimately means destroying both the parties to the relationship.

It is not only the nihilistic element in Levinas' brand of idealism, however, upon which Derrida focuses attention. He also seizes upon a no less disastrous utopian element that is closely linked with it. This utopian element arises from the extended sense in which Levinas uses the term violence, a sense that is not restricted to physical and mental harm, but is synonymous with the existence of any kind of mediation in the relationship with the other. Derrida rightly objects that, if violence is used in this extended sense, then there are in effect only two ways of dealing with it: either one can eliminate the element of violence by adopting the nihilistic strategy already indicated or, if that option is rejected, one can accept that violence is inescapable and try to come to terms with it, instead of trying to abolish it, as Levinas seeks to do. If the latter response is adopted, as it will be by any moderate person, then the conclusion (Derrida notes) must be the paradoxical one, that in order to have ethics at all, one must accept that even the highest ethical relationship (regardless of how that is defined) is inevitably a violent one.

It is clear, then, that Levinas' concern with affirming alterity does not yield a coherent politics of difference. Where Levinas fails, however, it might yet be hoped that Derrida, whose criticism of Levinas is so impressively sane, would manage to come up with a more viable political theory. Unfortunately, Derrida's own attempts to create a politics of difference appear to get little further than Levinas'. Consider, for example, his attempt to envisage what a society would look like in which all sexual discrimination had been eliminated and full sexual emancipation achieved. Derrida describes it as follows:

> The relationship [to the other] would not be a-sexual, far from it, but would be sexual otherwise: beyond the binary difference that governs the decorum of all codes, beyond the opposition feminine/masculine, beyond homosexuality and heterosexuality which come to the same thing. As I dream of saving the chance that this question offers, I would like to believe in the multiplicity of sexually marked voices. I would like to believe in the masses, this indeterminate number of blended voices, this mobile of non-identified sexual marks whose choreography can carry, divide, multiply the body of each 'individual', whether he be classified as 'man' or 'woman' according to the criteria of usage.[16]

A passage of this kind, needless to say, inevitably creates the suspicion that a politics of difference amounts, in Derrida's case at least, to a purely rhetorical celebration of difference. Matters are not much improved when Derrida indicates elsewhere that this celebration of difference entails a commitment to democracy, since the kind of democracy he has in mind is described in terms that are no less purely rhetorical. The relevant rhetoric emerges in the course of his recent convoluted broodings over the fate of Marxism:

> what remains irreducible to any deconstruction, what remains as unde-constructible as the possibility itself of deconstruction, is, perhaps, a certain experience of the emancipatory promise; it is perhaps even the formality of a structural messianism, a messianism without religion, even a messianic without messianism, an idea of justice – which we distinguish from law or right and even from human rights – and an idea of democracy – which we distinguish from its current concept and from its determined predicates today .... But this is perhaps what must now be thought, and thought otherwise, in order to ask oneself where Marxism is going, which is also to say, where Marxism is leading, and where it is to be lead ... where to lead it by interpreting it, which cannot happen without transformation, and not where can it lead us, such as it is, or such as it will have been.[17]

Other remarks he makes about democracy yield nothing more substantial than an appeal for a new International, whose nature he describes thus:

> The name of new International is given here to what calls to the friendship of an alliance without institution among those who, even if they no longer believe or never believed in the socialist-Marxist International, in the dictatorship of the proletariat, in the messiano-eschatological role of the universal union of the proletarians of all lands, continue to be inspired by at least one of the spirits of Marx or of Marxism (they now know that there is *more than one*) and in order to ally themselves, in a new, concrete, and real way, even if this alliance no longer takes the form of a party or of a workers' international, but rather of a kind of counter-conjuration, in the (theoretical and practical) critique of the state of international law, the concepts of State and nation, and so forth: in order to renew this critique, and especially to radicalize it.[18]

Not surprisingly, the vagueness of this vision of a new International has left Derrida's version of the politics of difference open to the charge of amounting to nothing more than 'the ultimate post-structuralist fantasy.'[19] It must immediately be added, however, that the principal theoretical deficiency of Derrida's political writings lies elsewhere than in the flights of rhetoric they contain.

It lies, more precisely, in his indifference to the problem of legitimacy. He displays, that is, a systematic failure to face the problem of what grounds, if any, can ever render exclusion defensible. In this respect, it may be added, Derrida merely displays the main weakness of the postmodern ideal of a politics of difference at large. The reason for this weakness is not hard to identify: legitimacy simply disappears from the postmodern political agenda, either because it is optimistically assumed (as by Derrida) that diversity will automatically tend to create harmony; or else because it is assumed that power is inescapable, so that legitimacy itself is merely power.

The latter view – viz. that power is inescapable, and legitimacy merely a way of evading this reality – has received its best known expression in the work of Foucault. Postmodern pessimism in the face of power does not, however, stop there. Foucault, it has been argued by fellow postmodern thinkers, does not take pessimism far enough, largely because he remained wedded, in spite of himself, to a traditional political vocabulary which simply cannot grasp fully the wholly novel character power is acquiring at the present day.

Deleuze, for example, agrees with Foucault's view that 'modern power is not at all reducible to the classical alternative "repression or ideology" but implies processes of normalization, modulation, modelling, and information that bear on language, perception, desire, movement, etc. ...'[20] He maintains, however, that Foucault is unable to convey the true significance of contemporary changes in the nature of power because he fails to appreciate the *immanent* character of the capitalist 'axiomatic' by which these changes are motivated. Instead of developing the immanent range of concepts necessary to comprehend this axiomatic, Foucault relied on the traditional vocabulary of political theory, which treats power as basically external or transcendent.

The reality, Deleuze maintains, is that we are now in the throes of a new form of enslavement which is neither external nor transcendent. This new slavery Deleuze describes as 'machinic enslavement'. The essence of machinic enslavement is that the machine is no longer experienced as a thing external to the self – as something, that is, made by man, to be used or consumed by him – but as an integral component of human identity. In other words, the gap which has hitherto always existed between the human world, on the one hand, and the technical or machine world, on the other, finally disappears. This occurs, more specifically, with the movement from the era of the 'motorized machine' which has dominated the past three or more centuries, to the era of cybernetic and informational machines. As Deleuze puts it:

> recurrent and reversible 'humans-machines systems' replace the old nonrecurrent and nonreversible relations of subjection between the two elements; the relation between human and machine is based on internal, mutual communication, and no longer on usage or action.[21]

Machinic enslavement, Deleuze stresses, 'is no more "voluntary" than it is "forced"', and attempts to analyze it in such terms merely illustrate why the traditional vocabulary of power is so woefully inadequate.[22]

The detail of Deleuze's portrait of the new machinic form of power in the present age is not relevant here; what matters is the fact that, like other postmodern theorists, he ignores the topic of legitimacy. The result is an ambiguity in his treatment of power that is endemic in postmodern political thought. This is his assumption that the new system of machinic power amounts to a system of enslavement. A vital part of that assumption is the premiss that juridical forms are at best of merely functional significance, as techniques (that is) of integration, rather than procedures that secure freedom and dignity by checking arbitrary power. Merely to raise this problem is of course to risk the charge of being enmeshed in old-fashioned (i.e. 'modern') ways of thinking about power. That charge, however, is not in itself an adequate defence of the postmodern refusal to consider the possibility that no significant distinction at all exists between power and authority.

The all-embracing concept of power deployed by postmodernism acquires its most fantastical form, however, only when a further step is taken by Baudrillard. This step brings about a strange inversion of the old Marxist doctrine of economic determinism. In opposition to Marxism, postmodern thinkers insist on the autonomy of a symbolic order of non-referential signs. This would be a healthy corrective, were it not for the fact that the autonomy of signs has been interpreted in a narrowly intellectualist way that first disconnects them completely from any roots in human desire, and then treats them as manufactured entirely by the media, with the result that the only 'reality' we can ever experience is said to consist of simulacra shaped by the media. It is on this flimsy ground that Baudrillard is led to treat the impersonal power of signs as so all pervasive that the modest kind of freedom secured by liberal democratic institutions is not worth a mention. The precise nature of the fantastical concept of power that fuels this contempt for liberal democracy is worth identifying.

For Baudrillard, liberal democracy builds on quick sands in so far as it takes for granted a distinction between subject and object that can no longer be made today. It can no longer be made, because the 'modern' world, in which it was still possible to think of subjects confronted by independent objects, has disappeared, to be replaced by what he terms the bubble world of postmodernity. In this world, he writes:

> We are all bubble children, like the boy who ... lived in his [NASA bubble] protected from all infection by the artificially immunized space; his mother caressed him through the glass with rubber gloves, as he laughed and grew up in his extraterrestrial atmosphere under the observation of science .... This bubble-child is the prefiguration of the future .... He is the symbol of existence in a vacuum, until now exclusive to bacteria and particles in laboratories, but which will increasingly become ours .... We will be thinking and reflecting in a vacuum, as illustrated everywhere by artificial intelligence.[23]

What distinguishes Baudrillard is the exhilaration with which he contemplates this eclipse of man (that is, of Cartesian and Kantian man) beneath an ever extending network of information and communication systems. In more sober moments, it is true, he enjoins, 'Let us be Stoics: if the world is fatal, let us be more fatal than it. If it is indifferent, let us be more indifferent. We must conquer the world and seduce it through an indifference that is at least equal to the world's.'[24] Whether he ends in an optimistic or pessimistic mood, however, is neither here nor there, in the present context: what matters is that, whatever his mood, the only vocabulary he knows is a vocabulary of power, even if it takes the gentle form of seduction.

On the basis of what has been said so far, one may have much sympathy with the wholesale indictment of postmodernism launched for example by George Steiner[25] and Roger Scruton,[26] both of whom regard it as completely destructive. Scruton in particular is emphatic in dismissing it as merely the nihilistic expression of the unqualified hostility to bourgeois society which has been particularly widespread amongst French intellectuals in the aftermath of 1968. More generally, post-modernism is merely 'a last spasm of romanticism', a romanticism that 'has given up hope of an otherworldly redemption, and set out instead to destroy the illusions in which others still believe ... '. It is, in fact, a new religion, rather than a philosophical movement. As with all religion, its key words, like *différance*, have a purely incantatory force for their devotees. The essence of this particular religion, however, is that it 'is defined by negation of "the Other"'.[27]

Although Scruton's misgivings command sympathy, his comprehensive indictment of postmodernism is open to two criticisms. One is the charge of exaggerating the nihilistic impulse in postmodernism, which may instead be seen as the story of how an increasing disillusion with radicalism has, in some cases at least, paved the way for the beginnings of an uneasy accommodation with that civilization. Julia Kristeva, coupled by Scruton with Derrida as an arch postmodern destroyer, is a case in point. What is notable about Kristeva is in fact her discovery of the delights of bourgeois ordinariness or banality, as she informed her interlocutor in a recent interview:

> People say: 'There was this group of people who were so intellectual, who were there in '68, and where are they now? At home having children! *Quel malheur!* What conformism!' But I say that this is not to be less, it is to be more .... I'm getting to know the banality in myself.[28]

As the interviewer commented, 'She finds it a pleasing discovery'. This is hardly the descent into nihilism described by Scruton in such unqualified terms. It is, rather, as if continental intellectuals hover on the brink of rediscovering, somewhat late in the day, the wisdom of Montaigne's verdict in the concluding words of his essay *On Experience*. 'The finest lives', Montaigne wrote, 'are, in my opinion, those which conform to the common and human model in an orderly way, with no marvels and no extravagances'.[29]

It is significant, secondly, that Scruton's critique of postmodernism concentrates on continental postmodernism and ignores Anglo-American sympathizers. The latter thinkers, whatever else they may be, are far from being nihilists. Their problems are, in many respects, merely those of well meaning liberals in an era of scepticism, in which the universality of western values can no longer be taken for granted. It is from this point of view that we may now turn to consider how they have responded to the disappearance of old hierarchies and the call for a politics of difference.

Four postmodern philosophies of difference

The Anglo-American literature reveals four different responses to diversity, in the form of four different political theories. Although none is unique to postmodernism, each has been formulated in what aspires to be a distinctively postmodern idiom. The four political theories are considered in some detail below.

The political theory of liberal ironism

The first theory, which is associated in particular with Richard Rorty, takes as its starting point a fact which is considered by postmodern thinkers to be the most important characteristic of the contemporary world. This is awareness of the contingency of individual identity. The recognition of this contingency, it is said, can arise only at an extremely advanced stage of culture in which it becomes possible to contemplate seriously *the possibility that one might have been born somebody else*. This was impossible in earlier stages, in which it was taken for granted that the self had an essence, and that life as a whole possessed an intrinsic necessity conferred by fate, or by God. In the apt phrase of Heller and Fehér, the sense of contingency is possible only when life is regarded as no more than 'an agglomerate of possibilities.'[30]

For Rorty, acknowledgement of the contingency of human identity is inescapable for those who have come to appreciate that the western philosophical tradition is largely a series of mistaken attempts to 'mirror' a supposedly objective reality that is completely separate from us. The appropriate response to contingency, he maintains, is not to flee from it but to embrace it. To those who fear that this response opens the door to irrationalism and relativism, he replies that such misgivings are only possible in so far as one is unwittingly committed to the old, 'metaphysical' view of morality and politics that must now be discarded, since it simply cannot provide the kind of ethical absolutism that it purports to.

In political terms, acknowledgement of contingency leads Rorty to three propositions. The first is that the appropriate attitude towards personal identity on the part of those who have arrived at the recognition of contingency is one of irony. A liberal ironist is one who is 'sufficiently historicist and nominalist to have abandoned the idea that [his or her] central beliefs and desires refer back to something beyond the reach of time and chance.'[31] For such citizens, irony is the secret of freedom, which consists precisely in the recognition and acceptance of contingency.[32] The second proposition is that the appropriate form of regime for ironists is what Rorty terms a liberal utopia. This is marked by universal irony in the private realm, in relation to an endless quest for self-perfection, and in the public realm by a ceaseless attempt to achieve an ever more inclusive ideal of solidarity, rather than in attempts to implement some supposedly pre-existing telos of the good society. This ideal – viz. of solidarity – takes the place in Rorty's thought of attempts to provide liberalism with universally valid metaphysical grounds.

The third proposition elaborates on the second by making explicit the fact that the sense of human solidarity cannot be given any rational foundation whatsoever. On the contrary, what is crucial in creating it is imagination, not reason. It is imagination alone that determines whether we are able to break through the them and us division which restricts the range of human sympathies at any particular time and regard a person as 'one of us'.

The most important problems created by this attempt to formulate a liberal politics of diversity arise from three concepts in particular. The first concerns the ambiguous character of Rorty's concept of contingency. Rorty contends that this entails recognizing that identity consists in a process of describing and redescribing a centreless self, rather than in acquiring knowledge of an ahistorical essence. The problem, however, is that the precise status he assigns to the process of self-description is never very clear. Sometimes, for example, he writes of identity as a thing to be 'tinkered' with, in a sense that assumes that self-description is an entirely optional matter, like the clothes one wears. So far as he acknowledges any criterion for choosing between the different identities available, it appears to be the relative degree of edification they offer. At other times, however, he treats self-descriptions that reveal awareness of contingency as superior to other kinds, on the ground that they display deeper insight into the kind of beings we actually are. To that extent, he appears to be offering a version of the very essentialism he claims to reject.[33] On still other occasions, Rorty writes of the contingent self in terms that suggest he has not in fact made the radical break he claims to have made with the traditional metaphysical vocabulary, but is merely offering a modified form of Kant's dualistic account of it.[34] More generally, the survival of the subject/object dualism which has shaped what he terms the metaphysical tradition is evident, for example, in remarks such as 'The world is out there, but descriptions of it are not'.[35] It is not clear, in a word, quite what Rorty's doctrine of the contingent self commits one to.

The second problem concerns Rorty's concept of solidarity. Specifically, it is that the central position he assigns to this concept entails the division of the political order into us and them – that is, into an in group and out group. As Rorty puts it, 'the force of "us" is, typically, contrastive in the sense that it contrasts with a they which is also made up of human being – the wrong sort of human beings.'[36] This them and us distinction immediately suggests two possibilities, neither of which, unfortunately, creates much confidence in liberal ironism. On the one hand, the 'we' may consist of nice, progressive people. As Charles Sykes has argued, however, the danger then is that postmodern idealism may easily become little more than an oppressive formula for political correctness.[37] On the other hand, if the 'we' consists of nasty, reactionary types, then Rorty cannot mount a very strong challenge to the potentially militant and exclusive concept of solidarity which may then arise. In either case, Rorty's liberal ironism appears to leave the core of liberalism, which is the ideal of the limited state, in a very precarious condition.

The source of Rorty's problems in this respect may now be more precisely identified: it lies in his failure to realize that throughout the modern period, solidarity has been the subject of two conflicting interpretations. One is that of Rousseau, for whom solidarity is identified with a substantive consensus on fundamental values. It is in fact in this sense that Rorty himself seems mainly to interpret it. The other interpretation is the formal or procedural interpretation of solidarity espoused by a long line of defenders of the model of civil association, from Hobbes to Oakeshott. The fact that this formal or procedural interpretation has been the basis of the American liberal democratic ideal makes Rorty's neglect of it all the more surprising. By siding with the Rousseauian tradition, Rorty automatically injects into ironist politics ambiguities that Rousseau originally exposed with inimitable clarity.

The third problem, so far as political theory is concerned, is the most important.

It is Rorty's attempt to underpin his version of liberalism with a distinction between public and private issues. Private issues relate entirely to the personal project of self-creation, whereas public ones concern the implementation of social purposes. There is, Rorty insists, absolutely no way of bridging the gap between these two types of concern in a single, unified, or 'organic' conception of politics. The great virtue of ironist liberalism is precisely that it recognizes this. The mistake of thinkers like Plato, Marx, and Foucault, by contrast, is that they have refused to accept the ultimate character of the distinction.

The problem with this distinction, as critics have rightly observed, is that it eliminates political disagreement altogether, replacing it by a discussion of mere classificatory technicalities. The result is that Rorty effectively de-politicizes liberalism, which becomes in his hands an entirely administrative affair. But why, it must be asked, does this de-politicization of politics occur? It occurs because Rorty assumes, with enormous self-confidence, that he possesses an almost god-like detachment when it comes to deciding whether a particular issue or thinker is to be assigned to the private or public sphere. He assumes, more precisely, that he enjoys the kind of supra-political status that Rousseau assigned to the Legislator. This is in radical conflict, however, with Rorty's own hermeneutic conception of philosophy, which permits only internal perspectives and accordingly rejects the very possibility of any kind of transcendental perspective. The net result is philosophical incoherence, in the sense that it is unclear about where, as the phrase has it, Rorty is coming from. Where he ends up, however, is not in doubt: in his hands, the radicalism with which postmodern deconstruction has been associated on the continent is effectively eliminated, and deconstruction becomes instead a formula for a somewhat complacent conservatism.

The postmodern theory of agonal politics to be considered next seems at first sight to have at least two advantages over ironist liberalism. One is that it drops the problematic concept of solidarity in favour of a concept of agonal respect. The other is that it does not naively assume that the distinction between public and private issues can be given definitive expression. Whether agonal theory finally succeeds in pulling the rabbit of unity out of the hat of diversity, however, remains to be considered.

The agonal response to diversity

The emphasis of agonal politics is on generating mutual respect for each other by fellow citizens through a direct personal encounter in the course of which their identities undergo significant transformation.[38] The outcome, postmodern political theory maintains, is one in which deeper, more secure but less complacent selves result, on the one hand, and a relationship in which mutual sympathy and acceptance replace the traditional, but patronizing, liberal virtue of tolerance, on the other. The most impressive case for this way of thinking about politics has been presented by

250

William Connolly.

The aim of agonal politics, Connolly maintains, is to foster an ethic of care for the protean diversity of being.[39] In practice, this means fostering a 'culture of pluralization' based, not on natural rights, or reason, or God, but solely on 'agonistic respect'. By agonistic respect, Connolly explains:

> I mean a relation of respect and forbearance between contending perspectives embodying appreciation by each side of the contestable character of the presumptions that vindicate it. Agonistic respect is an ideal relation to pursue between two contending perspectives that both have a definite foothold in the established culture.[40]

Agonistic respect, Connolly adds, is the basis of the supreme postmodern political virtue, which is 'critical responsiveness'. This is a 'delicate combination' of an affirmative response to new drives to pluralization with resistance to tendencies in each new drive to become a new, exclusive orthodoxy.[41]

Fundamental to agonal politics is a far more active fostering of a sense of the contingency of identity than Rorty's ironist liberalism, for example, permits. Agonal politics, Connolly claims, does this in four ways:

> first, by respecting the productive role of disruption and disturbance in politics, whereby congealed identities are pressed to come to terms with elements of historical contingency, uncertainty and difference in themselves; second, by honoring a role for genealogy and political disturbance in cultural life, as historical elements of artifice, power and chance in established unities are exposed through these intellectual strategies; third, by cultivation of critical responsiveness to new movements of pluralization proceeding from old injuries, differences and energies; and, fourth, by participating in coalitional assemblages that install the economic and political conditions of forbearance and generosity in relations between contending, interdependent identities.[42]

It is from this standpoint that Connolly interprets, for example, the troubles in the former Yugoslavia. The break-up of that state, he writes, 'is not due to the "proliferation of difference" but to war between contending and exclusive identities each of which is bent upon effacing its own contingencies and uncertainties.'[43] An unkind reader might of course dismiss this as just a rather elaborate way of saying that there are some pretty fanatical nationalists out there; but let that pass. What matters at present is that Connolly presents agonal politics as the only form appropriate for those seeking a positive, genuinely pluralized pluralism suited to 'the historic trend towards multiculturalism'.[44] The awareness of contingency which inspires this pluralism ultimately points, he adds, to a trans-national ideal of global democracy.

How viable is this fully pluralized ideal of agonal democracy? Connolly himself recognizes three problems. The first is that it is an extremely high risk ideal, since every pluralization movement is in danger of provoking a fundamentalist reaction from those who feel their identity threatened by it. The second is that a deep sense of contingency may provoke a sense of political paralysis among rulers. The third is that any attempt to apply the ideal under present conditions of economic and political inequality would impose unjust burdens on those not well placed to engage in the struggle for recognition. Connolly's response to all three problems is one of more or less cautious optimism, blended with a conviction that, in any case, no other option is open to those who clearly grasp our nature and our situation.

There is, however, a fourth problem with Connolly's agonalism that is, from the philosophical standpoint, more serious than these three, although he himself is almost wholly unaware of it. This concerns the fate of those who, for whatever reason, do not share the sense of contingency which is, in his eyes, the hall-mark of the truly civilized postmodern man. Amongst them is Nietzsche, whom Connolly particularly admires. What is puzzling is the fact that, despite Connolly's admiration, he appears to ignore the core of Nietzsche's teaching, which is a concept of fatality diametrically opposed to his own contingent concept of selfhood. 'What alone can our teaching be?', Nietzsche asked rhetorically (in *The Twilight of the Idols*). It is, he replied, that:

> No one is accountable for existing at all, or for being constituted as he is, or for living in the circumstances and surroundings in which he lives. The fatality of his nature cannot be disentangled from the fatality of all that which has been and will be ... one is a piece of fate, one belongs to the whole, one is in the whole ...[45]

Nietzsche's doctrine of fatality is not of course intended by him as a formula for moral egoism and political irresponsibility. It is quite compatible, for example, with the ideal of universal chivalry espoused by Santayana, who shared Nietzsche's sense of fatality. What it *is* incompatible with, however, is the moralistic desire to vindicate one's whole life that inspires Connolly's agonalism, by converting it into an unending struggle against evil.[46]

The righteous note which this desire injects into Connolly's attitude towards those who do not think of their identity as contingent is evident in the terms he uses to describe them. Their existence, he maintains, is basically anachronistic, and they are vilified as possible 'conduits for fascist unity'.[47] Connolly criticizes de Tocqueville for his exclusionism in relation to the American Indians,[48] but the lot of the non-global democrat who lacks a sense of contingent selfhood is not an altogether enviable one, in Connolly's supposedly non-exclusivist democracy.

In the light of Connolly's difficulties, it is worth considering briefly the compromise version of agonal theory recently proposed by a leading British feminist philosopher, Anne Phillips, who attempts to overcome them by resituating agonalism in what she terms 'the half-way house of remedial reform'.[49] Phillips' starting point is the claim that, in the established tradition of liberal democratic political theory:

> difference has been perceived in an overly cerebral fashion as differences in opinions and beliefs, and that the resulting emphasis on what I will call a politics of ideas has proved inadequate to the problems of political exclusion. The diversity most liberals have in mind is a diversity of beliefs, opinions, preferences and goals, all of which may stem from the variety of experience, but are considered as in principle detachable from this.[50]

In order to remedy the one-sided character of the traditional 'politics of ideas', Phillips maintains, we need to modify the existing system of representation by incorporating into it more provision for what she terms a 'politics of presence'.[51] She does not, she stresses, wish to disparage the place of ideas in politics but contends, rather, that:

> when the politics of ideas is taken in isolation from the politics of presence, it does not deal adequately with the experiences of those groups who by virtue of their race or ethnicity or religion or gender have felt themselves excluded from the democratic process. Political exclusion is increasingly – I believe rightly – viewed in terms that can only be met by political presence ....[52]

How then is one to create an alternative kind of politics capable of overcoming the exclusionist tendencies created by the excessively cerebral character of traditional liberalism? Phillips' reply deliberately eschews ambitious theorizing like Connolly's, on the ground that it fails to meet the pressing need for an immediate programme of action. Instead, she stresses the need for a series of practical reforms within the existing framework of democracy. The aim of the reforms is however to foster the agonal spirit, in so far as they gradually seek to create a system of politics in which citizens no longer passively settle for majoritarian decision-making but actively engage with one another in a democratic process that 'anticipat[es] some process of transformation and change.'[53] The authentic agonal note sounds even more loudly when Phillips explains that:

> Where the classically liberal resolution of difference relies on a combination of private spaces and majority norms (these in turn established by majority vote), the democratic resolution of difference expects us to engage more directly with each other. We bring our differences to the public stage; we revise them through public debate. Major disagreements then surface between those who anticipate a full 'resolution' in some newly achieved public consensus, and those who see

differences as contingent but never as 'difference' going away. The first position looks more utopian than the second, but both operate at a level of generality that barely touches on democracy as practised today.[54]

Bearing this in mind, the question posed by Phillips' work is clear: it is whether she succeeds in portraying a coherent half-way house by means of which existing liberal democracies can be steered in the direction she indicates. This half-way house, she writes, is made up of 'mechanisms' which:

> include the quota systems adopted by a number of European political parties to achieve gender parity in elected assemblies, the redrawing of boundaries around black-majority constituencies, to raise the number of black politicians elected in the United States, and the longer established power-sharing practices of those European consociational democracies that have distributed executive power and economic resources between different religious and linguistic groups.[55]

Although Phillips is in fact extremely cautious about the claims she makes on behalf of these mechanisms, her very caution serves only to magnify the misgivings she herself expresses at one stage, when she remarks that they may merely intensify the very problems of exclusion she hopes they will solve. There are, however, other, more theoretical problems presented by her attempt to combine a politics of ideas with a politics of presence. Of these, the most obvious concerns the question of whose presence is to be represented.

Here Phillips encounters two difficulties in giving a satisfactory answer. One is that any attempt to provide an official solution would immediately introduce rigidities by restricting access to the public realm to some groups at the expense of others. The other difficulty arises because she is careful to reject the essentialist assumption that gender, race and culture identify homogeneous groups. Having rejected essentialism, however, she has to allow that such groups as blacks, lesbians, Asians, or women all not only comprise multiple identities, but identities which may be in fact be dismissed by members of those groups as largely irrelevant to their own self-perception. In fact, Phillips readily acknowledges this; but that makes it all the harder to say precisely what the experience is that requires 'presence' to do justice to it politically.

A further problem is created by Phillips' candid recognition that, in the case of political identity, any attempt to analyze it in terms of an experience that can only be represented directly by 'presence' is in danger of becoming reductionist: that is, of denying the autonomy of political identity in the course of attempting to analyze it in terms of some wholly pre-political identity.

Finally, there is the problem of determining on what grounds anyone can ever claim to represent anyone else at all. For the politics of ideas, there is no difficulty in answering this question. For the politics of presence, however, the only consistent answer must be that given by Rousseau, who rejected the idea that one person could ever represent another and opted in favour of direct democracy. In seeking a compromise between these two wholly distinct and conflicting theories of representation, Phillips seeks a half-way house which is non-existent.

The conclusion must be, then, that precisely because Phillips is so commendably sensitive to the difficulties mentioned, no coherent position is left for her after the long series of qualifications she makes in order to take account of them. Ironically, the very subtlety with which she tries to work out a compromise between the politics of presence and the politics of faith means that, in the end, she is left at best with little more than an act of faith in the benefits of moderate reformism, rather than with a coherent theory of how an inclusive politics of difference might be constructed. To her credit, however, her problems arise because, despite her agonal sympathies, she is reluctant to take the agonal high road and run the risk of ignoring rights altogether, on the ground that what matters is to change self-perception, which a politics of rights does not do.

The discourse theory of political diversity

The postmodern version of discourse theory owes much to Jurgen Habermas, an anti-postmodern thinker whose influence is nevertheless evident, for example, upon the work of Seyla Benhabib. Benhabib has attempted to modify Habermas' version of discourse theory from a feminist standpoint that is sympathetic to postmodernism. Habermas, in Benhabib's view, takes uniformity too much for granted, with the result that he pays too little attention to the requirements of a politics of difference. Benhabib's ambitious aim, more precisely, is to combine the emphasis on difference characteristic of postmodern politics with the regard for universal ethical principles characteristic of traditional liberal democratic theory. She describes the outcome as 'postmetaphysical interactive universalism'.[56] More simply, it is an ethics of inclusion, based on 'a post-Enlightenment defence of universalism, without metaphysical props and historical conceits'.[57] What, one must ask, does this involve?

Benhabib's starting point is the claim that the traditional basis of liberal democracy is a morally untenable separation of public and private life. This separation is, in effect, an exclusionist strategy, of which women are a major victim. It is exclusionist because it relies on faith in the possibility of a formal or procedural framework of rules. In reality, this framework of rules does not stand apart from the play of power that it is supposed to regulate. The framework, that is, is not something that can be settled apart from and prior to the political process, as its defenders maintain. It is itself, on the contrary, a fundamental part of that process, and can only acquire legitimacy in the course of a public dialogue which is genuinely open to all.

Benhabib's central contention, accordingly, is that legitimacy and democracy (in her radical sense of that term) are synonymous concepts. This view, she maintains, is strongly supported by postmodern concepts of rationality, self, and moral argument. So far as reason is concerned, she appeals to a concept which is not legislative but discursive. So far as the self is concerned, she invokes the postmodern analysis of it as constructed through a narrative unity, rather than as the pre-existing, disembodied consciousness of Cartesian philosophy, or the equally disembodied transcendental unity of apperception found in Kantian philosophy. So far as morality is concerned, she turns in particular to Habermas for a concept of moral objectivity based on an interactive concept of rationality.

For the sake of argument, let us assume that all three of the philosophical positions with which Benhabib underpins the discursive concept of legitimacy are tenable. The question then is whether they yield a coherent politics of difference. There are three major reasons for suggesting that they fail to do so.

The first reason is that her critique of the classical theory of civil association is dangerously oversimplistic. For Benhabib, the main defect of the tradition is that it rests upon assumptions that have not been democratically negotiated. This criticism, however, ignores the most important feature of the tradition, as it is formulated by thinkers like Locke, Montesquieu and the American founding fathers. This is the fact that the inspiration of the tradition is a suspicion of power as such, regardless of how democratically its possession has been arrived at. In response to Benhabib, then, the classical thinkers would reply that the conception of democracy she employs entails what they regard as the height of political folly. It entails, to be specific, completely forgetting the virtue of prudence, which demands that power should be surrounded with checks and balances. To the extent that citizens seek to create a participatory democracy based on what they regard as an ideal speech situation, Benhabib is content to abandon any such suspicion.

Indifference to the virtue of prudence, however, is not the only problem presented by discourse theory. A second is that the concept of legitimacy upon which this theory relies merely replaces one form of exclusion by another, rather than creating the radically open or inclusive style of politics which was promised.

The problem, to be specific, is that the concept of democracy which Benhabib invokes is in fact a highly élitist one, in which the apolitical lives and values of the mass of ordinary citizens of western democracies enjoy at best only a residual moral respect. This, as Benhabib stresses, is because the discursive concept of legitimacy assumes that identities and institutions can only acquire ethical significance subsequent to, and not prior to, participation in the process of discursive will formation. In other words, no existing identities or institutions have ethical significance until they have first been 'renegotiated, reinterpreted and rearticulated as a result of a radically open and procedurally fair discourse ...'[58]

The third problem presented by the discourse model of democracy is that the elitism just mentioned is further intensified by the patronizing conviction that ordinary citizens, male and female alike, are such passive dupes of the media that their communicative capacity is in practice negligible. Thus Benhabib writes, for example – in a manner reminiscent of continental postmodern thinkers – that 'The autonomous citizen, whose reasoned judgement and participation was (sic) the *sine qua non* of the public sphere, has been transformed into the "citizen consumer" of packaged images and messages, or the "electronic mail target" of large groups and organizations. This impoverishment of public life has been accompanied by the growth of the society of surveillance and voyeurism on the one hand (Foucault) and the "colonization of the lifeworld" on the other (Habermas).'[59] The views of the ordinary citizen, then, are excluded from serious consideration by the discourse model at the outset. As was said, this exclusion appears to encompass male and female citizens alike.

One must conclude, then, that so far as the emancipatory and inclusivist claims made on behalf of the discourse version of postmodernism are concerned, their benefits are confined to a small elite. Even for this elite, however, the benefits of emancipation and inclusion are likely to prove oppressive. They are likely to prove oppressive because the distinction between public and private life is too fragile to protect the freedom of the individual, regardless of sex. Benhabib is emphatic, it should be stressed, that the discourse model does not destroy the basis of the public/private distinction, but merely rejects the traditional basis for that distinction in favour of a new, democratically renegotiated basis. We are in fact assured that:

> In principle, the discourse model is based upon a strong assumption of individual autonomy and consent; thus, even in discourses which renegotiate the boundaries between the private and the public the respect for the individuals' consent and the necessity of their voluntarily gained insight into the validity of the general norms guarantees that this distinction cannot be redrawn in ways that jeopardize, damage and restrict this autonomy of choice and insight.[60]

Now, the integrity of Benhabib's commitment to the limited state is of course not contested here. What is suggested, as was just said, is that, in spite of the assurance given above, her discursive form of democracy provides little protection for a private realm, for two reasons. The first is that many within it will be ordinary citizens whose views are not likely to be considered worth much protection, for reasons already indicated. The second is that Benhabib's concept of discursive democracy makes no allowance for the frailty of many mortals in the face of group pressure: she forgets that only the Solzhenitsyns of the world possess the kind of 'strong' autonomy necessary to resist fellow citizens who assume (once again, after the fashion of Rousseau) that the essence of politics is the remoulding of identities in ways that foster a sense of 'civic friendship' and solidarity.[61]

The civil theory of difference politics

The final version of the politics of difference to be examined here brings postmodern political theory full circle by reestablishing connection with the classical theory of civil association originally inaugurated by Hobbes. This development is most clearly represented by Chantal Mouffe. In Mouffe's case, however, it is more especially in the mature form in which classical theory recently has been restated by Michael Oakeshott that she sympathizes with it.

Specifically, Mouffe's concern is to identify a concept of the political that will permit the idea of pluralism to become 'a vehicle for a deepening of the democratic revolution ... [in a way that can] apprehend the multiplicity of forms of subordination that exist in social relations and provide a framework for the articulation of the different democratic struggles – around gender, race, class, sexuality, environment and others.'[62] For such a concept she turns to Oakeshott's idea of civil association as *societas*.[63] Civil association in this sense, she writes, is marked above all by the fact that it does not require fellow citizens to have a shared purpose of any kind. Instead, 'what is required is that we accept a specific language of civil intercourse [which Oakeshott terms] *res publica*.' *Res publica* consists, not of commands or orders or instructions or decrees, but of rules. These rules (Mouffe writes):

> prescribe norms of conduct to be subscribed to in seeking self-chosen actions. The identification with those rules of civil intercourse creates a common political identity among persons otherwise engaged in many different enterprises. This modern form of political community is held together not by substantive ideas of the common good but by a common bond, a public concern. It is therefore a community without a definite shape or a definite identity and in continuous re-enactment. Such a conception is clearly different from the premodern idea of the political community [viz. as held together by a common purpose, as provided by religion], but it is also different from the liberal ideal of the political association. For liberalism also sees political association as a form of purposive association, of enterprise, except that in its case the aim is an instrumental one: the promotion of common interest.[64]

The civil model offers, in short:

> a mode of human association that recognizes the disappearance of a single substantive idea of the common good and makes room for individual liberty. It is a form of association that can be enjoyed among relative strangers belonging to many purposive associations and whose allegiances to specific communities are not seen as conflicting with their membership of the civil association. This would not be possible if such an association were conceived as ... purposive

association, because it would not allow for the existence of other genuine purposive associations in which individuals would be free to participate.[65]

This then is the most fundamental feature of civil association: in it, diversity is accommodated by a non-purposive framework of formal rules. The model does not, it must be stressed, offer a formula for automatically deciding what kinds of diversity are to be permitted or excluded. It is, rather, an attempt to identify the conditions under which an endless, on-going debate can occur about that issue. More precisely, it specifies the conditions which such a debate must satisfy if it is to issue in rules that possess obligatory status. In this respect its aim is of course at one with ironism, as well as with agonal and discourse theory. In the civil version, however, such problematic notions as solidarity (in Rorty's sense), an ideal speech situation, and a demand for the politicization of personal identity, are all stripped away.

It is worth noticing, however, something that Mouffe ignores, which is that three considerations led Oakeshott himself to be deeply pessimistic about the future of civil association in modern mass societies. The first is that the civil model presupposes a culture in which there is a place for the non-instrumental spirit of play. It has plausibly been argued, however, that this spirit (which is not to be confused with the ideas of sport and fun, both of which may exhibit an instrumentalism excluded by play) is precisely what has disappeared from the contemporary world.[66]

The second source of Oakeshott's pessimism is that the civil model also presupposes that primary value is attached to freedom and dignity, rather that to security and prosperity. In this respect, Oakeshott's misgivings resemble those expressed by Alexis de Tocqueville a century and half ago. The third source of his misgivings is also one that was expressed by de Tocqueville. It is that civil association presupposes a respect for forms which is unfortunately somewhat alien to democratic culture. The reason why forms are alien is not hard to understand: the primary democratic concern is with intimacy and equality, with the result that forms are easily seen as merely sources of division and masks for domination. Sadly, Oakeshott's pessimism is the most striking feature of one of the last essays he published during his life time, which was a re-telling of the story of 'The Tower of Babel'.[67]

Conclusion

The main conclusion to emerge from this examination of the postmodern quest for a politics of difference has a paradoxical character: it is that what began as a demand for a more truly liberal and democratic politics of diversity has rapidly threatened to become the most sustained attack on the ideal of the limited state that the present century has witnessed. By way of conclusion, I want to ask why what one sympathizer has described as postmodern 'superliberalism, more pluralistic, more tolerant, more open to the right of difference and otherness' has disappointed expectations.[68]

In the case of continental postmodernism, the answer is clear enough. Especially in France, the postmodern challenge to the limited state must be seen as the latest episode in the long established hostility of the intelligentsia to modern mass society. Behind the complexities of postmodern philosophy, this hostility has a fundamentally simple structure. It consists of a sustained debunking exercise in which all knowledge and all institutions are reduced to ever more elusive, sophisticated and impersonal forms of power. The result is that the very concept of legitimacy is rendered unintelligible in continental postmodernism. In this respect, it has been justly observed, the continental postmodernists may be regarded as the modern heirs of Thrasymachus and his fellow sophists in the ancient world.

In the case of Anglo-American sympathizers with postmodern philosophy, the attitude towards power is diametrically opposed. Like their continental bed-fellows, it is true, they regard the established liberal democratic tradition as a mask for forms of power and exclusion. Unlike the continental thinkers, however, they reveal no tendency to carry the debunking impulse to an extreme which would make discussion of legitimacy an absurdity. Instead, they explore various conditions for creating a politics of inclusion in which power would be placed in the service of liberty. Unfortunately, however, this concern for otherness threatens to bring about the division of society into 'them' and 'us' – in Rorty's case – in a way that risks ending the rule of law. Alternatively, the concern for otherness threatens the rule of law from a different direction, which is through the enthusiastic politicization of personal identity by thinkers like Connolly. In either case, the Anglo-American thinkers invariably treat the whole system of checks and balances on power that has been the basis of more persuasive forms of liberalism ever since the eighteenth century in a cavalier fashion.

In a more sympathetic vein, however, it may be added that in both its continental and Anglo-American forms, postmodernism has freqently (thought not invariably) worked to create an agenda that contemporary political theory cannot ignore. At the top of this agenda stand two items. The first is the need for a more modest, less ambitiously moralistic reformulation of liberalism than that widely attempted by thinkers such as Rawls since the Second World War. The second item on the agenda is the need to restate liberalism in a way that does not take for granted assumptions, such as those relating to the definition of the public and the private dimensions of life, that can no longer be taken as self-defining. The present essay has sympathized with the school of postmodern thought that considers this restatement can best be achieved by extensive revision of the early modern ideal of civil association, rather than through a quest for some wholly novel kind of political theory. It is obvious, however, that this aspect of the debate is incapable of any final resolution.

It may be added, finally, that if this agenda is to stand any chance of being carried out, then it is necessary to break free from the principal delusion which has been prone to haunt the postmodern politics of identity. This is the dream of creating a wholly inclusive political ideal. In this respect at least Rorty is surely correct to emphasize the inescapably contingent nature of all human existence, including political existence. Given this contingency, every attempt at inclusion inevitably and necessarily creates a new form of exclusion.[69]

Notes

1   'Natural law, natural rights and the Enlightenment "science" of morals', unpublished Inaugural Lecture given at Boston University, 29 March, 1995.

2   Haakonssen has an interesting suggestion about the origins of the historical caricature of the Enlightenment which has played such an influential part in the modern/postmodern debate. The caricature began, he surmises, as 'the last gasp ... of Wilhelmine cultural imperialism. Through the nineteenth century, but especially in the latter half of that century, a vast amount of fine German scholarship was devoted to the dubious cause of inventing a peculiarly German contribution to European culture, and this had to be philosophical idealism, literary romanticism and cultural historicism – all of which had to be defined through the deepest possible contrasts with an empiristic, rationalistic, scientistic and ahistorical Enlightenment of the West. This cartoon history served Germany well during the first war and to ill repute during the second, but in the post-war period it has mainly survived outside of Germany. In France it became the subject of a deconstructionist vaudeville whose French domesticity could be obscured by a European target. And in the Anglo-American world the caricature Enlightenment has had its run extended due to the lack of a better show.'

3   The thought of Kierkegaard and Nietzsche would of course be highly relevant to a more far-ranging survey, as would that of Saussure.

4   The distinction between the two Heideggers is made most convincingly by Joanna Hodge, in the form of a distinction between the 'ontological' and the 'ontic' Heideggers. Hodge argues that the ontological and ontic inquiries cannot be allocated to different periods in Heidegger's career but are interwoven throughout it. Hodge (1995), p. 168.

5   Heidegger was well aware that Nietzsche was trying to do exactly the same thing, but believed that in the end he had failed to carry the project through. Nietzsche had failed, in Heidegger's eyes, because he himself had ultimately remained trapped within the web of metaphysics. Whether this is a just accusation is a question that need not detain us here.

6   Deleuze (1993), p. 46.

7   Kearney (1986), p. 50. Italics in the original.

8   Ibid., p. 125. Italics in the original.

9   Levinas (1994), pp. 21-2.

10   Ibid., p. 129.

11   Levinas (1989) pp. 53-4.

12   Ibid., pp. 282-3.

13   Ibid., p. 283.

14   Ibid., p. 290.

15   Derrida's critique of Levinas is in his essay, 'Violence and Metaphysics' in Derrida (1993). My remarks in what follows are based on this essay.

16   Quoted by Moi (1991), p.173.

17   Derrida (1994), p.59.

18   Ibid., pp. 85-6.

19   Eagleton (1995), p. 37.

20   Deleuze (1993), p. 241.

21   Ibid., p. 241.

22   Ibid., p. 244.

23   Baudrillard (1988), pp. 36-7.

24   Ibid., p. 101.

25   Steiner (1989), p. 134. Steiner describes postmodern thinkers as 'masters of emptiness'.

26   Scruton (1994), pp. 481-505.

27   Ibid., p. 501.

28   *The Independent on Sunday.* 9 February, 1992.

29   Montaigne (1958), p. 406.

30   Heller and Ferenc (1988), p.17.

31   Rorty (1989), p. xv.

32   Ibid., p. 46.

33   Bernstein (1991), p. 250.

34   Bhaskar (1991).

35   Rorty (1989), p. 5.

36   Ibid., p. 190.

37   Sykes (1994).

38   In the original Greek sense, 'agon' connoted, not agony, but a gathering or assembly, especially for the public games. By extension, it came to refer to a contest for a prize at the games. It subsequently came to mean any contest or struggle. It is in a sense that links the Greek ideas of a public assembly and a public contest that postmodern political theorists have taken up the term.

39   Connolly (1996), p. 70. See also Connolly (1991a).

40   Ibid., p. 73, fn. 24.

41   Ibid., p. 67.

42   Ibid., pp. 66-7.
43   Ibid., p. 68.
44   Ibid., p. 54.
45   Nietzsche (1990), p. 65.
46   See the Preface in Connolly (1991a).
47   Connolly (1991b).
48   Connolly (1996), pp. 55-6.
49   Phillips (1994), p. 89.
50   Ibid., p. 75.
51   Ibid., pp. 74-91.
52   Ibid., pp. 77-8.
53'   Ibid., p. 80.
54   Ibid., p. 80.
55   Ibid., p. 84.
56   Benhabib (1992), p. 6.
57   Ibid., p. 3.
58   Ibid., p. 110.
59   Ibid., p. 112.
60   Ibid., p. 111.
61   Ibid., p. 11.
62   Mouffe (1993), p. 7.
63   Ibid., p. 67.
64   Ibid., p. 67.
65   Ibid., p. 67.
66   Huizinga (1970).
67   Oakeshott (1983).
68   Benhabib (1992), p. 16.
69   See Beeser (1989), pp. 303-16.

References

Baudrillard, J. (1988), *The Ecstasy of Communication*, Semiotext(e): New York.
Beeser, H.A. (ed.)(1989), *The New Historicism*, Routledge: London.
Benhabib, S. (1992), *Situating the Self: Gender, Community and Postmodernism in Contemporary Ethics*, Routledge: New York.
Bernstein, R. (1991), *The New Constellation*, Polity Press: Cambridge.
Bhaskar, R. (1991), 'Rorty, Realism and the Idea of Freedom', in Malachowski, A. (ed.), *Reading Rorty*, Blackwell: Oxford, pp. 198-232.
Connolly, W. (1991a), *Identity/Difference: Democratic Negotiations of Political Paradox*, Cornell University Press: New York.

___ (1991b), 'Democracy and Territoriality', *Millenium*, 20, Winter 1991, Vol. 20, No. 3, pp. 463-483.

___ (1996), 'Pluralism, Multiculturalism and the Nation-State', *Journal of Political Ideologies*, Vol. 1, No. 1, February, pp. 53-71.

Deleuze, G. (1993), *The Deleuze Reader*, Boundas, C.V. (ed.), Columbia University Press: New York..

Derrida, J. (1993), 'Violence and Metaphysics', in *Writing and Difference*, Routledge: London.

___ (1994), *Specters of Marx*, Routledge: London.

Eagleton, T. (1995), 'Marxism without Marx', *Radical Philosophy*, 73, Sept.-Oct.

Heller, A. and Feher, F. (1988), *The Postmodern Political Condition*, Polity Press: Cambridge.

Hodge, J. (1995), *Heidegger and Ethics*, Routledge: London.

Huizinga, J. (1970), *Homo Ludens*, Paladin: London.

Kearney, R. (ed.) (1968), *Dialogues With Contemporary Continental Thinkers*, Manchester University Press: Manchester.

Levinas, E. (1989), *The Levinas Reader*, Hand, S. (ed.), Blackwell: Oxford.

___ (1994), *Totality and Infinity*, Duquesne University Press: Pittsburgh.

Moi, T. (ed.) (1991), *Sexual Textual Politics*, Routledge: London.

Montaigne, M.E. (1958), 'On Experience', in *Essays*, Cohen, J.M. (trans.), Penguin: Harmondsworth.

Mouffe, C. (1993), *The Return of the Political*, Verso: London.

Nietzsche, F. (1990), *Twilight of the Idols*, Penguin: Harmondsworth.

Oakeshott, M. (1983), *On History and Other Essays*, Blackwell: Oxford.

Phillips, A. (1994), 'Dealing with Difference: A Politics of Ideas or a Politics of Presence?', *Constellations*, Vol. 1, No. 1, April, pp. 74-91.

Rorty, R. (1989), *Contingency, Irony and Solidarity*, Cambridge University Press: Cambridge.

Scruton, R. (1994), 'Upon Nothing', *Philosophical Investigations*, Vol. 17, No. 3, July.

Steiner, G. (1989), *Real Presences*, Faber and Faber: London.

Sykes, C. (1994), 'The Ideology of Sensitivity', *The Salisbury Review*, Vol. 12, No. 3, March, pp. 14-9.

Acknowledgements

I am grateful to Daniel Kleinberg for comments on a draft of this paper.

10　The international origins of national sovereignty

Paul Hirst

Political theorists and sociologists commonly assert, following Max Weber, that a distinctive and definitive feature of the modern state is the effective control of the means of violence in a specific territory. Weber says: 'The claim of the modern state to monopolise the use of force is as essential to it as its character of compulsory jurisdiction and continuous operation'.[1] Yet in the sixteenth and seventeenth centuries, supposedly the key period in the rise of the modern state, this claim was frequently unsustainable. Many political entities could not consistently make this claim for the whole of their territories, and other rulers could not make such a claim. Thus, the French monarchy after the Edict of Nantes (1598) had explicitly ceded the control of certain fortresses to the Huguenots. Likewise, the Holy Roman Emperor's ability to regulate the use of force by lesser rulers within the territory of the Empire or to call on rulers to provide him with military forces was distinctly circumscribed. Some states were no more able to sustain this claim than the Lebanese state could control the armed militias in its territory in the early 1980s. France, at certain points during the religious civil wars, was close to the anarchy we have become familiar with in Beirut, Bosnia or Liberia today.

In what is supposed to be the period in which the larger territorial monarchies prevailed over other political entities, over feudal nobilities, universal institutions like the Papacy or the Empire, city states, and leagues of free cities (like the Hanseatic League), many major states actually had for long periods of time few means to control the loyalties of or the use of force by their citizens.[2] The supposed subjects of the monarch or ruler were committed to rival forms of social organization, to churches and religious sects, that had most of the attributes of states: that demanded a supra-political loyalty, that taxed their members' incomes, that imposed religious justice, and that controlled confessional armed forces. Given that religion was the main issue promoting dissent and conflict in the sixteenth and seventeenth centuries, dividing the populations of political bodies on primarily confessional lines, it inevitably became the main focus for political loyalty.

As Carl Schmitt argued, the issues that define the political are open-ended; ultimately they concern whatever drives people to group themselves into conflicting camps and compels them to create forms of political order – foci of loyalty and means of common decision-making – that enable them to contest with their enemies.[3] Schmitt's views remain controversial and certainly only capture one aspect of politics, but his was a position shaped in part by reflection on the religious civil wars, and it is sharpened in its contemporary relevance by the experience of Bosnia. The aspect of politics that Schmitt emphasizes, friend-enemy relations, remains central, and Schmitt stresses the uncomforting truth that what order there is in politics arises either from the stabilization of conflict or by the defeat of one of the contending parties within a given territory.

Religious conflict thus had the capacity to disrupt the processes of state-building. The Reformation was central in this respect because it allied religious dissent to political power, and it enabled lesser rulers to escape the hegemonic claims of the Emperor. Protestantism survived, unlike many previous movements for reform like the Lollards and Waldesians, because Luther was shrewd enough to ask for the support of disaffected elites and thus ensure that the new reformed religion did not become a 'heresy', wholly outside the orbit of established power.[4] But even though Protestantism attracted certain established elites and rulers, it also created dissent within and between states, in France and the Empire in particular. The Reformation also gave rise to radical sects, Müntzer and his followers, the Anabaptists and the like, who rejected any form of covenant with the powers that be.[5] In large areas of Europe rulers could not rely on the religious, and therefore the political, loyalty of their subjects whether mean or mighty. Noblemen and peasants, journeymen and members of the urban patriarchate could turn revolutionary under the influence of religion. Huguenot nobles and bourgeois Calvinist elders in Scotland show that radical religious dissent was not merely a product of revolt by the poor and excluded. Moreover, religious dissent was not merely a threat that came from the Reformed religion. The Catholic League was a revolutionary organization that was willing to browbeat and even to cast aside the French monarchy in the pursuit of its goals. In such circumstances state-building could not follow a steady course, prevailing over feudal lords and lesser political entities, steadily acquiring control and constructing uniform systems of administration within their own borders.

Large states did not enjoy the inherent advantages over lesser powers in military and taxation terms if in fact they were subject to extensive disruption by religious dissent – entire regions or social strata rejecting the rule of the centre. Indeed, given a certain tax base and a loyal local population, the new military means that developed rapidly in the sixteenth century did not necessarily favour central power.[6] The new artillery fortifications could enable dissident regions to survive, as the alliance of rebel provinces in the Netherlands which defied Spain, the greatest military power in the period, in an eighty-year war of independence demonstrates. This was a protracted war of sieges behind new fortifications and water lines. The protestant minority in France, led by local noble and urban elites, although outnumbered and geographically scattered, held out in a network of local fortresses until Huguenot power was finally crushed at La Rochelle in 1628.[7] In Holland's case Protestant foreign aid and access to the sea enabled survival at certain crucial moments in the war. La Rochelle fell because the English navy failed to break through and bring relief. Without that contingency, the course of absolutist state-building in France might have been rather different.

Whether in Germany or Holland, France or England religious dissidents could expect help from co-religionists abroad. In a genuine sense the Protestant and Catholic religions created true 'internationals' in the sixteenth and seventeenth centuries. Princes and apprentices alike were willing to make efforts and sacrifices for the cause. States aided foreign rebels and also made war to help other states. They promoted civil war and encouraged ideological rebellion. Catholic Recusants in England, Huguenots in France, could expect foreign help, whether it be secret Papal agents or subsidies, or bibles smuggled through concealed in herring barrels by Dutch traders. Elizabeth I or Gustavus Adolphus were of course pursuing the political interests of their states, but that *realpolitik* was conducted within an international system in which the religious affiliations of states mattered. Thus to see the Thirty Years War as exclusively a matter of conflicting *state* interests, as a Hapsburg bid for hegemony that was resisted by other powers and as a series of local conflicts caught-up in the bigger struggle, is as mistaken as it would be to view it as a *purely* religious war.[8]

States thus frequently could not begin to substantiate claims to 'sovereignty' in a given territory, nor were they under effective international pressure to abide by a rule of non-intervention in their neighbours' internal affairs. On the contrary, non-intervention could only come to be seen as an issue when the religious conflicts had escalated beyond all bounds. Religion promoted ideological internationalism and civil war driven by political ideas. In that sense they were comparable to the ideological conflicts of the twentieth century between left and right, between Communists and Fascists. Indeed, religious belief was if anything more international, since confessional allegiances could make existing frontiers irrelevant. Class conflicts remained stubbornly national by contrast, social interests struggling to seize power and sovereignty in nation states. Genuine popular acts of internationalism were rare among socialists, and the example of 1914 remains notorious. Confessional groups gave more than lip-service to international solidarity.[9] State-building could not have been effectively contained in several key European regions until the supra-national appeal of religious belief could be curtailed. The claims of loyalty to sovereign had to prevail over confessional loyalty, and the only way to do that was to make confessional loyalty and political loyalty coincident, to territorialize religion.

It is in this context that we should look, once again, at the Treaty of Westphalia. It has become fashionable to argue that the Westphalian states system is coming to an end and that the political universe will continue to diversify, to become more complex and pluralistic in the type of entities it contains, leading to the demise of the nation state as the predominant political entity.[10] On the other hand, Stephen

Krasner argues that Westphalia was actually not the founding moment of the modern system of states, and that it did not usher in an international arena made up exclusively of sovereign nation states interacting externally one with another. Both of these arguments may be true to a degree, but I want to try and make a case for a rather different proposition. My claim is that Westphalia *was* a decisive moment in the formation of the modern system of states, but not because an already internally-created and domestically-secured state 'sovereignty' was recognized there; rather the point is that by successfully reducing international religious conflict below a crucial threshold, states were able to gain control of their societies.

The negotiations of 1648 brought the Thirty Years War to an end.[11] In that sense the Treaty marked the end of a long century of religious civil wars and of inter-state conflicts with a strong religious dimension that had begun with the Hussites and had accelerated after Luther was able to win over some of the German princes. By 1648 religious conflict had begun to be seen as self-defeating; the miseries of the wars were perceived as bringing general discredit on religion. Much of Germany was devastated, or so contemporaries believed. Even the victors of the peace, France and Sweden, were close to exhaustion.

What the Treaty did was to attempt to stabilize religion and territory in Germany, and to make the main external powers who had intervened parties to and guarantors of that peace. The ruinous effects of the war led key political elites in Germany to put social peace before supra-territorial confessional ambitions and obligations. Westphalia worked in that it did strengthen the principle that the confessional status of a territory should be unambiguously clear, and that internal and external actors should not attempt to alter it. In this it follows previous efforts to end the religious conflicts but with more success. Thus the Peace of Augsburg of 1555 had attempted to stabilize religion and territory on the principle of *cujus regio ejus religio,* that the religion of the state is that of the prince. But it had failed to institutionalize it, dissident subjects and rulers who changed religion when the mass of their people did not were beyond control. Moreover, the peace of 1555 was an agreement within the Empire, it was not underwritten by the major non-German rulers, who were thus at liberty to aid their allies in Germany.

Subject to certain guarantees and concessions to particular interests, Westphalia attempted to legitimize and to reconstruct a religious *status quo,* to freeze the relationship between religion and territory as Augsburg had, but to generalize it so that non-German states accepted through religious division of power could be made to prevail within the Empire. States and the political entities in Germany had to accept that the confessional status of neighbouring powers was fixed and not subject to change by military force or by the support of sedition. Religious change thus ceased to be an object of inter-state policy. States became Catholic, Calvinist or Lutheran according to the will of their rulers or to local agreements as to consent by subjects, both principles being present in the Treaty.

Thus over the remainder of the century that followed 1648, religion became 'depoliticized' in Carl Schmitt's terms. That is, it ceased to be a matter that led different groups to organized conflict. Subjects could no longer effectively dispute the claims of their sovereign to rule on the basis that they wanted to pursue a form of religious belief different to that of their lord, and increasingly this was because they could not rely on other states intervening to help their cause or allowing co-religionists among their subjects to do so. If religion began to cease to be a source of conflict, at the same time economic affairs had yet to become 'political'.[12] Social conflicts were limited in scope and pre-ideological in nature, class war had yet to replace religious war. Hence as a consequence of the de-politicization of religion, the state could begin to assert more power over society than it had been able to do heretofore. The scope for 'political' conflict *within* states was considerably lessened and the main forms of conflict came to be those that took place *between* states. This change increased the claims that states could credibly and legitimately make on their subjects. As *enemies* became increasingly external, states were able to call forth new forms of loyalty on the part of their members, and the ruling elites could begin the project of identifying the subjects with a territory and with the state. The regimes that were most successful in this process could draw more deeply on the lives and property of their subjects to fight foreign wars. In this context of de-politicization and the externalization of military conflict, it become possible for states to construct or resume the construction of systems of relatively uniform administration in their territory, to subject their subjects more effectively to their hierarchical control and organizational hegemony. Given such administration, then the means of violence could be controlled, appropriated and monopolized. The development of a monopoly of the means of violence is thus closely associated with the limitations on the scope of political conflict that were at least in part brought about by agreements between states. The monopoly thus established is then used more effectively to direct violence outwards in a long struggle for territory and hegemony in the shifting balance of power between European states – from the 1680s onwards.

Westphalia established the principle that states agreed not to intervene in other states' affairs in matters of religion, to accept a world of religiously diverse territories. Catholics and Protestants abandoned claims to universalism. States accepted the legitimate existence of other religions in other territories. This was the case whatever their internal religious policy, whether they practised a policy of religious toleration, subject to minorities accepting conditions, as in Holland, or sought to impose religious homogeneity by force, as did Louis XIV when his regime revoked the remaining provisions of the Edict of Nantes in 1685, and began the dual process of the expulsion of the Huguenots and the 'Catholicization' of France. Either policy made possible the consolidation of political authority by making state power legitimate in religious terms.

Thus it is misleading to present the state as if it acquired its effective monopoly over the means of violence by its own internal efforts, slowly eliminating feudal military powers and the privileges of free cities. This is the case even if it is

269

accepted that this growth of military monopoly was stimulated by external conflicts and the need to further them. States could not consolidate by state-building alone – constructing administrative systems for their territories and steadily adding to their powers to tax, to make laws, and to regulate the raising of troops.

Even in England, where monarchical legal and administrative centralization had proceeded considerably by the later Middle Ages, the decisive periods of Renaissance state-building were closely connected with religious conflict. In Henry VIII's case religious dissent legitimated the acquisition of further powers and resources with the dissolution of the monasteries and the assertion by the Crown of the right to determine the form of religious belief. Later the struggle against Spain legitimated royal power and provided a basis for growing internal political supervision of belief. It is only in retrospect that England can be presented as a steadily growing monarchical-territorial state. In the mid-15th century it was in crisis. Its project of domination in France had been destroyed – but for that it would have been a supra-national *imperium*. Equally, the Wars of the Roses reduced England to anarchy in the aftermath of defeat in France. Thus to present England as an early example of a territorial sovereign state as Krasner does is hardly accurate.[13] It is so only if one constructs a teleology of the 'true course' of English state-formation, one that ignores or sidelines the crises, uprisings, the Civil War, and the Crown's dream of recovering its dominions in France that continued well into the sixteenth century. England remained a relatively backward and fragile Renaissance state. To ignore this is to indulge contemporary projects of presenting the stability and continuity of the English state, those of the late Elizabethan era, and those of the Whigs. The religious conflicts at times helped to promote state power, in that they provided the Tudor Monarchy with the means to construct and enforce a 'national' confessional homogeneity, and at other times, most notably the Civil War, they undermined central royal authority.

Until religious conflicts could be contained from spreading across borders, no state subject to religious dissent could hope to develop uninterruptedly those attributes of sovereignty claimed as definitive of modern statehood by Weber. Those states that were able to avoid such disruption had managed to preseve or construct forms of religious homogeneity – Spain did so by an early practice of religious 'police' directed against Jews and Moorish converts. Religion was *the* central political issue, and the capacity to prevent, eliminate or contain religious conflict was vital to building an effective *political* foundation for state power.[14] Thus by exploiting the freedom from external interference underwritten by international treaty and gradually extended throughout western Europe as the core principle of the emerging international law, states were better able to enforce 'sovereignty' on their societies. The agreement of most of Europe's most affected states to avoid interference in the religious peace of other states changed the terms of conflict between territorial authority and confessional groups in the former's favour. To a significant degree the capacity of state elites to assert 'sovereign' control over territory came from *without*, from agreements between states in the developing society of states. To a considerable degree therefore, the capacities of the state grow inward from the *international* recognition of its rights to certain key powers by other states.

This process was complex and by no means complete in 1648. But Krasner is wrong to talk down Westphalia as a watershed. States did not create fully uniform and effective administrations in most cases until the nineteenth century. France in 1789 was far from 'absolutist', it remained a patchwork of internal jurisdictions, status privileges and particular liberties. The process of state building from above, imposing royal or state power, was subject to many limitations even in the supposedly 'absolute' monarchies. But at least that project could be essayed once peace was assured in confessional matters, whereas it was radically delayed and undermined by the religious civil wars.

Krasner is right to point out that 1648 did not immediately result in a monoculture of sovereign states, displacing all other political entities both supra- and sub-territorial. But his interpretation of Westphalia in the matter of religious conflict seems somewhat forced. He is right to say that: 'Even the exercise of authority over activities exclusively within given territory, generally regarded as a core attribute of sovereign states, has been problematic in practice and contested in theory. The most dramatic challenge has involved efforts by external actors to control the way a state treats its own citizens or subjects'.[15] This is certainly the case; the content and scope of sovereignty have been subject to constant conflict and re-definition. But he treats Westphalia in matters of religion as if it were a limitation of sovereignty, rather than an attempt to reinforce it. He says: 'In the sixteenth and seventeenth centuries, states concluded international agreements containing provisions in respect to the treatment of religious dissenters'. This is true, but Westphalia was an attempt to *limit* the grounds on which states could intervene by cementing a religious peace and delimiting confessional territories.

Curiously, Krasner recognizes this, without drawing the conclusion that Westphalia was a turning point. He says that 'the more general problem therefore ... at issue at 1648 ... was to find some way of dealing with the religious disorders that had torn Europe apart for a century'[16] and 'Westphalia attempted to insulate religion from politics.[17] The latter terms might well be reversed to sum up the impact of the Treaties. Certainly the peace tried to freeze the religious *status quo* as it had existed, and thus to a degree limited the absolutism in religious matters of rulers within Germany. But to say that Westphalia 'was less consistent with modern notions of sovereignty than Augsburg' in 1555 is surely to miss the point of these provisions. The aim of the 1648 Treaties is to cement the provisions of the previous peace in the new context. Treaties are almost always complex amalgams of items agreed by difficult negotiations, and the agreements at Münster and Osnabrück were no exception. Nevertheless, key articles of the Treaty make clear that the aim was to reinforce Augsburg, not to set it aside.[18] 'The Religious Peace of 1555 ... shall, in all its articles entered into and concluded by the unanimous consent of the emperor, electors, princes and states of both religions, be confirmed and observed fully and without infringement.'[19] 'Whereas all immediate state enjoy, together with their territorial rights and sovereignty as hitherto used throughout the empire, also the right of reforming the practice of religion; and whereas in the Religious Peace the privilege of emigration was conceded to subjects of such states if they dissented from their territorial lord; and whereas later, for the better preserving of greater concord among the states, it was agreed that no one should seduce another's subjects to his religion, or for that reason make any understanding for defense or protection, or come to their aid for any reason; it is now agreed that all these be fully observed by the states of either religion, and that no state shall be hindered in the rights in matters of religion which belong to it by reason of its territorial independence and sovereignty'.[20]

In these provisions it is clear that Augsburg *limited* the powers of sovereigns radically: they could not enforce conversion and compel subjects to stay, subjects had a right to belief even if this meant exile. States thus had limited controls over their populations; they could not by right prevent emigration in the way that many states, especially the Communist regimes of the twentieth century, have done. This limitation was in the interests of religious liberty – perhaps the first internationally recognized civil right. At the same time rulers had rights too, under the principle of *cujus regio ejus religio*. Moreover, the principle of non-intervention is defined in the 1648 Treaty as reinforcing an attribute of sovereignty, the right of states to order their own affairs. The upshot of this parcel of rights – for subjects, rulers and sovereign states – is to cement the ties of confession and territory, to prevent arbitrary acts against this state of affairs by subjects (they may leave but not rebel in the name of religion), by rulers (they may not subsequently and arbitrarily alter an established religious constitution agreed by prince and people), and other states (they may not legitimately intervene to aid co-religionists). Therefore, the internationally-recognized rights of these diverse subjects reinforce state sovereignty rather than undermine it. The architects of Westphalia were not explicitly intending to create a new international order or to define sovereignty in a new way. But the effect of Westphalia was to cool the centre of religious conflict and make possible a form of connection between cultural homogeneity and political power, that is, confessional conformity and the exclusive control of a territory by one principal political body. That model of a coherent culture and a coherent territory being ruled by a single political entity could then subsequently generate 'nationalism', that is, the requirement that cultural homogeneity extend to far more than religion, to whatever defines the 'nation' as a specific socio-political construct. The notion of a confessionally coherent territory is thus the foundation for the idea that states and their subjects should have common and distinctive attributes. Before this notion of confessional conformity, peoples and rulers could have very diverse attributes, conflicting and overlapping loyalties and obligations, identities and beliefs.

Of course as Krasner argues, the Holy Roman Empire survived until 1806, but few contemporaries doubted that the Imperial Party were the main losers in the wars that followed the Edict of Restitution in 1629. The Edict was a bid by the Emperor to alter the religious balance between Protestants and Catholics in Germany in the latter's favour. It was backed by the threat of Wallenstein's army of 134,000 men. The Edict threatened not merely the Protestants, but the autonomy of the Princes of the Empire, and it also provoked the intervention of the Swedes in 1630. The main beneficiaries of Westphalia *within* the Empire were its principal territorial states, who gained both more autonomy and a greater say in the conduct of Imperial affairs. The Papacy was very clear that the Catholic cause was the main loser in the peace and in the changes in Imperial government. The Pope was not a party to the negotiations and he fired off an angry Bull 'Zelo Domus Dei' repudiating the terms of the Treaty. Innocent X clearly did not believe nothing had happened, rather the 'heretics' as he called them were accepted as a stable part of the political system of Germany both by Ferdinand III and the French.[21]

Krasner's scepticism is not unwelcome, since the conventional account of the rise of the modern state assumes too readily a sharp break between medieval and modern political forms. My difference with him is over the role of the Treaty of Westphalia in creating certain of the conditions for the territorialization of political-religious authority and thus the building of the modern state. In the last few years international relations theorists[22] have begun to ask new questions about the formation of the modern sovereign state and to take the discussion of the development of a monopoly of the means of violence beyond Max Weber. They recognize that both the units of political power and the relationship between them, the system of states, changed in early-modern Europe.

Brian Downing's *The Military Revolution and Political Change* emphasizes the impact of the military revolution of the sixteenth and early seventeenth centuries on state formation and as a determinant of the type of political authority that emerged. He argues that the fiscal exigences of the military revolution in conditions of intense conflict fostered the development of military bureaucratic absolutism. Where rulers were forced to tax the agrarian sector heavily in order to survive, they were compelled to abrogate the local powers and the representative institutions of medieval constitutionalism. Brandenburg-Prussia and France moved in the direction of absolutism, whilst England and Holland were able to use the advantages of an advanced economy, alliances and geographic position to finance war on a basis that did not threaten the limits to taxation that their representative institutions were willing to grant. Sweden escaped the worst effects of absolutism because to a considerable degree it could make foreigners pay for its wars.

The argument is well-marshalled, but it ignores how chaotic were the political and military institutional arrangements in much of Europe during the religious civil wars and the Thirty Years War. Often funds were raised for armies by mere extortion and pillage, forms of 'taxation' beyond the control of either medieval assemblies or

273

'modern' absolutisms. Again religious fervour could call forth resources that normal political purposes could not, changing the terms on which representative institutions were willing to act. Armies were far more makeshift than the term 'military revolution' implies, composed of mixtures of volunteers, local levies and mercenaries armed with whatever came to hand. Often in the French civil wars or the Thirty Years War, armed bands degenerated into an anarchy close to generalized banditry. A casual reading of Grimmelshausen's *Simplicius Simplicissimus* will reveal what was typical not only of the Thirty Years War in its later stages but of many other conflicts: a broken-backed form of war conducted by armed bands directly feeding off the people and beyond any form of central or bureaucratic control. Religious zealots, mutinous unpaid mercenaries, impressed ploughboys, and rebellious peasants made up much of the 'armies' of this period, forces far removed from the orderly schemes of Maurice of Nassau or Gustavus Adolphus, and principally armed with the cheap and cheerful pike and that low-tech, low-skill substitute for the crossbow, the arquebus.[23]

Hendrik Spruyt's *The Sovereign State and its Competitors* asks the entirely reasonable but very original question, if feudal authority was in decline and a new form of political order was necessary in a more commercial and urban society, why did it take the form of the modern territorial sovereign state? Spruyt examines the possible competitors, city states and city leagues, and attempts to explain why the territorial state emerged as the dominant form. Central to Spruyt's explanation is that the sovereign state was a more effective institutional arrangement than its competitors. He claims that: 'Organisational types that were fraught with free-riding and factionalism, that had problems rationalising their economies and reducing transaction costs – in short, those that could not make the transition to consolidated national economies – were less effective and less efficient in mobilising resources than sovereign states'.[24] The emergence of the sovereign state and the system of states went together: 'The system selected out those types of units that were competitively speaking less efficient'.[25] Thus the Hanseatic League was excluded as a distinct party at the peace negotiations of Westphalia, Spruyt argues, because it was not a territorial state. Rather the issue seems to turn on the delicate issue of religious power in Germany. The League was not a party to the Religious Peace of 1555 and its *German* cities were either directly or indirectly represented in the negotiations of 1648. The delicate balance between Protestants and Catholics could well have been undermined by such double counting, if the League were represented as a power and some of its member cities like Lübeck were also there because of their status in the Imperial constitution. The League's nature as a non-territorial form of organization seems less the point in and of itself, than the danger that it would alter the balance of forces further against the Catholic party.

Many of the 'territorial' states at Westphalia were hardly in the position where they could cope with 'factionalism'. The weaknesses Spruyt sees in city states and city leagues were real, confronted with a territorial state in which sovereignty was effectively asserted. But many states at different points in the sixteenth and seventeenth centuries were in a state of religious civil war, or of aristocratic or local revolt, they were thus not inherently superior to other forms. Authority remained fragile and provisional in this period to a degree that makes theoretical analyses of the competitive advantage of forms of state hypothetical to say the least.

Janice E. Thomson's *Mercenaries, Pirates and Sovereigns* concentrates on the issue of sovereignty as the state's control of non-state violence beyond its borders. As she argues that the monopolization of the means of internal violence by the state is only one aspect of sovereignty, what she calls its 'constitutive dimension' defines 'the state as *the actor* in international politics by designating the state, rather than a religious or economic organisation, as the repositary of ultimate authority within a political space that is defined territorially'.[26] This decisive element of sovereign statehood is in no way accomplished by the end of the seventeenth century: 'The state's monopoly on external violence came very late and through a process spanning several centuries. For three hundred years non-state violence was a legitimate practice in the European state system'.[27] She recognizes the extent to which this responsibility for external action and sovereignty over such action was internationally established and enforced. States gradually asserted control or were required to assert control over all actions emanating from their territory: 'Interstate relations and not domestic politics were the crucial determinants in this transformative process'.[28]

Her work draws on numerous sources, but in particular owes its key insights on the international aspect of national sovereignty to Charles Tilly. Tilly[29] sees state-building, the growth of territorial sovereignty and its legitimacy, in stark and brutal terms. He argues that states were built by power-hungry elites, who used the force available to them to amass wealth and the instruments of hierarchical control. Central to the legitimacy of such power grabbers was not the opinions of the mass of the ruled; given a certain capacity for coercion they could be ignored and compelled to obey. Power in early-modern Europe was seldom beneficial to the common people. Instead, states depended on the acceptance of their existence and their capacity to control territory by others: 'Legitimacy is the probability that other authorities will act to confirm the decisions of a given authority.[30] Anthony Giddens argues that the *nation* state, recognized within a definite territory and accepted as the legitimate agency for determining the scope and scale of governance within these borders, is a distinctively modern form. He argues that this extended sense of sovereignty depends upon mutual recognition by states; 'upon a reflexively monitored set of relations between states'.[31]

These various arguments confirm the role of inter-state agreements and international processes in generating and cementing aspects of state sovereignty. The forms of non-state and state-sanctioned 'private' violence that Thomson analyses clearly limited the capacity of the state to assert sovereignty in the sense of an *internal* monopoly of the means of violence in the seventeenth century. Private armies, mercenary forces for hire, privateers and pirates at sea, all contributed means of intervention in *other states'* territories and affairs, they limited the affected states' capacities to protect and monopolize control over their own citizens and commerce. The possibility of hiring mercenary armies and foreign troops (often on credit) strengthened some rulers against their peoples, but this could also provide rebel strata and provinces with the means to resist central power and royal authority.

Westphalia clearly did not end such practices as mercenarism and piracy, and they persisted until major liberal states made determined efforts to limit them or stamp them out in the nineteenth century. As we have seen, however, Westphalia did attempt to limit aspects of external intervention by controlling and curtailing the right of states to interfere in others' religious affairs, irrespective of whether they were Reformed or Catholic. In one sense Westphalia could be called the international triumph of the *Politiques*, the liberal Catholic faction in the French religious wars who argued for the primacy of social peace and a stable political order over the claims of purity of religious doctrine and the right to propagate one's religious practices at whatever cost.[32] As Reinhart Koselleck argues, there is at this period a fundamental shift in political theory towards seeing the state as a neutral public power, above society, that can impose order on the warring factions of citizens.[33] Civil society is seen as problematic and incapable of sustaining itself without political control over religious disputes.

Bodin and Hobbes both argue for the primacy of sovereign *political* authority within the state, determining what religious practices and beliefs are legitimate, and imposing its will as an uncommanded commander.[34] Given this conception of the state as a neutral power internally, it is evident why international relations should be viewed as a realm of de-ideologized power-technique too. Hobbes saw inter-state relations as an anarchy in which all powers are morally equivalent, states have interests and capacities but they are not part of a civil order. Thus the norms of inter-state relations are prudential and based on things as they are, not as they ought to be. This conception of the state as a supreme public power can easily be accepted by other states, it imposes no ideological condition for conformity or moral test of conduct. One can deal equally pragmatically with Turk or Christian, and treat Reformed and Catholic regimes as entities of the same kind, as potential allies or foes. The new conception of state raises guilty *realpolitik* to the status of legitimate behaviour, sanctioned by high theory. The way is then clear for the kind of international law based on sovereignty and non-intervention fully developed in the eighteenth century by such theorists as Vattel.

Koselleck's argument is a powerful one, linking political theory and practice; it explains why, in the context of the mutual exhaustion of the religious wars, the notion of the state as a power above society could acquire a definite legitimacy and an attraction to a wide variety of social actors. Kings, counsellors and peasants could all agree that Paris, and peace, is worth a mass. Thus although Tilly is right that most ruling elites were driven by a ruthless will-to-power, one has to explain why rulers and peoples were willing to forgo their strongly held beliefs to the primacy of their own religion, and accept beyond their borders other states legitimately practising alien beliefs. One has to explain why non-elite social actors also wished to stabilize political authority, to have order, and to reinforce domestic peace by international recognition in a treaty. Legitimacy did not just come from without, it was sanctioned by tired and frightened people within. Most citizens or subjects had few illusions about the state, but they had even fewer about the capacity of 'civil society' to live at peace unaided. Rulers who could offer order within had something to offer peoples, even at the price of foreign wars and taxes, if they put an end to the religious sects and zealots who tore the body politic apart in the reckless pursuit of their own beliefs. Westphalia marks a watershed because the ruler-sanctioned confessionally-stable state, recognized by other states, was part of the answer to the social crisis and crisis of authority brought about by the religious schisms.

The reason the analysis of the religious conflicts is not well-integrated into accounts of state building in the sixteenth and seventeenth centuries based on international relations theory and political science is that religious struggles tend to be fully considered in social and cultural history rather than political history. We forget how real and important was religious belief as a source of motivation for actors in this period, both princes and people.[35]

The burden of this paper has been to argue that the territorial sovereign state was able to develop its distinctive attributes at least in part because of international agreement between states to limit intervention in each other's affairs in matters of religion.[36] Modern nation states have been built on these seventeenth century foundations. Sovereign power did not originate at the national level alone. It is now widely claimed that the modern state is threatened with obsolescence as the processes of globalization and the trends towards localism that accompany them strip out its powers above and below the national level. Some people in consequence look back to the Middle Ages, before the formation of the modern sovereign territorial state, for models of the type of patterns of power that may prevail.

Perhaps there are still some lessons to be learnt from the period of the formation of the modern state and the modern states system. If the international and the national interacted so closely as they did in the seventeenth century, then it may be that they will interact in equally complex and surprising ways today. It is indeed the case that certain vital dimensions of governance are beyond the competence of even the largest states today, for example, creating a set of rules and an agency to regulate world trade, or controlling global environmental change. International governance is now a necessary part of the division of labour in government. It does not follow, however, that national states are therefore powerless and that all they do is cede sovereignty and competencies to international agencies and thereafter cease to have any role. On the contrary, international governance, no matter how indispensable, cannot exist without the continued consent and cooperation of at least a crucial sub-set of powerful national states. Without such nationally-derived consent, such international agencies will lack legitimacy. States can provide such legitimacy most effectively, because it is they alone who can speak for territorially-bounded populations. They can ensure compliance within their own territories and can also support supra-national bodies in dealing with other more refractory states. States with definite boundaries and at least minimally democratic governments can credibly speak for their people and commit their part of the globe to a common supra-national policy with authority. Without such territorially-derived democratic legitimacy, international arrangements and agencies will be ineffective.[37]

It is also the case that if effective economic and social governance increasingly depends on the actions of regional and local authorities, the national state retains a crucial role in providing the constitutional ordering for such governments. The national state distributes powers and competencies within, ensuring lesser authorities have the right scope, powers and access to resources. It provides local and regional governments with political stability and physical security. National states are thus not losing 'sovereignty' upwards and downwards, to the international system and to regional authorities. That would be so only if sovereignty could only conceived in narrowly Bodinian terms and no other, as an exclusive possession that can be neither divided nor delegated. That view may have made sense confronted with the religious strife of the sixteenth century, but in relation to the complex division of labour that is necessary to modern governance it is outdated. The new national sovereignty is above all the power to confer legitimacy and governmental competence to other agencies, international and local, but then to continue to support and sustain those agencies as a cooperative partner in a new scheme of authority. The nation state does not thereby become functionless, rather it becomes the key node (the main source of legitimacy that ties the whole together) in a complex web of governing powers. If that is so, then the new and emerging patterns of supra-national governance will not simply supplant the nation state but will continue to depend upon it. This relationship is quite different, indeed the reverse, of that postulated as an effect of the Treaty of Westphalia, when international agreements empowered the territorial state, but it a reminder that the national and the international levels have been closely and reciprocally interlinked since the beginning of the modern states system.

Notes

1   Weber (1968), Vol. 1, p. 56.
2   On this process of competition between different forms of political organization in early modern Europe, of which the sovereign territorial state has only one of a number of contenders to replace the feudal system in advanced decay see Spruyt (1994).
3   See Schmitt (1976)

4   On the history of heretical movements before Luther, Lambert (1977) remains a comprehensive survey. On the failure of an influential 'reform' movement and its decline into heresy and its defeat see McFarlane (1972).

5   See Cohn (1970), Ozment (1973) and Williams (1962) for the radical ideas, sects and movements spawned by the Reformation.

6   It is a commonplace of the literature on early-modern state-building in Europe to refer to a 'military revolution' that is supposed to have taken place between the early sixteenth century and the mid-seventeenth and to argue that the new military technologies and structures favoured large-scale authority and thus shifted the balance of power in favour of the central state and against aristocratic and municipal localism. The concept of a 'military revolution' between 1550-1660 derives from the classic paper of Michael Roberts (1956); for a sympathetic discussion see Parker (1979, 1988 ch. 1). In the 2nd edition of *The Military Revolution* (1996) Parker tries to defend his own version of the concept against criticisms, but in my view not wholly convincingly. The idea of a distinctive revolution in the art of war in this period is actually rather difficult to defend. Of course there was a great deal of change, but over a longer temporality of 1500 to 1800 and certainly not in one definite direction. What undermines the notion of a 'revolution' is that the conditions underlying military organization and military operations remained remarkably stable, a *longue dureé* in the underlying structures of conflict. These underlying constraints on warfare meant that innovations were rapidly absorbed into a set of circumstances that tended to impose continuity in the actualities of conducting operations. Given the fundamental limitations imposed on mobility by bad roads, on logistics by agricultural productivity and therefore surpluses in even the most advanced regions, and the inability to keep armies in the field in winter, warfare tended to degenerate into ineffectual sieges and into raiding the most accessible enemy province. Armies remained fiscally and logistically fragile, as the work of Parker (1972, 1979) on the most organized and competent army of the time (Spain's) demonstrates.

It is certainly the case that the size of armies increased dramatically from 1500 to 1700, but until remarkably late they were organizationally ramshackle. Most units were raised by military contractors for the duration of a campaign. The hosts assembled at the start of a war or campaign tended to melt away with astonishing rapidity. Most armies seldom stayed coherent or efficient for long; disease, desertion, the corruption of military contractors, mutiny for arrears of pay, and the general tendency of armies to scatter into bands to loot and forage for supplies meant that the numbers on payrolls meant little in terms of effectives who could be assembled to any strategic purpose. Black (1991, 1994) is sharply and tellingly critical of the notion of a military revolution. Anderson (1988) and Tallett (1992) are particularly informative on the composition of armies, military contracting and logistics, and the impact of war on society.

The problem with the notion of a 'revolution' is not that there are no changes, but that the effects of these changes are ambiguous. If there was no distinct 'military revolution' with a definite set of outcomes, then there are unlikely to have been effects on the process of state formation stemming from military organization that worked unambiguously in favour of the central state apparatus in this period. To take a key example; the new Italian-inspired artillery fortifications of the late 1520s/1530s. These are often presented as an inevitable effect of the French invasion of Italy in 1494, which finally demonstrated that medieval walls were obsolete. The new fortifications were expensive, as were the new siege cannons, and thus are supposed to have worked in favour of central authority.

Actually, what it meant was that effective sieges were difficult to conduct because cannons were scarce until the early seventeenth century; they were expensive because they were cast in bronze. Once the lessons of 1494 had been absorbed, military engineers and soldiers could devise cheap and cheerful ways of defending medieval town walls and castles: firstly, only building bastions at the most threatened points; secondly, erecting temporary earthworks in front of or behind breaches in old walls. As Pepper and Adams (1986) show, in the most detailed study of Italian siege warfare, weak places could offer an effective and prolonged defense, costly to the besiegers. Montalcino made an effective resistance, despite being a very weak place. Siena held out in the prolonged siege of 1554-5, the old walls being reinforced by bastions on the most likely avenue of attack and bolstered by temporary earthworks. A spirited defense could thus challenge and even repel central power at a modest cost. Fortifications limited mobility, and thus worked against larger armies, dissipating their advantages. Warfare is usually more subject to contingency than historians allow; in this period it was frequently chaotic and thus quite unsuitable for the neat generalizations of political scientists.

7   Historians have a distinct tendency to write victor's history in the case of French absolutism, which doubtless would have been comforting to Richelieu, confronted with liquidating the Hugenot state within a state, and Mazarin, faced with the multi-faceted revolts of the Fronde, had they been privy to the outcome. A.D. Lublinskaya (1968) esp. ch. 5, although stalwartly an orthodox Marxist, explains the political situation of the suppression of the Huguenots exceptionally well and also indicates that it was more of a 'close run thing' than many accounts of French state-building allow. On the siege of La Rochelle see Duffy (1979).

8   Reinhart Koselleck remarks on the status of the Thirty Years War that it
      was a *civil* conflict that subsequently became perceived as primarily an
      inter-state conflict: 'And if in Germany we do not refer to the Thirty Years
      War as a civil war – as corresponding events in neighbouring countries are
      called – it is because the Imperial constitutional character of this war has
      been altered with the termination of thirty years of struggle. What had
      begun as a civil war between the Protestant Imperial orders and the Imperial
      party ended in a peace treaty between almost sovereign territorial states.
      Our religious civil war could thus be interpreted *ex post* as a war between
      states'. Koselleck (1985) p. 44.

9   Michael Mann (1986) takes a contrary view: 'Up to the seventeenth century
      grievances expressed in religious terms were paramount in social struggles;
      yet they took on an increasingly state-bound form. Religious wars came to
      be fought either by rival states or by factions who struggled over the
      constitution of the singly, monopolistic state in which they were localised'
      (p. 435). This is not wholly convincing: co-religionists *did* aid others,
      religious mercenaries and volunteers were commonplace, and subjects
      struggled against their rulers for religious goals and against central state
      power. Luther's 'nationalism', for example, was *cultural* – addressed to
      'Germans', not to the members of a definite state – see Dickens (1974).

10   For examples of such arguments within international relations and social
      theory respectively see Zacher (1992) and Held (1995) esp. Part II. The
      'Westphalian model' it is argued is threatened by economic, environmental
      and cultural charges on a world scale that are undermining the governance
      capacities of the nation state and the system of international relations based
      upon it. For an attempt to argue that the nation state remains crucial and
      especially as a foundation for international governance, see Hirst and
      Thompson (1996).

11   For an exhaustive military, socio-economic and political assessment of the
      war, see Parker (1987) and for a modern historiographic survey see Limm
      (1984). For the text of the Treaty of Munster see Symcox (1973).

12   This should emphatically *not* be taken to mean that there were no conflicts
      over economic resources. For example, trade, piracy and warfare in the
      Mediterranean were inextricably intermingled in the sixteenth and
      seventeenth centuries: Guilmartin (1974). Rather the point is that such
      conflicts did not tend their protagonists *systematically* to group themselves
      as friend and enemy, they were episodic and shifting as specific crises or
      trade conjunctures developed and changed. Marxist historians attempted to
      portray the conflicts of this period as based on class struggles and as part of
      the general process of transition from feudalism to capitalism. Strong
      versions of such arguments, such as Porshnev's (1963) interpretation of

popular uprisings in France before the Fronde, or Hobsbawm's version of a 'general crisis of the seventeenth century' (1954), have not worn well in subsequent critical debate. Zagorin (1982) is an authoritative review of the modern historiographical literature and an examination of the major examples of localist, social and religious revolts and civil wars.

13   See Krasner (1993).

14   Without a stable relationship between confessional organization and political power it was difficult to impose religious discipline and to begin the process of 'Christianization' in terms of subordinating popular piety to elite beliefs and practices that began with the Reformation but in many Catholic countries was hardly accomplished in the Counter Reformation and only got under way in the late seventeenth century. See Delumeau (1977, 1988) and Muchembled (1978). Larner (1981) and Muchembled (1979) argue that the witch trials of the sixteenth and seventeenth centuries were part of this process of acculturation of the people and, in conditions of weak religious and secular authority, an attempt to assert social control. Catholic regimes in Italy and Spain were relatively efficiently able to control religious dissent. For example, in the Basque country in the early seventeenth century the Inquisition paid little attention to witchcraft as heresy, regarding self-confessed witches as self-deluding and mentally-ill – see Henningsen (1980). Even in Spain, however, religious dissent could weaken the state at crucial junctures, as for example the Morisco Revolt of 1568-70.

15   Krasner (1993), p. 237.

16   Ibid., p. 240.

17   Ibid., p. 242.

18   Treaty of Osnabrüch between Sweden, the Emperor and the German princes, article 5, para 1.

19   Article 5, para 30.

20   Cited in G.R Elton (1968) pp. 240-1.

21   Cited in Limm (1984) pp. 106-7. I am grateful to Dr Anthony Pagden for emphasizing this point to me during the discussion of my paper at the conference on which this essay is based.

22   See Ruggie (1986), Downing (1992), Spruyt (1994) and Thomson (1994).

23   This point about the low skill involved in the key weapons of the 'military revolution' is made effectively by Guilmartin (1984) pp. 150-5. He does so in the context of explaining why Lepanto (1571) was such a blow to the Ottomans. This was because so many highly-skilled archers holding land by military tenure were lost and they could not be quickly replaced – unlike galleys and their rowers. In effect the pike and the arquebus 'de-skilled' war – they made it easy to rapidly train urban militias, impressed men and

mercenaries. The effects of this were various: rebel armies could be improvised, as with the forces of the French or English civil wars; armies could become larger – as such low-skill soldiers were relatively cheap; and battles were thoroughly ineffective in settling wars, however 'decisive' the victory, since new armies could be raised relatively quickly. To illustrate this latter point, the Swedish victories at Breitenfeld (1631) and Lützen (1632) failed to end the Imperialist capacity to wage war, nor did the shattering French victory over the Spanish at Rocroi (1643) quickly alter the outcome of the war, as Spain held out in its dense network of fortified positions in Flanders.

24   Spruyt (1994), p. 178.
25   Ibid., p. 180.
26   Thomson (1994), p. 16.
27   Ibid., p. 143.
28   Ibid., p. 19.
29   Tilly (1975, 1990).
30   Tilly (1985), p. 171.
31   Giddens (1985), pp. 263-4.
32   For the religious beliefs and practices of the Huguenots and the relationship to their political and constitutional doctrines see Kelley (1981), this linking of ideas and political practice he argues represents the 'beginning of ideology. In that sense the *Politiques* represent an early and rapid disenchantment with ideology and political fanaticism – see Skinner (1978) Vol. II and Zagorin (1982) Vol. II for the political ideas of the French religious wars.
33   Koselleck (1988).
34   See Bodin (1992), Hobbes (1960).
35   Ruggie (1993) presents an example of this. Having extensively reviewed the literature and prospectus on the transition to territorial states in early modern Europe, he notes the role of the religious civil wars and remarks 'Still an international politics morally autonomous from the realm of religion did not become fully established until the Peace of Westphalia (1648), ending the Thirty Years War' (p. 163). The event is registered, but not its full consequences for state building.
36   Gourevitch (1978) is a useful review and analysis of the relationship between international and domestic policy and structures, but it does not explicitly examine the issue of the foundations of sovereignty in its international dimension.
37   For a fuller version of this argument see Hirst and Thompson (1996) chs. 6 and 8.

References

Anderson, M.S. (1988), *War and Society in Europe of the Old Regime 1618-1789*, Fontana; London.

Black, J. (1991), *A Military Revolution? Military Change and European Society 1550-1800*, Macmillan: Basingstoke.

Black, J. (1994), *European Warfare 1660-1815*, UCL Press: London.

Bodin, J. (1992), *On Sovereignty*, Franklin, J.H., (ed.), Cambridge University Press: Cambridge. First published 1576.

Cohn, N. (1970), *The Pursuit of the Millenium*, Granada-Paladin Books: London.

Delumeau, J. (1977), *Catholicism between Luther and Voltaire: a New View of the Counter Reformation*, Burns and Oates: London.

___ (1988), 'Prescription and Reality' in Leites, E. (ed.) *Conscience and Casuistry in Early Modern Europe*, Cambridge University Press: Cambridge.

Dickens, A.G. (1974), *The German Nation and Martin Luther*, Fontana: London.

Downing, B.M. (1992), *The Military Revolution and Political Change - Origins of Democracy and Autocracy in Early Modern Europe*, Princeton University Press: Princeton, NJ.

Duffy, C. (1979), *Siege Warfare – The Fortress in the Early Modern World 1494-1660*, Routledge and Kegan Paul: London.

Elton, G.R. (ed.)(1968), *Renaissance and Reformation 1300-1648*, Macmillan: New York.

Giddens, A. (1985), *A Contemporary Critique of Historical Materialism, Vol. 2, The Nation State and Violence*, Polity Press: Cambridge.

Gourevitch, P. (1978), 'The Second Image Reversed: the International Sources of Domestic Politics', *International Organisation*, Vol. 32 No. 4 Autumn, pp. 881-912.

Grimmelshausen, H.J.C. von (1964), *Simplicius Simplicissimus*, Weissenborn, H. and Macdonald, H. (trans.), 1964, John Calder: London. First published 1669.

Guilmartin, J.F. (1974), *Gunpowder and Galleys: Changing Technology and Mediterranean Warfare at Sea in the Sixteenth Century*, Cambridge University Press: Cambridge.

Held, D. (1995), *Democracy and the Global Order - from the Modern State to Cosmopolitan Governance*, Polity Press: Cambridge.

Henningsen, G. (1980), *The Witch's Advocate: Basque Witchcraft and the Spanish Inquisition (1609-1614)*, University of Nevada Press: Reno, Nevada.

Hirst, P. and Thompson, G. (1996), *Globalisation in Question - the International Economy and the Possibilities of Governance*, Polity Press: Cambridge.

Hobbes, T. (1960), *Leviathan*, Oakeshott, M. (ed.), Basil Blackwell: Oxford. First published 1651.

Hobsbawm, E.J. (1954), 'The Crisis of the Seventeenth Century', *Past and Present*,

Nos. 5 & 6, reprinted in Aston, T. (ed.)(1965), *Crisis in Europe 1560-1660*, Routledge and Kegan Paul: London.

Kelley, D.R. (1981), *The Beginning of Ideology – Consciousness and Society in the French Reformation*, Cambridge University Press: Cambridge.

Koselleck, R. (1985), *Futures Past*, Tribe, K. (trans.), MIT Press: Cambridge, MA.

____ (1988), *Critique and Crisis*, Berg: Oxford.

Krasner, S.D. (1993), 'Westphalia and All That', in Goldstein, J. and Keohane, R.O. (eds.) *Ideas and Foreign Policy: Beliefs, Institutions and Political Change*, Cornell University Press: Ithaca, New York.

Lambert, M.D. (1977), *Medieval Heresy: Popular Movements from Bogomil to Hus*, Edward Arnold: London.

Larner, C. (1981), *Enemies of God: The Witch-hunt in Scotland*, Chatto and Windus: London.

Limm, P. (1984), *The Thirty Years War*, Longman: London.

Lublinskaya, A.D. (1968), *French Absolutism: the Crucial Phase 1620-1629*, Cambridge University Press: Cambridge.

Mann, M. (1986), *The Sources of Social Power*, Vol. I, Cambridge University Press: Cambridge.

McFarlane, K.B. (1972), *Wycliffe and English Non-Conformity*, Penguin: Harmondsworth.

Muchembled, R. (1978), *Culture Populaire et Culture des Elites dans la France Moderne (XVe - XVIIIe siécles)* Flammarion: Paris.

____ (1979), 'The Witches of the Cambrésis – The Acculturation of the Rural World in the Sixteenth and Seventeenth Centuries', in Obelkevich, J. (ed.), *Religion and the People 800-1700*, University of North Carolina Press: Chapel Hill, NC.

Ozment, S.E. (1973), *Mysticism and Dissent*, Yale University Press: New Haven, Conn.

Parker, G. (1972), *The Army of Flanders and the Spanish Road 1567-1659*, Cambridge University Press: Cambridge.

____ (1979), 'The "Military Revolution, 1560-1660" – A Myth?', in *Spain and the Netherlands 1559-1659*, Fontana: London.

____ (1987) (ed.), *The Thirty Years War*, Routledge and Kegan Paul: London.

____ (1988), *The Military Revolution – Military Innovation and the Rise of the West, 1500-1800*, Cambridge University Press: Cambridge, 2nd edn. 1996.

Pepper, S. and Adams, N. (1986), *Firearms and Fortifications: Military Architecture and Siege Warfare in Sixteenth Century Siena*, Chicago University Press: Chicago.

Porshnev, B. (1963), *Les Soulévements Populaires en France de 1623 á 1648*, Paris: S.E.V.P.E.N., excerpted in Coveney, P.J. (ed.) (1977) *France in Crisis 1620-75*, Macmillan: London, chs. 3 and 4.

Porter, B.D. (1994), *War and the Rise of the State – The Military Foundations of*

Modern Politics, The Free Press: New York.

Roberts, M. (1956), 'The Military Revolution 1560-1660', Lecture at Queen's University, Belfast, printed in Roberts, M. (1967), *Essays in Swedish History*, Weidenfeld and Nicholson: London.

Ruggie, J.G. (1986), 'Continuity and Transformation in the World Polity', in Keohane, R. (ed.) *Neorealism and its Critics*, Colombia University Press: New York, pp. 131-57.

____ (1993), 'Territoriality and Beyond: Problematising Modernity in International Relations', *International Organisation*, 47-1 pp. 139-72.

Schmitt, C. (1976), *The Concept of the Political*, Rutgers University Press: New Brunswick, NJ.

Skinner, Q. (1978), *The Foundations of Modern Political Thought*, Vol. 2, Cambridge University Press: Cambridge.

Spruyt, H. (1994), *The Sovereign State and its Competitors*, Princeton University Press: Princeton, NJ.

Symcox, G. (ed.) (1973), *War, Diplomacy and Imperialism*, Harper and Row: New York.

Tallett, F. (1992), *War and Society in Early Modern Europe 1495-1715*, Routledge: London.

Tilly, C. (1975) (ed.), *The Formation of National States in Western Europe*, Princeton University Press: Princeton, NJ.

____ (1985), 'War Making and State Making as Organised Crime', in Evans, P.B., Rueschemeyer, D. and Skocpol, T. (eds.) *Bringing the State Back In*, Cambridge University Press: Cambridge.

____ (1990), *Coercion, Capital and European States AD 990-1990*, Basil Blackwell: Oxford.

Thomson, J.E. (1994), *Mercenaries, Pirates and Sovereigns: State-Building and Extraterritorial Violence in Early-Modern Europe*, Princeton University Press: Princeton, NJ.

Weber, M. (1968), *Economy and Society*, Vol. 1, Bedminster Press: New York.

Williams, G.H. (1962), *The Radical Reformation*, Westminster Press: Philadelphia.

Zacher, M.W. (1992), 'The Decaying Pillars of the Westphalian Temple: Implications for International Order and Governance', in Rosenau, J.N. and Czempiel, E.O. (eds.) *Governance without Government: Order and Change in World Politics*, Cambridge University Press: Cambridge.

Zagorin, P. (1982), *Rebels and Rulers 1500-1660, Vol. 1 Society, States and Early Modern Revolution, Agrarian and Urban Rebellions, Vol. 2 Provincial Rebellion Revolutionary Wars 1560-1660*, Cambridge University Press: Cambridge.

Acknowledgement

This paper is part of an ongoing project with Lars Bo Kaspersen, Aarhus University Department of Political Science, and I am grateful to him for advice and assistance.

287

Index

288